ROBERT ALTMAN

ROBERT ALTMAN

The Oral Biography

*   *   *   *

Mitchell Zuckoff

ALFRED A. KNOPF   NEW YORK   2009

THIS IS A BORZOI BOOK
PUBLISHED BY ALFRED A. KNOPF

Copyright © 2009 by the Estate of
Robert B. Altman and Mitchell Zuckoff

All rights reserved. Published in the United States by
Alfred A. Knopf, a division of Random House, Inc., New York.
www.aaknopf.com

Knopf, Borzoi Books, and the colophon are registered trademarks of
Random House, Inc.

Due to limitations of space, permissions to reprint previously
published material can be found following the index.

Library of Congress Cataloging-in-Publication Data
Zuckoff, Mitchell.
Robert Altman : the oral biography / by Mitchell Zuckoff.—
1st American ed.
p. cm.
Includes filmography and index.
ISBN 978-0-307-26768-9 (alk. paper)
1. Altman, Robert, 1925–2006. 2. Motion picture producers and
directors—United States—Biography. I. Title.
PN1998.3.A48Z83   2009
791.4302'33092—dc22
[B]   2009019847

Manufactured in the United States of America
First Edition

For Suzanne

CONTENTS

*"I don't think anybody remembers the truth, the facts.
You remember impressions."*

ROBERT ALTMAN

INTRODUCTION

ROBERT ALTMAN drew you in, enlisted you in his schemes, took what he needed and gave what you asked. He trusted that you'd be good, right for the part he'd cast you in, and unless you screwed up he'd give you free rein. He pulled you onto his pedestal, passed you a joint, then rocked so hard you'd fall off together in a happy heap.

Bob did all that with me, a writer he met near the end of his life, someone with whom he could talk movies, baseball, the glory of a well-turned female leg, movies, politics, family, friendship, and movies. At first, Bob was cool to the idea of a book. His medium was film, and he considered it dangerous and distracting to publicly analyze himself. He relented under the condition that I'd help him write a memoir of the art and craft of filmmaking, a book that would focus on his work and pay little attention to his personal life. He said his motive was a healthy paycheck from the publisher, and he meant it—Bob was far better at spending than saving. But he also knew he'd have a chance to talk about his movies, something he loved almost as much as making them.

The deal was that when we were working, we'd talk film, not life. He didn't want stories of his past deeds or misdeeds to fog the lens, and he didn't want anything to hurt his family, especially his wife, Kathryn Reed Altman. His one concession was a chapter that would sketch the broad contours of his past.

We began talking in long sessions at his homes in Malibu and Manhattan and at the New York office of his last company, Sandcastle 5 Productions. It soon became clear that the lines between his life and his work weren't just blurry, they were almost nonexistent. After he returned from flying bombers in World War II, planning and making movies defined nearly everything he did. The films he eventually made weren't overtly autobiographical—not even *Kansas City*, which is a sepia-toned memory of a world he glimpsed as a boy. Not *The Player*, either; there's no evidence that he ever killed a writer, though he might have fantasized about it. He didn't need to make movies about himself because the entire process of filmmaking *was* his adult life, a stage for his passions, his rages, his triumphs, his humor, his visions, his failures, his gifts.

We talked more, and I secretly fretted that the limits he'd set would make our book a clinical rendering of the outsized, extraordinary, flesh-and-blood man I'd come to know. Me: "Why'd you film the gunfight in *McCabe* in a snowstorm?" Bob: "Because it snowed that day."

My concerns got worse one night when we attended the Malibu Celebration of Film for a showing of his last movie, *A Prairie Home Companion*. The film had been out for months, and I can only guess how many times he'd seen it. But when we returned to his home, Bob was fuming. We'd sat in the second row, behind a couple and their antsy twelve-year-old son. "If that fucking kid got up one more time," Bob growled, "I'd have strangled him *and* his father." Separating the man from his film, physically or otherwise, wasn't a good idea.

A month later, Bob died. My concerns were trivial in context and swallowed by sadness. Academic, as well: Our work was unfinished. But a new idea emerged. Our talks, Robert Altman's final sustained interviews, would form the backbone of a book about his work *and* his life, rough edges and all. Kathryn agreed, recognizing that to understand the films Bob made and the man he was, the man she loved, meant examining the whole remarkable, complicated, combustible package.

What followed for me was an Altmanesque tour from birth to death. Scenes took place in Kansas City, California, and New York, with side trips to such places as Burlington, Vermont, and Plum Island, in Massachusetts, and phone calls throughout the United States, Canada, Europe, South America, and even to a movie set in Morocco. The cast was huge and varied, from A-list stars to complete unknowns, many from the world of film but some purely from the world of Altman.

Bob told me that he and his cowriters created forty-eight characters in *A Wedding* only because that was double the number in *Nashville*. It was a conceit, a caprice; he wanted to see how many individual voices he could establish in a celluloid choir without drowning the audience in cacophony. It took nearly four times as many characters to survey his life. Their thoughts, reminiscences, opinions, regrets, praise, criticism, and in a few cases their dreams, are presented here in something approaching chronological order.

That's not to say the result is a neat, complete tale, with a moral and a point and a bow on top. That isn't Bob. He didn't think much of linear storytelling, and he wouldn't have wanted his life rendered that way. In fact, he disliked the word "story," believing that a plot should be secondary to an exploration of pure (or, even better, impure) human behavior. He also hated the ventriloquism of a single writer's voice emanating from many diverse characters, as if a baker and a surgeon, or a phone-sex worker and a grieving jazz singer, would use the same syntax. See *Short Cuts* again if you doubt that. He loved the chaotic nature of real life, with conflicting perspectives, surprising twists, unexplained actions, and ambiguous endings. He especially loved many voices, sometimes arguing, sometimes agreeing, ideally overlapping, a cocktail party or a street scene captured as he experienced it.

Bob was no more conventional when he wasn't behind a camera, and I tried to reflect that, too. As James Caan says, in Hollywood "Trust me" is code for "Fuck you." Bob didn't speak in code. In a world of air kisses and backstabbing embraces, he spoke his mind. No, he roared his mind. He believed that every capitulation large and small was tallied somewhere, each one a new link in a chain that choked off creativity. His refusal to play along cost him, personally and professionally, but he wouldn't complain and he wouldn't change. He lived the way he made movies. At times it was messy, but it was completely of his own design.

There's no way to replicate in print what Bob accomplished on film and in life, but an oral biography seemed the next best thing. I hope he'd agree.

In the transcripts of our talks, there's a passage that I've reread more times than I care to admit. It's an interruption, really, the sort of thing a transcriptionist usually omits. But for some reason it's there, embedded in a discussion about viewing an artist's work through the prism of his life.

"Excuse me," Bob says, reaching for a ringing phone. It's his producer, Wren Arthur. "Lemme call you back," he tells her. "Mitch is here on the floor next to me. I'm lying on the couch and he's sitting on the floor, and our heads are next to each other."

I've held on to that moment, trying to keep my head next to Bob's, to fairly yet fully explore his work *and* his life.

Mitchell Zuckoff, Boston, 2009

ROBERT ALTMAN

Prologue

*

Announcement from the Academy headlined "Robert Altman to Receive Honorary Academy Award," January 11, 2006: Director producer-writer Robert Altman has been voted an Honorary Award by the Board of Governors of the Academy of Motion Picture Arts and Sciences. The Award, an Oscar statuette, will be presented at the 78th Academy Awards Presentation on March 5, 2006. The Honorary Award will be given to Altman to honor "a career that has repeatedly reinvented the art form and inspired filmmakers and audiences alike." Altman has received five Academy Award nominations for directing—for *M*A*S*H*, *Nashville*, *The Player*, *Short Cuts* and *Gosford Park*—as well as two additional nominations as a producer of Best Picture nominees *Nashville* and *Gosford Park*—but has never taken home the Oscar. He has directed 37 films, produced 27 and written 16 of them. "The board was taken with Altman's innovation, his redefinition of genres, his invention of new ways of using the film medium and his reinvigoration of old ones," said Academy President Sid Ganis. "He is a master filmmaker and well deserves this honor."

*   *   *

Presentation of Oscar for Lifetime Achievement, 78th Academy Awards, March 5, 2006

LILY TOMLIN (actress and comedienne): Boy, I didn't think we'd get past security out there.

MERYL STREEP (actress): Yeah, I know. Now we just have to get past all our insecurities up here.

LILY TOMLIN: Okay. Hello, I'm Meryl Streep.

MERYL STREEP: And I'm Lily Tomlin.

LILY TOMLIN: And, and tonight we . . .

MERYL STREEP: No, no.

LILY TOMLIN: . . . are pleased to honor . . .

MERYL STREEP: No, no. . . . Wait, wait a minute. No, no . . .

LILY TOMLIN: To honor a man . . .

MERYL STREEP: No, no . . .

LILY TOMLIN: We are honoring a man . . .

MERYL STREEP: A man who we honor, that's . . . a man who didn't . . . that's my, you're reading my line. A man who didn't play by the rules.

LILY TOMLIN: Yeah, that's what I said. Who didn't play by the rules or stick to the . . .

MERYL STREEP: Stick to the script.

LILY TOMLIN: I am, Meryl.

MERYL STREEP: No, I'm agreeing with you. I'm agreeing with you. I'm just saying that Robert Altman didn't stick to the script. He colors outside the lines.

LILY TOMLIN: And he wants actors to do the same thing.

MERYL STREEP: Yeah.

LILY TOMLIN: I, I personally know . . .

MERYL STREEP: He doesn't want us to act.

LILY TOMLIN: No, and I'm grateful for that. He, uh, he wants the kind of spontaneity that can only come from not knowing what the hell you're doing.

MERYL STREEP: Like, like now.

LILY TOMLIN: Like now.

MERYL STREEP: Right?

LILY TOMLIN: Right. Yes. He just starts to film and we watch the dailies and, and it's a magical point.

MERYL STREEP: The film just starts to wake up to itself. That's what. And you see, you see . . .

LILY TOMLIN: You say, "Oh I see, I see something's happening."

MERYL STREEP: Yeah, but usually you don't know what it is.

LILY TOMLIN: No, but, but Altman does, because otherwise it . . .

MERYL STREEP: Well, I would . . .

LILY TOMLIN: . . . wouldn't be happening . . .

MERYL STREEP: . . . hope so. And his moviemaking style just does seem to enhance our capacity to take in more sounds and more . . .

LILY TOMLIN: more . . .

MERYL STREEP: images than . . .

LILY TOMLIN: layered . . .

MERYL STREEP: . . . than we ever knew we had the, the ability to process. You know, because the movies seem to have a different metabolism than other movies . . .

LILY TOMLIN: It, it, it . . . Well, well, he's always been . . .

MERYL STREEP: . . . and it's almost as if he's just . . .

LILY TOMLIN: . . . been ahead of the curve.

MERYL STREEP: He's just kind of . . .

LILY TOMLIN: And he's able to capture the . . .

MERYL STREEP: He moves out . . .

LILY TOMLIN: . . . curve . . .

MERYL STREEP: . . . densely layered . . .

LILY TOMLIN: . . . on film, with floating cameras . . .

MERYL STREEP: . . . soundscapes . . .

LILY TOMLIN: . . . extended zooms.

MERYL STREEP: And it's just incredibly living, almost like it came from a parallel universe.

LILY TOMLIN: And, well, and to some moviegoers it seems as if the popcorn they've just been munching . . .

MERYL STREEP: Yeah . . .

LILY TOMLIN: . . . had suddenly turned into peyote buttons. Oh, it's just . . .

BOTH: Wow.

MERYL STREEP: I wouldn't know. So . . .

LILY TOMLIN: Well, no, I mean just . . .

MERYL STREEP: Well . . .

LILY TOMLIN: Figuratively speaking.

MERYL STREEP: If, if, if you . . . Yes. *M*A*S*H. McCabe & Mrs. Miller. Kansas City.*

LILY TOMLIN: *Nashville.*

MERYL STREEP: *The Long Goodbye. Thieves Like Us.*

LILY TOMLIN: *Short Cuts.*

MERYL STREEP: *Gosford Park. California Split.*

LILY TOMLIN: *The Player.*

MERYL STREEP: Yeah, uh . . . *Come Back to the Five and Dime, Jimmy Dean, Jimmy Dean.* So many others. And television. He does plays, he does . . .

BOTH: . . . operas.

MERYL STREEP: It's amazing.

LILY TOMLIN: Oh, and you know. Did I say *Nashville?*

MERYL STREEP: Yes.

LILY TOMLIN: It bears repeating [*audience laughter*]. Um, I must say you're, uh, you're worried now, that I got a laugh that you didn't get.

MERYL STREEP: No . . .

LILY TOMLIN: I can see it. . . .

MERYL STREEP: No, it's okay.

LILY TOMLIN: I can feel it.

MERYL STREEP: It's all yours.

LILY TOMLIN: [*Laughs*] Over the years, he has fired our neurons, opened our eyes. . . .

MERYL STREEP: Um-hum. And bloodied a few noses.

LILY TOMLIN: Well, yes. Even his own. Um, he's a satirist, he's a sage . . .

MERYL STREEP: He's examined the minute particulars of human behavior and he's doing it right now and he's dying for us.

LILY TOMLIN: [*Laughs*] And we, we are all richer for it.

MERYL STREEP: [*Laughs*] But if . . .

LILY TOMLIN: . . . dialogue . . .

BOTH: We leave his movies knowing that life is many things . . .

MERYL STREEP: . . . at once . . .

LILY TOMLIN: . . . at once . . .

MERYL STREEP: Let's look at the clips!

* * *

ROBERT ALTMAN (*Recorded voice-over to Oscar audience, during a montage of film clips*): I equate this work more with painting than with theater or literature. Stories don't interest me. Basically I'm more interested in behavior. I don't direct, I watch. I have to be thrilled if I expect the audience to be thrilled. Because what I really want to see from an actor is something I've never seen before, so I can't tell them what that is. I try to encourage actors not to take turns. To deal with conversation as conversation. I mean, that's what the job is, I think. It's to make a comfort area so that an actor can go beyond what he thought he could do. I've done almost every kind of job. I love to take them and then kind of turn them over a little bit. Look at them a little differently. I purposely don't go into a project that I know how to do. It's just such a joyous collaborative art. When you start looking back, the real reward is the process of doing it and the people that you do it with. And man, it goes fast.

*   *   *

After Robert Altman's Death, in November 2006

ALAN RUDOLPH (director): You know he directed that thing at the Oscars, right? I was watching the Oscars on television, like ninety-nine-point-whatever percent of people. The day after, he called me, and I told him, "That thing with Lily and Meryl Streep was really the highlight for me."

And Bob said, "You know, I directed that. When they were rehearsing, I heard one reading her lines and then the other, back and forth. I went over and said, 'Just talk on top of each other.' "

MERYL STREEP: He told us, "This is a lot of horseshit. Just fuck around with it." Of course we were terrified. It's a big responsibility to honor this man we had admired so much. We wanted to make him laugh. That was our whole m.o.—make Altman laugh, and to hell with everybody else.

ALAN RUDOLPH: I wasn't surprised. These were two actresses in Bob's latest film, playing sisters, and they talked about Bob and how he does it in a way that Bob would have done it himself. Which means he wouldn't take it too seriously, but the truth would come out.

ACT I

1925–1969

Robert Altman is born, torments his sisters, judges his parents, collects snakes, chases girls (and catches them), goes to war, tattoos dogs, marries three times, becomes a father or stepfather six times, learns how to make movies, impresses and insults "the suits," says "cheese," and sets his sights on Hollywood success.

*

CHAPTER I

Kansas City

*

ROBERT ALTMAN: Kansas City? *[Starts to sing]* "Everything's up-to-date in Kansas City They've gone about as far as they could go. They went and built a skyscraper seven stories high. About as high as a building ought to grow. They've got a big theater that they call a burleseque. For fifty cents you can see a dandy show." *[Stops singing]*

Yep, Kansas City. I think it was a rather uneventful, American middle-class community I grew up in. I don't think it makes a hell of a lot of difference where you grow up, except if you can't shake the prejudicial influences. Whether it was Kansas City or Bangladesh. If you grew up in an Amish family in Pennsylvania, and you're fifty years old today, even if you shed all the main tenets of what you learned, you still retain something of that. A lot has to do with how strong the influences are, where you were placed in the world, and whether you're inhibited by that perspective. Have I shaken these influences? I don't know that I have, really.

KATHYRN REED ALTMAN (wife): Kansas City, born and bred. He's the boy next door. He was very influenced by that whole environment—it's always been a big part of him.

JOHN ALTMAN (cousin): Our great-grandfather, Bob's and mine, was Clement. He came here from Germany. They're the '48-ers, the failed revolutionaries of 1848. They're from Schleswig-Holstein and they're Catholic. And like a lot of those Germanic principalies and duchies, they pretty much took sides at the end of the Revolution of 1848. A lot of the minor nobility and the smaller principalities and rulers were really freaked out by 1848, so they tended to wrap themselves in the flag of either the Lutheran or the Catholic, depending on where they

Robert Altman at two and a half, in his parents' home in Kansas City

were. If you were in Schleswig-Holstein, it was mostly Protestant, so a lot of the Catholics took off. Clement probably was born around 1835—he died about 1888. So he probably came here, to America, as a boy. They settled in Quincy, Illinois. From the way they're dressed in photographs, they're probably petit bourgeois, they're probably shop-keepers.

Clement is the father of F.G., or Frank, our grandfather, who's born in approximately 1860. F.G. comes to Missouri in 1878, so he's eigh-teen or so. He may have come first to Edina, Missouri, which is in northeastern Missouri, a tiny little town. He was here in Kansas City by 1880. He apparently had some money, because he opened a jewelry store on Main Street in the 700 block, which was pretty much right in the center of downtown. And then he moved progressively south over the next few years.

In 1888, he began building what became the Altman Building. He also took on the two buildings immediately next to that, which are very similar but a little bit different. Both had bellied up, and he bought them and then he kind of clapped an iron front on all three of them, so it looked like it was one building. But as you were walking through the building you would know that it was a façade—you would go up sometimes and then go down, on what was supposed to be the same floor. That was at the center of what was known as Petticoat Lane, Eleventh and Walnut, which as a result made it just a dynamite location to build the family fortune. But he didn't own the land, and there were three different owners of the land underneath these three separate parts of the building. I have had friends of mine from law school call me and say, "Hey, I'm reading about your family's ongoing lawsuits over this land and how it's an example of how never to build." The lawsuit continued for generations and ate up a lot of money.

F.G. marries Nettie, and they're Bob and my grandparents. They had six children, two of them boys. One was my father, Frank, Jr., and the other was Bob's father, B.C., for Bernard Clement. The children viewed F.G. like *Life with Father,* as standing at the head of the table. F.G. was always spoken of in somewhat forbidding terms. Whereas Nettie—God, she was great. She was lovely, she was wonderful. You know in *A Wedding,* Bob named the matriarch, the Lillian Gish character, Nettie, right?

JOAN ALTMAN SARAFIAN (sister): Our father, B.C., had one brother, four sisters. Frank's the oldest, then comes Annette, then comes Marie, then comes Dad, then comes Pauline, and then comes Ginny. Annette, Marie, and Pauline were put in Europe, in France, for their education. That's what they did in those days. Grandmother Altman—Nettie—and Ginny stayed in England. They studied art, music. Annette played the harp beautifully. Pauline played a little bit. Marie was a wonderful pianist.

Grandmother Altman was a wonderful pianist, too. But she wasn't a concert pianist like everyone keeps saying. She wasn't—she played in movie houses. And she was a wonderful woman. I mean really great. Just alive and happy and fun to be around.

JOHN ALTMAN: The family story is that in about 1916—B.C. would have been around fourteen—our grandfather's brother, Uncle Clem, gave B.C. a hundred dollars and said, "Go to Riverside Park and bet that on a horse called Feather Duster." B.C. goes down to the paddock, sees Feather Duster, and decides, "I don't like the look of him." He decides he's going to save Uncle Clem that hundred dollars. Of course Feather Duster wins at something like twenty-two to one, and B.C. has to go back and tell Clem he didn't place the bet. That might have been the last bet that B.C. *didn't* place.

B.C. and my father were only about a year or two apart, and they were virtual twins, physically. They were products of Kansas City in the teens, which was an ebullient, growing, we-can-do-anything kind of place. I'm sure the country was too, but this city especially. And then the Roaring Twenties in this city, my God, with Boss Pendergast, if you were in your twenties and you had money, which they did then, I mean the world's your oyster, or at least the world bounded by Kansas City.

The Altman Building initially had twin motion-picture theaters on the first floor. And they opened with *Birth of a Nation*. The distributor at that time hadn't figured out this was a twin theater and sent the reels of one print. So they staggered the showtimes by fifteen minutes, and B.C. and my father, who at that time would have been fourteen and sixteen, respectively, were the projectionists. They would quickly hand-rewind it—no electric-power rewinds in those days. They quickly rewind the first reel as it comes off Projector One and run it over and stick it on Projector Two. They quickly solved that, but the first week was really exciting. So maybe that's how film—like an infection, like dengue fever, you know?—gets into the system, and then it mutates genetically and takes over the lives of your children.

Our grandfather F.G. died the night my father graduated high school. As was the wont of *The Kansas City Star* in 1917, the obituary says, "Frank Altman, prominent Catholic businessman. . . ." The Altman Building was one of the last big buildings in Kansas City built primarily out of wood. Huge wooden beams. F.G. would have been fifty-seven, and he was helping some of the workmen move a huge wooden beam. It slipped and he got a huge sliver, which infected. And before antibiotics, he was gone in a few days. He left Nettie, six kids, and enough money for Nettie to live just fine for the next forty years.

Dialogue from *Kansas City*:

BLONDIE O'HARA *(Played by Jennifer Jason Leigh):* Can I have my husband back now?

SELDOM SEEN *(Played by Harry Belafonte):* How do you want him, in a box or a sack?

* * *

BARBARA ALTMAN HODES (sister): Mother's family was a very wealthy family, the Matthews, but her father died when she was young.

JOAN ALTMAN SARAFIAN: Jack, her grandfather, raised walking horses. When he died he went out to the barn and he died there.

Did someone say our mother's side was from Mayflower descendants? No. Absolutely not. Grandma said they came over with all the other criminals. They got here in about 1701 or 1702, something like that.

TIM ROBBINS (actor/director/producer/writer): My great-grandmother on my maternal side was a Matthews from Missouri. I'll bet Bob and I are cousins. We've got to be some way, right? I mean how many Matthews were in Missouri in the late 1800s? When I heard about the Matthews thing, I said, "Holy fuck, he's from Kansas City, my mom's from St. Louis." Wouldn't that just be a mind blower? I only learned about it at the memorial, so I never asked him.

ALAN RUDOLPH: My mother's maiden name was Altman. I didn't tell Bob for a few years—several years, actually. When I did, he just looked at me for the longest time. And then he said, "I'll be a suck-egg mule."

* * *

BARBARA ALTMAN HODES: Mother's name was Helen, but she was called Rose, because she always wore a lot of red. And B.C. was a good-looking son of a gun—a full head of hair, and quite the guy in town. But Mother wouldn't tip her hat to him. Mother was seeing this man from New York. Anyway, she finally gave in and they started dating, and she said, "I'm not interested in marrying you." And she would write letters to this guy from New York. B.C. would come pick Mother up, and he'd see that letter, and say, "Oh heck, I'll mail that." He'd take

Bernard (B.C.) and Helen Altman with their toddler son, Robert

it home and steam it open and read it. Then he'd seal it and mail it. He wanted to find out about the guy in New York, to help his own chances.

So one Christmas, B.C. walks in with a beautiful box of candy. And in the center was this ring box, wrapped in foil. And of course Mother's mother was there, and her sister and her brothers were there. B.C. said, "Take that middle one." She said, "You know I don't eat candy. Why would you bring that?" Finally she took that middle piece and opened it up with the ring inside and oh—"Congratulations!" and everything from her family. She said, "Bernard"—it wasn't "B.C." with her, it was "Bernard"!—"in the other room." Well, Mother was older than Dad and she wasn't Catholic, though she became one later. She told him, "I'll marry you under two conditions. Never bring up my age, and never bring up religion, no matter what kind of knock-down, drag-out fight we have." And that was the deal.

Susan Davis (actress and cousin): Bob's mother was before her time in many ways. Helen was into nutrition. She was very charming. Not, in quotes, "social" or "chic." The Altman girls—Bob's aunts—were very chic. They all belonged to the Junior League. I don't think Helen did. Uncle Bernard was much more out there. She was quieter, a very good mother, a very conscientious mother.

John Altman: B.C. always had a twinkle in his eye. He never seemed to talk down to you. He seemed to be interested in what was going on with you. And he also would let you in on masculine things like hunting and drinking underage and things like that. Not terribly— it wasn't a structured thing, and he wasn't trying to garner your affection. He was just, you know, "Come on in and be part of the men's club." And he was a member of many men's clubs.

B.C. operated at all these different levels, and always smooth. He had friends from what my father called the "joints" around town all the way up to captains of industry and Ewing Kauffman, who eventually owned the Kansas City Royals. B.C. would be playing cards with the boys and then raising money to put Christ the King parish into existence, without skipping a beat.

Jerry Walsh (friend/lawyer/executor): My father ran for Congress in 1944, and B.C. was his campaign manager. They lost by something like six hundred votes out of twenty thousand or thirty thousand. It was a very close election. My father was not somebody who ever would have been a good politician, I think, but he had the ambition. As for B.C., Bob once said to me, "It's a good thing for the Republic that they failed in this operation." He thought his father's interest, and probably my father's, too, would have been primarily to find a way to get money out of the federal government for themselves.

*   *   *

Barbara Altman Hodes: Our parents had a great marriage. I'm sure Mother went through a lot with Dad, mostly because of the money he always gave away, but they had a great marriage.

JOAN ALTMAN SARAFIAN: Their relationship? Very good. He took her everywhere, till he had his affair. Even after, I think, he still took her everywhere.

JOHN ALTMAN: Helen was a sweetheart. Sweetest lady. And when she suffered a severe stroke, B.C. did not leave her side. No way was he putting her in a facility of any kind, he just waited on her in every way you could imagine, hand and foot, for years. He loved her, and that was the right thing to do. It was his duty, and I'm sure he wanted to do that very much. He just put his head down and did it and it was a lovely thing to see. It was a lovely example of what a man should be.

BARBARA ALTMAN HODES: Yes, all the women loved B.C. Everyone loved him. I mean the men *and* the women. Why wouldn't they all adore him—he complimented them from head to toe: "Oh my God, you look great," and all this blah, blah, blah. All the men really liked B.C., too. My God, he gave them an arm and a leg and a nose to go along with it. It didn't bother Mother. Mother was never jealous of

The wedding of Pauline Altman to John Walsh was a gathering of the prominent, prosperous Altman family in Kansas City. The ring bearer, fifth from right, was Robert Altman. His father, B.C., is the third man from left, and his mother, Helen, is the first woman on the right.

Dad, of other women or anything. It wasn't that she decided not to let it bother her. It *didn't* bother her because she knew B.C. I can't put it any different. I'm sure he was not a complete angel in his life, but I mean, she knew my dad. And Mother was a very classy, elegant lady.

JERRE STEENHOF (high school girlfriend): The Altmans were an old-time, very well-to-do family in Kansas City. B.C. was almost like the scallywag of the family. Helen was the sweetest, most considerate, charming lady. She was just one of the most beautiful, charming women who ever lived. But in my opinion B.C. was the dirtiest old man who ever lived. He used to speak fresh to all the young girls.

LOTUS CORELLI ALTMAN MONROE (second wife): B.C. was a woman-izer, a gambler. Helen was in another world. She was somewhere in the vapors. Just so nice, but she had made her own world because that was how it was. D.C. was a con man. He made his living off the people he knew at the country club, selling insurance policies to them over and over again. He'd play golf, play cards. All he did was play. Bob did take after B.C. in that he could sell anybody anything.

SUSAN DAVIS: It was a funny balance. My family, the Kigers, were in diamonds, and the Altman family was in insurance. My family was so much more serious and responsible. Uncle Bernard made and lost I don't know how many fortunes. You know that was a little rocky there. Everybody loved Bernard, and who wouldn't? He was the salesman of the world. But the family was always concerned, "Are they going to have enough money to get by?" Everybody was concerned. And there was a "take care" quality in the family—"Well, we've got to buy more insurance over there from the Altmans"—to get them money.

JERRY WALSH: It happened more than once where B.C. would call on a Monday morning. The phone would ring early, the kids were eating breakfast or getting ready to go to school, and my father would answer the phone. There'd be kind of a mumbled conversation. He'd say, "Okay, okay, good. Well, I'll wait for you." And my mother would say, "Who was that?" My father would say, "Oh, that was B.C., he's going to give me a ride to the office." And my mother would say, "I know what happened. He lost money on the golf course yesterday and he needs to borrow a few hundred dollars to cover a check, isn't that right?" *[Laughs]* B.C. would sell some policies and get some money and whatever.

RICHARD SARAFIAN (director/actor/former brother-in-law): B.C. had breakfast in bed until ten o'clock, served by Helen, and then from there he'd go to the Kansas City Club for an hour or two of gin rummy. By three o'clock he was on the golf course. He was a great salesman. He could sell anywhere. He was never a high-pressure salesman, though. In the waiting room, waiting for his daughter Joan to deliver my second son, he sold three policies.

When hunting season came around, B.C. would practice his duck calls months before. Every year he had a new device. One year he manufactured a slingshot out of metal and he was all excited because he had these ball bearings as big as marbles. He was going to shoot the slingshot. He was hard of hearing, but somehow he could always hear the ducks first. On one occasion, he called out, "Here they come!" He pulls back on the rubber band and holds up his thumb to get a good aim and smashes his thumb with the ball bearing. He passed out from the pain, and that was the end of duck season.

CHAPTER 2

Into the River

*

ROBERT ALTMAN: I was the eldest child. Born in 1925. Had I been born in 1935 instead of 1925, my life would be totally different. I would be a totally different person. Same if I had been born in 1915.

It all depends on when you're placed into the river, and where that river takes you—it couldn't happen the same way a week earlier or a week later. You're in your time and space in the river. Now, you can swim over toward the bank where the current isn't as fast, but basically from that point you're going down the river. You can swim upstream. But just for a little bit. If you swim up against the current a lot, by the time you die you have only covered a short distance along the bank. If you go over to the edge and go with the mainstream, you cover a lot more territory, but you're not exercising. I don't think you ever have the energy to beat the river. The river is always going faster than you can swim against it. The reason I think you fight against something is simply because it's there to fight against.

I think I go upstream because it's the easiest place for me to go. But I'm over at the edge, not in the center of it. In other words, I'm not out there making the long-distance swim across the channel. I take the easiest path upstream.

SUSAN DAVIS: Bob was the first baby of that generation, and he was the apple of everyone's eye. One day my mother was over there at the house with Helen Altman and Annette Altman Kiger and probably Marie Altman, and they were taking care of Bob. They were all so excited and crazy.

Helen said, "You know, he's getting ready to walk, he's pulling up."

From left, Barbara, Joan, and Robert Altman, circa 1937

But they were paying no attention. Bob lifted himself up, grabbed the table, and my mother said he didn't walk, he ran. And he was not even ten months old. They were so stunned. And he never walked after that, he ran. He set a very high bar, the gold standard, for kids to walk. I mean, if you didn't walk or run by nine or ten months in the family, you know, too bad. You were measured up to Bob.

ROBERT ALTMAN: My mother was okay [*laughs*]. I think she found being in the background comfortable because she kept going into it. I have a picture of her with a big laugh on her face, holding an apple, a close-up that was taken at some sort of country-club event. It showed her in a way I rarely saw her. I don't know. I feel elation for her, but I've thought: "I don't believe her in that picture."

I don't think that we were terribly close. I don't know much about her. I only know her in our relationship—that was the job she had in my life, being my mother for a short period of time. She was very kind. But in the best and worst ways of the word. She was, I think, kind of ineffective. I remember a situation where I was eight or nine. I was never a great baseball player, or even a good one. But it was in the culture. I remember what I really wanted was a baseball mitt. And I knew I wasn't qualified to get it. It would be like getting your first bicycle, you know? And my mother came home—most of my memories of her were from when I was lying on a couch sleeping when I'd have a fever. I was lying on the couch and she came in from a shopping trip.

She said, "I have a surprise for you. I bought you a baseball mitt."

I went, "Wow!"

She takes this package out and it's a baseball mitt that she'd bought at the drugstore. It was just wrong, a thing for a four-year-old. And I just got furious.

I realized, if not that day, then shortly after, that I'd hurt her feelings a lot. I understood it. And I didn't know how to correct it. But I knew that whatever pain it caused me was my fault, not hers. She had no way of knowing. She had the best of intentions, but the worst came out of it. And consequently I think I scared her a little. I think she was afraid of [*pause*] getting on the wrong side of me.

But I was always proud of her. I mean, I was always happy to introduce her to my friends. And if people would come to my house, I was content and proud. I never had a sense of "Oh God, how am I going to explain her?"

I knew my father a lot better. I mean, I can pinpoint him a lot easier than my mother. Nobody called my father Bernard. He was "B.C.," but "Nag" was his nickname. I never called him that, but when he was a kid, he was called Nag, 'cause his older brother, Frank, used to say, "Quit nagging me!"

I'd say he was a gambler. But that was an avocation. He was an insurance salesman. And he got his business, I now realize, by being in the country club, and by playing gin rummy, and all that. The more friends he had, the more insurance policies he could sell to all those people. He was kind of a hail-fellow-well-met.

He would come home at night—I didn't see him a lot. I remember a long session of homework, where I had to write something a hundred times or something like that. And my mother would always have to sit up and do those chores with me. I can't recall my father and school ever crossing paths.

He was very careful about his appearance, how he appeared to people. He was a natty dresser. I find myself emulating him. Many times I've been in a situation where I've said, "God, I'm dressing like my father." But I did that more ten years ago and twenty years ago and thirty years ago than I do now. That's gone now. But I remember being in military school and he came down to visit once on parents' day or something, and he had a camel-hair coat on, and he was really natty-looking, and he stood out from the crowd. I thought, "I kind of like that. But that's not a quality."

His good qualities are not the kind of qualities that I admire in people today. He was a good guy, people liked him. He went out of his way with strangers. He'd be the first one out on the street with a snow shovel, or if somebody's car would break down he'd stop; he'd be the first to stop and change their tire. But it all came from himself. It was all about those things that served himself. It was about having everybody like you. If you lose three hundred dollars to that person, that three hundred dollars you get back when you sell them an insurance policy.

Barbara Altman Hodes: How can Bob say Dad served himself? When you do something nice for someone, who gets the best benefit? You do, right? Well, in that sense maybe Bob's right. But Dad was always helping others. A couple of guys that Dad sold insurance said, "Hell, I don't care, I want to cancel that insurance policy. Hell if my wife can't take care of herself." And Dad would keep those policies current with his own money. I remember him going over when the guy died, and he'd go over and give that policy to that woman. Can you imagine the feeling she had? He must've felt good, too. There's nothing more satisfying than if you can help someone. Dad always wanted Bob to go into the insurance business with him. Of course you know that didn't happen.

Kathryn Reed Altman: My father-in-law was a real player, a gambler, a swinger, anything goes. I know there were even times when Bob was in his twenties when he and Bob would be going after the same girl and all that kind of stuff. He always had a big wad of money. Bob always had to have a lot of cash, which was so unusual to me. For security or something. A big tipper. I'm sure he was influenced a lot by his dad and his dad's behavior.

Jerry Walsh: When my father ran for Congress they had a storefront headquarters downtown, and I would go and be a messenger boy. Bob's cousin Frank Altman, who is the son of B.C.'s older brother and was a friend and contemporary of mine, he and I would go down to the headquarters. We used to love it that B.C. had a receptionist there who was a very sexy little blonde woman named Ginny Hewitt, and she would be nice to us.

Bob later told me that, after the war, when B.C. lived in Los Angeles for a few years, Bob met Ginny Hewitt and he asked her for a date. B.C. took him aside and said, "Listen, son, I've got to tell you something here, you know? Ginny and I have a little thing going on." And Bob said, "Okay, okay, I won't . . . !" *[Laughs]*

KATHRYN REED ALTMAN: His mother was a Catholic convert—his father was born and raised Catholic—and you know what they say about converts. So Bob did all the childhood stuff of the Catholic boy—Catholic schools and an altar boy and all that kind of thing. I

With his mother and sisters

nicknamed her the Billie Burke of Kansas City. Billie Burke was an actress in all the old MGM pictures and she was the fluttery one. She never accepted reality. Everything was always just fine, nothing would get serious.

*   *   *

JOHN ALTMAN: He was the oldest cousin of about fourteen from our generation, and the hero to all the rest of us. I mean, my gosh, Mister Charming and a sweet guy, you know? To his sisters, too. You could tell they just idolized him.

ROBERT ALTMAN: Growing up, my sisters were just a couple of toys for me to torment, as I recall.

JOAN ALTMAN SARAFIAN: My first memory of Bob is when he was running away from home. I would have been four or five. I went and got my doll suitcase and packed it with whatever was in the bottom drawer of my dresser. Then he came in and said he wasn't going, maybe because I was tagging along.

BARBARA ALTMAN HODES: I remember one time we were down at the Ozarks. He said, "Mother, I'm going to take Barbara and teach her how to swim." Oh, I was so excited. We go down, he throws me in the deep end and says, "Swim." That's not a very good thing for me to tell, is it?

I just worship my brother, okay? Let's get it out. Let's just lay it on like it is. He couldn't do anything wrong in my book.

JOAN ALTMAN SARAFIAN: My baby sister was the sweetest, most adorable child you could ever imagine, and we both adored her. She always called Mother "Dolly." So Bobby and I took Barbara out to the side of the house.

Bob would say, "All right, say, 'Mo.' "
She said, "Mo."
"Now say, 'Ther.' "
She said, "Ther."
He went over and over it, "mo" and "ther." I'm watching him and I'm looking at Barbara and she is so adorable. And he would say, "Now put that together."
And she'd say, "Dolly."
That was the end of that.

BARBARA ALTMAN HODES: We were reared, the three of us, with etiquette, class, to take people for who they are when you meet them, not what they have on, or their citizenship papers, or FBI record or library card.

SUSAN DAVIS: You have to remember we were brought up Southern. We weren't brought up Midwest. It was going to cotillions, and we had Negroes, we had black folks. We had nannies. They were the ones who helped raise us. Our mothers were there, but the nanny was the one that put you to bed.

ROBERT ALTMAN: We had a black maid, Glendora Majors—we called her Glen—and she was very important, maybe more important than my mother. A person like that in a household becomes someone in between a parent and a sibling. She was a parent I could manipulate more. She was more of a confidante.

JOAN ALTMAN SARAFIAN: Glen was unbelievable. She was so smart. Played all our games with us, taught me my multiplication tables. She loved Bob. Rabbit, she called him. I don't know why. Bob loved her, too. And Barbara she called Ducky. It broke my heart because I didn't have a nickname. Mother was different from Glen. Glen was more of a mother than Mother was. Mother was just so dear and so sweet and so captured; I mean, she had no life but us. She was a very gentle, kind, loving woman. Glen was tougher. Glen was tough love.

BARBARA ALTMAN HODES: When we'd get on the streetcar to go down to Brookside to the drugstore, Glen would say, "All right, I want you girls to sit up front there and be sure you act like ladies." Well, I'd get up and run back and sit with her. I never knew the difference between black, yellow, green, or orange, Catholic, Jewish, Methodist, Protestant, or whatever. You take people for what they are. And she'd say, "Oh no, now, you go back up there and sit with Joan, and I want you to act like a lady."

I never knew there was a Depression. We had a nice house. It wasn't an expensive home. I mean, it wasn't big, big like if you'd drive down Ward Parkway, the big homes. No, it was just a little house on a street. And we had a formal dinner in the dining room every night. First thing, we'd have to say grace before meals. Glen would go put a clean uniform on, a clean apron, come in and serve dinner. We all had to clean up before B.C. got home. You know, take a bath, put a nice little outfit on. I don't know if it was a cold bowl of chili, a rotten egg on dark toast, but we ate it, and I had a bottle of ketchup to go with it all, every time. We didn't know Dad was working at night downtown in a garage where they parked cars to make ends meet. But every night, that ice-cream man would come by, and every kid on our block would be waiting, and Dad would buy every one of them an ice-cream cone.

JOAN ALTMAN SARAFIAN: I was born in '29, but in June, just before the Depression. So Dad had already bought "Blue Boy," which was a Pierce-Arrow. And he used to take us for drives on hot summer nights. I remember Bob there, because he asked me why I was crying, and I said I felt sorry for everybody because they weren't as happy as we were. I can't imagine anyone having better parents than we did.

BARBARA ALTMAN HODES: Dad took care of Glen all that time, and he took care of Bud, who did the yard work and really was a bum, and of Geneva, who used to come and make our little pinafores with our little matching underpants, and Mabel, who would come and iron and make the biscuits. Dad and Mother always had these cocktail parties, and Mabel would make these little biscuits with ham in them that were just succulent, you know?

ROBERT ALTMAN: I have an image in my head of Glen sitting me down and saying, "Now, you listen to this—the best music that ever was." She introduced me to jazz. I've told people that "Solitude" was the first piece of music I remember hearing. I heard it from her.

Music from the last scene of *Kansas City:* Duke Ellington's "Solitude," performed in bass duet by Ron Carter and Christian McBride.

HARRY BELAFONTE (actor/singer/activist): Glendora Majors did something to him, opened him up on race. He'd see through her eyes. She played an important part in his growing up, maturing, and in that maturity he found his own center.

*   *   *

JOHN ALTMAN: I don't know that we felt it was anything special to be an Altman in Kansas City back then. Maybe it was to other people. I don't think Bob felt that we were any great shakes, not at all. I don't ever remember Bob having any kind of preconceived, egotistical position about anybody. I mean, he did not suffer fools gladly, but you had to prove you were a fool first.

ROBERT ALTMAN: My grandmother, my mother's mother, lived with us all through the time I was growing up. Momma, we called her. She called my father Mr. Altman, and she'd make a face at him when he turned his back. I remember one time she said, "Bobby, get all of your friends in the neighborhood and bring them over there. I want to talk to them. I have a surprise." So I went running around and I got four or five of these kids, my group who lived in the neighborhood. We went down in the cellar of the house and she came down and sat on the stairs. She said, "Boys, I have a surprise for you." I just felt so good about this. And she said, "One of you broke my lamp"—or something like that—"and I don't know how, but you're going to pay for it. It's going to be a quarter apiece." I just exploded. And I called her— I said dirty words, and I screamed at her and ran out. She was just a mean person.

BARBARA ALTMAN HODES: Bob had a doll when he was little. A little boy doll. You'd push the stomach and it would whistle. And the little doll's lips were puckered. Momma, our mother's mother, kept it when Bob was away. I would ask to see the doll and she'd bring it out. She wouldn't let us touch it. She had it wrapped in tissue paper. When Momma died, we gave it to Glen. It was the cutest little thing.

* * *

JERRY WALSH: When Bob was about twelve or thirteen years old, he went to a Boy Scouts meeting one evening each week at a location that was near the Kansas City Art Institute. Walking home after the meeting one evening, Bob and several other Boy Scouts discovered that they could climb up a wall and look through a window at a naked woman posing in a life-drawing class that Thomas Hart Benton was teaching at the Art Institute. They spread the word to other Scouts, and for several weeks there was quite a crowd of boys on the wall. Eventually, someone noticed them and told Tom, who came outside and chased them away. Bob concluded the story by saying, "It greatly improved attendance at the Boy Scouts for a while!"

JOAN ALTMAN SARAFIAN: Bob was a Boy Scout, and he went to camp. That's where he made friends with Phil—I don't know his last name. Phil was the snake man, and Bob loved snakes and collected snakes. When he came home he brought the snakes with him and he turned the bookcases—you've seen those legal bookcases—into snake cases

At Boy Scout camp in Osceola, Missouri, circa 1938,
when he was about thirteen

and put them in the back of the garage. B.C., our father, wouldn't let them in the house. B.C. had a phobia about snakes, but he still pulled his car into the garage every night; it made him very, very nervous.

We went on summer vacation and Bob brought Phil with us, which Mother and Dad didn't understand because he was so much older than Bob. Bob and I went out tracking snakes. And he caught a cotton-mouth by the tail. Bob got his height early—he had zoomed out to six-foot-two by then. So he pulled the snake out by its tail and he was just turning around to hold it out straight, 'cause it was really long, huge. I was barefooted, which I always was. And he wanted me to step on the head. So he kept turning around with this huge snake, round and round, and I'd get up close as I could and I'd look at that mouth. Have you ever seen a cottonmouth? This was a big one; I'm not exaggerating, it must have been over five feet. And I couldn't do it. He was furious with me. So he said, "Run up and get Phil." So I ran up—my feet were bleeding—and I got Phil, but by the time I got back, Bob was worn out and he had tossed it. I felt so bad about that. That was his best snake for the whole time.

The next vacation we were on was in the Ozarks. We had a cabin on a high cliff. And again he was collecting snakes. There was a group of goats and for some reason they were chasing me. So I was running. Bobby had trapped a copperhead. He had just lifted up the rock. I ran over it and stepped right on it and killed it, and then I tripped on a log. And I would have gone over the cliff, which was oh, maybe five hundred yards down—it was really, really up there—but Bob grabbed me, saved me. The next day, Bob tied a rope around one of the aspens at the edge, and he hauled himself over that cliff and swung himself into a cave. I thought this was the end. Evidently the cave was filled with stalagmites and stalactites, and as he described it to me, it was just gorgeous. Of course somehow he got out, made his way back up top.

That night, after he was in the cave, the sky had turned just coral. The whole sky was just absolutely gorgeous. We were staying in a cabin. We had our dog Teddy with us. Teddy was a great dog, half husky and half chow. We were all lying out on this sleeping porch—me, my cousin Louise, my baby sister, Bobby, and I think one or two of his friends. The wind started coming and you could hear it from miles away, hitting those trees. This wind was unbelievable, but approaching slow. You knew it was coming. Bob was telling us that he had already chartered a spaceship. They're coming to pick him up, and he's going up to the moon because the world is coming to an end. And he can only take two people. Well, it just scared the shit out of all of us. Of course we were all begging, begging him, "Please let us go with you. Why only two?" Barbara, I think, was crying. He really was very convincing. At first we pooh-poohed him, but he convinced us.

* * *

ROBERT ALTMAN: I loved movies, but it was like all kids—they were just movies, just entertainment. I must have been seven or eight, and I remember climbing out of the window. I had the mumps. It was maybe a mile, two miles, from my house to the Plaza Theater, and I have this memory of running down to that theater and seeing *King Kong*, sitting through it a couple of times.

The Four Feathers and *Viva Villa!*, too. I liked *Gunga Din*. There was something about the adventure of those films—every one of them took me into a culture and a place, a space on the Earth that was different than anything I knew. Later, *The Treasure of the Sierra Madre* was another—I like that movie a lot. It had a different convention from other movies—the hero was not a hero in the conventional sense. It was all fresh to me at that time.

BARBARA ALTMAN HODES: Oh God, one night Mother took Joan and me to see *The Hunchback of Notre Dame*. Bob was home when we got back from the movie. And I've always had a yellow streak down my back. The baby, you know. Joan and I were sleeping in one bed because I was scared to death and everything. And Mother said, "Now it's time

Robert Altman, at right, dressed as a woman for Halloween at age thirteen

to go to bed." All of a sudden we heard this loud noise. Bob had put on some of Mother's makeup and got a hanger. He hooked it in his mouth and hooked it around his neck to pull it back, and stuffed this big pillow up his back. All of a sudden here he comes—the hunchback—leaping into the room. Joan pushes me and Bob grabs me. I about had a heart attack. The neighbors called, thought there'd been somebody murdered.

ROBERT ALTMAN: My first interest in dramatics was radio. I remember listening to the radio a lot as a kid in the 1930s, lying on the floor like all the kids at that time. My big idol when I was a young man was Norman Corwin, who pretty much created the radio drama. . . . Anything I know about drama today comes more from Norman Corwin than anybody.

NORMAN CORWIN (radio pioneer): I went to dinner in Woodland Hills with some friends one night and I got in my car—it was midnight or so—to drive back to the city. I turned on the radio and there was a man being interviewed, and the first thing I heard was, "Mr. Altman, have you had any influences in your life?" He says, "Yes, I was influenced by Norman Corwin." He proceeded to utter the words with which you are familiar—"Anything I know about drama today . . ." It was an astounding thing to listen to, having just turned on the radio.

He was most generous in his evaluation of my own work, when I was not conscious of having contributed to his art at all. I tried to figure out in what way I might have influenced him, and the only thing I could arrive at was the tackling of subjects that would normally defy dramatic reconstruction. Bob tackled difficult subjects and made them palatable and organized.

I know he said that I was a hero to him growing up. He became a hero of mine as a man. That's remarkable and rare, to go from being someone's hero to having him as your hero. That's what happened between us.

Letter from Norman Corwin to Robert Altman, thanking him for writing an introduction to a broadcast, May 13, 1996: I tend to worry at times that maybe I've fooled a lot of people a lot of the time, but when the Altman Seal of Approval is stamped on the product, I say to myself, what the hell, man, a giant has paid you a great compliment, so accept it, relax, and store it in your heart. Which I do. You continue to hit line drive home runs, and I rejoice in them all.

*   *   *

JOAN ALTMAN SARAFIAN: Bob and Dad clashed, but I think that's normal because he was extremely gifted. Bob was always being punished. Our parents were not brutal, but the hairbrush would come out on any infraction. And you know it hurt. One time Bob got a spanking and B.C. came out of the room and he says, "That's it, never again." Bob wouldn't cry. And B.C. said, "That's the end of it. I don't care what he does, I'm never doing that again."

RICHARD SARAFIAN: One time when Bob was brought into court for something, as a kid, B.C. went to the judge. This is how deeply he felt about his son—he pounded his fist on the table so hard he broke his hand. Bob got off.

BARBARA ALTMAN HODES: Dad pounding his hand—Bob used that later. It was a scene in *Bonanza*, I think.

Robert Altman to Hal Hinson, story headlined "Robert Altman, His Way; on Art, Money and *Vincent & Theo*," *The Washington Post*, November 18, 1990: I did introduce comedy to *Bonanza*. . . . I had Lorne Greene go into the sheriff's office and demand that his son be released. He said, "You're not going to keep my son overnight in jail," then, pounding on the table, breaks his hand. Well, this is something that happened to me and my father when I was sixteen. My father broke his hand telling a cop that he wasn't going to keep me in jail. And he wouldn't show that he hurt himself, but from my cell I could see his face go bright red and then white. And I just had Ben do the same thing.

Dialogue from *Bonanza*, Episode 63, "The Secret," directed by Robert Altman, originally aired May 6, 1963:

BEN CARTWRIGHT *(Played by Lorne Greene):* If I were to start doubting my son at this point, everything I've lived and worked for would be lost.

* * *

BARBARA ALTMAN HODES: The girls from school would be calling Bob all the time. All the time.

JOAN ALTMAN SARAFIAN: I remember his first love—and he's had many—was a girl with white-blonde hair at Southwest High School. I believe he was a sophomore and she was a senior.

JERRE STEENHOF: Of course I dated him. I was blonde. Every blonde in our high school knew him. If they were blonde he dated them. Most everybody would have one date and that was it. Why? Ha! I think he considered himself pretty fast. My best friend said to me, "How come you went out with him twice?" You know what she was implying!

He was tall and handsome. He had beautiful blue eyes and they sparkled liked nobody's business. He had a delightful sense of humor. Bob was so neat and so precise in his dress—he had all the class. He knew how to act. My mother thought he was a good kid. He would stand up when she came into the room. He had all the graciousness of any well-raised young man.

One of the reasons he used to come over to my house was my father had one of the first Zenith radios that had a recorder on it. Bob was fascinated by that. Someplace I still have one of the recordings he made. One side was him reciting from Poe, "The jingling and the tingling of the bells," and the other side was *Gunga Din*.

JERRY WALSH: Once my parents were disagreeing about whether I should be allowed to do something or not, and my father said something like, "Well, you know, when Bob was that age, B.C. let him do it." And my mother said, "Well, I certainly don't want him to grow up and be like Bobby Altman!" The reason behind that was that Bob had had kind of a checkered career as a teenager at different schools.

JOAN ALTMAN SARAFIAN: Bob didn't like school. In fact, he hated it. I remember when he was in Catholic school, sitting outside while Sister Hildegard was chasing Bob around the room, trying to catch him with a stick to beat him up. Now, most of the nuns were great, but Hildegard was very old—she must have been in her eighties—and Bob was testing her.

JERRE STEENHOF: He went to St. Peter's for grade school, then he started out at Rockhurst—the Catholic high school—and I think he lasted there two years. Then he came to Southwest High School,

Robert Altman, center, as a member of the
Wentworth Military Academy track team

which was a public school. I don't think a teacher or anybody at school really tapped into his abilities. He had a wonderful imagination about things. He was smart, but he was trying to find himself. There was more talent there than people knew. He just didn't care too much for organized school. He didn't hit the books. And everybody who talked in class got the seventh-hour study hall. It was detention. He was in there as much as anybody.

As it turned out, he really wasn't at Southwest all that long. I think I can take credit for him being expelled. He knew the combination of my locker, up on the fourth floor, because he didn't want to carry his books from one floor to another. So one day he put his books and this cotton-picking green snake in my locker. The snake's in a jar. He also put a pistol in there. He was in ROTC at Southwest, and I think he wanted to show it to his commanding officer after school. It was a pistol, I think, from World War I. Well, I opened the locker and I let out a scream like a crazy person. It wasn't long until he was sent to Wentworth Military Academy. I felt badly afterwards.

Norma Maring (Wentworth Military Academy alumni director): On September 8, 1941, he entered the academy in his senior year. While he was here, he lettered in basketball and he lettered in track.

Robert Altman: Back then I perceived myself as being in the higher echelon of the people I knew. Anytime I wasn't, I had a reason—not an excuse, but a reason. For instance, I ran track in high school. We ran on cinder tracks with shoes with those spikes in them. The mile was the first race of the meet, usually, and the half mile was the last. They'd have me run the mile, and I was, say, third or fourth all the time. Then I would run the half mile. I could have been first in that, but I'd just had the energy taken away from me by running the mile. So I ended up always being second in the half mile. And I'd go, "Well, goddammit! I could have been first if I hadn't run the mile."

One time, it was one of those outdoor meets where lots of schools come together. They'd line up maybe twenty, thirty guys, so the take-off is a sprint. As the mile started, either I hit somebody's heel or somebody hit my heel, and I went down in the cinders. And these guys ran over me. I actually had holes, spike holes, in me, plus a lot of cinders in my hips and legs. By the time I got back up, they were a hundred yards ahead of me. Instead of just walking off the track, I took off after them. It was a quarter-mile track. And by the end of the half mile, I was in first place. I had caught up with all of them. I had these thoughts—you know, in those races you have a lot of time to think. I'm imagining that I'm going to win this race after falling down, which is inconceivable. I'm running along and I'm seeing these headlines. And then I don't remember anything—I passed out. And these guys ran around me again. I never even finished the race, but I tried. I think it was because there was a crowd there. I was playing to those unknown people for the first time. I think that's kind of an important event in my life.

Norma Maring: He graduated from high school January 23, 1943, but remained the rest of the school year through May. He had not only his high school degree but also some college credits. His first year he took English comp and rhetoric, algebra and trigonometry, general and organic chemistry. He had physics, economics, salesmanship, and physical education. His second year, which ended up being his one semester of college, he had analytic geometry, international relations, and weather and climate.

ROBERT ALTMAN: Mathematics was my first subject. That and weather. I took a course in meteorology and I liked it a lot. I liked the idea of how the different cooling levels of a lake affect the atmosphere. And the whole predictability or nonpredictability of weather. I still keep that in my mind. Under the right circumstances, I would have signed up to go into weather. Although I don't think I would have liked to be one of these weathermen today. But now I can follow these programs and understand the philosophy of weather and climate. I take that more seriously, or I look at that subject more seriously, than most people. And I think that it helps me in terms of the balance of elements.

NORMA MARING: Every time he came to Kansas City, you'd hear him on the news, he would always say, "I went to Wentworth Military Academy in Lexington, Missouri. I was more of a social student than an academic student." His record tells you right there he was academically doing fine. He was a member of Alpha Company, and he had the rank of sergeant, which meant he was trusted with responsibility and leadership.

CHAPTER 3

307th Bomb Group

*

ROBERT ALTMAN: I enlisted because I was going to be drafted. I don't think it was anything I would've chosen otherwise. I went into the Army Air Force because I was in Wentworth and we found out that if we wanted to take the Air Force exam, they had to let us go—and the test was going to be in Kansas City.

It was one of those multiple-choice things, about a two-hour exam. I didn't even read the questions. I just went down and arbitrarily marked the answers, 'cause I wasn't there to take the exam. I didn't care about going into the Air Force. I cared about having a night or two in Kansas City. They came back and said I got a fairly high score, so I went into the Air Force.

JOAN ALTMAN SARAFIAN: I remember when he was leaving. He was in this truck with all these kids, and we followed in the car down to the Union Station. We weren't supposed to upset him or cry or anything, but it was heartbreaking.

ROBERT ALTMAN: I went to Jefferson Barracks in St. Louis, and we did more tests. And they said, "You tested equally well for all these three things"—you were either a pilot, a bombardier, or a navigator. Most of the kids in there all wanted to be pilots. I didn't care about that. In fact, I was saying, "Oh, I think I want to be a bombardier," because I was good at math. But when they said I scored equally well on all three and I could make my choice, I said, "Oh—pilot." I think I picked pilot because that's what most of the kids I was there with wanted the most. I don't know if that means I had a competitive nature or that I wanted to please other people.

Copilot Robert Altman of the U.S. Army Air Force

I went to pre-flight training at Jefferson Barracks, and then I was sent to flight training. Muskogee, Oklahoma, then to Coffeyville, Kansas, then Frederick, Oklahoma. Eventually, before going overseas, I got to California, at March Field in Riverside. The P-38 was what I thought I'd like—a twin-engine fighter—but I ended up getting put into multiengine bombers. You were put into those categories according to what their needs were. So in that part of the river, that's what I was pushed into.

I was ordinary, middle-of-the-road. I was fairly coordinated. In training, I thought I was hot stuff—everybody thought that they were hot stuff. I don't know what makes a good car driver or aviator, but I know now I would never have been at the top. I know I would never win an auto race or an aero race.

JOAN ALTMAN SARAFIAN: When he was in training, he hooked up with a girl named Daphne. She used to go down to Muskogee to see him. I think Daphne would be every young boy's dream. Gorgeous. She was about four or five years older than him. Her husband had been killed in the war—he flew a Black Spider, and when you're hit there's no way you can get out of those, so he died. I think she really kind of introduced him to a more interesting sex life than what he was used to. I remember how she would put on her lipstick, because we'd all watch her. She would powder her lips first, then put on the lipstick. Then powder it again. Then blot them. And we all thought that was something, because we weren't even allowed to wear any.

FRANK W. BARHYDT (screenwriter): There's a story about Bob losing his virginity in a whorehouse. I don't know about that, but he had a girlfriend who his father didn't particularly like. So he didn't want Bob to marry her, and he figured that if Bob got laid his mind would be off it. I'm not sure that's the beginning, middle, and end of that story. But I do remember his father kind of setting him up.

BARBARA ALTMAN HODES: Bob met LaVonne, LaVonne Elmer, when he was in training, though he didn't marry her until later. Blonde, very attractive, and had a real nice figure, very nice.

JOAN ALTMAN SARAFIAN: He met her in Salinas, California. She was a phone operator. Incredible figure. Always in high heels, and she couldn't even walk barefooted because her feet were curved for heels. She cooked great breakfasts for him. He didn't love her. He said he didn't. But I guess she was a good lay and he liked that. She was wild, but she loved him. God, she loved him so much.

CHRISTINE ALTMAN (daughter): My mother was from a small town in Nebraska. She graduated and she decided she wanted to go out and see the world and do things. So she went to California and stayed with one of my aunts. That's when the war was going on, and she would go to these dances at the NCO clubs, and that's where she met my dad.

She was very beautiful. She was a knockout. Her hair was brown and she always had a white streak coming down one side. I don't know if she did that. She was very exotic-looking. She was thin and she was just gorgeous. My dad told me one time she was the most beautiful woman he had ever seen. Of course they hooked it right up, I guess.

* * *

Robert Altman at the beach with his first wife, LaVonne Elmer

BARBARA ALTMAN HODES: When he'd come home during training, he'd say, "All right, now you better go on upstairs and get your good clothes on. We've got a date tonight. Not you, Joan, I'm taking Barbara." And we'd go down to the drugstore, sit up at the fountain, and we'd have sodas, me in my dress and him in his uniform. I must've been about twelve. I thought, "My God, he's wonderful."

JOAN ALTMAN SARAFIAN: We were a very, very close family. When Bob went into the service and was stationed in California, our father moved our family out there, to be with him.

BARBARA ALTMAN HODES: When we went to California, I was dating R.J., Robert Wagner. You know, he was in high school when I was. He was just a nice person. From a well-to-do family, but, you know, just a nice guy.

We'd come home and Bob would grab R.J. "What in the hell, where in the hell have you been with my sweet sister?" He used to do that every once in a while. He'd be in a bad mood and grab R.J. and put him up against the wall. B.C. would say, "Come now, Bob. Everything's fine. She's home early." God, it was funny. But Bob used to drink, you know, quite a bit.

ROBERT ALTMAN: When I first went to California, I really was kind of a star fucker. I mean, I got as close to all that stuff as I could. And I think I fell for the glamour of it, and the girls. I had an aunt and uncle who lived out there, my aunt Pauline and her husband, John Walsh. She had written a song that had been a hit, and he was a hustler of some kind—a lawyer. They were on the edges of people who knew people. And I just decided I wanted into that world.

JOHN HOROSCHAK, JR. (bomber crew gunner): We were in the 307th Bomb Group. Just before we were going overseas, Bob got together with his aunt Pauline and decided to have a party for the crew. There were ten of us—I was the armor gunner. She supplied cars and chauffeurs to bring us up there. Bob had a convertible Cadillac and he and I were in there. He got stopped for speeding and he talked fast. Somehow he got away with it.

So we got to his aunt's house, in Beverly Hills, overlooking Hollywood and L.A., a big, beautiful home with a swimming pool, a tennis court. A bicycle rack maybe fifty bicycles long. We opened the door and she had a band in one corner of the big living room and they played a welcome to us. They had ten girls from UCLA dressed up in evening gowns and they were there to greet us—to dance with us and play tennis with us. We stayed overnight—not that there was anything done, of course. The next day she let the servants off for the day and she made breakfast for all of us and the college girls. My room had a Plymouth-type bed with an overhang. Like something from the movies, you know?

The party was going on and a lot of us were in a rec room off the living room, a beautiful big room. His aunt came in and Bob says, "Aunt Pauline, you see John over there, the little fella? He's in the ball turret on the bottom of the airplane."

"What's that?" she says.

"It's a steel ball with two guns on it."

And she says, "That sounds complicated."

She had a big glass table in the middle of the room, oblong, maybe ten feet long by three feet across. Cactus plants underneath.

Bob tries to show her. "John gets into the turret"—and he sat in the middle of the table—"and he'd be on his back." Well, Bob broke through the glass and went down into the cactus.

She says, "Oh, I'll call an ambulance."

And Bob says, "Nah, I'm all right."

That's the way Bob was.

WILLIAM STUCKEY (bomber crew gunner): We all acted like gentlemen. When the evening was over, Bob Altman's father and I drove the girls home. He was a very nice guy. I'm not sure where Bob was.

JOHN HOROSCHAK, JR.: We were in San Francisco on the night before we were leaving. We sat around as a group, the enlisted men, and we decided that since our pilot was named Dale Dennison we'd call ourselves Dennison's Dragons.

WILLIAM STUCKEY: Yeah, Dennison's Dragons. I thought it was kind of silly.

JOHN HOROSCHAK, JR.: When we were going overseas, we stopped at different islands in the Pacific. Bob and Lester Goldschlag, the first officer, would always get hooked up with Army nurses. The first night, they both shacked up with them.

Unbylined story headlined "Exploits of B-24 'Long Rangers' to Provide Lively Post-War Yarns," *The Washington Star*, October 20, 1945: Here's what Daddy did in the Big War if he was in the "Long Rangers" group, one of the famed B-24 outfits of the Jungle Air Force.

He was a member of a team which: Reached out from its South, Southwest Pacific and Netherlands East Indies bases to plaster the Japanese over an area of more than eight-and-a-half-million square miles, considerably more than the area of the United States; Struck the enemy on more than seven hundred days of its three years in action, usually flying two or more missions a day; Earned two Distinguished Unit Citations, awarded by direction of the President, for cracking the tough Turk and Balikpapan bases; Helped neutralize the bristling bases of Turk, Yap and Palau in less than four months to pave the way for the invasions of Guam, Saipan and the Caroline Islands; Threw the Standard Operating Procedure book on B-24 Liberators out the window to put all four squadrons of the group in the air for one-hundred-eighty-seven days with only one twenty-four-hour period of inactivity in a six-month climax ending June 28, 1945—dropping ninety-eight hundred tons of bombs in thirty-seven thousand air hours logged.

Garrison Keillor, writer and radio impresario, from the Los Angeles memorial for Robert Altman, DGA Theater, March 4, 2007: This was an amazing plane for a nineteen-year-old kid from Kansas City to be piloting. It had a crew of ten people, four gunners, it had the pilot, the copilot, it had the navigator and the bombardier, a flight engineer who doubled as a gunner, and it had the radioman who also doubled as a gunner. It had six people manning guns on a plane with four engines, a twin-tail plane that was stripped down to carry a maximum of fuel and bombs. It carried a bomb load of more than two tons, about five thousand pounds of bombs, flew at twenty-five-thousand feet. He told me all this, reeled off all this information about the B-24. It had a range of up to two thousand miles.

He was flying all over. And it was in the Pacific, and all of the navigation was by celestial navigation and by landmark. There was no radar on board the plane. And the navigator had been trained just as rapidly as you had been. So if you lost your way, you were in trouble rather quickly. At twenty-five-thousand feet.

I said, "Well, what is it like up there?"

He said, "It's cold."

It's thirty below zero and the plane was not insulated at all. He said it was as loud as a steel foundry inside. The wind came blowing through the cracks and the gun turrets and the bomb bays. You could barely hear yourself in there. You were on headphones on the radio and you had oxygen and you were flying this thing that had the power of about ten semitruck engines and weighed about as much as one, so that you could fly at three hundred miles per hour at twenty-five thousand feet, thirty below zero.

Any crewman who flew more than thirty missions had only about a thirty percent chance of coming back. And Bob flew almost fifty.

ROBERT ALTMAN: I was stationed in the Halmahera Islands, on an island called Morotai. We flew missions over Borneo, which was a long way. It was like a six-hour flight, maybe a four-hour flight to the target,

Flight Crew F8–360–AW 8, aka Dennison's Dragons. In the top photo, Robert Altman is kneeling, second from right; in the bottom photo he is kneeling, second from left. In the top photo, the front row, from left, are Lester Goldschlag; Charles W. McKay, Jr.; Altman; and Dale Dennison. Behind them, from left, are John P. Lister, Jr.; Harold Nichols; William Stuckey; John Horoschak, Jr.; William Keel; and Harold Eleson.

and then the time over the target was usually twenty minutes. And then back. We were just constantly hitting those oil fields in Borneo, at Balikpapan. We'd fly in echelons of six, or in threes that would come together to make a group of six or nine. Once there was a plane, and I was on its left wing. I saw it get hit—*blap!*—by a piece of antiair flak. The whole front of the plane just disappeared out of the air.

The flak is there and you're there, and you can't fly away from it. It either hits you or it doesn't.

I don't remember any specific feelings about dropping the bombs. I was more concerned with watching the flak, the antiaircraft stuff going on around us, than I was about what the bombs were doing. I didn't have any ethical response to it.

JOHN HOROSCHAK, JR.: Almost every mission we had flak coming up from the targets trying to shoot us down. Also, the Japanese would fly above us and drop phosphorous bombs on the formation. Some were dropped clean and some were on parachutes. They missed us, but they hit other aircraft. There's danger, but you live with it. You get back to the base and say, "Well, that's one out of the way, we've got another mission to go." That's the way you looked at it.

WILLIAM STUCKEY: Bob was an excellent copilot, every bit as capable as the pilot, Dale Dennison. On some missions Bob did the takeoffs and landings and so forth. I was the nose-turret gunner, and he was sort of in charge of me. He'd get on the intercom and tell me that we had aircraft coming at us and keep an eye out but don't fire. More than once they were Navy aircraft flying around someplace. We didn't want to entertain them.

JOHN HOROSCHAK, JR.: Our pilot was like an old man. Even after the war he wasn't friendly.

Bob actually saw himself more as a fighter pilot—he liked the excitement of a fighter plane. He was not happy about becoming a copilot of a big bomber. In a fighter plane, he's all alone. His personality was more suited to that. But he was a good B-24 pilot, too.

DALE DENNISON (pilot): Yeah, I knew him. He was a good pilot. That's all.

Entry in wartime diary of John Horoschak, Jr., June 8, 1945: Took off at 0740 for Balikpapan. Took a cameraman. Put on my flak suit and broke my oxygen bottle. Cameraman was hit in shoulder by flak. [Waist gunner William] Keel was hit on his shoe. I stood still and watched flak bursts all around us—black and all colors—sounded like buckshot. Pilot's windshield was blown out and left landing gear was shot out. Big flak hole on right vertical stabilizer.

JOHN HOROSCHAK, JR.: That entry is from a mission to Balikpapan, over in Borneo. It was an oil-refinery center—very big among the Japanese as a source of fuel for their boats and their planes. The Japanese didn't have the sophistication that we did with antiaircraft guns. They had maybe four or five batteries of aircraft guns, and each one would fire at a different altitude, with a different color. It was like a big cloud of bombs—blue smoke at one level, red at another altitude, orange, and so on. They'd have guys on the ground with binoculars. When they found out which was the right altitude, which color was closest to our plane, all the other batteries would go to the same altitude. Depending on how long it took to get there, most of the time we could get the hell out of there, but not always. That's what happened on this mission.

The windshield on Bob's side, the right side, got hit with shrapnel. It ran up the side of his arm. There was shrapnel flying all over the place. It tore his flying suit off on the left-hand side. Gave him a gash on the side of his arm—he was hurt, but not that bad. He wrapped it in white cloth and came back to see how the fellas in the back were doing. We had a photographer on that mission, and he was hit. He went out like a light.

WILLIAM STUCKEY: The waist gunner, Bill Keel, got on the pipe and said, "I've been hit. I've been hit." But he wasn't hit—it was just the heel was taken off his shoe. Flak came through and took the heel off his shoe and ended up in the photographer's shoulder.

JOHN HOROSCHAK, JR.: We were up at twenty-six thousand feet—it was cold as anything. We took our jackets off and gave him whatever blankets we had. We were able to put the intravenous solution in him to try to take away his nerves, to calm his nerves down.

To make it back we had to strip the plane of all the heavy items. We lost an engine, so we were running on three engines. We lost fuel, too. We took all of the guns out of the turrets and tossed them overboard. Any bombs we still had, we dropped. We dropped the bombs over neutral territory over the island of Borneo—we let the bombing wire go with them, so they wouldn't explode. We made it back and landed, with ambulances and fire trucks all around, and we found something like twenty-seven holes in the plane.

WILLIAM STUCKEY: There were thirty-two holes in the ship. We lost one engine. I didn't know we took so many hits until we got down on the ground, back at base. We were a lucky crew.

JOHN HOROSCHAK, JR.: They covered all the holes with pieces of aluminum. You pop some rivets in there. The crew that took that plane up next, they got as far as the northern part of Borneo. It started to vibrate terribly, and they crash-landed on the island and everyone died.

JOAN ALTMAN SARAFIAN: A friend of Bob's, a man that he knew in the Air Force, came over to visit and to pay his condolences to Mother and Dad. Well, they hadn't heard anything, and I don't know if Bob ever told them anything about getting hurt. But B.C. found out he wasn't dead.

ROBERT ALTMAN: There were more good experiences than bad. I'm talking about setting up an officers' club on Morotai, and I remember doing the paintings on the windows. We'd get Australian girls and invite them to party. The whole idea of setting up this officers' club was so we could have a reason to attract these Aussie women in there. It worked pretty good.

Entry in wartime diary of John Horoschak, Jr., June 9–13, 1945: Altman came to visit us every night and drink beer.

* * *

JOHN HOROSCHAK, JR.: Bob wasn't like the other officers. He was friendly. He'd introduce us to girls. He was a good friend. The Australian Army occupied Morotai. Bob and another officer, Lester Goldschlag, got familiar with a couple of the Australian nurses and they invited me over there to that side of the island. There was a beach. They bought a package of beer. So they introduced me to this girl. This girl and I made out good. We were up in the coconut grove at the beach.

Bob got hell from the pilot, Dennison, for that kind of thing. The pilot made sure he was the boss. The copilot—that's Bob—he's got to be the boss, too, so Dennison didn't like when Bob spent time with us. After a mission, we'd go play cards at the officers' club. Bob would take us in. He was losing money at cards, so he'd come over to our tents and borrow money. When his father sent him money, he'd pay us back with a tip for loaning him the money. The pilot didn't like that one bit. Dennison was going to court-martial him for borrowing money from the enlisted men. In the end it got blown over, because Bob was a pretty slick talker. He talked his way out of it.

ROBERT ALTMAN: I didn't like the military. I didn't like anything about it. I wasn't a big in-line-for-promotions person. I was not interested in that. I did not try to become a successful Army person, and I'm usually interested in being successful in whatever area I'm in. But the Army was never part of that. It wasn't anything I wanted. I didn't want to be a major—well, I would have loved that, but only because it would have given me more girls, you know?

Dialogue from *M*A*S*H:*

CAPTAIN WALTER "PAINLESS POLE" WALDOWSKI (*Played by John Schuck*): I wasn't gonna fool around out here, because I got these three girls I'm engaged to back home.

ROBERT ALTMAN: When I was discharged, I could go back on a ship or I could get a plane and fly back. I signed up to fly back because I wanted to be in California as fast as possible. It was five days to fly back, so I took five pair of pants, five shirts, five pair of socks, and my flight suit. At each stop I'd take a shower and throw those clothes away. When I landed in Sacramento, that was it, I was out. I didn't even have a bag to carry.

Undated letter from General George C. Kenney to Bernard C. Altman: Recently your son, Robert B. Altman, was decorated with the Air Medal. It was an award made in recognition of courageous service to his combat organization, his fellow American airmen, his country, his home, and to you. . . . Your son took part in sustained operational flight missions during which hostile contact was probable and expected. These operations, consisting of bombing missions against enemy airdromes and installations as well as attacks on naval and cargo vessels, aided considerably in the recent successes in this theater. . . . I would like to tell you how genuinely proud I am to have men such as your son in my command, and how gratified I am to know that young Americans with such courage and resourcefulness are fighting our country's battle against the Japanese aggressors. You, Mr. Altman, have every reason to share that pride and gratification.

BOB BALABAN (actor/producer/director): Bob told a great story. When he was a pilot he wasn't at all scared when he thought he was going to die. But when he realized he was going to live, he really had to work on it. He was like, "Oh shit, I have a chance. I really better be good now."

Garrison Keillor, from the Los Angeles memorial for Robert Altman, DGA Theater, March 4, 2007: Nineteen, twenty years old in the Pacific. When you have done that at the age of nineteen or twenty you really have crossed a bridge. You really have left your youth in Kansas

With his parents, in California, in his uniform

City behind you. And that's how you get the chance to die old and beloved and distinguished in California, is by being extremely lucky when you are nineteen and twenty. He really was a man who believed in his luck. When you've flown fifty missions in a B-24 Liberator bomber over the Pacific, what's the worst they can do to you in the movie business? Nothing. Nothing whatsoever. So that was Bob's life.

*   *   *

JOHN HOROSCHAK, JR.: After the war, Bob got the plane to fly over the ranch where his mother and father lived, and we were just throwing toilet paper out the plane at the ranch.

ROBERT ALTMAN: When we came back, we were able to get medals, these ribbons. You had a list of things that you had earned—so many service, so many good conduct, this and that. I remember going immediately to a store in Los Angeles that sold those medals. I'm sure I wore those things once or twice, but I got out of that uniform pretty fast.

BARBARA ALTMAN HODES: The first night Bob came home, Joan and I doubled up in the other bedroom. All of a sudden we hear this "HA! HA!" And my God, I'm grabbing Joan. I hear Dad: "You're all right! You're all right!" Mother said, "Oh my God!" We went down the hall and Bob's up on the bed like an ape. He was in a nightmare, you know, and he did that almost every night automatically. He had these horrible, horrible nightmares. Dad would try to wake him up and Mother says, "My God, he'll kill you!" Bob's swinging at everything. That was the only change in him after the war—at night. In the daytime he was great, no problem at all. But the nightmares went on for two or three months.

*   *   *

JERRY WALSH (friend/lawyer/executor): In 1986 or '87, I read an interesting novel called *Paper Doll* by a young writer named Jim Shepard about the crew of a B-17 bomber that was bombing Germany from a base in England in 1943 or 1944. Knowing that Bob had flown a heavy bomber during the war, I sent him a copy and suggested he might like it. About a week later, he called me full of enthusiasm about the book:

"That kid must have known someone who was there because there are so many things in the book that are exactly what I remember. The way the ten crew members, instead of being buddies and teammates, just hated each other. And the way it felt when all the fifty-caliber machine guns were firing at the same time—you were afraid the plane was going to shake to pieces."

Jim Shepard (author): I had been out walking the dog. A friend of mine was staying with me at the time, and when I got back he said, "Robert Altman called." I didn't believe him. There was a callback number, and I called back skeptically and it was, I think, his New York studios. He kept me on the phone for about forty-five minutes. He just rhapsodized about how accurate he thought the book was. He said, "I don't understand to Christ how you did it." He talked about how it felt viscerally to have these things flying at you at such speeds, and the balance of invincibility and vulnerability you felt. You felt like you were depending on a large group of people and you felt completely alone, isolated in your little station.

I teased him, naturally, about turning it into a film. He said, "I can't get something simple off the ground, much less something that requires a thousand-plane raid. Goddammit, if I ever got three or four dollars together I am going to try to make this movie." The book was published in '86, so it was probably in early '87. I kept fantasizing that he would call back after *The Player.* We never spoke again.

Frank W. Barhydt: You couldn't really drag things out of Bob. If he wanted to talk about something, he'd talk about it, but otherwise you couldn't really engage him on that subject. The war was like that. He'd never see any of those guys he served with, never went back to meet with them again. But all that he saw and all that he experienced, and how long past the longevity of an average pilot he lived, all that had an effect on him. It had a lot to do with how he lived his life.

Robert Altman: If we keep talking about the metaphor of the river, this is the part where a bunch of natives on the edge of the bank are shooting and throwing darts at you. You say, "Well, I'm glad we're past this part."

CHAPTER 4

Making Pictures

*

ROBERT ALTMAN: I know where it started, this thing of making pictures, or what eventually led into making pictures.

I think you could walk down the street and see a kid—a seven- or eight-year-old kid—and he's throwing a baseball. You stop him—you're a stranger. And you say, "Hey, throw that ball again." And the kid throws the ball again. You say, "Hey, you could be a major-league pitcher. You've got the stuff for it. You really know how to throw the ball." You leave, and you never see that kid again for the rest of your life. But that kid has a better chance of being a big-league pitcher than if you hadn't stopped.

I was overseas, and I had a cousin—it was actually my father's cousin—a woman named Mary Rector. She was the secretary to the guy who was the emcee on the Camel cigarette weekly variety show. I wrote her a letter because I thought that she was a star. I mean, she rubbed shoulders with those people. It was a real funny letter—I mean, I was trying to be funny. And she wrote back, "Oh, you're a born writer. You should be a writer—your letter was so good." From that day on I was a writer.

After that I wrote a couple of pages of something. I can remember, almost, the first line: "The scallops of lights on Wilshire Boulevard emptied into the shallow ocean, and a glaring sign blinked on and off. And it said, THE BROKEN DRUM; YOU CAN'T BEAT IT." That was a restaurant. And then I took this character into the restaurant. I never got to the real character. It was all just atmosphere, and it was always somebody else's character that I had in mind. But I stuck with that piece of writing a long time.

After the war, looking for what to do next

Untitled work from Robert Altman's personal files: There was just the hint of dawn in the East, and Wilshire Boulevard was quiet and dark, save the scallops of light that bordered the curbing. A few blocks from where the file of streetlamps emptied into the blackness of shallow ocean, one small building gave evidence of life. Evidence in the form of a blinding neon sign which illuminated in red and white neon the words, THE BROKEN DRUM. Beneath this glowed another neon tube shaped like a drum, and to a tom-tom rhythm the irritating phrase, YOU CAN'T BEAT IT, flashed on and off.

ROBERT ALTMAN: The first film that made the difference in my mind between a movie and a film, if you can use those terms, was *Brief Encounter.* This was after I got out, after the war. I remember going to the Fairfax in L.A., going over by myself for some reason. I remember thinking, "What is this about?" This girl, Celia Johnson, was not pretty. She wore those sensible shoes. And suddenly I'm in love with her. I walked out of that movie and I went for a long walk. I realized the difference, and from that point on I started looking for those kinds of experiences in films.

* * *

JOAN ALTMAN SARAFIAN: After the war we went back to Kansas City and LaVonne followed him there. There was a terrible car accident. It was a red Buick, and the guy driving was wealthy, rich and wild. He had a bad leg or a limp or something. There were, I think, six people in the car. LaVonne was sitting on Bob's lap and they hit a Greyhound bus, or the bus hit them. The entire car was gone. LaVonne's face was pretty broken up—her face was all wired. No one died that I know of, but everyone was injured badly and thrown. Except for Bob. He was fine.

BARBARA ALTMAN HODES: Bob gets out and wanders around. They didn't even know he was in the wreck.

JOAN ALTMAN SARAFIAN: He married LaVonne as soon as she got out of the hospital. He felt responsible.

CHRISTINE ALTMAN: I imagine that they were going to get married anyway, but she was going to have to stay there at the Altman house when she got out of the hospital. B.C. said, "Son, you should do something about this."

BARBARA ALTMAN HODES: He married her because she was pregnant, with their daughter, Christine.

Twenty-two-year-old Robert Altman with his first wife, LaVonne,
and their daughter, Christine, in 1947

CHRISTINE ALTMAN: Pregnant with me? I don't know. I was born in '47, and I don't know the date that they got married. I'm not sure. The way I got it was they were just married and I came along. If it was before or after I'm not really sure. It was never an issue.

BARBARA ALTMAN HODES: After they got married, here in Kansas City, they came out to California. She looked like a skeleton, she was so thin. Her mouth was still wired. He used that in *A Wedding*. You know, the bride with braces.

*　*　*

ROBERT ALTMAN: After the war, I took singing lessons from my aunt Pauline. I had no aptitude for it at all. But I remember I took some singing lessons from her. I didn't know what I was doing, or going to do.

I got into this Identi-Code thing. I don't know how I got into this, but I bought this bulldog called Punch. The guy that sold me the dog was a guy named Skimmerhorn.

Dialogue from *M*A*S*H*:

(Hawkeye and Duke race off in a stolen Jeep.)
MOTOR POOL SERGEANT *(Played by Jerry Jones)*: Skimmerhorn, get that son of a bitch! He just stole my Jeep!
[Skimmerhorn runs past, bumps into sergeant, spilling hot coffee on him]

ROBERT ALTMAN: Skimmerhorn was from Detroit, and he had a partner named H. Graham Connar. He was an English guy, and he had introduced indoor polo to America, as I remember. He wore one of those English moustaches. So they told me about this thing they were doing called Identi-Code—tattooing identification on dogs, in case they were lost or stolen. I thought, "That's a great idea." I got very enthusiastic about it and somehow I joined them. I became the guy who did the tattooing.

I went down to buy the tattooing machines from a guy in downtown L.A., a guy who had been a tattooed man in a circus. And the wife was the fat lady in the circus, called Dainty Dottie. All around his garage he had designs, drawings of eagles, all that stuff. So the fat lady is typing up the invoice on this portable Royal typewriter and I was trying to be polite to her.

I'd say, "You know, this is really nice. I saw your drawings up there."

And she'd make a mistake on the invoice and she'd put a new piece of paper in. We did that a few times and I remember he leaned over to me and said, "It's better if you don't talk. Dottie can only think of one thing at a time."

I'm sitting there and I'm thinking, "I'm here with the tattooed man and the fat lady from the circus, and a little Royal typewriter. I bought some tattooing machines and she's writing up a receipt. Is this my life?"

JOAN ALTMAN SARAFIAN: He went in with Dad on that dog-tattooing thing. That was the first time they worked together—Dad on the financing, I think.

One time Bob went down to the corner grocery store and his bulldog followed him. A German shepherd was coming out of the grocery store and the bulldog grabbed it by the neck. He wouldn't let go of this dog, and Bob grabbed a broom and stuck it up his ass. That's how they got him to release his hold on that other dog. But the dog was docile with people, great with people and great with babies. Bob's daughter, Chrissy, was an infant, not even crawling, and that dog just loved her.

ROBERT ALTMAN: Punch was the first dog I tattooed. We would shave an area on the inside of the right hind leg, up near the groin, shave it with an electric razor. Then we'd put on the oil, which was a lubricant and also antiseptic. Then I would write in these numbers. The number system we set up was that each state had its number, like Alabama was "1" and Arizona was "2" or so on. Then each county in the state had its own number. So Aaron County, Alabama, if there even is one, would be "1–1." Then there was the dog's individual number. That was our system.

Then we made a deal with all the sheriffs in America, through the sheriffs' organization, that they would keep records of all those numbers in each sheriff's office. We would pay a dollar for each record they'd keep. So all they had to do was stick that in a file someplace and they'd get that dollar. That came out of what we charged for the tattoo, which I think was five dollars or ten dollars. Then we went to Washington and tattooed Harry Truman's dog.

Through John Walsh, Pauline's husband, we got through to someone who knew Truman. Truman had this dog he didn't even care about, a little dog of some kind. They sent it over to us and we tattooed it. That was part of our promotion of Identi-Code. Then we went to the Pure Food and Drug folks to get certification for the oil and the ethyl chloride we used to freeze the area.

Our hope was to sell this whole operation to the National Dog Bureau, which was owned by Purina. We'd sell it to them and come out with a few hundred thousand dollars and walk away. We even got the Hearst papers behind us because we said this was for antivivisection. They were a big antivivisection voice. It was part of their crusade, but for me it was a scam. I mean, although I did this stuff sincerely, it's like any salesman. You tend to believe in what you're selling, even though you really don't know what it is. Was it my goal to safeguard all the dogs in America? No, not at all.

We got to the point where we went to the ASPCA, or whatever it was at the time, and said we had all these funds behind us, seeking their endorsement. But Connar had taken the funds and gone to Ireland—he took, I don't know, fifteen thousand dollars or so. The indoor polo player went east with our money. It fucked us with the ASPCA, and the whole thing just fell apart. That was it. It almost worked.

I went back to California and declared myself a writer. My dad had a place in Malibu, up in the hills, and in the downstairs of the house lived a guy named George W. George and his wife. George was Rube Goldberg's son. We met and I said I was a writer. He said he was a director. So we started to work together.

GEORGE W. GEORGE (writer/producer): I had no idea who he was. He was just a guy whose parents lived upstairs who had some ideas for stories for movies and things like that. He seemed like a nice guy. We immediately started talking about stories, and we wrote a crime story for RKO.

Bodyguard *(1948; Robert Altman received story credit, with George W. George)*

GEORGE W. GEORGE: Bob was always a good collaborator. Work is a difficult thing to divide. Work is something you do as a personal issue among yourself and your gods. Sometimes it's easy and sometimes you suffer. It's either professional or it isn't professional, and Bob was always professional. Sometimes you can't work with people because they don't know what you're working on. They've been in the movie business all their lives and they have no idea what a movie is.

I worked once with an agent who told me, "Mr. George, anybody can write the first act of a play. The hard thing to do is a second act of a play." Think of it as your own life. You lived the first act of your life pretty good because you just did it. You think you know everything about life because you're young. But you've made a pretty good mess of your life so far. That's the first act. How do you write the second act? Well, very few people can write a successful second act. That's why it's such fun. Everybody wishes they could do it over again, do something over again, or at least live a full life. Most of them have no idea what they lived through or how to do a second act. Very few people live a successful second act. Bob knew how.

Robert Altman: George had an uncle named Eddie Marin. He was a director at RKO, kind of a B-movie director. We sold *Christmas Eve* as an original story through his uncle. I wasn't credited. And then we sold *Bodyguard*. And they were both made into films.

Joan Altman Sarafian: Bob and George wrote two Hollywood scripts together. I think they made thirty-five thousand dollars.

Robert Altman: They wouldn't let me do what I wanted. I remember, I went to them on *Bodyguard* and said, "I'll do the screenplay—let me do the screenplay for free." And, of course, that really turns them off. I could never even get on a set to learn how these pictures were made.

CHAPTER 5

The Calvin Company

*

RICHARD SARAFIAN (director/actor/former brother-in-law): Bob's career was delayed for about ten years. When he'd had some success with George, he took it for granted that this was easy money. Then nothing sold. Had he stayed in California he probably would have written another one and found his way. But going back to Kansas City grounded him in terms of learning his craft. He learned to produce and direct documentaries. From that point, he could glue it all together and give it life.

ROBERT ALTMAN: Film schools happened after I was making films. There was no such thing as a film school when I was going to school. There were writing courses you could sign up for, there were script-writing courses, little things like that going on. To make films, I went to Kansas City and got a job with the Calvin Company.

Select Industrial Films Robert Altman Made
at the Calvin Company

Modern Football (1951); King Basketball (1952); The Sound of Bells (1952); How to Run a Filling Station (1953); The Last Mile (1953); The Dirty Look (1954); Better Football (1954); The Builders (1955); The Perfect Crime (1955); The Magic Bond (1956).

FRANK W. BARHYDT: My father, Frank G. Barhydt, was in charge of production for the Calvin Company. He hired Bob. They made industrial films, which were really like advertisements for the company but

*The headquarters of the Calvin Company, coincidentally located in the
Altman Building, built by Robert Altman's grandfather*

also they were training films for the employees. I've heard various versions of how Bob got hired, but one was that Bob sort of limped in
there trying to find a battery for his car or something. He was like a lot
of starving artists—he didn't have a lot of money and lived paycheck to
paycheck. But he'd been in Hollywood. He'd been in a movie—an
extra in *The Secret Life of Walter Mitty*—and he'd had a screen credit as
a writer. He parlayed that into claiming to be a very experienced filmmaker.

ROGER SNOWDALL (sound engineer): We were the biggest sixteen-
millimeter company in the world. At one time Calvin had six hundred
fifty employees. We had four buildings.

  For Bob, it was his apprenticeship. He managed to stay busy all the
time. There never was a time I actually saw Bob not doing some-

*Robert Altman, center background, playing an extra, "Man at bar,"
in the 1947 film* The Secret Life of Walter Mitty, *starring Danny Kaye, at right*

thing—he was filming a new one or editing the last one. He earned his money while he was here, there's no doubt.

When we first met I was a helper in the sound department. The atmosphere on Bob's sets at Calvin was always very professional, but it was casual, too. When we were doing the scene, it was very professional, everything had to be right. He didn't do a lot of retakes. We rehearsed quite a bit, and we'd almost always take at least two good takes. Bob ended up doing almost all his own editing. When he didn't he'd hang over the editor's shoulder and the editor would wish he would do it.

FRANK W. BARHYDT: I think he used to drive Forrest Calvin, who was the owner, crazy at times. He just did things different ways. He had this passion for sound. He was always looking to do sound a different way, different than everybody else.

ROGER SNOWDALL: He was an innovator on sound even then. First of all, his use of the directional microphone. People weren't using that prior to Bob to any extent. They used omnidirectional microphones, which picked up all directions, and of course with that type of microphone you had ambient noise. Even though the soundstage is quiet you still get ambience. We were able to get closer to the subjects using the mike boom and the directional microphone. That's what he taught me to do.

He liked sound effects. Sometimes we'd have some artificially generated sound. And we had an ambience track. If we were in a factory he'd have me record five minutes of just ambience, which he could edit in as a background track to go along with whatever dialogue was taking place while the factory was shut down. It was a fixation on sound. He wanted the proper ambience. He wanted it to sound real, not artificial, and he worked toward that end. That's why his industrial pictures were good, because they had this quality.

With dialogue, he'd cut back and forth. Instead of this guy talks and that guy talks, he'd cut back to the guy listening while the other guy was still talking, which is what you'd do if you were a natural observer of the scene. He did that in *industrial* films. They'd write a script and A talks, then B talks, then A talks, and the camera is cutting back and forth. Well, he did things differently.

Still, we were pretty straitlaced at Calvin. Bob wanted to do things real. Of course he couldn't do that completely at Calvin.

ART GOODELL (cameraman): The cinematographers at Calvin considered him innovative, always coming up with something different in the way of camera angles, the way he accomplished shots. For instance, if he had guys sitting around playing poker, in order to get various shots of various players he would have them change chairs so we wouldn't have to make as many setups.

ROGER SNOWDALL: In all the time I worked with him, he never got upset with me. He might have got upset about the way the scene went, and I might not have done it to suit him. But he never said, "You messed up." It was, "Let's do it again, and would you try to do it this way." He always made it seem as though he blamed himself, as though "I didn't tell you right."

ART GOODELL: He was always respectful of the people he worked with. If you had a suggestion for a little different camera angle, he always listened to those suggestions. But he was also very encouraging about wanting you to learn more. He was great up to the last minute. When the action started he was in charge.

ROGER SNOWDALL: Caterpillar had a Number 12 loader-grader, and we went and shot motion pictures of this loader-grader in every aspect of its use—on the road and how it worked. The motion picture was shown to prospective customers. It was a sales tool. Bob tried to make it a more personalized thing. He'd shoot over the driver's shoulder instead of out on the roadway. He'd talk to the operator—"What do you like about this?" "Why do you like this one better than something else?" "Does it fulfill your needs in the snow? On the gravel roads?"

FRANK W. BARHYDT: One time he was doing an agricultural film and he figured how to rig a camera on the side of the car or mount it in a way that gave it a different look. The Calvin Company was a place where he could learn the craft, be around people he could learn from. He learned the basics so he could springboard into a higher realm.

Robert Altman, with foot on bumper, directing a Calvin Company film

ROGER SNOWDALL: We did this one safety show around Kansas City and we staged a crash on Truman Road out toward the armaments building, near Seven Highway. We staged this wreck where one car came down and hit another car—a beautiful, beautiful scene. Bob made arrangements to buy the automobiles, because both of them were going to be destroyed. Somehow or other he ended up with a new Ford Mustang, which somehow or other got buried in the cost of these pictures. Everybody knew it, but I guess nobody knew how to do anything about it [*laughs*].

He was a wheeler-dealer, I know that. He'd spend your money until it was gone and then he'd spend somebody else's. You'd go on a road trip with him, you bought the booze, you bought the drinks, and when you ran out somebody else would have to buy because he never had any money. If he did, he didn't spend it.

One time we almost got thrown out of a restaurant. Bob and I were discussing religious things. He was three sheets to the wind and he got a little loud. The people next to us left and we didn't realize that we had driven them away. We went up to pay the bill, and the woman said, "You know of course that you ran those people out of here because of your loud talk about religion." And I said, "No, I didn't know that. I'm really sorry about that." Bob made some comment to the effect of, "Who cares? If they don't like it, it's too bad." His take on religion was just being argumentative. It's not that he had a strong opinion one way or another, he just wanted to argue. I think he would have liked to be a practicing atheist, but nah, he wasn't.

Another time we were going down South, to Bartlesville, Oklahoma. We were shooting a Phillips Marlex plastics show. Bob and Art Goodell and another cameraman and myself were on this trip. They took the light fixture down from the ceiling in Bob's motel room, and put in a bunch of fruit and a bunch of booze, and they made a punch bowl out of it. Everybody got really soused. They started cleaning the place up, and somebody poured this stuff in the toilet, and of course it stopped up the toilet. The next morning somebody flushed the toilet and this stuff ran all over the bathroom floor—red water and booze and fruit and everything. Bob called the manager, and the lady came in who ran the place, and she was all aghast. With a straight face, Bob said, "Somebody must've killed a fruit-eating monkey." She screamed and ran out of the room. And we very quickly left the motel.

* * *

JOAN ALTMAN SARAFIAN: I'd go down to Calvin and watch him directing. He seemed to know what he was doing. I tell you, if you wanted to see a really good film, you would film Bob making a film.

SUSAN DAVIS (actress and cousin): He treated all of us as part of his own rep company. "Suze, I've got to use your baby." It was a Calvin Company thing and Bob needed an eighteen-month-old baby, and he had to be able to take direction. I said, "Bob, you're kidding." And he said, "Let me just work with him. And you can be the mom." I said, "Sure, why not?" I was always the mom or the wife or the widow. So I hand my son Jeffrey the spinach and Bob is directing him. And Bob said, "If you throw that on the floor as hard as you can, I will give you an ice cream." So there's film somewhere of my oldest son, after Bob bribed him, throwing spinach on the floor. It was brilliant.

JERRE STEENHOF: After high school, I saw Bob again when he was at Calvin. Some of us girls acted for him. In one scene I was pushing a perambulator. And he thought that was just the funniest thing in the world—me, his old girlfriend, with a baby buggy.

ROGER SNOWDALL: He made a lot of these service-station films, driveway-type scenes where you'd see the customers driving through. Phillips Petroleum made a big deal of that. That was in the days when you had a full-service filling station, and in the movie they made a point of describing what a good driveway technician should do—check the water, check the oil, clean the windshield, check the fan belts, make sure they don't need new ones. They had an opportunity to sell, and they emphasized that.

LOTUS CORELLI ALTMAN MONROE (second wife): I was an actress, and I got a casting call from the Calvin Company. Bob was going to be directing. This was one of his first directorial things—he was very new to it. They had hired William Frawley—you know, Fred Mertz from *I Love Lucy*. He had a continuing role in the Phillips Petroleum movies that they made. Each one of these little half-hour films was to demonstrate different things to the Phillips company employees—how to keep a station clean, how to sell TBA—which I learned was tires, batteries, and accessories—how to run their gas stations. The first one I did for them was *Keeping the Station Clean*.

My little bit was that I was supposed to be getting out of my car and walking up to the ladies' room. They had a guy cleaning the ladies' room, and I was supposed to try the door. He was supposed to say something, and I was to turn around and leave.

So I walked up to the door and tried the handle and this voice came out, "I'll be through in just a minute, ma'am." At the sound of his voice, I stepped back in shock to see if it was the ladies' room—I looked up to the sign in bewilderment, then turned around and left immediately. Bob cracked up.

I'm an actress, and that bit of business is what I do. I think that's the first time Bob realized that if you hire an actor, you tell him what the situation is and let them go. That's what he's always done with his women, particularly. And that's why everybody, every actor, loves him.

JOAN ALTMAN SARAFIAN: Lotus was a New York actress who had come to Kansas City with her first husband. She was very smart, very hip, and he fell in love with her.

CHRISTINE ALTMAN: My parents fought a lot. They got into a huge fight and he broke the mirror before he went out. This mirror was like the Empire State Building to me, and this mirror came crashing down. That's the memory that keeps coming back. It was a catastrophic memory. The wood in it was six inches wide, with carved cherubs. A few years ago was my fiftieth birthday, and he had it restored and fixed and sent it to me for my birthday. That was wonderful. But my parents weren't together very long.

Why'd they divorce? I think it's because of his unquenched desire to do and be whatever he wanted to do or be. From racehorses to tattooing dogs to all kinds of strange little scams on his way to trying to figure out what he really wanted to do, which he figured out at the Calvin Company, which was to make movies.

LOTUS CORELLI ALTMAN MONROE: After that film for Phillips, we became acquainted. He asked me if I wanted to have a drink afterwards. I was amenable. I was having kind of a little split in my marriage, and I was very unhappy. We were not separated, but he was going his way and I was concentrating on my work and keeping busy. So Bob and I went to dinner a couple of times and of course he's a delightful raconteur. Most women like a man with a sense of humor.

He was already divorced from LaVonne. I had to straighten Christine out about that. She thought, "You came along and took my father away." But her mother was already living in Fremont, Nebraska. I had nothing to do with their breakup.

Bob came to a couple of our parties when I was married to Max. Bob was looking for a hostess, and he decided that I was a perfect hostess. Just before I left my husband we had a big bash. Bob looked at my husband and said, "I'm going to marry your wife, you know." Max laughed and said, "A lot of people have said that." I turned to him and said, "I think you should listen to him." Later on my husband and I talked, and I said, "Yes, I'm going to leave." This was during the holiday season. I said I was leaving on New Year's Eve, and I did.

Bob said, "Well, let's move in together." I said yes—I was ready to leave. It was New Year's Eve, 1951, and so we lived together for almost a year. We didn't tell anybody. He continued to work at the Calvin Company. I continued to do my plays and my television. I had a series of little things. One was called *Name That Sketch*. We had some of the announcers who were popular in Kansas City in that time. We had a panel and a sketch artist with a huge sheet of blank paper who would draw these charcoal sketches and we were supposed to figure out what they meant. A long fence with a knothole with a fish looking through it. I said, "Pike's Peek!" That's how dumb these shows were.

Bob wanted to get to California, so he quit Calvin. I think it was November 21, and it had to be 1952. We rented a house right off Sunset Boulevard in West Hollywood. Bob was trying to get work, but he wasn't getting any. Bob and Jim Lantz, who had been an anchorman in Kansas City and was a very good friend, collaborated on writing things. He and Bob worked up one idea where they were going to make millions: Play-A-Tune. It was a strip of paper with musical keys on it. They had numbers on the keys. You put the strip of paper behind the keys on the piano. The book was written so it had numbers under the notes. You'd play the number under the note and that's how you'd learn to play the tune. Jim and Bob filmed an ad, and it ran on television. They got a P.O. box and waited for the orders. They had about ten responses. Well, that wasn't going to work.

This was about the time they came up with the all-purpose country song "Give Me a Girl Who Will Love My Dog and Teach My Kids to Pray." They tried to get a truck in there somehow but they couldn't manage it.

Lou Lombardo came out with us, too. Louis latched onto Bob when he was in his late teens or something—he had done work on the sets at Calvin. Bob was a flame that attracted lots of moths. Louis claimed to have quasi-gangster affiliations. "You want anybody taken care of, I can get their knees broken. Just one if you want." Louis attached himself to us. So he was part of our little crowd.

Nobody was making any money, so Bob said, "I've got to go back to the Calvin Company." So we went back, but Louis stayed on and got a job in the studios.

FRANK W. BARHYDT: Bob would go out to Hollywood for a while, and when he could not find work he would come back to the Calvin Company. I think he did that three or four times.

ROBERT ALTMAN: I was broke. I couldn't get a job. I couldn't do anything. And I went back to them. And each time I'd go back, I'd take a salary cut.

Robert Altman, from a speech to the Calvin Company, circa 1964: I started in the film business not too long ago, right here on this soundstage. It was a stormy beginning, and as I remember, I was in such a hurry to "make it" that I often forgot to stand still long enough to do what it was I was trying to do. I'm not sure—even today—that I knew what it was I was trying to do, but I do know that I tried very, very hard, and ran around and around my goal until either I or it became like tigers turning into a circle of melted butter. And never once stopping to wonder what it was I was chasing—or was it, by then, chasing me.

Anyway, I was hired and quit. Rehired and fired. Came and went. Until one of the brighter fellows around here remarked—as I was storming out of the front door one day with a chip on my shoulder, and none in my pockets—"If Altman comes back a third time, they'll get to keep him."

LOTUS CORELLI ALTMAN MONROE: When we came back from California, we lived outside Kansas City, at Lake Lotawana. It was a charming little place, built like a little lighthouse. It was two cabins on one lot. The inside wall was also the outside wall. It wasn't meant for winter living. To heat the place was a fireplace. The stove and the sink weren't important—we had a bar.

Bob got me a job at the insurance company where his father was working, Kemper. They gave me a job to send out notices to people that their premiums were due. We went out on the lake and Bob taught me how to cast for bass. We'd get home from work and change our clothes and get in our boat and fish for bass.

With his second wife, Lotus, in 1952

RICHARD SARAFIAN: One time Lotus managed to catch a big one. I don't know what kind of fish it was. She kept it on a string in the water, for weeks. If anybody floated by and asked her how she was doing, she would pull up this fish. She had humor, not just humor but mischief.

LOTUS CORELLI ALTMAN MONROE: Bob's sister Joan and her first husband, Chet Allen, and Bob and I were a little group. They moved into the cabin next door. Chet and Joan were absolutely the most gorgeous couple you've ever seen. Joan was classic. She looked like she'd just stepped out of *Vogue*, this porcelain beauty and this naturally dark blonde hair. Joan was brilliant. She and I got along very well. We would catch fish and cook and feed all these people. Nobody had any money. It was a fine time.

JOAN ALTMAN SARAFIAN: Lotus was the greatest cook in the world. She could cook anything, and it would taste good. Out at the lake, we would hunt frogs at night, because she cooked frogs' legs. Bob and I would go out with our spear. The lake had been populated by hundreds of frogs, but by the end of that summer there wasn't a sound. I always felt bad about that, but not too bad.

LOTUS CORELLI ALTMAN MONROE: So then I got pregnant. We all had gone to see *The Bridges at Toko-Ri*, and I'm waiting for this kid to pop. We'd already been to Bob's sister Barbara's wedding, and we decided to play poker. This is like midnight. Finally I said to Chet, "Does your watch have a second hand on it?" Joan said, "What are you doing?" I said, "I'm timing my contractions." They did the situation-comedy thing. They all jumped up and ran around and I'm standing there with my bag. They forgot me!

It was a fun time. Our first son, Michael, was born in 1955. Bob said, "We're going to call him Michael Bernard, for my father."

What kind of father was Bob? Terrible. Michael was in his crib and Bob was lying on the couch in his usual position, with his arms on his head. I come home and Michael is screaming—he has his head between the bars of the crib. "Why didn't you go in there and help him?" And Bob says, "I thought he always did that."

The child could do nothing for him, nothing to bolster his ego. In fact, one night Bob and some friends were playing poker, and he ran out of money and picked up Michael and put him on the table and said, "Okay, I'll bet the kid." The men who were with him were horrified. I just came over and took Michael off the table. Was he joking? He wasn't laughing when he did it. Well, he was drunk.

*   *   *

RICHARD SARAFIAN: I was working for the Army Hometown News Center in Kansas City. I rented a house right near him, in fact, right next door at Lake Lotawana. I remember he floated by in an inner tube. As he passed me he tried to get into a conversation with me. I was pretty much a wise-guy New Yorker. Whatever he said, I told him to fuck off. Subsequently I was cooking shish kebabs for my Army buddies. The aroma from the fire pit lured him. He came over and tried to talk with me again. I said, "Listen, I told you before, fuck off." He sent Lotus over, and then we got friendly.

LOTUS CORELLI ALTMAN MONROE: Dick Sarafian lived near us at Lake Lotawana with some Army buddies. One day, Bob said, "Go down and ask those guys if they want to come over here for a drink."

We ended up singing and dancing. They all became good buddies, and Dick and Bob hit it off immediately.

RICHARD SARAFIAN: One day we marched into a restaurant. Bob had the hots for the waitress. I looked rough—needed a shave, a clean shirt. He said, "Pretend you're blind—but underplay it." He held out his arm and marched me in. Sat me on a stool next to him. The waitress was well-endowed. I went along with it. He was talking to the waitress. She asked about me, and Bob said, "He's blind, but he doesn't want anybody to know it." All of a sudden she became the earth mother, the one who wanted to hold me. It's like her milk flowed—like a mother to a needy baby. Drinks came at me from every direction. The waitress was now in my lap. He slammed the keys on the bar and said, "Sarafian, you son of a bitch, you drive her home!" [*Laughs*]

LOTUS CORELLI ALTMAN MONROE: The beginning of our marriage was the affair part, when we were madly in love. The song "It Was Just One of Those Things" reminds me of Bob, especially the lyric, "It was too hot not to cool down."

He was still young and hadn't gotten into a pattern yet, but I should have recognized it. He was pretty wild. One night he got very drunk and he smashed one of my mother's tea sets that I was very fond of. Then he took a knife and tore up these posters that my mother had sent from her silent-movie days. Later, I had one of his mistresses calling me and saying he broke this or that. I said, "Why are you calling *me*?"

He would say things to people if he got to know them, if he could see any chink in their armor, he would strike verbally and could tear a person apart in a second. And not in private, but in front of large groups of people. He had to have an audience because that was the point. He had to destroy people to make himself feel real. I don't know. He had a tremendous ego, and God knows he knew he was brilliant and so did everybody else. But he was just compelled to do this.

*　　*　　*

REZA BADIYI (director): I was invited to the United States in 1955 by the State Department, for an exchange program, and I was brought here from Iran. I was twenty-five. I was sent to Syracuse University because I was graduated from the branch of Syracuse University in Iran. But they put me in a class at a very beginner level about how to approach documentary. At the time, I had over forty-five documentaries in my name. I went to the dean and explained, and twenty-four hours later they told me, "Pack, because you're going to Kansas City, Missouri. There is a center there where they're making film for overseas, named the Calvin Company."

I got there and they took me to a stage where they were shooting. And I noticed they're using a camera named Cine Special. Now, in my training in Iran, I learned with a Cine Special, but I graduated to Arriflex. So I asked them, "Why don't you use Arriflex?" They said, "What is Arriflex?" I said, "There's a camera that you can look through the lens." They shook their heads. I said, "By the way, I have one with me that belongs to the Ministry of Iranian Education." So they sent me back to the hotel with the taxi and I went over there and brought my Arriflex. It looked like a revolution took place, everybody looking through the lens. The director asked me, "Let us shoot one scene with

Robert Altman playing a fallen soldier in a scene from The Magic Bond, *a Calvin Company film he directed that was sponsored by the VFW*

your camera as well as with the Cine Special, and we can compare it." That director was Robert Altman.

That very first day, he asked me, "Where are you staying?" I said I was staying at this hotel called the YMCA. He said, "Oh, no, no, you don't want to stay there." So he called his mother, Helen, and by seven o'clock I was moved to a spare room. I stayed there for several months.

When I first came to their home, B.C. tells me, "You have to have insurance." So he sold me life insurance, which I still have. Kansas City Life, a hundred thousand dollars. In those days, whenever you'd go on a trip, you'd buy some extra insurance. I didn't have anybody in America, so I write the beneficiary for B.C. One time Bob and I went on a trip, and I had a million-dollar policy.

B.C. calls Bob and says, "Did you guys arrive safely?"

Bob says, "Yes."

B.C. says, "Everything's okay? Nothing happened?"

Bob says, "No, why?"

B.C. says, "Shit, son, Reza put the million-dollar policy in my name, and you couldn't push him out the door or do anything to help me?"

*   *   *

RICHARD SARAFIAN: Bob drew people around him and made them part of his circle. Sometime after we became friends, Bob asked me if I wanted to act in a play he was directing—*Hope Is the Thing with Feathers*. I was playing some sort of a tramp, a New York–type hobo. It was at the Resident Theatre at the Jewish Community Center in Kansas City.

SUELLEN FRIED (friend): It was kind of a hub for the Jewish community. It was a large building, like what a YMCA would be. So there were basketball courts and it was this big square building, and there was this wonderful theater in the building. The theater was a way for the Jewish Community Center to connect with non-Jewish people. Up on the roof, it was the whole square of the top of the building, and somebody came up with the creative idea of having an outdoor summer theater. That's where Bob directed plays.

It was very hard to get a terrific role because there was always competition. There were marvelous actors and actresses who earned their living in other ways—these were people who would have loved to have a lucrative career, but it wasn't easy to support yourself as an actor. The Resident Theatre had such a wonderful reputation; to have that on your résumé was something very special.

I remember meeting Bob at a reception after his first play. There was such a liveliness about him. He had such a zest for everything he did, and such enthusiasm for the process and the experience and the people that he worked with.

One play we worked on was supposed to end with a kiss. I was not a professional actress, and this was back in a time when kissing and things like that were things you only did with your husband. I was very self-conscious and uncomfortable about kissing this young man who I hardly knew at all. When we got to that scene, I tweaked his nose and I patted his cheek and I did all these little things, everything to avoid the kiss. And Bob allowed it to be just like that. He did not insist. I was so grateful.

Even then, Bob was such an authentic person in a world of make-believe. I think people, actors, wanted to work with him so much because he cherished authenticity and he was much more interested in bringing to life something that felt genuine. If somebody had something to offer that was real and genuine for them, Bob had great respect for that. He stayed true to his authentic integrity in a world where everything was dramatic and created but nothing was real.

LOTUS CORELLI ALTMAN MONROE: Joan was doing *My Little Heiress* at the Resident Theatre. She said, "Don't you dare come backstage and tell me how wonderful I was." So she's backstage and I walked in and everybody turned around. I said, "Oh Joan, you were . . . adequate!" She later used that line with Richard Sarafian.

JOAN ALTMAN SARAFIAN: Bob directed plays there while he was still working at Calvin. I would sit on the seawall, take his notes, tell him what I thought when he was auditioning people, who was good, who wasn't. I never looked at the people because my idea of an actor or actress depends on if they have a voice or not, and most of them don't. But one voice was this voice of Richard Sarafian. I heard this voice and I told Bob, "There's one in there. You got one."

RICHARD SARAFIAN: After the Army I went back to New York University but quit after about a month. I had a job working for Time Incorporated. I must've done something to charm everybody at the Christmas party. A few days later, I was called to personnel and asked,

Directing the model Carolyn Cross in a "fifteen-minute editorial fashion show" for the Kansas City–based dress designer Nelly Don

"Richard, how would you like to work for *Sports Illustrated*?" I went upstairs, thought about it a few hours, and quit. The reason was that I thought, "For me to relive the moment I became accepted into this high-class fraternity of reporters, I'd become a drunk." That's what went through my mind. Of course there was the other lure of Bob Altman and his sister and working in the documentary business. As soon as I quit Time, I got on the phone and called Bob.

He said, "Come on out." I got a job in the Calvin Company as a flunky. I can honestly say that Bob was the instrument by which I got started as a director. With what savings I had I met him in Salina, Kansas. He was doing a documentary for the Missouri Farmers Association. For about a month we went on a drunk. We drank all my money. However, with everybody gone at the Calvin Company, I wrote and shot with a short crew and put together a short documentary for the United Fund. The result was that I was promoted to director.

LOTUS CORELLI ALTMAN MONROE: Around that time, Joan fell madly in love with Dick Sarafian and left Chet. This was quite a time. Chet didn't know what happened to him.

JOAN ALTMAN SARAFIAN: Dick married me, I think, to be near Bob.

REZA BADIYI: During the time I was living at his parents' house, Bob quit Calvin Company. And he said that I have to go with him. He called the State Department and became my sponsor. The first project we did together was in Florida for spring training American League baseball. It became *Grandstand Rookie*. Bob wanted me to be one of the cameramen. There was another Kansas City gentleman by the name of Charlie Paddock, from the Calvin Company, and he was Bob's first cameraman. So we all moved to Palm Beach, Florida. Bob had just bought a brand-new station wagon, and on the door was painted "Robert Altman Productions." That was our production.

JOAN ALTMAN SARAFIAN: We went down to Florida when I was divorced—Dad and myself and Bob and his daughter, Chrissy, down to Palm Beach while he did the Kansas City baseball-team show. Reza went with us and he couldn't drive. He drove the car off a short ledge. Bob kept saying, "Just keep going, you'll pick it up" [*laughs*]. He finally did learn how to drive. Bob always made everyone feel so confident around him. I think that was one of his gifts.

CHAPTER 6

The Delinquents

*

The Delinquents (1957)

"Film Capsules," *The Bridgeport Post* (Connecticut), May 21, 1957:
"The Delinquents" is a realistic, shocking, frank treatment of the problem of juvenile delinquency. A presentation of Imperial Productions, "The Delinquents" was written and directed by Robert Altman. The cast of young, unknown, but talented performers is headed by Tommy Laughlin, Peter Miller, Dick Bakalyan, and Rosemary Howard. There is not a single manufactured set in "The Delinquents." The entire production was shot on location sites—interior as well as exterior—in Kansas City. Some 22 different locations were utilized in the picture—ranging from public institutions, through crowded streets and highways, to gas stations, private homes and a drive-in theater.

* * *

JOAN ALTMAN SARAFIAN: I had my first real job, at a collections company. I wrote tough letters to soldiers who owed money to the Arthur Murray Dance Studio. I told Bob, "I can't do this anymore. I'm not going to ask those guys for money for cruddy contracts they signed." Bob said, "You've got to quit anyway because I'm making a film and you have to come and work with me."

He had rented a church downtown, and I mean it was just a broken-down church, no pews or anything—just an office, a table, and an altar. Elmer Rhoden, Jr., a wonderful guy but a real alcoholic—he died of it—he was financing it. Elmer's dad was president of a theater chain,

Working on the script for The Delinquents *with his sister
Joan and his protégé, Reza Badiyi*

and Elmer was kind of a philanderer. Wonderful wife, daughter, but he loved this little blonde gal and he wanted to be near her and she was in California, so he wanted to be a producer.

Anyway, I would go and get the money from Elmer. I think I first got about ten thousand from him. Bob immediately took the money and bought two tuxedos, one white and one black, and a ticket to New York. Of course, nothing in *The Delinquents* called for black and white tuxedos.

He dictated the script to me in about an hour before he was leaving.

ROBERT ALTMAN: I wrote a script because I felt I had to. I wouldn't have gone into the process any other way. I think one of the main reasons for a script is the actors, when they get it, they agree to do it, they tend to want to hold on to it. They want a certain security. They want a safety net.

Another thing about a script is that it determines what set you build and what costumes you build. And you don't want to build those things and not use them. So the script is—well, it's a diagram. The car breaks down in the middle of the highway and the tow truck comes along. And while the tow truck is pulling the car up, these people have a discussion. Well, I have to get that tow truck or rewrite that scene. What happens when they're waiting for the tow truck, or what they say to each other, we can loosen up in there and see what happens.

The danger of writing a script is that everybody has the same voice. I think when they don't have the same voice it makes the film better. So when you have five different sources in there, five different voices, it seems closer to reality. I'm trying to push the actor into becoming a real creator—creating that part. Bringing things to it that the writer and/or myself couldn't bring. Many of them are not comfortable with the burden of having to become the author. They're like a deer in the headlights. They go, "Whoa-whoa-whoa, wait a minute." But if they're doing somebody else's line, that somebody else has written, the unkind way would be to say that they're relieved of the responsibility, and if it doesn't work it's not their fault. And it's true. It's the director's fault, and the director has to be the one that fixes it. I prefer actors who take the responsibility. I feel like I'm getting more bang for the buck. Sometimes it's the smallest of subtleties that you acquire in doing something that makes it real.

Many writers have hard feelings about what I do to their scripts, but my idea is, it's not their script. Their script is my tool to work with, and consequently I have been as responsible to their writing as I am to my own. I don't owe them an apology. Whether it's their script or my script, it's just a marker on the path that says, "This is the way to go." And so you kinda follow that. But you don't follow it to the point where you walk off the cliff.

With *The Delinquents*, it was written overnight, really in a weekend. I just dictated it to my sister. Then when we went to do it, we improvised the scenes.

JOAN ALTMAN SARAFIAN: After he finished the script, he gave me three or four names to call for equipment and then told me to call the union in Chicago. He gets on a plane, goes to New York, and he's gone a week. In the meantime, I get all the catalogues, I order all the lighting, I talk to a lighting man, a cameraman, I talk to the union in Chicago. Awfully nice people. I mean, they must have thought, "this person is so stupid we've got to help her."

ROBERT ALTMAN: When I got the wherewithal to do *The Delinquents*, I called the only agent I knew, a guy named Bob Longnecker, who was married to Ruth Hussey. Remember her, the actress? He had represented me as a writer when I was trying to be a radio writer. He said, "Well, there's this kid I have, Tommy Laughlin." I cast him from that. You know, later he was Billy Jack.

JOAN ALTMAN SARAFIAN: Bob got some actors—Tom Laughlin, Richard Bakalyan, Peter Miller—and he also brings this woman back from California. Helene something, who was about twenty years older than him. She's the kimono type. I mean really sleazy. Dyed black hair that's down to her shoulders, but she must have been a terrific lay because he was really smitten with her.

LOTUS CORELLI ALTMAN MONROE: I was five months pregnant with Stephen when *The Delinquents* started. I'm playing the mother of one of the girls, and his next mistress, Helene Hawley—her actual name was Pollock—she was going to promote Bob. So Bob hired her to be the mother of the boy involved in this Romeo and Juliet thing.

It was painful and I was very, very much in love with Bob. It wasn't working. I couldn't handle the women, all the extracurricular things.

REZA BADIYI: Lotus was a regular Kansas City wife. There wasn't any disagreement ever between them that catches the eye. But it was one of those things that was never openly said. Bob was always facing something, not knowing what was bothering her. One night Bob comes home and she brings the dinner on a tray and puts it in front of him. Usually in those days, people eat about six thirty to seven o'clock. And this is like ten o'clock. She ate and the children are in bed. Then Bob is looking at the food and then looking at her. And she picks up the plate and drops it, and walks out. That kind of thing.

LOTUS CORELLI ALTMAN MONROE: I was concentrating on the job I was doing. We were separated. When we first had our cast reading, we were sitting around the table and I got through and everybody's smiling. And Bob said, "That's the worst reading I've ever heard in my life." It was a stressful time for me.

His daughter, Chrissy, was hired to be the little sister. Joan was the script girl. Her husband, or ex-husband, Chet, was still around. He was set director. Bob also brought in some Kansas City friends to act.

SuEllen Fried: Even though I was already married and pregnant with my second child, I was young and Bob asked me to be a delinquent. I thought that would be fun. There was a lot of beer available, and we were told just to drink and have a great party. That was the extent of our direction. All the other delinquents—they pretty much all knew each other. Bob had gone to Rockhurst High School, and he may have pulled in a group from there.

Reza Badiyi: They didn't let Bob bring back a cameraman from California, so he had to use the local cameraman, Charlie Paddock. I became his assistant. It was a good time—I was also acting as an extra and a stand-in and a go-getter. And sometimes at night after everybody finishes and goes, and they were in the middle of the street, they put everything together and I was the night watchman.

Bob didn't jump to it with both feet. He worked on the story, developed it. Sat around and everybody read it for a while. And then talked about this and that. And then Bob needed some of the friends to come, like Louie Lombardo, who became a very good film cutter later on. Sarafian was around, just to talk about the story. And of course Joan.

Joan always was idolizing Bob. It wasn't just a big brother. Joan is absolutely a believer. She's one of those kind of people at that age that usually wouldn't give you an idea unless you asked for it. But in this case, she had many notes and discussed it with Bob. And I remember every time it brings a shine in Bob's eyes.

You have to realize Bob was that kind of guy. I learned that the philosophy that he had, it was never "It's *my* movie, so everybody shut up and listen to me." He said, "We are going to work together. Anybody has ideas, bring them to me. If it's good we use it, if it's not, we're not using it. But don't be ashamed of it." If you go on the set of a Sam Peckinpah and you want to tell him anything, he kills you right there.

Tom Laughlin (actor): Very amateurish. It was like neighbors getting together and making a film.

But I was very impressed with Joan. She did everything. She'd get people in place, she'd negotiate the salaries, she did everything. I think she did everything but make the lunches.

JOAN ALTMAN SARAFIAN: I was the script girl, but I did a little of almost everything, and the script was the least of it. I would get the money from Elmer, stick it in the back of my jeans, and bring it to Bob. I used Bob's Thunderbird as the office.

The first day of shooting, Bob came up to me and said, "My God, everyone keeps asking me questions."

I said, "I'll work that out." I got a chessboard and I set it up in the back of the Thunderbird. I said, "You just come over here and stare at that board, and no one is going to bother you, or if they do, you look annoyed."

That's what he did. Of course after the first day he was fine. But he was really nervous. He was so cute, he really was.

I was supposed to get forty dollars a week for my work. I had left a job making three hundred dollars a week, but Bob was never able to come up with that money.

LOTUS CORELLI ALTMAN MONROE: At that time I was doing a TV show sponsored by the Presto pressure cooker and GE stoves and refrigerators. He wasn't working at the Calvin Company, so this was keeping us going at this point.

JOAN ALTMAN SARAFIAN: Helene was really disappointed with the accommodations. But she lived with it. Tom Laughlin also was really disturbed. He'd just come off something; he thought he was an actor now. I have heard through the grapevine he speaks very highly of me, though I can't say the same of him. He was going to walk off the show.

Bob said, "You've got to talk him up. Give him lunch and talk him out of it."

So I did. He said he couldn't stand the girl that Bob hired from Kansas City. Pat Stedman, I think. Nice girl. She had been one of the Resident Theatre actresses and she was very good.

Laughlin said, "I can't look at her. She looks like a pig."

I felt like saying, "You look more like one." But I was able to talk him into staying.

TOM LAUGHLIN: I don't remember her name. Some local kid. She had never acted. She struggled. I felt badly for her and I felt for the picture, but there was nothing I could do about it. She was just very amateurish and very raw.

ROBERT ALTMAN: That was terrible. He was just arrogant, and he had an idea about how he thought the film should be made, and what the other actors should do. I had a different idea, and we just did not get along.

TOM LAUGHLIN: He was disorganized. He didn't have a precise plan to shoot all the time. Sometimes he showed up pretty late. That's how I started to be a director. Bob would come late and I showed up on time, ahead of time, very professional. One morning, I got rambunctious. The crew, everyone else was there. I said, "Well, the scene is written. Let's do it. If Bob doesn't like it he can throw it out. Why sit around wasting time?" It was Elmer Rhoden's money. I felt guilty. So I directed. I shot a scene. I never heard directly from him, but I understood he was furious.

I didn't have much of a relationship with Bob. He was a great party

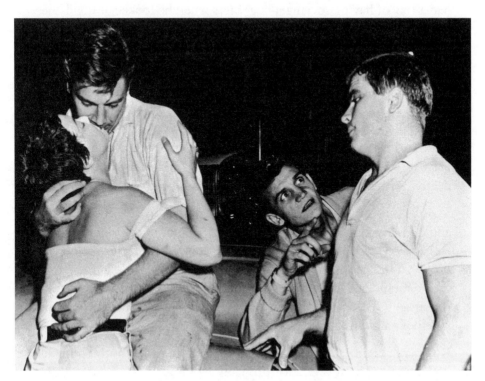

A scene from The Delinquents, *with Tom Laughlin at far right*

guy. I didn't party with him. I was very serious about my craft and career. When it was done I went home and got ready for the next day.

RICHARD BAKALYAN (actor): Laughlin was a very strange guy. I think he thought he was Marlon Brando and James Dean wrapped together. He was into performing as a Method actor, I guess.

TOM LAUGHLIN: I don't consider myself a Method actor. I consider myself a Stanislavsky actor.

RICHARD BAKALYAN: I loved Bob. I thought he was a very good director. He knew what he wanted and he worked to get it.

The real conflict was between Laughlin and Peter Miller, who played the other gang leader. Only because Laughlin threw his weight around a lot. He was a karate guy or some crap. You can go around talking about how tough you are, but the real guy is the one who keeps his mouth shut and goes around doing his business. Laughlin wanted to be the main man and that's the way he behaved.

TOM LAUGHLIN: In the script I was the hero. Peter was the villain. Bob had a way of having social get-togethers when he looked at the dailies. He and Peter became very close. Peter wanted to change his image from the rapist in *Blackboard Jungle* and be the hero. So they would come back and make script changes, like I'm supposed to get down and cry and beg for my life, and he's the hero. I refused. That was totally in contradiction to everything I was hired for and contracted for and was promised. I went to the Guild on it and won, of course.

RICHARD BAKALYAN: Bob was a gentleman. He never lost his temper, even at times when one could. Like trying to do it on a shoestring and dealing with Laughlin.

TOM LAUGHLIN: One night we were shooting a night scene and Peter and I were having a verbal confrontation in front of the car and it escalated. He changed the scene and I think I threw Peter over the hood of the car. That ended the night's shooting.

I remember that night Joan trying to intervene and trying to stop the tussle. I was pretty hard on Peter. Though he was my size he wasn't much of a fighter.

ROBERT ALTMAN: He was just a horror, but there was nothing I could do about it. That experience probably had a lot to do later with me making sure there wasn't a presence like that around.

The minute an actor comes into a cast, into a group, it's like DNA. They're there. And if you take them out and replace them with someone else it's a different creature—it's an elephant instead of a rhinoceros. To think that you can control this animal, you know, you're wrong. All you can do is assemble it.

From the movie poster:

THE DELINQUENTS: THE HOODS OF TOMORROW!

THE GUN-MOLLS OF THE FUTURE!

THE "BABY FACES" WHO HAVE JUST TAKEN THEIR FIRST

STUMBLING STEP DOWN SIN STREET, U.S.A.

* * *

REZA BADIYI: Night and day we shot *Delinquents*. When it was finished, the film was shipped to Hollywood. Bob arranged to edit it there, to get himself there, too. Then Bob threw a big good-bye party. He invites a hundred people to a certain hall and orders the food and booze and then gets the most famous black singer and their band to come over there and perform. It was a hell of a night, a hell of a night. And in the end they bring the bill and he's writing a check and the guy from the hall says, "Bob, wait a minute. I have three of your bad checks. I don't want any more checks." So Bob reaches in his pocket, he brings out twenty dollars. He says, "I pay, everybody pays!" And we did. I mean, I never ever heard of anybody else doing that.

He had bought himself this brand-new Thunderbird. And for some reason he didn't like the color of it. He sent it to be painted, because he used it in the movie for one scene or two, and there was a scratch. It was red, and he wanted to change it to be white. Well, it came back and it's red again. Now he was upset, but that was the last day before we were leaving, so that was that. The plan was that I'd go with him, because I haven't seen the West. The good-bye party went till almost midnight and everybody drank to his health and he drank to everybody's health. At the time I wasn't familiar yet with alcohol. Being born a Muslim it wasn't something that I was interested in. So Bob came out, and we have our suitcases in the trunk and in the back. He drove us to the turnpike, and then he says, "Reza, I'm not doing well, I'm going to lay down. You drive west." I said, "Which is west?" And he pointed, "That way."

It was after noon that we got to mountains in Colorado. And it is a bright, bright day, but somehow it started snowing a little. I pulled out the camera and I started shooting as Bob is driving. He used to be a flier in World War II, so he had these flier glasses. So he's wearing his flier glasses and he's driving and it's snowing and we have the top down and he said, "Fabulous."

When I think about the good part of life, it was that. It was those days. And it was beautiful.

CHAPTER 7

California

*

REZA BADIYI: The next day we drove all the way to Las Vegas. This is 1956, during the convention of the Republican Party in San Francisco. We were listening to that on the radio, and Bob was analyzing what was happening in the country and reciting the speeches of Winston Churchill. I realized at that moment that Bob is a Democrat. He had such an ear for politics, and such respect for Harry S. Truman. And he was troubled by seeing an Army man in the White House.

Ahead of time, before Las Vegas, we stopped at a place to eat. Bob called long-distance to a lady that was in our movie, Helene, and a few other friends to meet us in Las Vegas. We went to the hotel that he wanted to stay in, and there wasn't any room. We went to second hotel, third hotel. He was very unhappy. So we went to a motel and Bob told me to take a shower and get ready—"Get your good suit out and send it to be pressed." Bob went out and shopped for a few things that included dark sunglasses for me and a cigarette holder, a black one with a silver end. Then Bob put me in a suit and tie and said, "Reza, let's see if we can do this."

He called the Sahara, and he says, "This is Robert Altman. Is our suite ready? It's Prince Reza Badiyi from Tehran, from the State Department. Is his suite ready?"

And they ask, "Who?"

Bob said it again and they said, "Would you please hold?" They came back and said, "Yes sir, it's ready." So he sent the car to be washed and we went over. He told me, "Never talk to anyone but to me."

We arrived and I'm having my cigarette holder in my hand and I have my tie and a carnation. And it was just too much. It was like a bad

Working with his first writing partner, George W. George,
the son of cartoonist Rube Goldberg

high school play. I was graduated out of the Royal Academy of Drama
in Iran. I won the gold medal from the king. And now I'm playing
somebody that Bob imagined!

The elevator door opened and Bob didn't allow anybody to go in
but me and Bob. We went up to our room—fabulous! Champagne, the
beautiful fruit baskets and everything. We were not there ten minutes
and management called. They say, "You are invited tonight to have
dinner and a show." Bob was in hog heaven. And the call came from his
friends, all these guys that he knew from before and Helene. They
arrived, so it became an entourage for me.

Judy Garland was entertaining and her daughter Liza was ten years old. They came on the stage for one end of the show. Then they came down to be introduced to me! I got up and did my impression of being great and I kiss her hand and so forth and then they took pictures of us. Great. Now, of course there wasn't any bill. Bob tells me, whispers— "Under the table." With no one seeing, he hands me a one-hundred-dollar bill. He said, "When we get up, drop it for the boys who clean."

This is what I did. It was like a bomb—"The man threw a hundred-dollar tip on the table when he left!" So this whole play is being written by Bob, and he is of course starring in it.

Second day, third day. I'm getting tired. I sit at the gambling table with Bob. Bob is playing craps, and he says, "Push the entire stack on number eight." And he wins!

Helene is staying in the suite with Bob, and I have a separate room. She comes to me and says, "Bob is winning so much. You know, Reza, he's going to lose it all. You know that's the nature of Bob." She had started gathering anything that was not a dollar or five dollars—ten dollars, twenty dollars—gathered all of that and put it in one of the drawers. The next night she was going to go back to California. She had one of those heart-shaped hatboxes. It was something like twelve grand in there, and she left.

Bob came back and now he was losing, and he says, "What happened?" So now we are coming to the end of our drama, and all of a sudden there's a telephone call from management. And they said, "Prince Gholam-Reza from Iran has arrived. We told him Prince Reza is here, and he is very anxious to meet him."

Oh shit, now what? Bob says, "We run for it." I said, "No, no, no. When I was on my soccer team, he liked me very much. After I became a cameraman for the palace, he was saying to me, 'Why don't you play more soccer?' So maybe he recognizes me." So I called his room and in very polite Farsi I said, "Hello, I'm Reza Badiyi. I do not know if you remember me from the soccer days. The fact is, we wanted to come stay here, and there was no room and my friend and sponsor said I'm a prince." He laughed. He says, "You're kidding me! This is good, I like those things. I like those things." He says, "Tonight, you come with me." So we went down with his entourage. The two princes, arm in arm, we walk in and the cameras are taking pictures. I didn't know it, but he paid for our room, without me asking for anything.

And Bob lost everything that he had. We got back to our car and started driving. When we got very close to L.A. we were out of money, out of gas. I find something like five dollars and that put gas in it, just enough to get there. We went to Helene and she had a dinner for us. After dinner, Helene went and brought the hatbox and put it in front of Bob. Bob says, "What's that?" She says, "Let's open it." He opened it, sees all the money, and says, "Where did that come from?" She explains and he says, "Goddammit, that's why I was losing! You took my seed money away."

He picked up the money and flew back to Vegas from Burbank. He lost it all that night and came back. That's how Bob and I came to Hollywood.

LOTUS CORELLI ALTMAN MONROE: When we went back to California, Bob's with Helene, so he finds an apartment for me in Brentwood. Bought all this furniture and for about two months couldn't decide between me and Helene. He'd go back and forth.

I told him once, "You should get a large apartment building for all your women." He laughed and said, "But you have to remember, seniority doesn't count."

Lotus Corelli Altman with her sons, Michael (left) and Stephen Altman

One night I got a babysitter and when I got back Bob was with the kids and he's in a rage—"Where have you been?" I said, "I've been to the movies." He was so furious. This was the first time he was violent. He pulled the phone out of the wall, and this was one with a heavy base. He swung it and hit me in the back and broke two ribs. I called the police and the doctor, and I was running out in the driveway and he realized he'd better get out of there. When the police called him, he said, "You woke me up. I haven't been anywhere."

JOAN ALTMAN SARAFIAN: Bob was in California, editing *The Delinquents*. I had to go to California with him. I did not want to. I had to go with him.

I called his apartment the largest ashtray in L.A., and I was the only one who did the cleaning. All the young Hollywood kids would come over. Reza's friend would fix a pilaf that would melt in your mouth. I've never been able to match it. And who was in *Easy Rider*? Dennis Hopper, yeah, he would be there. He would come and all these girls who were really, really ultra, little shiksas, I call them, wandering around. Every night there was a party. One day I was upstairs cleaning the floor, a red-and-white linoleum floor, and Reza came in. He sat down and he always thought he was in love with me. I said, "If you really cared about me, Reza, you'd pick up a mop and help me!" He was always so cute, though. He was sweet.

B.C. kept sending me tickets to come back, but Bob needed to cash those in and use them, which he did. The last one, I said, "No, I'm not going to give it to you." He stood at the door, and I can see him today. I said, "You know, Bob, you have a red hue around you. It's like looking at the devil. I'm not giving you the ticket. I'm going to go home. I'm in love with Dick Sarafian."

Bob did not like Dick. He told me, "Don't marry him, he's"—what was the word? Not a user, but some word like that. I was pregnant, but I didn't marry him because I was pregnant. I didn't know I was pregnant.

Anyway, I went back to Kansas City and Bob stayed in California.

HARVEY FRIED (friend): After Bob left Kansas City, SuEllen and I saw him a handful of times in those early years in California. Bob was always a very generous guy, even when he was down on his luck. Trying to take us out to dinner, have us up to dinner, that sort of thing. He was frequently short, financially.

He insisted we go one evening to a small stadium to see tennis matches, because Pancho Gonzales was playing. He didn't have the tickets when he got there. So I got tickets and we saw the tennis. I kind of felt sorry for Bob at that time because I think he was having financial difficulties.

SuELLEN FRIED: One time we went to a tennis match with them, in California. The marriage was kind of coming apart at this point. Lotus confided to me that evening when the guys were into the tennis that she was very concerned about their relationship. They got divorced, and the next time we saw him he still hadn't become famous yet. He was living off the Hollywood strip. He was sharing a place with two other men, and so we offered to take Bob to lunch. He suggested the Brown Derby. Harvey can tell you how many martinis Bob had, which was kind of shocking to us.

HARVEY FRIED: He just had a series of martinis for lunch. Four or six martinis and that was all. "Is this the way Hollywood types have lunch?" I asked him. He chuckled. I thought it was strange. It didn't seem like a wholesome lunch.

SuELLEN FRIED: Then he said, "Why don't you have dinner on me?" We said, "That sounds great." He told us to be back and meet him at this little place that he was sharing. He went to a delicatessen and got a roast chicken and some pickles, and this was dinner. These were the days when he was trying to find his place in the sun, and it hadn't happened yet.

We were living here in the middle of the world in Kansas City and here was Bob out in Hollywood, with all these irons in the fire, and it was very exciting to us. For us, it was worth the cost of the thirteen martinis or whatever it was.

CHRISTINE ALTMAN (daughter): When he went to California, I missed him a lot. He would send me things on my birthday. And he would, I imagine, try to get me out there as much as he could in the ragged lifestyle that he lived at that time. He was getting divorced here and married there and having kids here and having kids there and not knowing how to pay child support. It was really kind of a mess. I'll give everybody ninety percent credit for at least trying to make it work. There were a lot of people involved to deal with when he was young.

DR. MARTIN GOLDFARB (friend): I was at a poker game up in the Hollywood Hills. I knew a few of the people there, mostly just Bobby Altman. I had met him a few times but I didn't really know him. So about two in the morning I'm home in bed. I had a little house right at the top of King's Road, toward the end up in the mountains, so it was pretty quiet. Suddenly somebody threw pebbles at my window. I'm thinking, "Who in the hell is doing this?" We were too dumb in those days to become afraid of anything. So I walked outside and there was Bobby Altman throwing pebbles at my window.

I said, "What the hell are you doing here, Bobby?"

He says, "Well, you know, the cards didn't run with me tonight, and I broke up with my girlfriend, Helene, and she doesn't want me to come home, at least not now. Can I stay with you for a while?"

I said, "Sure."

He said, "I don't have any money."

I said, "I don't care, you can stay as long as you want."

So he stayed two years.

Robert Altman in 1958, trying to get his career rolling

Why'd he come to me? I was there. And it was free. And I never begrudged him anything. I was a cardiologist, and anytime I could help him I would. If had to slip him a few bucks I did, and that was okay. He was paying his way just by being around, telling stories and laughing and making fun and introducing you and bringing people by. Worth his weight in gold. You could tell right away he was going to be a big winner. It was a pleasure to see a meteor about to take off.

*   *   *

The James Dean Story *(1957)*

Bosley Crowther, review in *The New York Times,* **October 19, 1957:** What should be an effective contribution to the perpetuation of the legend of the late James Dean is achieved in "The James Dean Story." . . . This eighty-two-minute memorial . . . is edited into a sort of cinematic elegy, with a commentary that throbs with deep laments. Obviously, it is angled to that audience that found in young Dean a symbol and sanctuary for the self-pity and self-dramatization of youth. It says he was wracked with doubts and torments, nursed a childish belief that he was "bad" and did reckless things as rebellion against the insecurity and loneliness in his soul.

GEORGE W. GEORGE (writer and producer): One day I sat in my apartment and nothing was happening. I was desperate to make a living. I had some money, so I didn't need to be desperate, but I was. Suddenly I saw that James Dean got killed in his car. That was it. I called up Altman—he had given up the motion-picture business by then, he had gone back to Kansas City, but now he was back in California, trying again. I knew a guy at Warner Brothers who I thought could help us.

I said to Bob, "You want to do a picture about Jimmy Dean? Have you thought about it?"

He said, "That's a good subject."

He hadn't made a documentary. I hadn't made a documentary. I didn't even know what a documentary was.

He said, "Do you know Jimmy Dean at all?"

"No, I never met him. What about you, you know him, ever have a meeting with him?"

Bob said, "No, I never met him." Then he said, "Let's go do it."

Which is just like Bob. Fearless. If I had been by myself I wouldn't have done it. It would have been too much. I would have figured out a reason not to do it. You find out in life most things in life are not done. Fear of failure, fear of stupidity, fear of some shortcoming on your part. Luckily, we were all there at the right time, including Jimmy Dean.

We made the picture. We went to Indiana—everybody else was talking to his representatives. We went and did it. We went and made the picture.

ROBERT ALTMAN: After Calvin, I had the experience of being able to make these documentary films. George still wanted to be the director. I said, "I'm the director now." So we shared—written and directed by together.

George fronted the money for *The James Dean Story* because we took a trip to Fairmount, Indiana, and interviewed Dean's uncle and aunt and little brother and the farmer down the road, all that stuff.

GEORGE W. GEORGE: I got the guy who wrote Dean's movie *Rebel Without a Cause* to do our screenplay. Stewart Stern. That was the making of our picture. It gave it a point of view. Our picture dealt a lot with his loneliness. Our picture in a sense grew out of their picture.

STEWART STERN (screenwriter): I was, I think, the first after Henry Ginsberg who heard about Jim's death. Henry had produced *Giant* and was a close friend of my cousin, Arthur Loew, and an acquaintance of mine since childhood. The phone rang and it was Ginsberg looking for Arthur. He said, "The kid was killed an hour ago," or something like that. He had just had the call from the head of publicity at Warner Brothers.

This was an odd situation. Jim's death was a terrible personal loss to me, and I felt it as I had felt no other death in my life. I almost can't explain why because it was such a short relationship and so scattered. But he was an absolutely unique human being. He was an astonishing person, and given the background he had—which never would have pointed in that direction—it was a kind of visitation. You couldn't account for it any more than you could account for the genius of Mozart as a child.

They began calling me, various producers in Hollywood. "Hey, we got to make this documentary. Got to document Dean's life because he's such an icon and it's just going to build." When all these offers came I really didn't want to do it. I really didn't want to contribute to what I felt was a kind of quick-buck mentality, to make profit out of a relationship with Jimmy. I didn't like it. So I turned down two or three.

Then I had a call from George George, who said, "I know what your feeling is about doing this, but it's not going to be that kind of film." He said, "At least come in and talk with us. I have a partner I like—Altman." So I did and he convinced me. He said, "We will not put anything in that you do not want in. You're going to be the writer and you will have access to all the interviews that we shot with people. You can write your script and I promise you that script will stay intact." That sounded safe to me.

I made it poetic because I felt that Jim was poetic. It was succulent. It was purple. It wasn't nice, crisp, uninvolved, objective storytelling because I didn't feel that way. I wanted to be very sure that Jim came across as human, flawed, searching, lonely, complicated, all those things. But I didn't want to get into anything that I didn't know about and I didn't want to add to the unhealthy side of the legend.

GEORGE W. GEORGE: When we were making it, one incident was pure Bob. You know Dean got killed on the road, running into that car. So Bob said, "We'll get that for the picture."

I said, "How the hell are you going to do that?"

He said, "I'll figure it out."

Well, son of a bitch, he goes and figures it out by lashing a camera onto the end of a long piece of wood and putting it on the bumper of his car. And driving down the road that Jimmy Dean had taken that day! It looked like Bob was going to have a crash, but son of a bitch, he missed crashing by about two feet. He was driving the car!

I said, "Bob, you're crazy."

He said, "Yeah, I guess I am."

STEWART STERN: I tried in the worst way to get Marlon to do the narration. He said, "I'll only do it if it's for free, but nobody else can take any money either." I said, "Well, that's not the way it's going to be." There was too much money in the movie and they needed to make it back. Then I said, "Dennis Hopper. You need to have a young voice. It's a young subject." They came to me with the idea of Martin Gabel. He was a great narrator with a deep, booming voice. I said it would ruin the film to have that voice, and it did. You might as well have Rabbi Magnum. I had no power. They got him, and whatever was pretentious about my script, the narration only added to it.

I liked Altman very much personally. He was going through analysis at the time. I forget who it was with, but Altman absolutely worshipped him. He used laughter, humor, the analyst did, and Altman so respected that. It made it possible for him. He never felt judged. He felt freed and better, and it was really all he talked about. I was being analyzed too, and so we shared that in odd moments. But we almost never talked about Jimmy or the picture. I don't know what he did or when he did the work. It might have been in the editing room with George. When I finished the script that was it for me. He liked the script very much because even if it didn't mention analysis, it certainly was talking about the movements of the psyche. We just found that in common. I was even thinking of going to his analyst. Altman might have been encouraging me to try. He was so smitten with him.

I had no idea that he was a talented director until years later, when that first movie came out, *That Cold Day in the Park*. That was a revelation to me.

ROBERT ALTMAN: When we got it all together, we met a guy named Lou Stoumen who had this method of shooting stills where it was like animation—it was ahead of its time, really. I hired Lou Lombardo, who had been a cameraman on the set, and I taught him editing, and he became a rather famous editor. It came together pretty well, I think.

STEWART STERN: Afterward, the only thing I kept saying is "When am I going to see any money?" I never got a red cent out of it. After finally battering George George, I think I got fifteen hundred dollars out of all the profits. It just seemed to pass from hand to hand and nobody saw anything, at least not according to George.

*   *   *

Robert Altman, to David Thompson, from *Altman on Altman*: My agent at the time showed *The Delinquents* to Alfred Hitchcock. I went and had a meeting with Hitchcock, who had liked the picture. He thought it was different. He hired me to go to New York to produce on *Suspicion*, a series of hour-long shows.

BARBARA TURNER (screenwriter/actress/producer): The first time I met Bob he was working for Alfred Hitchcock. I got the part out here in California and I went to New York. Bob came to the hotel to pick me up in the car. David Wayne was the star. Warren Beatty had a bit part in it. It was about a guy who had a bad heart and had a new doctor and he goes to the office and gets checked out. They say, "There's something wrong with these X-rays, there's nothing wrong with your heart. You're fine." But they've mixed up the X-rays. So the rest of the episode is them searching for him. So he does all the things he's never done before. And goes to Coney Island and we're all on the same bus and the guy I'm with, Warren Beatty, sort of dumps me and Wayne befriends me. We spend the day at Coney Island and I'm supposed to be sixteen. Then we go back to the city and we sit and have coffee and he asks to see me again and I say, "Well, my folks wouldn't like it," or some such thing. But I thanked him for the day and I leave, and he collapses and he dies.

My first impression of Bob was that he was kind. He was kind and funny and Bob, you know? You know how much he loved actors. He just loved actors. I was very, very shy then, so I didn't say too much and he didn't press. He was just funny and kind.

ROBERT ALTMAN: I realized early on to rely on the people you work with. When you have a crew, the crew becomes kind of a mirror, or a barrier that you don't go beyond. In other words, your first audience for your film is your crew. The minute we start rehearsing a scene and I say, "Well, let's put the camera here, and so and so," a collaboration starts.

I remember I was doing *Hitchcock Presents*, directing, and I did one at Universal and there was a cameraman named Curly Lindon. Curly Lindon was a big-name cameraman. I'm doing a Hitchcock with Joseph Cotten and Christine White, and Curly Lindon was the cameraman. And I went in and I said, "Okay, there's a phone on the desk. Let's have the phone in the foreground and you'll see these people back there, and she'll come in the door and he'll be over there. And you've got the phone and then they'll come over and pick the phone up."

He kinda looked at me and said, "Yeah? What kind of lens are you going to use?"

I was asking for something that was not in the range of the tools that I had. So I was embarrassed in front of everybody, because this was out on the set and I realized that I didn't know what the fuck I was talking about.

I had a friend, an actor named Johnny Alonzo, who later became a rather well-known cinematographer, and he worked with me on a lot of things. He was a still photographer. And I said, "You've got to teach me how to shoot stills." And he did, and we'd do our own developing and printing. I bought a camera, and I had a long lens on it. I had a zoom lens on it. So I spent three or four years shooting still photography. And I became pretty good at it. It was one of those things where I would take my camera wherever I went, and by doing that I think I helped myself learn the tools that I needed. I learned the responsibility of what I could do and couldn't do. And the zoom lens got me.

* * *

Robert Altman, to David Thompson, from *Altman on Altman*: I decided that television was the world I was shooting for. There were lots of opportunities at that time to do low-budget, offbeat films, but

Directing an episode of Whirlybirds

they were always bad, and I always said I would keep doing television until I got a film that I really wanted to do. I didn't want to go out and make a feature just for the sake of it and then find out that was the end of it.

From a letter to Alfred Hitchcock from Robert Altman, February 26, 1958: I want to preamble this presumptuous little note by stating that it is neither a complaint nor an indictment, but rather a vague query. Sometime ago, in a meeting at your office, you and I discussed, in the presence of Mr. Manning O'Connor, several ideas relating to the possibility of doing a television show against a ready-made realistic background of some scope, such as the building of a dam, the waterworks of the city and things of that ilk. . . . This is the last I heard of the matter until yesterday. My agent called me, quite upset, and said that you were going ahead with the project, but without my services. . . . I have no legal claim to any participation in this project and I believe that words like "integrity" and "moral obligation" are primarily used by people as a sort of dubious court of last resort. I am merely writing these facts because I feel sure that you are not aware of these events and I would like you to be informed. *(No response from Hitchcock found.)*

Television Directing

Alfred Hitchcock Presents—1957–58 (2 episodes); *Peter Gunn*—1958; *Bronco*—1958; *The Troubleshooters*—1959; *U.S. Marshal*—1959; *Whirlybirds*—1957–59 (14 episodes).

ROBERT ALTMAN: Television gave me Kathryn. I met her on *Whirlybirds*. She was an extra. She came out one day with her own white stockings and played a nurse.

CHAPTER 8

Kathryn

*

KATHRYN REED ALTMAN: Everybody has their own interpretation of what happened. I say it was April Fools' Day, 1959, and he says it was April 2. So we never clarified that. He just assumed he was right and he always felt that way, and I just assumed I was right. I was working different jobs within the film business. I had a daughter I was helping to support—supporting, actually. And so it was a great way to work because I could work in blocks—whether I'd be swimming or standing in, or doubling, or working as a showgirl, or as an extra, or whatever, and I had time to be a mother. So it was ideal.

I got into doing all that because of swimming, on an Esther Williams picture. They had a call. I knew how to swim—I was born and raised in California. They had a call for girls with showgirl looks who could swim, and, God, what a huge call it was. A couple of girl-friends and I went on it, and I ended up getting it. But I had to do a lot of stuff—diving out of trapezes and going down slides. It was a famous number in *Million Dollar Mermaid*.

It was perfect timing for this meeting. I got the call because of Tommy Thompson—unfortunately he passed away. God, he was such an important part of Bob's early career—he was his assistant director. Anyway, I knew him. We were buddies and all that.

He had said to a girlfriend of mine, "God, Kathryn would love this guy. He is so clever and he is so funny." Her name was Dee Sharon, and she told me, "He's getting a divorce, he has two little kids." He really had three, with Christine.

And I said, "Oh boy, that sounds just great."

"But he's funny and he's interesting," she told me.

Kathryn Reed Altman

So I got the call to be a nurse and bring my own white stockings, which became a joke for forty-seven years. Actually, the truth is I didn't bring any white stockings. The night before I had done something very social and very late, and I had really a terrible hangover. I had to be on this bus with everybody else at about seven in the morning. By the time we got to the location, which was up in the Malibu mountains somewhere, on a ranch, it was so hot, oh horrible. As I stepped off the bus, I was surprised, because no director ever comes to the bus to meet the extras. And I knew why he's there, because they set him up with me, too. Tommy was sure I'd be crazy about him, and my girlfriend was, too. She and Tommy were kind of dating, and they both arranged it. I had kind of forgotten about it, I was feeling so crummy, and I hadn't dwelled on it much. Until I started getting off the bus, and then I realized this was the guy. And he just looked terrible. He was overweight. He had his shirt off. Sweaty. He had a wet rag on his head. He was standing next to Tommy, who was terrific looking and a terrific guy. And so I got off and he introduced me.

He said, "This is Bob Altman. Kathryn, this is Bob Altman."

He didn't say hello, he didn't say anything. He just said, "How are your morals?"

I was so annoyed. And I said, "A little shaky, how are yours?"

That was the beginning.

He invited me—ha!—over to have a cappuccino, which meant going over to the bench that was set up with hot chocolate and hot coffee in the middle of this hot day, and he mixed the two together and made a cappuccino. And that was it.

He was directing all day. We hung around during lunch, and then he made sure I was on the callback. That day his boys were visiting the set and Lotus was there, too. She was still his wife, though they were separated. At lunchtime he came walking through the lunch tables with the littlest boy, his Stevie, and he had him on his shoulders.

Dee, my girlfriend, said, "His pants are on backwards." He was two and a half years old.

Bob said, "I know it and I'm going to keep it that way."

I'll never forget that line. That was the first line that really broke me up.

Then he invited me to go up in a helicopter, which I didn't really want to, but I did with a couple of other people and the kids. It was just a helicopter ride. I didn't like them.

LOTUS CORELLI ALTMAN MONROE: Bob called and said, "We're out in Thousand Oaks and we're making *Whirlybirds*." Thousand Oaks was the place they shot when they needed wide-open spaces, for cowboy movies and things like that. "Why don't you bring the kids and we'll give them a helicopter ride?"

They had a lunch break and Bob and I and the kids were walking along. There was a long table to the right and the lunch was out for the cast and crew. Kathryn was standing at the table with her back to us. Bob looked over to her, and I said, "Well, Bob, you don't have to bother with lunch now." He just devoured her with his eyes. He just snorted and said, "You caught me again."

MICHAEL ALTMAN (son): Bob put me and my mom in the helicopter with Stephen strapped to her. He told the pilot to take 'er up. The pilot turned the thing upside down and there's no fucking doors on it, and my mom just started screaming and pounding on him and flipping out. And Bob was down there laughing his ass off. That's what I remember.

STEPHEN ALTMAN (son): I remember a helicopter ride, but that's it.

MICHAEL ALTMAN: Steve and I grew up with our mom and my step-dad. It wasn't like she would, like, rag on him all the time, but there was some heavy-duty resentment there. In the early years it was really tough on her, but then, he didn't have anything going on. That day at *Whirlybirds*, she just went down there probably to get twenty-five dollars for groceries. I'm sure she was down there trying to get a couple of sacks of pinto beans, you know?

I don't think he was maliciously withholding money from my mother. I think it was just, you know, he didn't have twenty-five dollars to send her. You know that joke about the producer who says to the other producer, "Hey, I got this great deal on this property, it's only a million bucks. The bad news is they want a hundred dollars down." Right? It was that kind of deal. He was always in hock up to his . . . He lived well, but he was living off the next paycheck. And God only knows how he managed it.

STEPHEN ALTMAN: There was not a lot of friendship for him on my mom's side when we were growing up. It was always, "We don't have any money for the rent and da, da, da. He's an asshole." Kids are pretty perceptive, I think, and I kind of threw that part out. You know, "I think you're being emotional, Mom." Sometimes kids are a little more rational than the adults can be. I never grew up with a chip on my shoulder for him. I only got it later after working with him [*laughs*].

KATHRYN REED ALTMAN: He didn't appeal to me at all at first. But by the end of the day I caught on. That night we all went out for a drink on the way home, probably to Nickodell's, which was the hot spot at RKO. After I'd settled down and we had a drink I got the whole idea.

The next day I showed up—we hadn't gotten really intimate—it was all kind of polite with everybody else around. The next day the call was at a church and I was sitting in a pew reading *The Diary of Anne Frank* between takes. He was going up and down the aisle, setting lights, and he said, "Oh, you like that book?" We were still very distant, we weren't buddies.

I said, "It's terrific, did you read it?"

And he said, "Oh yeah. It was great."

Well, he never read it, I found out later. Courting behavior.

That night we all went out. It was a Friday night, "Tight Shoe Night," an assistant used to call it, and Bob and I always laughed at that. And it's been "Tight Shoe Night" for the rest of our days. So we had a whole good time after drinks. That was fun, and the next day Konni, my daughter, and I were doing Saturday errands and all that kind of thing. We got home and there was a card under the door—I still have it—and it said, "That's showbiz." That's all it said. I remember Konni immediately got that jealousy thing. And so she wrote on it, "Whoop-dee-doo."

KONNI CORRIERE (stepdaughter): I was moody and pouty and shy, but he never did try to win me over, at least not the way her other boyfriends did. You know, try to get in good with me or whatever.

KATHRYN REED ALTMAN: I spent Sunday afternoon with him, and he was trying to show off that whole day. He was going with this girl, Ricky Barr. She was real aggressive; she was an agent. I guess they had a date on this Sunday night. And he wasn't returning her call. I don't know how it all worked. She came over and beat on the door and he went outside and had this big conversation with her. So we went out to dinner and came back and she was still there. It was a big deal. I don't know who else she called, but the next day Tommy Thompson had this great line to Bob: "I hear they were bunching up at the gate at your apartment last night." It was fun.

Lotus, his estranged wife, came over one of those nights, too, to meet me. She probably would have been one of my best friends if I had met her a different way. We both cooperated with the little boys all of the way through. I was comfortable enough and she seemed to be. I think she hoped up to that point there was a possibility, and she said she realized then there wasn't. We never had any problems and we've been through a lot.

LOTUS CORELLI ALTMAN MONROE: That evening I was going to a play with a bunch of kids from Los Angeles City College. After, I called him up and said, "You want some coffee?" He said, "Yeah, sure, come on up." I went there, and Kathryn was there. He said, "Kathryn, meet my wife." Well, it was very convenient for him to stay married because he would tell his girlfriends, "I can't marry you. I'm already married." So I was kind of a safety net.

We chatted, and I was wound up from drinking coffee and seeing the play. I said, "I'm sorry I interrupted." So I left. I thought, "She's nice." He was still coming and going. I knew that it would never work. We had tried it. It was supposed to be the two of us together. Before

Stevie was born he'd call me and we'd talk, and he'd play me the whole music score from *My Fair Lady*. It took me a long time to get over this, but I knew it wasn't going to work. It was not working for me.

I didn't know her that well from that short meeting. I graduated from Hollywood High the same year as Kathryn. I didn't know her there, but I found out later we had mutual friends. They started living together and we became better acquainted. Kathryn was perfect for him. We were divorced that same year they got married.

Kathryn and Robert Altman on April 5, 1959, during the first week they met, at what they came to call their "engagement dinner"

Robert Altman, from an undated,
unpublished poem titled "Infatuation":

Infatuation,
May fool this heart of mine
Infatuation
May seem like love at times

Knowing that it's light romancing
Hoping that it's love advancing

Infatuation
Came when we met by chance
Infatuation
Sprang from a subtle glance

Then you kiss me
My heart soared high above
Infatuation
Became love.

SUSAN DAVIS (actress and cousin): When I think about Kathryn, I think about the older generation of Altman girls—[his aunts] Marie and Annette and Pauline and Ginny. Ginny is interesting because I think she's the prototype of Kathryn, I always have. Ginny Altman was funny. She was only a teenager when Bob was born. See, it was like having the groovy, sexy aunt. That's who Kathryn is. I met Kathryn the day Bob had me doing P.R. for *Troubleshooters*. I thought, "God, she's like Ginny. He found a redhead who's just like Ginny." She has the same sense of humor, same kind of laugh, and knows just how to handle Bob.

KATHRYN REED ALTMAN: We went right into a full-time relationship—I never worked again after *Whirlybirds*—with a lot of ups and downs, a lot of adjustments. When you first meet somebody and all of a sudden you're tight from the beginning, of course all kinds of things come up. And then I found myself pregnant, with Bobby. I don't know if you want to go into the pregnancy thing or not, but that was the reason we got married.

KONNI CORRIERE: The next thing I know, we're getting all dressed up because he's taking us to dinner, my mother and myself, to some really fancy restaurant. He literally did it in order to ask me for my mother's hand in marriage. I was thirteen. He did all the talking: "Konni, what would you think if I decided to marry your mother," or whatever. I don't know where my voice came from or who I thought I was, but I said, "Well, I think it's all right, but actually she just came out of a marriage, her second marriage, and I think she needs some time by herself or something." I said, "No, I think it's too soon for her to do that." I didn't know she was pregnant.

KATHRYN REED ALTMAN: I'm not sure I would have married Bob if I hadn't been pregnant. I was stuck to marry him at that point. There wasn't anything I could do about that pregnancy. I had Konni and I had gotten her into the whole situation, and I was stuck. I never told him that and probably shouldn't be saying it now. "Stuck" is probably too strong a word. I was crazy about him and I wanted it to work.

He was very much in love with me. He was determined. A couple of those episodes, those partying behaviors, I pulled back a couple of times. But he always convinced me. It was his charm, absolutely.

We went to Ensenada to get married. We couldn't just live together. I wouldn't even consider it because of my daughter. And he

Robert Altman and his stepdaughter, Konni, in December 1959, at the Crescendo Nightclub, on the night Kathryn Reed Altman gave birth to Robert Altman's third son, Robert Reed Altman

wouldn't have, either. He still had a little of that Catholic upbringing that had come to the fore, as they say it will.

KONNI CORRIERE: When they got married we had to move, and I had to go to a father-daughter dinner at Paul Revere Junior High School. So Bob came. I was completely new and scared and he was there, and it was just the two of us and we didn't know each other that well. We put name tags on, and I was Konni Pederson. So all night long, everyone introduced themselves to "Mr. Pederson" and he went with it. He played the part of Mr. Pederson, which was so sweet.

CHAPTER 9

Cheese

*

KATHRYN REED ALTMAN: When we got married Bob was in the middle of *Hawaiian Eye*. He was doing a lot of TV. After we were married, it was *Bonanza* and *Combat!* and all kinds of things. We were getting out of debt. We were terribly in debt when we got married. We were living off my child support, practically. Then we got a really good business manager; his name was Charlie Goldring and he got Bob straight. He had us on a regular budget. It worked out very well because he got us out of debt and on our feet. I just kind of thought that was going to be our life. We bought a house with a swimming pool in Mandeville Canyon. We lived there for nine years. We bought a house and we had a baby and we had the other kids coming over. It was a great house and we had lots and lots and lots and lots and lots of parties.

Television Directing

Hawaiian Eye—1959; *The Millionaire*—1958–59 (five episodes); *Westinghouse Desilu Playhouse*—1960; *Sugarfoot*—1959–60 (two episodes); *Gale Storm Show*—1960; *Maverick*—1960; *Lawman*—1961; *Surfside 6*—1961; *The Roaring Twenties*—1960–61 (nine episodes); *Bonanza*—1960–61 (eight episodes).

DAVID DORTORT (producer): I produced *Bonanza*, and George W. George was someone I respected. I knew his father's reputation. I had hired George to write an episode of *Bonanza*, and he did an excellent job. I mentioned how struck I was by the use of the camera on the James Dean movie, and George said, "How about giving Bob a chance

Directing Ray Danton (left) and Roger Moore
in an episode of The Roaring Twenties

to direct?" We were number one in the world and I didn't know anything about this guy. I met him and he was so overweight, heavy, and
drinking. I said, "If I hire him, he must promise that he would stop
drinking." That was no easy thing.

He was fantastic on *Bonanza*. He was the best director I had. The
series became sharper, more focused. He was born with a camera in his
brain. The guys on the show immediately recognized his talent compared to the other directors. But he told me that as much as he liked
working for me, now he wanted to be able to direct a feature.

Television Directing

Route 66—1961 (one episode);
Bus Stop—1961–62 (eight episodes).

ROBERT BLEES (producer): I did the television adaptation of *Bus Stop*
from both the William Inge play and the Fox movie, which starred

Marilyn Monroe. When I realized that I had to make thirty-nine hours the first year—thirty-nine new shows—I fought to get some assistance.

We were going along and I couldn't get the talent that I wanted for behind the camera, and I knew there was a show at Warner Brothers, *The Roaring Twenties*, that had gotten a little bit of talk. I looked at some reels of that show, from three different episodes, and all were good. The director on all three was Bob Altman.

We learned we were both from Kansas City originally and we hit it off. When I called up the producers of the Warner Brothers show, I said, "Tell me about Altman." They said, "He's trouble. He's good, but trouble. Fights over everything. There were almost blows exchanged." Nevertheless, we hired Altman, because he was good.

He was doing overlapping dialogue, even in those days. He was very good about casting—he wouldn't go the obvious ways. On *Bus Stop*, he cast Robert Redford, the all-American boy, as a member of a criminal plan. And Barbara Baxley, everybody's sensible grandmother, as part of a criminal enterprise.

SUSAN DAVIS: I was commercial looking, so I could pay the rent, but it was a constant struggle. He hired me on a show called *Bus Stop* and Robert Redford and Barbara Baxley were on there. I was hired, and we were going to shoot my part in one day. It was very simple. He rehearsed it, but we didn't shoot it, and I'm sitting there for the rest of the day. It was a Friday, and about five thirty he said, "Okay, the scene with Susan Davis and so-and-so, we can't get to that. We'll have to bump that over to Monday. Can you make it, Susan?" And I'm thinking, "Whoa, that's two rent checks, two days." He knew exactly what he was doing, taking care of me. He never mentioned it, but I thought, "Wow."

ROBERT BLEES: Bob responded to provocative ideas and sometimes wanted to do things that were too provocative. Not from a censorship point of view, but for the sake of being provocative. He was always pushing it. Sometimes, to my mind, erroneously.

FABIAN FORTE (singer and actor): The *Bus Stop* episode I was in that Bob directed was about evil. It walks among us. That was the title, "A Lion Walks Among Us." Evil. It's out there. And you never know where it's coming from. It was perfectly written. I played a drifter, a psychopath. He was very, very charming. Wandered into this little town and took advantage of anything he possibly could take advantage of. He repaid anyone who was nice to him by killing them, and he almost got away with it.

I met with the producers, Roy Huggins and Bob Blees. They said the only way you could possibly get this, me being Fabian, is you have to meet with Bob Altman. So I drove up to his house in Mandeville Canyon. I don't think anybody knew anything about Altman at that time. I knew I was going to have to read for this guy and convince him I could do this. I was nervous as hell. I walked in, and he reminded me of a hippy-dippy kind of guy, which I loved. He was cool, he was warm, he asked me a lot about my personal life, I guess to put me at ease.

KATHRYN REED ALTMAN: When Fabian came over to the house, Konni and Christine just couldn't believe it. They served him a sandwich, and the potato chips he didn't eat, they put them under their pillows or something. They were just gaga over him.

FABIAN FORTE: At first he wanted to improvise a few things about the character. I read with him. We read from the script, and I think it was because of his input I totally transformed myself into this really

Teen heartthrob Fabian, star of Robert Altman's
"A Lion Walks Among Us" episode of Bus Stop

fucked-up guy. He opened windows into the guy—"How would you feel if you had this in your past?" He really wanted you to have that power to see if you could do it. We did it eight or nine different ways. He didn't say much, just a word here or a word there. He had the power to make you go to another dimension. He was that way on the set, too. He never bludgeoned you or was harsh with you. He was very astute—very few words but right to the point emotionally. Then he'd walk away. He did that with all the actors. To me it was, "Wow, if this is the way acting is, this is what I want to be part of."

ROBERT BLEES: Bob, of course, saw this as an opportunity to make a shockingly violent picture. We had to reshoot two different scenes because of the gore and the violence. One was the opening scene, in which Fabian murders the little store owner. That was enough to make anybody gag except Bob. Still, it was a powerful piece.

Jack Gould, story headlined "TV: An Hour of Ugliness," *The New York Times*, December 4, 1961: An hour of dark and sordid ugliness— cheaper than anything yet seen on television and its crude reliance on primitive violence and such—was presented on "Bus Stop" last night. . . . The vehicle was entitled "A Lion Walks Among Us," and starred Fabian, one of the wiggling vocalists created for the TV market. . . . A play often can be extremely unpleasant but still command interest and respect because of the depth of its insight into characters. But last night's presentation had no such justification or excuse; it was unrelieved exploitation of the base instincts of an animal run amuck.

   Censorship on TV is certainly odious, but restraint does have its place. Given tact and delicacy, almost any scene can be handled, but last night's onslaught of mayhem and suggestiveness surely was misplaced in an hour known to appeal to a substantial young audience.

ROBERT BLEES: You know who wrote the book that episode was based on? Tom Wicker of *The New York Times*. I was amazed he never stepped forward to defend it.

FABIAN FORTE: The reviews were the best I ever got as an actor. I give Altman a lot of credit for that. But then the advertisers got scared about the content of the show, and then it got brought up in the congressional hearings they had going on.

Marjorie Hunter, story headlined "A.B.C. Head Backs 'Bus Stop' Episode," *The New York Times,* **January 25, 1962:** A network president testified today that he did not cancel a controversial episode in a television show because he feared his action might discourage creative talent. Oliver Treyz, head of the American Broadcasting Company, appeared before a Senate subcommittee investigating juvenile delinquency and the impact of television crime and sex shows on teen-agers.

Senator Thomas J. Dodd, Democrat of Connecticut, who is subcommittee chairman, reminded Mr. Treyz that he testified last summer that networks could police themselves. "How do you square that statement with your refusal to let the code authority preview your show?" the Senator inquired. Mr. Treyz replied that he felt a preview would have opened the door to possible prior censorship of program content.

Robert Blees: In the aftermath I thought it was ridiculous. I think it was Senator Dodd who said on the floor that he had never seen it, but had heard enough to know it was evil. I thought that was bullshit. It has a very moral point. Roy Huggins was a very devout Catholic—it was sometimes almost impossible to keep his Catholicism out of the show. All the people who criticized it for being evil or approving of crime are absolutely wrong.

Fabian Forte: Dodd had a bug up his ass about what was on television, and they used this show as Exhibit A. A lot of people loved it. It was only the tight-asses that were saying it was going to bankrupt our young people. You know, like the "devil music." Now here it comes on TV. Bob Blees and Roy Huggins wanted to make a feature out of the episode, it was that good. I was praying they would make the motion picture. But because of the heat, the advertisers, and the hearings with Senator Dodd, they buried it. That would have changed my whole life. Well, it might have.

Robert Blees: The show wasn't picked up after that first season. It was the controversy, but it was also the ratings. We were against *Bonanza* on Sunday nights. No show survived against *Bonanza.*

We got some very good notices from good critics and we ended up like number three in some poll. We took our shots and failed. The uproar? It might have helped Bob. He got print. And in this business that helps.

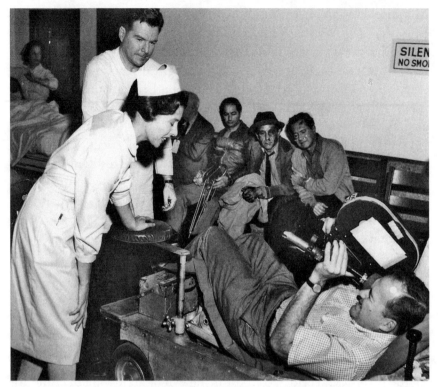

*Filming a pilot for Fox in 1962. The actor at left is Bert Remsen, who
became a close friend of Altman's and acted in eight of his films.*

*   *   *

Kraft Mystery Theater—*1962 (TV, one episode)*

JOHN WILLIAMS (composer): At Universal studios, I'd been working in
the music department since 1958 as a composer. I was assigned to *Kraft
Mystery Theater* for two years. Bob was very different from other directors. I didn't meet them; there wasn't contact. But once I was assigned
to Bob he practically lived over in the music department with me—
inviting me to his house, wanting to have drinks after work. I was fascinated with him because he showed so much unaccustomed interest in
what I was doing. He became a collaborator in a way that wasn't usual
in those days in TV.

Television Directing

The Gallant Men—1962; *Combat!*—1962 (ten episodes).

ROBERT BLEES: After *Bus Stop* came *Combat!* I saw what they wanted to do was take a World War II squad from almost D-day to Berlin's fall. I was hired and the first thing I said was, "I'd love to do it. I can improve it, but I want Bob Altman under contract." It was a unique contract for Bob—he would be under contract for the entire year, and he would shoot one episode and would be preparing the next one when he finished shooting. He'd be doing every other episode. That was unique, to commit to that many, but he was the best director. I had used fifteen or twenty directors, including some of the best. Arthur Hiller worked for me, Don Siegel. Other top, top guys. Bob was the best fifty-five minute television director I had ever encountered. No one had his instincts.

TOM SKERRITT (actor): I was right at the end of film school at UCLA, and I met this director guy who lived in the neighborhood near UCLA—he had seen me in this little antiwar film I had done. He said, "Come on over and be in this show, *Combat!*" It was Robert Altman.

The day before I'm supposed to start shooting, I went over to the set to see him to thank him for the job. I walk up and see him from behind. He was sitting in this tall director's chair, and I knew it was him. He had this wonderful Australian hat on. A Jeep drives up and the guys in the scene jump out. Bob's head is leaning over. Generally a director will say, "Cut." He says nothing. The A.D., the assistant director, comes over and shakes him. "Bob, the shot's over." And he woke up. "Oh, how was it?" he says. "It was fine, Bob." "Okay, print it. Let's move on." That was the first time I saw him in action. And I said, "He's my kind of director" [*laughs*]. But imagine falling into a mentorship with a guy like Altman. You work with other guys and you realize they're not half of what Altman is. Put them all together and they weren't half of what Altman was.

So then it's my first day on the set, my first *Combat!*, and I'm sitting next to Bob. There was a tense scene being lit. And I'm watching an electrician walking around with an empty five-gallon bucket, walking from one light to another on a catwalk. I'm thrilled, taking it all in. I've never been on a Hollywood soundstage before. I'm brand-new to all this, and I think this is really something. I'm watching the guy with the bucket and Bob is watching me, reading the whole situation as only he could. I've got this look on my face, "Gee-golly-whiz." I'm still looking up, and just then, the guy throws up in his bucket.

Bob points up there and says, "Hollywood."

JOHN CONSIDINE (actor and screenwriter): I was a young actor and I got this audition to read for this new show, *Combat!*, as guest lead on an episode. I was supposed to dive into this moat to swim across where we could get to this German machine-gun nest. He shot it and I thought we were done—there are such time constraints, everybody in television is pressured to get things done. But Bob realized he could shoot the whole scene in the reflection of the water. It was certainly more interesting that way. So he did the whole thing over. It was the only time I ever heard a director in television say, "Hey, I've got a better idea." Right there I saw a little of what Bob was going to be like later.

ROBERT REED ALTMAN (son): There's a story from the *Combat!* days, when Vic Morrow would walk down a crowded street with a hundred and fifty extras and no one could talk except that one actor and the guy that was with him, because they were being paid to do that. And my dad would go to the extras every morning and say, "Who wants a line today?" And the assistant directors were like, "No, no, you can't do that!" My dad would pick five people to shout things out as Vic walked down the street. The next day, the A.D. said, "Here come the producers. They're going to fire you for doing that." They came up and said, "Whose idea was it to have these guys do that, call out things as Vic walked by? That was great—we loved that. It made it real." He never had fear. If something creatively grabbed him, he would do it.

BARBARA TURNER (screenwriter/actress/producer, ex-wife of Vic Morrow): Vic adored Bob. Every actor in the world adored Bob. It was the sense of freedom that Bob gave actors. When I worked with Bob as an actress it was stunning.

MICHAEL MURPHY (actor): He was doing *Combat!*, and Joan Bennett, who is a longtime friend of Bob and Kathryn, said, "You should go out to MGM and meet Bob Altman. He's doing this Army thing and they're using a lot of young guys." So I went out and met him and he couldn't have been nicer. I knew from the minute I walked in that he was just this very unusual guy. Something about him, I was completely enamored. He knocked me out. Here was a guy, he was in his thirties, he was probably thirty-seven or thirty-eight, and he'd flown fifty missions over the South Pacific. So he was a fully formed adult male. He was a guy who you looked up to. He had older sensibilities. He had stories to tell and he knew how he wanted to tell them and it wasn't like some twit from film school. There weren't any film schools. He learned what he had to say by practical experience and he'd been through things that most people never go through.

So he said, "Are you sure you want to do this?"

I said, "Yeah."

He said, "Well, okay."

I opened my door one morning the next week, and there was a script from *Combat!* and I almost fell down. There was an offer in the envelope and I was to play Tank Driver Number Two. Tank Driver Number One was Matty Jordan—you know, the guy who owned Matteo's and ensured Bob a good seat on Friday nights.

So I went out to the lot when the day came, and you'd have thought I was the star of the show. He was so nice and I was included in everything. Remember, this was Hollywood. There was no reason for him to be hanging around with me [*laughs*]. But he was just this very, very nice guy and he seemed genuinely interested and he seemed to care that I was there. I remember saying, "Should I rehearse this with Vic Morrow?" He said, "Oh, we're not going to shoot that stuff." And we didn't. We sat out there in the weeds—they used to give you those box lunches in the old days out there. I remember sitting under a tree and he says, "Well, what do you want to say in this scene?" And I said, "What do *I* want to say?" I remember going home that night and thinking, "This isn't like acting. There's no anxiety. It's just so easy. It's just people talking to each other." Of course that was his whole point. That's how you operated.

Well, it turns out the bosses had told him not to shoot this episode. They told him that it was too dark and nobody was speaking English. The only people that spoke in the episode were the Germans and me. And Vic was wandering around hurt. He's burned and he's wandering. The bosses went to New York for some kind of business meeting, and he shot it anyway [*laughs*]. So of course he was busted, fired, for insubordination. And of course the episode, it's called "Survival," turns out to be the best one they ever shot.

Vic Morrow in the best-known episode of Combat!, *"Survival,"*
directed by Robert Altman

*   *   *

Kraft Suspense Theater—*1963–64 (TV, three episodes)*

KATHRYN REED ALTMAN: Bob was doing the *Kraft Suspense Theater*
shows. After he did the third one, he did an interview. He had to leave
for Chicago the very next day on something job related. I didn't go. I
had a small baby. And he gave this interview—I don't know what
prompted the interview, he wasn't that well-known. But the headline in

Variety the next day says, "Robert Altman says the *Kraft Theater* plots are as bland as their cheese." And he's gone, of course, and it hit the front page and I get all the phone calls. And I didn't know at first what anybody was talking about. Really funny. For Bob's next birthday, John Williams, the composer, and his wife, Barbara, brought Bob a whole case of Velveeta. I loved that.

GEORGE LITTO (agent): The show is as bland as its cheese. He said that. He didn't tell Kraft, he told *Variety*, which is worse. I was an agent in town, but I didn't know him at all. I knew of him, but I did not personally know him nor had I ever met him. I knew him as a filmmaker in the community—he was known for having directed many *Combat!* episodes, and good ones. He was known as a very skillful director.

Once I saw a show he did on television, just turned it on and saw the show, and there was a nice story. The story was good but not extraordinary, but what was extraordinary was the way the film was shot. And what was new and exciting was that it was the first time in a commercial program by a major studio where high-speed Ektachrome film was used, with which you could shoot night for night, with minimum light. And the way the film looked with this high-speed film, and the style he used to photograph and direct the movie, was extraordinary.

Nightmare in Chicago
(aka, Once Upon a Savage Night; *1964*)

Albuquerque Journal television previews, April 2, 1964: This chase tale is a sleeper, with a particularly terrifying moment out on a tollway. It involves a murderer, "a butcher," who throttles blondes. It was filmed around Chicago at night, and it's most effective in color. Black and white footage is not quite as suspenseful, because the star of the film is variations in light.

DONALD FACTOR (producer): He was hired to do this pilot, which was a cops-and-robbers thing. Some of his old Army Air Force friends told him that Eastman Kodak had developed some kind of new film stock, for photographing missiles. It was very high speed. He said, "With this, we can go out in the streets and shoot outdoors at night and have a really good, realistic film." He went to Universal and they talked to

Kodak and they refused to give him any. They said it wasn't tested for that kind of use. Bob simply went behind their backs and bootlegged a bunch of it and shot his pilot. Kodak found out and raised all kinds of hell. Of course it was a big success and everyone was impressed with the look of it. So after that the people at Kodak called Bob and wanted him to become the spokesman for that film stock. He did things like that and he usually came out on top.

BARBARA TURNER: After the Hitchcock show, the next time I worked with Bob was *Once Upon a Savage Night*. Bob called me one day and said, "We've got this script, but we're not going to be doing it. We're just going to rewrite the whole thing. Let me take you away from all this, and we'll have a good time." That was '63, because I got on the plane about two days after Kennedy was shot. And we had to change a large piece of the script because it was originally about a presidential convoy coming through, and somebody who was out to kill the president. He changed it to a missile being driven on the thruway. So the whole cast stayed up until three or four in the morning covering a gasoline truck to make it look like a missile.

Filming Once Upon a Savage Night *in Chicago with Reza Badiyi*

It was like camp. You know, everybody had to be together all the time. We ate together, we slept together, we did everything together. Everybody had to be around all the time. He would take from everybody and it was just fun. And it's not like it all went smoothly. The weather didn't go smoothly. It was so cold the cameras froze. We stopped for two weeks because he couldn't finish the movie. And we all came back to finish it without pay because everybody loved him so much and loved doing it.

We're all sitting around one night and he said, "You know, when I was a little boy, it was so cold in the morning that my mother used to make hard-boiled eggs and put them in my mittens in the morning to walk to school. Then when I got to school, when they'd cooled off, I would eat them."

I said, "Oh my God, can I have that? Can we put that in the script?"

He did, and it wasn't until the show was over that he said, "I made that up." But it was great, and it was in the movie. After, he had a little statue made of an egg. It was an "Eggie," and he gave it to me for "the best performance in twenty-below-zero weather."

George Litto: So Bob had a reputation as being very individualistic or a maverick or difficult or worse. But I was accused of being the same way, so none of that ever bothered me. As a matter of fact, I was attracted to people who had strong personal views and I liked people with a new and individual take on their work. I was always looking for it.

Robert Altman: Pretty much all the stuff I did in television, the style of it, the color of it, or the feel of it came from movies I liked. On *Combat!* I copied everything. I remember once on *Combat!* saying, "This is gonna be my *Four Feathers*," or I'd name some other movie. I'd have a movie in mind that I could apply to the script we were shooting. I was really stealing someone else's style and applying it to my work.

But that's no different than someone telling you, "Do a painting of the ocean," or "Do a painting of mountains." Well, you've got all these paintings of mountains and oceans, and that doesn't mean your painting of either of those things is diminished just because you're doing something similar to what somebody else does. We all do similar things.

* * *

Reza Badiyi (director): Bob loved actors, but he had an enormous disagreement—I wouldn't say hatred, but almost like the neighbor who puts up the fence—toward the management. So he always becomes a champion of the crew, to go and yell at the producers and the upper-up, the money. He would fight for their causes.

Barbara Turner: He taught me a lot. He got a letter or notes from Universal, because the show was from Universal. Something about being too dark or too light or something, and he sent them back a letter saying, "Fuck you. Rude letter follows." And I thought, "This is the greatest man in the universe." Bob was the most extraordinary man that ever walked the face of the earth. I mean, he didn't bend for anybody.

Bob was I think the closest reincarnation—except they lived at the same time—to Hemingway. They were the same guy. The same demons, the same passions, and the same ego and the same vulnerabilities. Larger than life. Incredibly gifted. And Hemingway could turn on people on a dime, for no reason, just attack, you know? But then would get over it. Bob, too.

Bob had a shit list of sorts, so you could get on that. It took a while to get off of it—when he decided to take you off of it—but I don't think he could hold a grudge. It was the same with Hemingway. He would get in raging fights with people, I mean fistfights, and then start to laugh. That was Bob, you know? And Hemingway loved women, like Bob.

I never thought of Bob as an alcoholic. I don't think Bob thought of himself as an alcoholic. I don't think anybody thought Bob was an alcoholic, but he drank a lot. And he was a big guy so he could pretty much carry a lot.

George Litto: He used to mix these fucking crazy drinks—the Green Death. It was all part of the fun. He'd have all this shit he'd order, and he'd mix all the things up and [say], "Everybody, try this, try that." It was a whole ceremonial thing. He used to captivate everybody's attention while he made all these drinks. He could have been a great entertainer. We'd all get shit-faced and roll over, fall asleep on the floor, wake up at six in the morning—we didn't know where we were. Well, when you're young and strong. Green Death. I'll never forget that.

*   *   *

RICHARD SARAFIAN (director/actor/former brother-in-law): I had written a script called *Andy*. It was a very sensitive story about someone I knew when I was a bartender in New York. He was retarded and he ultimately froze to death in a doorway. This film was a tribute to him. After I got my first job at Warner Brothers, I met Bob at Nickodell's and he had been drinking. He wanted to direct the script I had written. I wanted to direct it myself. I said no. He was furious. He said, "I'll tell you what, Sarafian, I'll become your worst enemy in Hollywood." There was a competitive side of Bob, and for whatever reason—marrying his sister, being a director—he saw me as competition in those days.

JOAN ALTMAN SARAFIAN: That's not true. Dick would love to have been Bob's friend. He would have loved it more than having me. He would much rather have had Bob.

JOHN WILLIAMS: Bob was uneven when he drank. He could always be very sweet, but more typically he would be cutting and sarcastic and apply that soul-destroying gaze of his. His eyes were fantastic instruments of reprimand and reproach.

When he drank, he seemed to find an excuse to go penetrating and in-depth at people's foibles. He could go right for the jugular with people in a way that could be devastating. He was so perceptive in his analysis of people at various levels that he was very well equipped to do it. A lot of that came out when he was lubricated, or liberated, by alcohol. I don't remember him aiming it at me. But my kids—he was hard on my kids.

I don't think it's very unusual. But Bob was also so attractive and elicited so much loyalty from his friends that I don't think there were too many relationships in his inner circle that were broken by this cruel behavior.

KONNI CORRIERE: He gave parties every weekend, loud and late and drunk, and he always got drunk and always got cruel and evil and terrifying. He was so perceptive; he'd go for a person's weakness and then crucify them. It was loud. It was frightening. It was the main attraction and no one ever stood up to him.

Once at the house in Mandeville Canyon, he was so drunk and so angry, he took the television and threw it through the plate-glass window into the swimming pool.

KATHRYN REED ALTMAN: He was a big drinker and a party boy. His good traits outshone his bad ones, but he had some pretty bad results with all the drinking. Telling people off at the wrong time. Really the problem was not that person. I would have to tell them, "You are not the target, don't take it personally." I won most everybody back. There were times when I would just walk on eggs and sit in fear before the evening was over that there was going to be an explosion. When he was good he was very, very good, but when he was bad, oh man.

REZA BADIYI: He wasn't scared to just say his mind. But sometimes he was just saying it for effect at that moment. But it has a resonance, an echo that bothered him dearly in life, to a point that he was truly not working and he needed some money.

KATHRYN REED ALTMAN: Some people are motivated by security. And then there's the gambler. He takes chances, risks. That's Bob Altman, the rebel and the renegade and all those names they called him. It was a given. His dad was a big hustler, player, gambler, so Bob grew up in it, knew all the tricks.

It was our fifth anniversary and he was at the track. I heard about this later. He had this last three hundred dollars or something, and he was saying, "If this horse doesn't win I can't go back home because Kathryn is waiting and I don't know what I'm going to do. I'm just going to put it all on one horse." And Martha Raye was there, and she said, "Put it all on this one."

Robert Altman, from an essay called "Risk" in *Esquire*, October 1993: Martha Raye came by and said, "Here's a tip. I don't know if it's any good but there's a horse called Pal Fast." I looked up and saw that Pal Fast was going off at thirty to one. "Thanks a lot," I said. . . . I'm thinking, "What the fuck am I going to do? I can't cover a check for Las Vegas and I can't lose face." Finally I said, "Oh what the hell."

KATHRYN REED ALTMAN: He bet it all and he won. He came up with a few grand and we had the greatest weekend—we laughed the whole time. It could have been a horrendous story, and I might not be sitting here very easily had it gone down the other way. That was our last ten cents. Make that our last nickel.

Robert Altman, from an essay called "Risk" in *Esquire*, October 1993: I've gambled all my life, but I've managed to gamble within my loss range. I've been lucky, because I haven't always been careful. My attitude is, "Why not?" Professional gamblers are the most uninteresting gamblers of all because they're like the banks. They play the odds and cut it right out of the middle. They don't even *think* about the long shot. Absolutely boring. I put them alongside the studios. . . . We don't rely enough on instinct in this culture. Sometimes you just feel the heat and you know the fucking number is going to come out and finally it does. Waiting for it is part of the joy.

*   *   *

GEORGE LITTO: So the *Variety* piece comes out, where he says the thing about the cheese, and when I read about it in the paper I said, "Jesus, what a stupid son of a bitch [*laughs*]. Didn't he have enough trouble? Can't he keep his mouth shut?" And he gets dropped by his agency, Ashley-Steiner. And before I knew it, Ray Wagner, who was an executive at MCA/Universal, called me on the phone. I had many clients working under his auspices. And he said, "George, I'm calling you because I'm planning to leave Universal."

I said, "Why, Ray? I know they like you there."

He said, "Well, I'm going to go into production. I want to produce pictures and I'm going to go into a partnership with Bob Altman to produce pictures and some television, too."

I said, "Are you out of your fucking mind?" My thought was, Bob Altman couldn't get a commitment to be a dogcatcher at this point in time.

He said, "George, you don't know Bob. You got to meet him and you got to come to breakfast with him."

RAYMOND WAGNER (producer): I liked Bob because he was a rebel. Bob was always Bob. He was not a man that enjoyed the big commercial process so much or the corporate structures, but liked doing whatever it was he liked doing.

GEORGE LITTO: So we had a breakfast meeting at the Beverly Hills Hotel. My first impression? He was angry. He was a little surly. I'm a first-generation Sicilian Italian, okay? I'm not intimidated by anybody. So he said to me, "If you're interested in working with us, I'm not going to do any more television."

I said, "You don't have to worry about that. I don't think anybody will let you."

It was true. It was a long time before he did television.

CHAPTER 10

No Milk

*

JOAN ALTMAN SARAFIAN: I don't think TV was right for him. TV is too regimented. Making a film is different. He can control it. He was not a soldier. It's not that he was a general, either. Just a free, free soul.

KATHRYN REED ALTMAN: He laid off for a year waiting for a feature film. We were out of money. We were cut off by the milkman. Oscar the milkman. That's pretty bad. And we had a Japanese gardener, Kenny, and he came to me, "I'm sorry, madam, I will have to halt the service" [*laughs*].

It was very brave of him to do that. We managed. We never fought over money. It wasn't one of those marriages where there's pinchpenny behavior. We were generous with each other. "You've got some money, okay, then, we'll pay that bill. Next month we'll have more and pay the other one."

MICHAEL MURPHY: He couldn't have found a better woman. I mean, she truly devoted herself to him, but he really met his match in her. She was fast and she made him laugh and they both had that same "I've been around the block a few times" outlook on life. His pet name for her was Trixie, and that just kind of fit who she is.

When times were rough, she was the kind of woman who could plow through it with him. She could live on the edge and do it with great style. But it must have been hard.

ROBERT REED ALTMAN: I went to Carlthorp from grade one to three; it was a private school, because they did want me to have a good education. But at times, when they couldn't pay the bill there, I would be put

Robert Altman in party mode

in the waiting room and they would come and get me. And that kind of confused me. "Why am I being picked up by my parents? Did I do something wrong?" So psychologically I think that did something to me, not knowing. My dad was always juggling money to try to make things work.

REZA BADIYI: It reached a point where he was truly not working and needed money. He was going to do some commercial for an automobile company. I was working at the time, but I went. Louie Lombardo came. Brian McKay, who was a writer, and Robert Eggenweiler, who did a little of everything. All of us, we gathered and shot it for him. And we did it all for free. We had to.

ROBERT BLEES (producer): I loaned him money personally. Bob was desperate. He was broke, broke, broke. Real broke. I wouldn't say promptly, but he paid me back.

Bob was a huge gambler, which is one reason he was broke most of the time. We almost bought a horse together named Earl the Pearl, a three-thousand-dollar claimer. Bob said the horse was going to run at a claiming race at Delmar. Bob said, "We've always wanted to buy a horse, let's look at the race." I said, "Bob, you owe me fifteen hundred dollars right now. I'd rather have the fifteen hundred than half a horse." So we didn't buy the horse. He ended up winning his next five races.

GEORGE LITTO: He didn't want to do television anymore, but he had kids, he had a wife, ex-wives, you know. I used to lend him money. That's a whole 'nother story. He had to put food on the table. He owed me at least a year's salary [*laughs*]. A year's income. What he would be happy to make in a year, let's say. He was always on the brink.

Ray Wagner was always a very diplomatic, soft-spoken guy, a nice guy. He was a bright guy, and he said, "George, we've developed two projects. We know you like unusual material."

I was saying to myself, "So I like it, what then? What can I do? This guy is just the most untouchable guy around. You know, it's one thing to get fired from a studio. But fired from your agent, too? I mean, that's almost unheard-of. Clients fire agents, agents don't fire clients." So I said, "Well, I don't know whether I can do anything to help you guys get started in the movie business."

He said, "We'll do television, too."

I said, "Ray, I don't know about that either." I turned to Bob and said, "Bob, I don't want to seem insensitive, but I think people are a little afraid of you."

He just said, "Grrrrrrrr." He didn't give a shit. He was not intimidated. I liked that about him. Ray said, "Please read the material." And I said, "Okay." I said to myself, "Ray's always been a good guy, and I've made a lot of money with him and his company, and I owe him that courtesy." Though I wasn't very hopeful that I could do anything. Because Bob really got everybody uptight.

So I read the two scripts. One Bob did with Roald Dahl, which

I think was his story or one he inspired, called *O Death, Where Is Thy Sting-a-ling-a-ling?*, which I thought was a brilliant script. As a joke, when people said "I've got a great script," I'd say, "I don't want it." They'd say, "What do you mean you don't want it?" I said, "If I agree you have a great script, imagine how frustrated I'll get if I can't sell it?"

PATRICIA NEAL (actress): I met Bob when I was in Hawaii doing *In Harm's Way*. I'd just won the Oscar and it was just great, and Roald was there with our three children. Bob Altman came to see Roald with Jackie Cooper, who had been a child actor. They came to see Roald because they wanted him to do the screenplay for an idea that they had. And they were so drunk from the minute they arrived till the minute they left. Dead drunk, but that didn't stop them from thinking. They had this gorgeous idea, and they thought Roald should do the script. It was very good, and Roald decided to do it. He did quite a bit of work on it and it became very attractive to people.

GEORGE LITTO: So I thought he truly had a great script. Roald Dahl is a great writer, and included were some letters between Bob and Roald Dahl. I could read the way this thing evolved and Bob's thought process. I said, "This is a brilliant guy." He's even better than I thought he was from seeing his film. Then I read the other script, which was the comedy that Barbara Turner did, based on a novel by a dentist, John Haase: *Me and the Arch Kook Petulia*. I read that and I said, "Absolutely charming, wonderful movie." First time I've read two good scripts in a row in years. I said, "Holy Christ, what am I going to do? Do I want to get involved in this?"

BARBARA TURNER: Bob came to me with *Petulia*. I wrote that on spec, by the way. But he asked me to do it. He said, "Do you think you can do it?" I said, "I have no idea." But Bob saw me as a writer. What appealed to Bob was the character. The character is this creature, and I think Bob liked creatures. She's feisty and unconventional and just wonderful.

GEORGE LITTO: I pondered it a bit because I knew it wasn't going to be easy. Even though the script material was great, Bob's going to want to direct them and there's going to be lots of resistance. So I had a meeting with them. I said, "Look, I love the material. I know you've got the talent to do it, Bob. Ray, I think you're a very good executive;

you should be a good producer. But this is going to be tough to pull off and I don't know if I can do it. I'm willing to try but I'll not promise you anything." And they said, "If you're willing to try, we want you to represent us."

RAYMOND WAGNER: At one time we had Henry Fonda and we had a cast and Bob was going to direct it and I was going to produce *Petulia*. We were almost within weeks of getting started at Warner Brothers and at the last moment they just pulled away. They were worried about Bob. They were always a little worried about someone they can't control. I think they felt concerned that Bob might be off doing something on his own and they might not be in full accord with it.

GEORGE LITTO: I went to work, and it was quite an adventure. I couldn't get the movies going initially. But we got a deal from folks at CBS who saw the same show I saw in Chicago. They wanted to do a police show in Chicago and they wanted Bob to do a pilot—Bob and Ray, in Chicago, for a series. I said, "Guys, what can I tell you? You don't have a movie, and this is a great opportunity if you want to do television." CBS was the best company to work for in those days, and they decided to do it. They did a terrific show, but it did them in. First Bob was upset because Ray tried to edit some of the footage when Bob wasn't there. And Ray got upset because Bob told him never to do that again.

RAYMOND WAGNER: We had different ways to approach certain problems. It's like a marriage. You face each day and many things go along wonderfully and smoothly and other things you're just not in step with. Bob loved the socializing, the after hours of sitting around having a drink with whomever, but I wasn't into that. It wasn't my style. I preferred to make myself an omelet and read. We had a mutual respect. We just approached important stuff differently. He had his own attitudes about certain things and I had mine and they weren't meshing, and it really impacted on both of us.

One place we parted ways was Bob was less interested in story than working with character. Bob loved character, and he was extraordinary with character. He could bring these people off on the film. Story was less interesting to him. Not consciously, at the time. It just wasn't as important to him. You have to have a combination, in my mind, and we often had bouts about that.

GEORGE LITTO: I could see this partnership beginning to crack. I don't remember exactly the timing, but it did crack, and they came to me to be the arbitrator because they were going to split up.

They wanted me to help them arbitrate this, and the way it was settled basically was that CBS wouldn't do the television show without Bob being the producer and the director. So Ray got a lesser percentage. I think he got twenty-five percent and Bob got seventy-five percent of the ownership if the show sold, something like that. Ray got *Petulia* and Bob got *O Death*.

LORING MANDEL (screenwriter): Bob was very bitter about that and about Ray Wagner. The way he explained it to me was he had gone down to the Caribbean to shoot a commercial—he was doing that to make money—and Wagner had taken *Petulia* from him while he was gone and ruptured the partnership. That's what he told me.

GEORGE LITTO: Then Ray sent the *Petulia* script to Dick Lester's agent and manager in London. Lester had just directed all the Beatles pictures so successfully, and he was interested to do *Petulia*. Meanwhile, Cary Grant got interested in the *O Death* script, and then United Artists and the Mirish Company got interested in *O Death*. But the Mirish Company or UA wouldn't accept Bob as the director. He had never done a feature, and in those days to make the transition from television to movies was very difficult. Only a few directors did it. And even fewer did it successfully. George Roy Hill was one. John Frankenheimer. Arthur Penn. Not too many more.

The irony of this whole situation for me was that Bob had to commit to the Chicago television series—they called it *Chicago, Chicago*—because they wouldn't do it with Ray without Bob, but they'd do it with Bob without Ray. For which he gave up *Petulia*, thinking we might make a deal with *O Death* because Cary Grant was interested. And if not Cary Grant maybe it would be somebody else. It was an ensemble piece, which obviously became Bob's signature later. Out of all these failures came the causes for his later success.

At the last minute, CBS decided not to do it. So Bob's interest in *Chicago* is worth zero. Then nothing happens with *O Death, Where Is Thy Sting-a-ling-a-ling*. Cary Grant drops out, and other opportunities didn't materialize. We had no deal, and Bob needed money desperately. I was helping him as much as I could because I really believed in him at that point. And Irving Lazar, Swifty, called me up one day and said Roald Dahl wants to sell the script to the Mirish Company. Bob reluctantly agreed to sell it, and at that time we got a very big price of a hundred fifty thousand dollars, of which he got half. He felt like he was selling his soul to the devil. It was brinkmanship, financially. He was on the edge. He sold it and was very unhappy about it.

PATRICIA NEAL: Roald had this agent, Swifty Lazar. And Swifty said, "Get rid of him." Meaning Altman. Because he hadn't done anything. "We're going to go out and get a great director" and that sort of thing. Bob was nobody, absolutely nobody at this point. He was angry with Roald, which I think he should have been.

I thought that was terrible, I really did. But by then I had had my terrible strokes. That was when I was unconscious. I didn't know anything about it until later. So Roald said he had to sell it, because he needed money. He said, "Okay, I'll do it." I think that was very bad of Roald. I think you stick by people.

So they started shooting in Switzerland. It began to snow and snow, and they couldn't finish it. I think they had three days of shooting at the end of five weeks. Isn't that something? So that movie was killed,

Patricia Neal with John Wayne, filming Otto Preminger's In Harm's Way *in Hawaii, where she met Robert Altman*

and soon after Bob Altman—boing!—he shot to the top. I think that's really fun—betrayal and comeuppance. That's what I like about it. I think, "Ha, ha, ha!" Then, of course, Roald did the same sort of thing to me [*laughs softly*].

GEORGE LITTO: On top of this, we sold *Petulia* without him, after he had given it to Ray Wagner. I put an ad in the trades that I just returned from London, where I'd made a deal with Julie Christie, who had just done *Doctor Zhivago*, and Dick Lester, who had directed all the Beatles pictures—the two biggest things in the film world at the time. In the ad I said I'd just made a deal with them to do a picture, and no major studio commitment has been made yet. My phone just rang up like a Christmas tree, and I orchestrated the symphony. I made a fantastic deal for Ray Wagner in the days when one hundred thousand dollars or one hundred fifty thousand dollars would have been top, top deal. I got him four hundred fifty thousand dollars to produce the movie. It was an "oh my God" deal. Of course Bob heard this. Bob called me, but not to say congratulations [*laughs*].

He said, "George, you know I have great respect for you and I appreciate everything you've done for me. I know you tried hard. But I cannot have an agent that represents me and Ray Wagner."

I said, "Bob, I cannot have a client who tells me who I can represent."

He said, "Well, I'm sorry, I have to go."

I said, "I'm sorry, too." And we ended it there.

I kind of lost track of Bob and went on with my other business.

BARBARA TURNER: He didn't get to direct it, but *Petulia* happened because of Bob. He was really good with women. He really liked women. I mean *really* liked them, and I think his career shows it. He gave women tremendous opportunities, writers and actresses, and he just liked them.

The movie's not bad. I was pleasantly surprised when I finally saw it. And I thought Julie Christie was glorious. And so is George C. Scott. However, I would love to have seen what Bob would have done with it. He should have directed it.

When you were working with Bob, it was always an adventure. Just this huge, wild safari. And you never were sorry for it, no matter how painful. And in an odd way, you kind of always felt he was watching your back. You always felt like he wouldn't do you in.

In the meantime, even before *Petulia*, I had read a story in *The New Yorker* called "At Lake Lugano," about a woman who's a Holocaust survivor. I wrote the screenplay without the rights. When I finished I went to the author's agent and I said, "I have no money, how much can I get the option for?" I think it was twelve-fifty. And at one point I showed it to Bob. Sometime after that, I found out that Anouk Aimée was interested in making the movie and Bob said he would do it.

We met Anouk in Paris. I think we were all at the Hotel George V. I don't know how Bob pulled that off but we were all staying there. We all met in Bob's room, and it was a very strange meeting because Bob was, like, loaded. He said to her, "I want you to see my movies." And she said, "I don't need to see your movies because you could make great movies and if we worked together and it was terrible, we'd make terrible movies. I just feel good rapport with you." She loved the script—she said that when she came in. That's why he said, "I think you have to see my movies," because I think he felt that it couldn't be just about her loving the script. And she said, "That's not important." And I think for Bob it was very important. So he said, "The first thing we have to do is get rid of *her.*" Meaning me, the writer [*laughs*]. That sort of started the evening. So one thing led to another and it just got worse and worse and worse. He said, "You know, the person I really wanted for this part was Annie Girardot." I was like, "What are you doing?!"

Reza Badiyi: Anouk just came out of her experience with Fellini, and she was talking about the richness of the experiences, and Bob got annoyed. He said, "I'm sick up to here. Let's talk about me a little bit." To make matters worse, Brian McKay was with us, and the night before, Bob accused him of stealing something from him. Brian had spent prison time for stealing, so that was sensitive. Brian hit him, and Bob had a huge black eye. It became very obvious that this is not going to work with Anouk.

Barbara Turner: He finally passed out at the table. He sort of went into his plate. It was weird, and at that point the way I rationalized it is that if he did his worst and you were still with him, then he trusted you. She was very cool, actually. I mean she was fine, except later she said to me, "I don't think I can work with this man."

Anouk Aimée (actress): Yes, I met him for *Lake Lugano*. He was very different. He was a little bit more noisy, less sensitive than I could imagine he really was. He was more rough, less delicate. But very brilliant and very funny. More brutal—not physically, but the way he talked.

I don't remember the story that Barbara tells. Or Reza. I don't know where she got that. He never told me he wanted to get rid of Barbara, and he never talked to me about Annie Girardot. Bob wouldn't tell one actress about another one. I don't remember him drunk, even. I think I would remember that. I do remember he was like a bomb. He had a strong personality. He was tall, and he had a big voice—"I want this," and "I want that." I remember thinking it would be very difficult to work with him, and we didn't make the film.

BARBARA TURNER: After, I wrote him a letter saying, "I don't think you want to make this movie, and it's very important to me because I love it." He didn't forgive me for that, not for a long time. It didn't get made anyway, because she picked a director who was . . . it got nowhere. But I think he felt that I didn't stick by him. Reza and I got married after that, and he did come to the wedding. But it was a big rift.

REZA BADIYI: Bob needed an audience. Bob was feeding from the admiring eyes of people sitting around him. It was his food, his oxygen. When there was a period that goes by and there wasn't anything going on, Bob physically feels sick.

That was one of the reasons he loved to take each movie that he's making out of town. When he's staying at the hotel with the cast and his crew, usually always having dinner with them, it's a continuation of him in the center and everybody's around him. And the medium, the thing that he created with them, is not broken. He often said, when he works in town, the crew, the cast, at night they go home and they get polluted with their family, with their problems, with the life things, with the delinquent daughter or this and that. But when you are away from it, very little of that gets to them, because they're still in that atmosphere of location. He could keep them tuned. That was very clever of him.

With us, the parting came when I wanted to direct. He said, "There are so many directors, but there's a rare cameraman with your talent." And he says to me, "You know what, two actors work together, two writers work together, two producers work together, but never two directors work together. So I wish you good luck and adios."

Bob had this theory: if you're my friend, you're going to stay till the last breath of your life. And the day that you go, you're gone, you're on the shit list.

It hurt, yet at the same time anywhere I did anything, when I looked at it critically, before I jumped in it, I would say, "Let's see how Bob would like this." He always stayed in my mind as a critic, as a mentor. Sometimes when I'm thinking about him it became almost like a spirituality, to that extent.

*   *   *

DANFORD GREENE (film editor): I met Bob when I was sixteen years old, maybe seventeen. My best friend, Jack Devlin, went with Bob's sister Joan, who later married Dick Sarafian, and who I used to take out, too. A couple of times we'd double-date with Bob's younger sister, Barbara. Bob had just come out of the service and I remember being at their parents' house once and he was in the other room with a piano with another guy collaborating on a song.

That was the last contact I had with him until I ran into him again when I was a film editor at Universal. He was doing *Bonanza*, and one of the producers of *Bonanza*, Bob Blees, came to Universal, and Bob Blees and I became friends. Then Bob Altman came to Universal and we immediately hooked up and I edited his pictures, Louie Lombardo and me. Then we did several *Kraft Theater* films at Universal, until Bob said that thing about the cheese.

So Bob left, and he started Westwood Films. He asked me to come with him, and this was a huge jump for me, because I'd been at Universal from the time I was a splicer out of USC. With Bob Blees we made a series of little films called Color-Sonics. They were three minutes long, the length of a song. He did one with Lili St. Cyr, the famous stripper. Then I came with him and we did a thing called *The Party*. We shot a bunch, all of this at Bob's house around a pool. Just a big party.

ROBERT BLEES: They were supposed to go in video jukeboxes, to be put in restaurants. It was MTV thirty years before its time. I do not know why it was not an economic success—the customers were delighted with them.

DANFORD GREENE: Through his contacts, Bob had development deals with the networks—CBS, NBC, and ABC. He was the leader. He would come up with ideas for series and we would try to get those off the ground. All that time, he would hold court every night, practically. The ice would come out and we'd have cocktails. He loved grass. He was trying to create his own independent studio even back then. He wanted control. He didn't like to be told what to do and how to do it. I think that cost him a few big pictures and some knocks around the business.

During that period when we had Westwood Films, he would be really broke. He'd owe money to the liquor store, the camera store, you name it. He'd be offered a job and he wouldn't take it because he didn't like it. Didn't like the script. With my whoring ways, I'm trying to get him to do it. "Oh, it's a beauty—when do we roll?" But I always admired him for that, that he just stayed with his guns, even broke. He could have used the dough for the mortgage, the whatever. He was really a guy of strong conviction.

*   *   *

KATHRYN REED ALTMAN: Bobby went to kindergarten when Konni went to college—the same week. Bob would never want me to get a job—like my first husband, who was also midwestern. If I took a job it would say something about his inability to provide. We really needed the money. We always needed money. I was offered some part-time things that would have been fun, but he wouldn't hear of it. So I tried all those volunteer things, the candy-stripe ladies at the hospital, that stuff. We bought a piano because I always wanted to take piano lessons, and I did that. I took tennis lessons because he loved tennis and I never played. But it was just all too dull.

I couldn't safely have any more children. It would have been a real risk physically. That was the year they were begging people to adopt. The first year of single adoption—1965. It was Christmas; we were in the car going from party to party. I remember asking what he thought about adoption. I said, "I'm really not through mothering. It'd be great for Bobby"—which it wasn't. To make a long story longer, he said, "Okay, I'm up for that, but only if we can adopt a hard-to-place child." I felt the same way.

We weren't prepared for a physically or mentally disabled child. So we went for the racial mix. That was the end of December. The day after New Year's Day, we made the appointment. We had the first orientation meeting in January of 1966, and we had Matthew in July. So to hell with the tennis lessons.

STEPHEN ALTMAN: Kathryn was always the unifier in the family. She made a real special effort to include Michael and myself into his life as much as she could. She was never, "Oh, Bobby is my actual child, and Matthew is my adopted baby, and Konni . . ." She was the one who was always the most diplomatic and kept everybody together and doing the loving thing. She's really a good person.

CHAPTER 11

Countdown

*

Countdown *(1968)*

Howard Thompson review in *The New York Times*, May 2, 1968: Say one thing for "Countdown," a limp spaceflight drama that landed at neighborhood theaters yesterday. It makes the moon seem just as dull as Mother Earth. This color package from Warner Brothers–Seven Arts is simply stultifying. The bulk of it is a slack, cliché-ridden prelude to the climactic space ride, as we see the conditioning of three astronauts at a simulated Cape Kennedy. . . . Finally, one of the men buckles in and roars aloft, thanks to some documentary footage, as the music rumbles ominously and the rest of the cast hang around a winking control board. By then slow death has already set in, since Robert Altman's direction is almost as listless as the acting of a dreary cast. The space rider is played by a squinting chap named James Caan.

Robert Altman, to Professor William Parrill, at Southeastern Louisiana University, April 14, 1974: *Countdown* was a book called *The Pilgrim Project* that I tried to option, and the Warner brothers got it. They had a low-budget program, and they had called me about doing three or four films, which I had turned down, and I accepted that. We had a very low budget. Jack Warner was still at Warner Brothers, and he saw a television program I had made in Chicago, and it infuriated him, and he said, "You can't hire that person." Bill Conrad, who was the producer of that program—he plays Cannon, the fat guy—he was the executive producer on this thing, and he said, well, he was going to hire me.

Robert Duvall handing a flag to James Caan in Countdown

LORING MANDEL: *Countdown* was my first produced screenplay. The first phone call that I received from Bob, he introduced himself as the director and said he had some questions about the script. He asked me about the overlapping dialogue. I had been doing overlapping dialogue in all my shows going back to the mid-1950s. I said, "I've been in Houston, I've been at the Cape, to the real space program. What's in there is as close as I can write to the way it was happening." In those complicated scenes where people are talking at the same time, it gives it a sense of reality. Obviously, he liked it. In later films he took it steps farther than I did, but that's where it came from.

Pauline Kael, critic, from unused footage from a Fox Movie Channel documentary, *Robert Altman: On His Own Terms*: Altman brought some kind of realism and spontaneity into movies, by overlapping the dialogue. It had been done in the theater by McArthur and Hecht in *The Front Page*. It had been done in almost every good American work, and he simply carried it further. Made it more of a group overlap. And it was wonderful because you heard exactly every line you needed to hear. People who complained weren't really listening. . . . They were used to the Broadway sound where you get a line and then a dead space. What Altman did was get rid of the dead spaces.

MICHAEL MURPHY: Bob figured he could do something interesting with it. It was Jimmy Caan and Bob Duvall and myself. We were three astronauts. The Russians had gone to the moon—you've got to remember, we were in the middle of the Cold War at this point—and Bob was already talking about the futility of it all. So Jimmy, being the biggest name, gets to go to the moon. And Duvall wants to go, he's like the military guy, and I'm a civilian astronaut who says, "I'm not going to go, they're not ready."

ROBERT DUVALL (actor): There are directors who want to control it. I remember one old-time director said, "When I say, 'Action!' I expect you to tense up, goddamn it!" Can you imagine what that does to the work? What do you think would happen if a coach told that quarterback up in New England that every time you get hiked the ball, you better tense up?

It was always a very relaxed scene with Bob. We shot one of those scenes out at his house at Mandeville Canyon, a party scene, and there was drinking but nobody served food. I ended up eating one of their kids' lunch. Kathryn never let me forget that.

MICHAEL MURPHY: What Bob did that was interesting was he focused a lot on the wives. They all drink too much. They all live in their husbands' shadows. The guys are outside showing each other the engines in their Corvettes, and they're kind of adolescent in a way. And the women are more mature and half of them are whacked by noon. That's what interested him. He shifted it off the action of the space shot into the sociological thing of being married to one of those guys. What it does to your soul to live on one of those bases.

Something happened on *Countdown* that had a real impact on me. I went out to Hollywood and I thought, "Well, you know, I'll be Dr. Kildare or somebody like that." I knew I had a look that they used. Then I got to know Bob. I mean, suddenly I thought, "Whoa, this is interesting. What the hell is going on here? This is great." So while we're doing *Countdown* an offer came in for me to be in some movie with an elephant. They wanted some young guy to go on a safari or something. Bob was laughing about it. He said, "You know, you'll make some money if you do that kind of stuff. But if you use your head and make good choices, you'll do interesting work. You'll never be a movie star, but you'll lead a more interesting life." And I went in and turned it down.

I'm just crazy about the guy. In ways that have nothing to do with the movies, he was probably the biggest influence in my life. Yeah, I really think he was. I was just at the right age, I was interested, I was naïve, I didn't know much about these things, about politics and how everything works. And he just led me.

JAMES CAAN (actor): Bob was great. He was a wild man, but he was so far ahead of his time. He drove the sound department nuts. Everybody was wired. He was basically the first guy to do this—you would be at a party and hear three, four conversations at once. It was like real life, by God.

So one night we're working all night. We have a lunch break around midnight or one in the morning. He wanted to show us this little movie he did—*The Party*. They put up this stand-up screen, we sit down and we're eating and it starts. Maybe halfway through it there is a shot of a girl coming in with a tray—she kind of turns to the camera and then she walks out. Five seconds go by—I scream, "Back that fucker up!"

Bob goes, "What?"

I say, "Just stop it, stop it!"

"What's the matter with you?"

"Just stop it, back it up. Please! Stop!"

He does, and I go, "Who the fuck is that? Oh my God, is she gorgeous."

And he goes, "It's my daughter."

"Oh God, I had no idea."

Well, it was his stepdaughter, Konni. We started dating. She was a really great girl.

KONNI CORRIERE: Jimmy was wonderful, just so sweet. He would pick me up at UCLA—he would wear a letterman's jacket and he would have a piece of licorice for me. He'd open up my textbooks and read in different dialects. He was just as charming as could be. We dated quite a while, both before and after my marriage.

MICHAEL MURPHY: So in the movie we have a way we figure we can get Jimmy to the moon, but we haven't got a way to get him back. So they shoot a shelter up on the lunar surface, they send Jim up, and he has to find the shelter and stay in it until we can get him down [*laughs*]. That was the idea of the movie. So Bob shoots all this, and at the end of the movie you see James Caan arrive on the face of the moon and he's walking around and he finds the three Russians and they're dead, the cosmonauts. And there's a Russian flag there. So Jimmy takes out the American flag, he's got it in his pack. Jimmy put the American flag under it or beneath it or to the side of it. And you see him start to walk off, and the camera pulls back, and you see the shelter, and he's walking in the wrong direction, and that's the end of the movie.

Well, Jack Warner thought it was a Communist plot [*laughs*].

Robert Altman, to Professor William Parrill, at Southeastern Louisiana University, April 14, 1974: I had a meeting with Mr. Warner, and he said, "I don't like what you do. I call it fog on the lake." Not understanding that, I accepted it. We shot the film, and we really tried to talk about this astronaut program in terms of real people rather than heroes. The film was shot on that level and to underplay the hardware and the suspense. Warner never saw it until about the time that it was finished and the film was just getting into assembly, first cut, and one night—I had gone home—and he, which he did quite a bit of, he called to look at the film. And then I got a call which said, "Don't come in tomorrow because the guards won't let you in the gate." And he said, the quote was, "That fool has actors talking at the same time."

LORING MANDEL: As Bob was working on it, the talk about the film was very positive. I remember Bob calling me once and saying, "I'm getting invited to parties I never got invited to before. Everybody thinks this is going to be a terrific picture." But Jack Warner was furious about the overlapping dialogue. So Bob was off the picture and Bill Conrad came on. Conrad did a little rewriting of the last part of the movie and reshot a little of it, and that's the movie that came out. Before the movie was released I was brought to Hollywood to see a screening of it. I was really appalled at what happened at the end. I wanted to take my name off it but my agent convinced me that was a disastrous thing to do on a first solo-credit screenplay.

MICHAEL MURPHY: So they take the picture away from Bob and they reshoot the ending. And Jimmy is walking *towards* the shelter and now the American flag is positioned *above* the Commie flag! *[Laughs]* I remember going to a screening of it. Bob wasn't there. For a young guy, Jimmy Caan took no prisoners. He was a tough guy. And he stood up at the end of the thing, he said, "Well, you cut Altman right out of the goddamn movie." He just really let them have it. Everybody sort of sat there in shocked silence. I thought it was great. Because that's exactly what they had done. But nobody knew, of course, at the time, that *M*A*S*H* was crouching in the wings.

JAMES CAAN: Bill Conrad took the picture away from him at the end. It was so comic book, so corny, and Bob is anything but corny. The original ending, you don't know if he sees the beacon or if he's going off the wrong way. Conrad said, "No, we can't do that." There was this whole bullshit with this toy mouse in my pocket. I spin the mouse and I head off in the direction of its ass or its nose or whatever it shows— obviously toward the beacon. I think they called us back without Bob, and that fat bastard Conrad called us back to do a day of shooting, with that spinning mouse thing. I remember that screening. They said, "Oh, we probably won't use that ending." You know how they say "Fuck you" in Hollywood, right? "Trust me." I remember thinking about Bob when I saw what they did. It was his first real movie, so what is he going to do? I sent Conrad a ten-pound box of chocolates. He was such a big, fat guy. I think he got the message: "Here, have another chocolate."

Bob and I kind of stayed friends. Then Bob had this book he wanted to option. We got to talking, drinking of course, and I think he needed some stupid little amount of money—to buy a book was like seventy-five hundred bucks. I haven't the faintest idea what the book was—I knew he liked it, and that was enough. Anyway, I loaned it to him. I gave it to him. Then this terrible thing happened. He was in between jobs, he was broke, and consequently when he saw me it was awkward. It was an unspoken thing. He never mentioned it again. Neither did I. His friendship was worth more than that. As time went on he started avoiding me because of the embarrassment of it. I never said a word about it until the day he died. After that when we saw each other we were friends, but it put something between us.

Robert Altman, to David Thompson, from *Altman on Altman*: Actually, being fired from *Countdown* was great for me, because each time something like that happens, you get a battle scar and you know how to protect yourself in that situation again. It was the choice I had to make at that time in my career. Was I going to try to keep going in television? Why was I staying inside this bubble? Am I the artist here? And I made the only choice that was really available to me, because I would never have survived inside the system. I would have been chewed up and spat out.

*   *   *

That Cold Day in the Park *(1969)*

Charles Champlin, review headlined "A Sick Character Gets Sicker," the *Los Angeles Times,* June 26, 1969: Perish forbid every movie should

Sandy Dennis searches for a prostitute for the boy she holds captive in her apartment in That Cold Day in the Park. *At far left is Michael Murphy, playing the Rounder, who supplies girls for hire.*

have a message. But the movie which has nothing to convey to us beyond the sequence of its own events had better concoct some pretty special events or generate a very special atmosphere or else it is in trouble. Which brings us, shivering, to "That Cold Day in the Park" . . . a small, well-directed but still unsuccessful movie. . . . [Sandy] Dennis is a sex-starved spinster who rescues [Michael] Burns from a rainswept park bench and sets him up in her spacious Vancouver apartment.

GEORGE LITTO (agent): Everything was fine with me—everything was fine and flying. Then I heard from a social friend of mine. His name was Don Factor; he was the son of Max Factor. He told me he wanted to be in the movie business. And before Waldo Salt wrote *Midnight Cowboy*, I got Don to advance Waldo twenty-five thousand dollars, which was not a small amount of money in those days. Don wanted to do more things, and I went to a restaurant one night called Dolce Vita. I went to my booth and I looked over, and there were Bob and Kathryn and a group of people. I hadn't seen him, it must be for over a year. I walked up behind him and I kissed him on the cheek.

I said, "How are you?"

He turned. "George," he said, "I'm lousy."

I said, "Come on, how are things going?"

He said, "Terrible."

I said, "You need an agent?"

He said, "Yeah."

I said, "I'd like to be your agent."

The next day, he said he's got this book called *That Cold Day in the Park*. He sent me the project and I said, "This is good." I told him, "I want you to meet a friend of mine who wants to be in the film business. He's a good guy, his name is Don Factor."

I put them together in a company called Factor Altman. Later on, I brought in a business-affairs guy to be their partner, to take care of the business because otherwise they bothered me too much. And I owned a piece of the company too, but I didn't put my name on it. So we got going with *Cold Day in the Park*.

DONALD FACTOR (producer): Before I made the deal with Bob I talked to a friend of my father's who was an old-time agent. He said, "He's a big talent, but keep away from him; he's trouble." That was the kind of advice I wouldn't listen to in those days. Bob wasn't very popular until he became a superstar himself.

The two of us went off to England. I took him—Bob was broke. No one wanted to hire him. What had happened was, he wasn't working, so we agreed we would make a little short together. It was called *Pot au Feu*. It was a jokey film about smoking pot, and it was a takeoff of a cooking show, only it explained rolling a joint instead of making a meal. It was a piece of therapy for us. It was great fun because it was still rather daring to admit you did that kind of thing. We shot it in sixteen millimeter and took a print of that with us to London and used that as a calling card. We hired a screening room in London and called everyone in the industry who might be of value to us. We had drinks and hors d'oeuvres and we kept running it over and over again, but we didn't succeed in putting a deal together.

We got along great, but I can remember one argument in London. I had rented a service flat in Mayfair, a two-bedroom affair. My girlfriend at the time, Vanessa Mitchell, and I were in one bedroom and he was in the other. One night he was rather drunk and we got into an argument and we were both rather pissed. It was a terrible argument and he ordered me out of the apartment. Of course I went, and when I got out into the street I realized, "Hey, I'm renting this place!" But most of our time together was very good. He fell out with almost everybody, but we never did fall out.

ROBERT ALTMAN: One thing I remember about Don Factor is one of the great pot-smoking stories of all time. We were in Palm Springs.

DONALD FACTOR: We came to an intersection with a red light. Bob was driving and we stopped. Chatting away, chatting away, and I said, "Why doesn't that light change?"

KATHRYN REED ALTMAN: Bob says, "God, that's a long signal. Is it broken?" Finally, Don Factor says, "That's not the signal! The signal is over there on the corner, and it's green."

ROBERT ALTMAN: I'd been looking at a red light on the dashboard, thinking it was a traffic signal.

DONALD FACTOR: It was the battery light. That was really being stoned. I don't know how long we sat there, but it was wonderful.

GEORGE LITTO: Factor and Altman were two very different guys, but they got along famously. Don Factor was very low-key, very intelligent, very sensitive, very unassuming, very wealthy, loved the adventure of being in the film business and he really had a high I.Q. for talent and taste. And he really liked Bob's work. I got him together with Bob, and he could identify. He had the sensitivity and the brains. What he didn't have is the backbone to put up with all the bullshit you have to put up with. That's another side of the business; you got to be like Teflon to survive. But he was a terrific guy. So they got on great.

Bob got Sandy Dennis interested in doing the movie. And Gillian Freeman was the writer. She had a reputation for *The Leather Boys*, a film that Sidney Furie did which got some distinction.

GILLIAN FREEMAN (writer): I had a phone call sometime in March 1967 and a voice said, "You won't know me, my name is Robert Altman, and I'm here with Donald Factor looking for a writer. Are you free to have lunch with us today?" Of course I said yes, and we met at L'Escargot, a restaurant in Soho that was—still is—a popular place for writers, publishers, film and TV producers, and various celebrities to meet. I felt that there was an immediate rapport between the three of us; both men were very laid-back and easy to talk to. Looking back, sartorially we epitomized the sixties. I was wearing a very short black coat cut like a man's, with a velvet collar, and a black-and-white-check flat cap. Don Factor was in a turtleneck sweater and sports jacket and Bob was wearing a leather bomber jacket and also a rather British flat cap. They outlined to me the story of a novel, entitled *That Cold Day in the Park*, by Richard Miles, and seemed full of imaginative ideas, and I very much wanted to work with them. The story was about a lonely woman who, from her window overlooking a park, sees a boy sitting alone on a bench on a cold day. The boy appears mute and never speaks. She takes him in and becomes possessive about her "captive," who sneaks out at night. Bob and Don appeared to look no further for a writer, and within two weeks I and my two daughters, Harriet and Matilda, aged nine and six, were on our way to L.A.

Script sessions proceeded at Bob's rented offices at 1334 Westwood Boulevard. We would talk each section of the story through in general terms, then in detail, before breaking for lunch at restaurants in Westwood. Then I would go off to my apartment for a couple of days and write up each scene we had discussed. Then we'd go through it, make any necessary changes, and discuss the next section. Don sat in on most meetings, occasionally making suggestions. Much of the money for the film came from his cosmetic inheritance from Max Factor. Bob ran showings of his previous films and TV work for me and I was impressed with the way he used the camera, with his atmospheric night shots, and by the way he made one conscious of the weather and general mise-en-scène. He was an easy and stimulating man to work with, and his concern with each scene was whether it seemed right for the story rather than what the film might gross.

ROBERT ALTMAN: I sent that script to Ingrid Bergman, and she sent me back a note—she was rather insulted by that part. And I sent it also to Vanessa Redgrave. That's how Sandy Dennis came up. She said, "Try her." She read it and agreed to do it. It was just this story of this woman and this younger guy. I'll tell you who I turned down for that part—Jack Nicholson. Jack wanted it—he came to my office and we talked about it. And I said, "Jack, I think you're too old for it."

GEORGE LITTO: So we got Columbia interested. The film was supposed to take place in London originally. The park was Hyde Park. Again, they were close to a deal but couldn't get it together. I flew over with Bob to try to get the deal made, and after several meetings with Columbia and other things, I said, "Bob, this isn't going to work. I've been here for, whatever, ten days. I can't spend any more time on this, and these guys are screwing you around. They're screwing us around. They can't make a decision. We've got to leave."

He said to me, "Well, I can't pay my bills. I need five thousand dollars to get out of here."

I gave him the five thousand. And that night we went out to dinner. We ended up at the Colony Club, a gambling place. George Raft, I was very friendly with him, he was the maître d' there, the "Mr. Lucky" of the Colony Club. Bob says, "I'm going to throw a little craps." I told him to be careful. I'm talking, we're drinking, we're all having a good time, and I see a crowd at the table, and I look over and I see Bob rolling the dice. And I hear the crowd roar. I go over there and what I find out is he got permission to put five thousand dollars on the line and he crapped out. And I said, "I'm going to fucking kill you."

DONALD FACTOR: After London, Bob flew up to Canada and rang me up and said, "You've got to get up here right away."

GEORGE LITTO: We came back here and Bob had this idea of going to Vancouver, where they had no unions and the atmosphere was good.

He could make the picture for a price, three hundred fifty thousand or four hundred thousand. That movie would have cost a million in London, let's say, with Sandy Dennis. She went along and we were able to get the deal made with her.

DANFORD GREENE (film editor): When we did *Cold Day*, Bob found this wonderful house in West Vancouver, which I shared with Bob and Bob Eggenweiler, who we called Egg, who was a producer. We had a cook, a big Prussian woman. Anyway, it was a very family-oriented situation and we would talk about the picture at night and this woman would make dinner along with Egg, who loved to cook.

One time, I had this girl over, and she got up and left early. I'm in the bedroom doing push-ups. Bob walks by, looks in, and says, "Danny, your girl is gone." We had that kind of fun.

They built this set on a big soundstage in West Vancouver, and Leon Ericksen built it. It was a set that was a whole interior of a very large apartment. He made it extra large so that Bob could get a camera into every place in that set. I learned so much from Bob—knowledge just fell off him onto me. I always loved the way he could walk into a set that he'd never been in, a place where you were going to shoot, and look around and in thirty seconds, if that, he'd say, "Okay, the camera goes here and we'll put the tracks over there." He just laid that shot out so fast.

We used to watch a lot of the pro games and he would bet—you know, in those days he was betting five hundred dollars a game. That was a lot of dough then. He liked to gamble. He liked to live. Liked his Scotch and grass and good food.

Dialogue from *A Wedding*:

REVEREND DAVID RUTELEDGE (*Played by Gerald Busby*): Dr. Meecham, as a physician you should know the body is the temple of the Holy Spirit.

DR. JULES MEECHAM (*Played by Howard Duff*): You mean you don't drink?

REVEREND DAVID RUTELEDGE: No.

DR. JULES MEECHAM: In other words, when you get up in the morning that's as good as you're gonna feel all day.

*   *   *

DANFORD GREENE: There was another side of him, too. There was this girl, a hairdresser, married, and really a dynamite sex-looking thing. So I put that together one night and borrowed the car. The next morning he's grilling me about what I did, and I didn't have a good story made up. I didn't want to tell him what happened. Anyway, he finally gets me to say who it is. And I say, "Jesus, it's really touchy, so please don't say anything." Well, the next day this girl comes up to me and just lays me out. That prick just went up to her and said, "Oh, you got fucked last night by my editor," or something like that. I was so embarrassed. That's a terrible situation. But he liked to do things like that, embarrass people that he shouldn't put on the spot, because they were part of him, you know? I've thought about all the things it might be—control? envy?—but he had all of that stuff. He didn't need to do that at all. I don't know. I talked to guys that he kind of got rid of or bounced out, and they've all said the same thing, that he kind of likes to hurt the people he loves.

He could be a prick sometimes, but he had too much good in him. It's Kansas City or something. There's no Hollywood horseshit. That's one of the reasons I liked him so much. We were two Kansas City boys playing Hollywood. Playing movies.

MICHAEL MURPHY: *Cold Day in the Park* is an example of Bob just picking himself off the ground. To me that was his major, major virtue. I mean this guy, I'd seen him just flattened by studios and no money, and he just gets up and starts casting, you know? Which is exactly what he did with that movie. And there was a time when the money fell out. He had a little billfold together, and then that fell out, and he just pushed ahead.

GRAEME CLIFFORD (assistant director): He had a preproduction speech at the beginning of the movie that just captured his whole approach. He said, "Anybody can come up to me at any time and give me any ideas they have or discuss anything they want. Sometimes I'll use them and sometimes I won't. I may not always have time to tell you why I'm not going to use your idea, but I'll always listen." I didn't work for anybody else for the next five years, and I just assumed everybody worked this way—the way he treated the crew, the way he treated actors. I stole that speech and I use it on any movie I make, but you think many directors say that?

DONALD FACTOR: Everyone came to rushes every evening to watch each other's work. That became a trademark of Bob's—getting everyone together, letting them know they were all in it together. Bob would have a bottle of whiskey and a few joints and we'd have a party until Bob was out and had to be carried off to bed. The next morning, we'd all be dragging and Bob would be full of energy and raring to go.

I saw how talented Bob was in the scene where Michael Burns's character, who's called The Boy, sneaks out of the apartment and Sandy Dennis's character finally gets her nerve up to make a pitch to him, except it's to an empty bed. Sandy objected. She said, "I would know there was no one there." Bob took her aside and said, "Look, Sandy, let's just try it my way, and if it doesn't work, we'll try it another way." She couldn't say no to that. She went in and it was a long monologue to an empty bed with pillows stuffed into it. It was a single take and Bob said cut. Even the crew in the scaffolding was applauding. That was it. It was Altman magic.

GILLIAN FREEMAN: The next thing I knew was a phone call from Canada at two in the morning. Bob's voice said, "You know that picture we worked on, well, we just finished it five minutes ago." Don Factor had put up more of his money, half a million dollars on a budget of one-point-two million dollars.

I liked the film a lot. It had a lot of those qualities that made so many of Bob's films marvelous and memorable, although I have to admit that Bob's habit of letting the actors skip the written dialogue I found irritating, thinking that their ad-libbing was less succinct, less illuminating of their characters, than the dialogue I had written.

A year or two later Bob outlined another story idea of his own to me and gave me permission to flesh it out as a novel, which I did. Entitled *An Easter Egg Hunt*, it was set during the first World War and involved the mysterious disappearance of a young French teacher. It proved to be one of my most successful novels, going into several editions. For many years Bob talked about developing it as a film, but there was always another project that he wanted to do first.

GEORGE LITTO: So he made *Cold Day* and I sold it to this new company, Commonwealth United. It was well regarded and liked, and it was a very well made, good film. But it was no hit. It was a small company and they were new and they didn't know how to promote a hit, you know?

DONALD FACTOR: It wasn't very successful. Critics didn't think much of it until Bob became Bob. Then they discovered things to like about it.

GEORGE LITTO: After *Cold Day*, one night I was having a party at my house. I said, "Bob, before you go home I want to give you a script to read."

ACT II

1970–1980

*Robert Altman directs a creative and commercial
blockbuster, becomes an international star,
builds a dream house, is a darling to critics,
is a disappointment to critics, threatens his marriage,
comes to his senses, creates his own studio,
brings arms to Malta, and gets written off.*

CHAPTER 12

*M*A*S*H*

*

M*A*S*H *(1970)*

Pauline Kael, review in *The New Yorker,* **January 24, 1970:** *M*A*S*H* is a marvelously unstable comedy, a tough, funny, and sophisticated burlesque of military attitudes that is at the same time a tale of chivalry. It's a sick joke, but it's also generous and romantic—an erratic episodic film, full of the pleasures of the unexpected. . . . It's a modern kid's dream of glory: Holden Caulfield would, I think, approve of [the heroes played by Donald Sutherland and Elliott Gould]. They're great surgeons, athletes, dashing men of the world, sexy, full of noblesse oblige, but ruthless to those with pretensions and lethal to hypocrites. . . . I think *M*A*S*H* is the best American war comedy since sound came in, and the sanest American movie of recent years.

*   *   *

From the *M*A*S*H* **theme song, "Suicide Is Painless,"**
lyrics by Michael Altman:

A brave man once requested me,
to answer questions that are key.
Is it to be or not to be?
And I replied, "Oh, why ask me?"

[Refrain] *Suicide is painless. It brings on many changes,*
and I can take or leave it if I please.

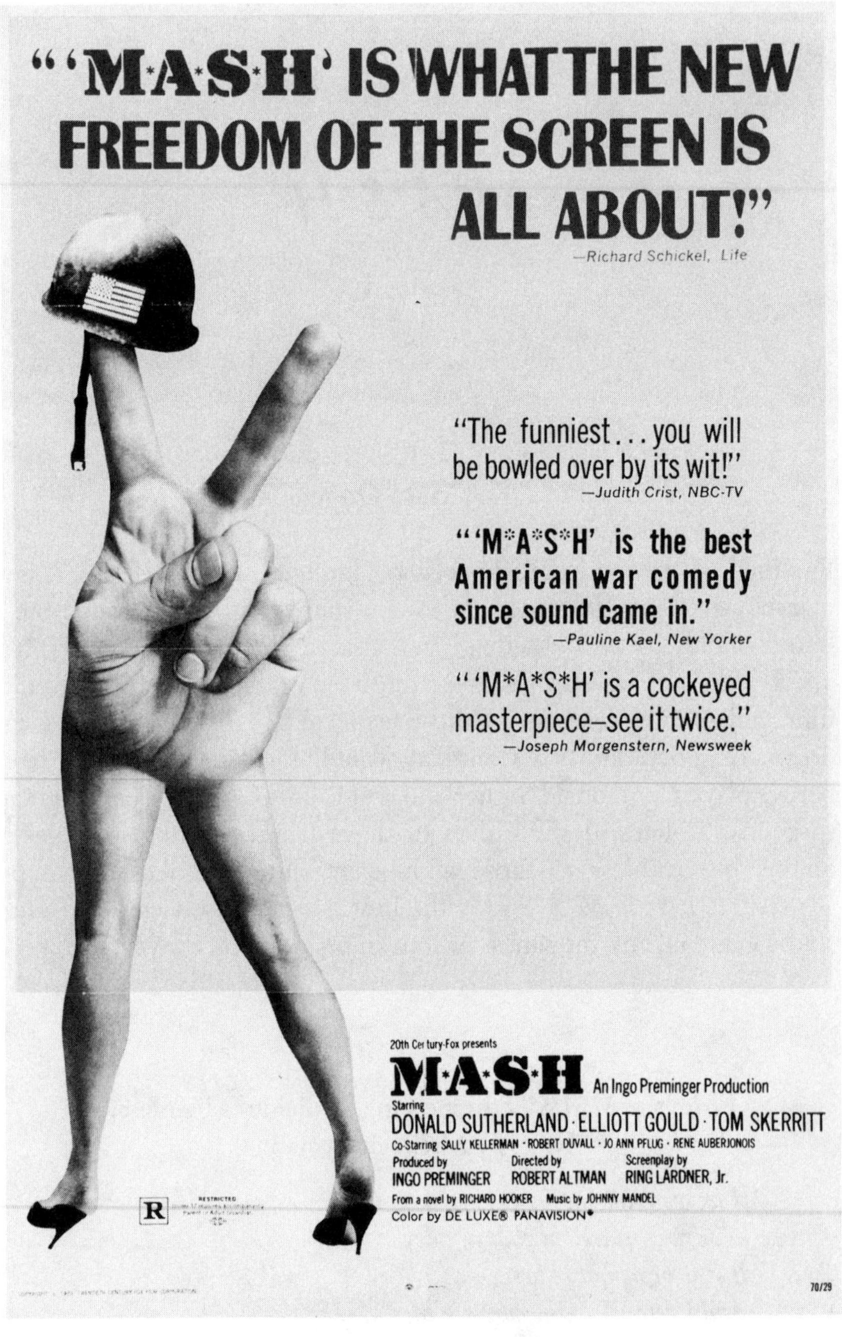

A poster for M*A*S*H *with the iconic peace-sign-on-legs image*

Memo titled "Synopsis of *M*A*S*H*" from James Denton, director of publicity, Twentieth Century Fox, July 16, 1969: Soon after Hawkeye Pierce (Donald Sutherland), Duke Forrest (Tom Skerritt) and Trapper John McIntyre (Elliott Gould) join the 4077th Mobile Army Surgical Hospital (MASH), Col. Henry Blake (Roger Bowen) ruefully realizes how placid his Korean War command had been before. The three surgeons have two things in common: They are the best in the Far East and they are hell-raising lunatics who make a shambles of army bureaucracy.

MICHAEL MURPHY: George Litto was an unsung hero of this movie. As brilliant as Bob was, studios worried about him because he was really an artist and he was rebellious and he wouldn't do it the way they wanted it. That's where George came in.

GEORGE LITTO: The way it started was my client, Ring Lardner, Jr., was asked to review the book *M*A*S*H* for *The New York Times.* You know Ring's story? He was one of the blacklisted guys from the Hollywood 10, a brave guy who went to jail not to name names. I'm not a Communist. If anything I'm a capitalist—if anything I'm a royalist [*laughs*]. But I was very sympathetic to the fact that the blacklist was unfair. People have the right to disagree, they didn't do anything in my mind illegal; you know, believing in something that's not popular is not a crime. They have their First Amendment right. And they were treated terribly.

Anyway, he called me and said, "George, I think it would make a terrific movie." Well, Ingo Preminger was Ring's agent before me, and we were very friendly, and he was moving into producing. So I called up Ingo, and I said, "Ingo, your ex-client just sent me a terrific book. I read the book and I think it would make a wonderful movie. But one condition: If you like it and you buy it, you've got to hire Ring to write it." He said, "No problem."

RICHARD ZANUCK (studio executive and producer): Ingo Preminger came into my office one day—he had a big literary agency—and he came in and he said, "I've read a book I'd like you to read over the weekend. If you like it I'll sell the agency if you let me produce it." I said, "Jesus, Ingo." He had substantial clients. It was a thriving agency. Ingo was much more civil than his brother Otto, who was an arrogant prick. Well, I read it, and I called him up and I said, "I have your office ready."

GEORGE LITTO: I had a house in Benedict Canyon. We had a poker game there on Sundays with a lot of people in the industry—writers, directors, producers—and Bob came to the poker game, and at the end of the poker game he said, "George, I read *M*A*S*H*. I think it's great. Do you think you can get me this movie?" I said, "I don't really think so, but I'm going to try."

So Ingo and Ring wanted to have a meeting. "George, who should direct this movie?" And I said, "Stanley Kubrick." They say, "Yeah, that's a good idea." So I say, "How could you get him? You can't. Or, Bob Altman." And Ring said, "Who's Bob Altman?" Ingo said, "George, we can never get Bob Altman this job." I said, "I'm telling you right now, you want to know who can direct this movie? Stanley Kubrick or Bob Altman. That's all I got to say. You know everybody in town, Ingo. But I'm telling you who can make this a terrific movie." Ingo says, "George, I can't get him the job." So, dissolve.

Ingo and Ring called me up some days later. They said, "George, we got a problem. Practically every meaningful director in Hollywood has turned down the script." Fifteen, sixteen top directors turned it down. I learned later that many directors turned down *M*A*S*H* because it had a group of characters, but it was a series of vignettes, and they were used to the traditional beginning, middle, and end. You have to have a motor to get you to the middle and a motor to get you to the end. And this series of vignettes didn't seem to have a motor. The way Bob fixed that was brilliant, but that comes later.

So Ingo said, "George, if we go to Fox with another turndown, they're going to cancel this project. We need a director who won't turn us down." I said, "Well, you know Kubrick probably will turn you down." He said, "George, stop being a smart-ass." I said, "But Bob Altman won't turn you down." That was the only lie I ever told Ingo. Because, you know, he did turn it down [*laughs*].

Ingo Preminger, from "Remembering *M*A*S*H*: The 30th Anniversary Cast and Crew Reunion": To get rid of George Litto, I went and met his client Robert Altman. And at that time he played a little film for me that dealt with the smoking of pot. It was short, it was sweet, and I loved it. I called Richard Zanuck and said, "We found the guy." He said, "You're crazy."

RICHARD ZANUCK: Ingo said, "Look, this guy has done some talented work. Not much, but good work." That's when we ran the picture *That*

Cold Day in the Park and something like fifteen episodes of *Combat!* He came in and we talked about his concept and how he would shoot it and all the rest. It was a gamble 'cause he really hadn't done anything quite like this.

DAVID BROWN (producer): We were absolutely bowled over by the book, but not by Altman. Ingo convinced us to go with Altman. Well, we weren't convinced, but we supported the producer.

GEORGE LITTO: So I call up Bob, I tell him, "You won't believe this, but I got an offer from Ingo Preminger for you to direct *M*A*S*H*." It was like a hundred and twenty-five thousand dollars and five percent of the picture profits, but Ingo had two other options for more pictures. So that was the deal I made with him. Ingo was a good, smart guy. So Bob agrees and great, fine, I make the deal. Dissolve.

A few days go by. I get a call from Owen McLean, who was head of business affairs for Fox. He said, "George, we got a problem." He said, "Ingo did not have the authority to make a deal with you for Bob Altman. We're canceling that deal unless you agree to our terms." He said seventy-five thousand, flat, no profits. That's it, take it or leave it. I said, "You know, you're a big shit, Owen." He said, "George, are you leaving it? I guess you're leaving it." And you wonder why Bob had such an attitude about studios? I said, "Hey, Owen, I'm just a humble agent. I can only deliver your message. I cannot accept or reject your proposal" [*laughs*]. He said, "There's not a fucking thing that's humble about you" [*laughs*].

RICHARD ZANUCK: When I made *Jaws* with Spielberg, he didn't have points and he had done a lot more work. He got no points and that was much later than Bob. In those days points weren't thrown around unless you were Bob Wise or Willie Wyler or somebody like that.

GEORGE LITTO: So I called Bob and every profane word you can think of he uttered through the telephone about Owen and Fox, because he had a bad experience there. I don't know if you know this. He was doing a television show with a singer from Philadelphia, Fabian. Yeah, the *Bus Stop* thing.

So I said, "Bob, do you really want to fuck them?" He said, "Yeah, I'd love to fuck them." I said, "Take the deal." He said, "What?" I said, "Take the deal. You think it'll be a great movie. If it's a great movie, after that I'll get you anything you want. Any picture you want to make. I'll get you the biggest salary in Hollywood. Just take the deal." So I called Owen and I said, "Owen, I got bad news for you. Bob's taking the deal."

RICHARD ZANUCK: When he was gearing up he came in and said, "I want to go scout Korea." I said, "Why? We're not going to Korea. We're going to the studio ranch in Malibu." He said, "This is ridiculous." I said, "Go out and look. I'll show you pictures of mountains in Korea. They match perfectly with what's out at the studio ranch." It was probably more Korea than had we gone to Korea. Nobody knows what Korea looks like, anyway. That's what I said to him and he got very angry.

He said, "We're going to shoot that golf scene in Tokyo." I said, "No we're not. We're going across the street to Rancho Park. There's a golf course. All you have to do is get a couple of Japanese girls and dress them up and they're caddies." One golf course looks like another. Why would we ever do that?

During the filming of M*A*S*H

In those exchanges, Bob was a guy who didn't like authority. He was a real rebel. I always felt that underneath that anger there was kind of a playboy. I would see the way he would dress, in the Paris airport, with the hat, the flashy white suit. I think there was a rogue element about that.

GEORGE LITTO: Now he's doing the picture. He's working with Ingo and Ring. They're doing the rewrite. They're planning the movie and talking to the production department. There's a guy by the name of Doc Berman that's like their executive in charge of physical production. Bob calls me up one day. He says, "I fucking hate Doc Berman. I'm planning a shot and they said, 'Well, you can cut it off here and you don't have to finish it now, you can finish it next week.' They're telling me how to make the movie. I'm sick of this shit. I don't want this shit. I don't want to do the picture." I said, "Come on, Bob. I'll have Ingo talk to Doc Berman. It'll be okay." Ingo talks to Bob, to Doc. Dissolve.

I think everything is okay. My phone rings about six o'clock in the morning. It's Kathryn. She says, "George, I'm very upset. Bob couldn't sleep all night. He's on his way to see you. He's not going to do the picture. He's going to walk out on the picture." I said, "Don't worry about it." She said, "What do you mean, don't worry?" I said, "Don't worry about it. You've told me he's going to walk out of the picture, you've told me he's on his way. I am up, I will have the coffee on, I will talk to him, and he'll do the picture." She said, "Why are you so sure?" I said, "Because he owes me so much fucking money" [laughs].

So Bob comes in, he said, "George, we got to talk. I don't want to do this movie." I said, "You want some coffee?" He said, "George, I'm serious." "I know you're serious, Bob, but come on, you like those eggs I make with sausages? You want some eggs and sausages?" "George, stop fucking with me. I'm telling you, I don't want to do it." I said, "I hear you. Can we have a little breakfast? I got to eat alone? Just take it easy. You're not going to do the movie. If you got good reasons, I won't be able to change your mind." We eat.

I say, "Okay, now tell me the reasons you don't want to do this picture." And he gives me a whole thing about, "I can't pick my own editor, I can't pick my own cameraman. . . ." He gives me a whole list. I said, "Okay, here's what I think. I think you're right. You should be able to pick these people. They shouldn't be telling you what to do. I'm going to call Ingo Preminger, and I'm going to tell him that you have problems about making this movie and you're very upset about it, and he has to resolve it for you to continue with this picture. And I'm going to ask him if he could see you this morning and you can go right from my house to his house"—which was in Brentwood.

So I call up Ingo and I said, "Ingo, you got a pencil and paper?" And I read him the list. He said, "George, I got to get all this?" I said, "What the fuck is the difference? Just go get it for him. Somebody's got to make the decisions. Say it was your decision." Bob went to see him, they worked it out.

ROBERT REED ALTMAN: My mom's desk had a piece of glass on it, and under the glass was a little piece of paper with my dad's writing on it. I said, "What's this?" And she said, "That's from when your dad decided that he would make the movie *M*A*S*H.*" The note said, "Oh fuck it, I'll do it."

*   *   *

ROBERT ALTMAN: When we were making *M*A*S*H*, Twentieth Century Fox had two other wars going on—*Patton* and *Tora! Tora! Tora!* Those were big-budget pictures, and we were cheap. I knew that if we stayed under budget and didn't cause too much trouble, we could sneak through. You could say they were distracted by those other films.

RICHARD ZANUCK: Whether we were making *Tora! Tora!* in Japan and Hawaii had nothing to do with anything. He was right under our thumb, but he claimed we were asleep while we were making the picture. That was ridiculous. He was a hundred feet away. I was at the ranch many, many times. I was seeing dailies every day, sending him notes every day—notes of praise. Of course we were busy with *Tora! Tora!* But what is it he did behind our backs? Nothing. Maybe he smoked pot on the set. He was just an authority resister. If you say "studio" he immediately becomes paranoid.

ROBERT ALTMAN: What's that expression about success having many fathers and failure being an orphan? Something like that, right?

When I got started, the only two people who were already cast were Donald Sutherland and, I think, Elliott Gould, though that might not have been finished. I went up to San Francisco to cast the rest of the film. I don't know what kind of theater you call it, theater of the absurd, I suppose, but there were like forty people onstage all the time, and it was highly improvisational. And I cast the film right there. If you look at the credits of *M*A*S*H*, it says, Donald Sutherland and Elliott Gould and "Introducing," and there's about twenty names. Well, those were all those people from San Francisco.

BILL BUSHNELL (theater impresario): It was the spring of 1969 when he came to ACT, the American Conservatory Theater, in San Francisco. I got a phone call one Saturday morning from my then-wife, Scotty, who was working with the casting agent. She gave me Bob's number at the Fairmont Hotel and I went up there and spent the afternoon and the evening drinking and smoking with Bob and took him down to ACT to a party that night where he met John Schuck and René Auberjonois and G. Wood, among others, and that was the beginning of a relationship between Bob and myself and eventually between Bob and Scotty.

* * *

JOHN SCHUCK (actor): I thought he was fascinating because I hadn't met anybody quite like him. There was no artifice about him. He had a way of simplifying the most complex of ideas that at first you weren't sure if he had much intelligence at all, you know? But that was part of my snobbery. I was used to articulate theater directors who could expound on the literature and history. Bob could have done all that but he wasn't that kind of a person. He was a great equalizer that way. He had—I don't want to call it a common touch, but his appeal was much simpler, much more basic.

He was fourteen or fifteen years older than me, but he had a weariness, like he'd really lived, you know? I don't want to say he looked beat up—he didn't—but he was craggy and with a beard and he had lost some of his hair.

SALLY KELLERMAN (actress and singer): I was going out for the part of Lieutenant Dish, so I thought, "Okay, I better wear some red lipstick." I never wore red lipstick, because I always hid my mouth because my sister used to say to me, "Shut up, big lips." But that day I wore bright red lips for Lieutenant Dish, and it was probably Ingo Preminger and the casting director and Bob and maybe my agent. We're just sitting there talking and suddenly Bob said to me, "I'll give you the best part in the picture: Hot Lips." I said, "Really? Oh my god." I went outside so excited, and I remember standing against the wall, and I quickly thumbed through the script. What a frigging amateur I was, looking for the part. It looked like there were seven lines and I just turned to granite. I was just bitter, thinking, "I'll never get in the movies."

Someone said, "You really should go back and see him, because he's really talented." So I read the script again, I went back to meet him, and I was just all puffed up and I was so angry, I mean that's how desperate I was. I remember saying, "I'm not a WAC, I'm a woman," and tears are in my eyes. I said, "Why does she have to leave the film so early?" And, "Why couldn't she do this?" and, "Why couldn't she do that?" He's just sitting back, and I was just mad and tearing up. And he goes, "Yeah. Why couldn't she? Why don't you take a chance? You could end up with something or nothing." I was coming from television, and in those days you couldn't change one line and if you did, the entire suite of suits from Universal had to come down to the set to check it out, you know? And here's this director saying, "Take a chance." So, needless to say, I grabbed it.

Tom Skerritt: I hadn't spoken to him in a year or two. I was writing something and having a difficult time with it. I called him one day. He says, "Skerritt. Hang up, I'll call you back." The next day I was in *M*A*S*H*. If I hadn't called that day I really doubt I would have been in *M*A*S*H*. The studio was pushing for a bigger name—Burt Reynolds. Bob was pushing back.

Bud Cort (actor): I got a call asking me to come in for a meeting. It was the middle of winter and I took buses and had to trudge through snow. I remember I was wearing new Army boots, light tan suede with gold buttons on them. I was shown into this room and there were probably five people there. The only one I remembered was Ingo Preminger. I focused on him because I thought, "My God, he's probably related to Otto Preminger." This one guy kept focusing on me. "Where'd you get those shoes?" I told him, "Army-Navy store." Then, "Those glasses real?" I had on little John Lennon glasses. I looked at him and lied and said, "Yes." He bored through me with these blue eyes and he says, "Yeah, right." And I ignored him. About a month later, I get a call: "You have an offer to do a movie in California in the summer."

They checked me into a little hotel on Pico Boulevard, right there by Twentieth Century Fox. Before we started shooting, we all went there as ourselves to be fitted. I had hair down to my shoulders and I was wearing a beige suede Indian vest with these long beaded tassels that hung like a bird's feathers almost down to the floor. This guy came up to me and just stared at me and started barking orders. Same guy who gave me a hard time at the audition about my glasses. He says, "I want his hair shaved." I turned to the guy next to me and I said, "What is *with* this hairdresser?"

"No," he says, "that's the director. That's Bob Altman."

RENÉ AUBERJONOIS (actor): He told me, "I won't even give you a script because you wouldn't think the part was interesting, because he doesn't do much or say much. If you were going to play a priest, what would you do with it?" I just started talking about a guy I had been in acting class with, a guy who had been a priest. He was a well-meaning guy, but humble. I described this character to him and he said, "Well, that sounds good."

I love Dago Red, Father Mulcahy. I thought he was everything I would want a priest to be. I thought of him as this sweet sort of a character. It never occurred to me that the audience would think of it as an insult, or anti-Christian or anything like that. I thought of him as a character full of humanity.

MALACHY MCCOURT (raconteur/writer/professional Irishman): Bob originally cast me as Father Mulcahy, you know. He wanted a real Irish priest. But the producer, Preminger, what was his first name, the brother? Ingo, yes, Ingo. He didn't like me. At the time, Bob didn't have what it took to overrule him, so I was out. There went my acting career. Every time I saw Bob after that, here at Elaine's, wherever, he always said, "I owe you one, Malachy. I owe you one." True story.

RENÉ AUBERJONOIS: I never heard that! But I love it because my son's beautiful, wonderful actress wife did a little independent movie this summer in Philadelphia called *Our Lady of Victory*. She told me, "There's a part of a priest that they'd like you to play." We had a back-and-forth with the director and producer. They couldn't even afford to fly me in. In the end, Malachy got to play the priest. So if he thinks I took his part of the priest, *he* took *my* part of the priest!

ELLIOTT GOULD (actor): I was asked by Twentieth Century Fox to meet Robert Altman. He asked me if I would consider playing the role of Duke, the American Southerner in *M*A*S*H*. I said, "I've never questioned an offer, and I'm really delighted and flattered that you would ask me to work for you. But I'll drive myself crazy validating me being an American Southerner. I'm sure I can do it, but I mean I'm going to be so intense as far as how it's going to sound. This guy Trapper John McIntyre, if you haven't cast him and your mind isn't set, that's the guy that I would like to play." I was blessed that Bob gave me the part.

*   *   *

JOHN SCHUCK: From the minute we started, he was creating this world of insanity with blood and guts and all the horrors of war. You have to realize, at the time, the Vietnamese conflict was still unresolved, really, so he couldn't make a movie about an anti-Vietnam thing at this point. I don't think Hollywood would have allowed that, so that's why putting it in Korea was very smart. It gave it twenty-five years' distance. But that's what he did, he created this world that fit his message.

TOM SKERRITT: The extras were basically this improvisational group that he found in San Francisco. I would go around and tell them that Bob's got mikes everywhere and he's floating a camera, and it would be a good idea to pay attention and come up with stuff on your own. And they did that. It made it crisp every day, the idea that you may be on camera.

I just loved the guy from the first. He made me realize early on that you could do no wrong, as long as you tried. The worst you could do was make an ass out of yourself. And that's the first thing you have to be willing to do as an actor, is be willing to make an ass out of yourself. Bob gave me that.

But as we're going along, I'm aware that Donald and Elliott are not too happy. They didn't quite allow Bob in. He's the director and all he's saying is, "Free yourself up, we're all in this together. Yeah, I'm the captain of the ship, but we're all guiding the ship through the fog, and the fog is the movie system." They did not respond to Bob's style. I'm thinking, "This is a classic." I'm saying that to Donald and Elliott, and they're saying, "We can't wait to get off this thing."

ELLIOTT GOULD: One of the peculiar things was that Donald and I had a problem working with Bob at the beginning. I think you may have either heard or you read that Donald and I had complained about what we thought was his style of direction, or his being lax in terms of what our expectations were.

One time Bob had the camera on a crane, and the crane had to be moving to come over and shoot each of us. It was a complicated shot and we were fighting time and we weren't quite coordinating the camera, the crane, with us. Bob was getting a little uptight about it and he was not happy being under the pressure of having to get this shot by a certain time. Then we broke for lunch and I got my lunch on a tray and there were a few people around, and Bob said to me, "Why can't you be like somebody else?" Which was the worst possible thing he could say to me, you know? I don't know if he said I was ruining it for him then, but he pointed to Corey Fischer and said, "Why can't you be more like him?"

COREY FISCHER (actor): I was playing Captain Bandini. At one point, Bob had me just walk across the compound. I think he was shooting

Discussing a scene with his unhappy stars,
Elliott Gould and Donald Sutherland

from very far away. He followed me walking out of the surgery tent, by myself, in the rain, trying to light a cigarette. No drama, no subtext, except exhaustion. And he wound up just loving that piece of film. He kept saying, "That was it." That was the spirit he wanted. Bob wanted actors who were quirky but minimal. He knew that just by doing something ordinary, they would be interesting.

ELLIOTT GOULD: I started . . . it was the only time when I've ever started to shake and it's the only time I've ever thrown up my food before I ingested it. I threw my lunch up in the air and I said, "You fucking prick. I'm not going to stick my neck out for you again. You tell me what you want and that's what you'll get. I started out in the theater. I was a chorus boy. I was a tap dancer. I understand all that stuff. You know, you fucking asshole, you telling me to be like somebody else . . ." And he said, "I think I made a mistake." And I said, "I think so." And he said, "I apologize." And I said, "I accept."

Donald and I had the same agent and we spoke to our agent. His name was Richard Shepard, Dick Shepard, at CMA, Creative Management, and we went in and had a meeting with him and we complained.

Robert Altman, from DVD commentary: The biggest problem I had, about halfway through the film . . . was that Donald Sutherland and Elliott Gould had gone to the studio and tried to get me fired because they said . . . they were the stars and I wasn't paying enough attention to them. I was spending too much time with all these extras, background people. And I think had I known that at the time, I would have resigned. I mean, I could not have gone on if I had known they had that attitude. But I didn't find out until later. And Elliott told me, called me up and said, "We made a terrible mistake because we thought you just didn't know what you were doing."

ELLIOTT GOULD: I think that, in hindsight, Donald and I were two elitist, arrogant actors who really weren't getting Altman's genius.

*   *   *

COREY FISCHER: People talk about improvisation in Bob's movies, but it's often a misnomer. It wasn't as if people were improvising on camera. What Bob loved to do was to create a scene that had a lot of density, a lot of levels going on, all these simultaneous conversations and overlaps. He liked having more than one center to a scene or a shot.

Take the scene at the beginning where Hawkeye and Duke are arriving in the stolen Jeep. He started with a shot inside the mess hall with me and Danny Goldman and Roger Bowen. I remember he had us create our own little intro to the scene. At one point I'm talking about these two new arrivals. I had my glasses up on my forehead, and one of the other guys flipped them down and said something like, "You don't even know what you're looking at." That's not in the script, but by the time he actually got to shooting it, it would have been set. He would have made suggestions, tinkered with it, and signed off on it.

With Bob I have this image of a Renaissance painter, where Michelangelo would be working on the main figures and his helpers would be working on the figures at the edges. I think that's what Bob wanted and needed, this entourage of actors who were not playing primary characters who would enliven those edges and give the final work a special feel that he became known for.

RENÉ AUBERJONOIS: For all of us who had never been in a movie before, other than being a day player, it's almost as if he ruined us for the rest of our lives. We thought that's the way movies were. That they were that joyous an experience. If you had any kind of career, you quickly saw that most directors don't really trust actors, don't really want to see actors acting. That was the difference with Bob Altman. He loved actors and wanted to see acting.

* * *

MICHAEL MURPHY: When they started to make M*A*S*H, I thought, "Good. Bob got a little break here. He'll deliver this film, put a few bucks in his pocket, and get out of debt." I go out on the set, it was like the third day, and there he is with this picture of the Last Supper in his hand and he's laughing at it. I'm thinking, "Jesus, now it's going to be blasphemy and they won't want to release it."

JOHN SCHUCK: So my character, Painless, is some dentist from the Midwest who is physically endowed and has trouble on a sexual level. The interesting thing about that scene at the Last Supper, when he's decided to commit suicide, is the doctors and all the others could have been mean-spirited how they handled Painless, you know? But it wasn't. Bob made sure there was an understanding that we are all failing on some human level and would like to get out of it, just go to sleep and not wake up.

The "Last Supper" scene from M*A*S*H

Dialogue from *M*A*S*H:*

*(Captain Walter "Painless Pole" Waldowski, played by John Schuck,
is feted by his friends at a "Last Supper" arranged to visually
echo the Leonardo da Vinci masterpiece.)*

HAWKEYE PIERCE (*Played by Donald Sutherland*): I just— I just
   wanna say one thing. Uh, nobody ordered Walt to go on this
   mission. He volunteered for certain death.

DUKE: That's true.

HAWKEYE: That's what we award our highest medals for.

DUKE: That's beautiful.

JOHN SCHUCK: By using the image of the Last Supper, he was taking
on another establishment, of course. Almost anything that was institu-
tionalized was game for him. Didn't matter whether it was the church
or the school of art or the Army or anything. Anything that was organized and was a group, he could be counted on to be cantankerous
about. Studios. The Hollywood system was an ongoing battle all the

time. Banking, finance, every aspect of it. How you shoot a picture. How you pay actors. It doesn't matter, he had his own iconoclastic ideas about it.

I sensed that he was a renegade from day one. He was out gunning for anybody that was hurting the little guy. You see that just in the sheer humanity of his films. He had a great sense of right and wrong, but if I was to use the word "justice," it would be in a moral sense. And that's why he didn't like institutions, because to a certain extent, they dehumanize. And he didn't like that. He liked human beings, with all their foibles.

JOHNNY MANDEL (composer): When I got there, the first thing he was going to shoot was the suicide scene. We're sitting around one night and he says, "This is the first thing I have to do. It's just dead air with everyone walking around putting Scotch and *Playboy* in the casket. We need a song. It's got to be the stupidest song that was ever written." I said, "Well, we can do stupid."

He starts thinking and says five minutes later—we were a bit ripped at the time—he says, "The Painless Pole is going to commit suicide. The name of this song is 'Suicide Is Painless.' I used to write songs. I'm going to go home and see if I can come up with something." The next day, he tells me, "There's too much stuff in this forty-five-year-old brain of mine. I can't get anything nearly as stupid as I need. But all is not lost. I have this kid who is a total idiot. He'll run through this thing like a dose of salts."

MICHAEL ALTMAN: I was writing a lot of poetry at the time. I was really heavily influenced by Bob Dylan, Donovan, Leonard Cohen. And I was really into the music scene. My stepsister Konni was a classic poster flower child, lived on Speedway in Venice, and I just idolized her. It was 1968–69, Summer of Love. I had a psychedelic guitar. Well, I bought the guitar for ten bucks and I painted it all up with Day-Glo paint and had the Nehru jackets and I was all about that shit. I was writing tons of poetry, and it was all pretty basic, four-four, even-steven stuff, very typical, classic kind of folk poetry.

I came into the living room one night and my father was sitting there with Mr. Preminger and they were having their Scotch and smoking dope and talking about their thing. And I said, "I'm sorry, I didn't mean to interrupt you." And he goes, "No, come here, what do you want?" And I went, "I was just going to show you some stuff that

I'd written." So I showed him some silly poetry and stuff that I was writing and he goes, "We were just sitting here talking about this scene for the movie, and we need a song. Why don't you write it?"

And I went, "Oh. Well, I probably can't do that." And he goes, "I'll tell you what it is. We got the name of it, it's called 'Suicide Is Painless' and blah, blah, blah." He describes the scene. He says, "You go write it. If it works we'll use it."

The next day I left and went to my grandmother's. I was staying with her 'cause nobody else would have me. And I wrote like a hundred and twelve verses. Just the most atrocious crap you've ever heard in your life. It was just awful, I mean, "I hear the sound of gunfire from over the hill. Come on, boys, let's kill, kill, kill." You know, just terrible shit. I tore it all up and threw it away and called him up and I said, "I can't do this. Forget it, I tried, there's nothing that I'm willing to give you."

So the following week I went back to Bob's and I'm in the backyard and I grabbed a piece of paper and wrote the whole thing in about ten minutes. Just boom, wrote it out like that and I walked in and handed it to him. I go, "This'll work." He goes, "Oh, okay. Put some music to it." So I grabbed my guitar and I do this C-F-G, you know, Bob Dylan chords. I did a little A-minor. Maybe C. Just real basic crap. So they got one of those crappy little cassette recorders, you know, where you hold both the buttons down, and I recorded the thing. They took the tape and shipped it to Johnny Mandel and he threw some sevenths on it and put a bridge in it and there it is.

JOHNNY MANDEL: It's the only song I ever wrote dead drunk. I only wrote sober, but this particular song I couldn't get together. I had to get loose enough to come up with that. Finally, out of desperation, I got bombed and wrote it. I don't recommend that.

I didn't have to make any changes—verse, chorus, verse, chorus construction. Threw in a couple of odd bars to make it sound home-made. He wrote a very good lyric for what it was. When we were done, they liked it so much they started putting it in over the main titles. With the helicopters. I said, "That doesn't belong." They said they liked it. I said, "That's the stupidest answer I ever heard." They said, "Well, we like it." I said, "I'm not going to be part of this stupid conversation." I'm glad they didn't listen. It became my biggest copyright.

MICHAEL ALTMAN: They paid me five hundred bucks and gave me fifty percent of the song. I went and took that five-hundred-dollar check and bought myself a big, beautiful twelve-string guitar. Fucking gorgeous, man; it was amazing. That was the most beautiful thing I'd ever seen in my life. And then a couple of years later, after the TV show came out, it went into syndication. You know Bob hated the TV series, right?

Anyway, after the series came out, I got another check for, like, twenty-six bucks. And then the second check was like a hundred thirty dollars. And I'm going, "Oh, this is nice." And the next check was like twenty-six thousand dollars. And then it started, the whole thing started with the royalties. I think I ended up making close to two million dollars. And Bob had gotten paid seventy-five thousand dollars to direct the movie and no points, right? And it made Fox Studios what it is, right? It was their biggest hit ever, you know. Then the TV show and stuff like that. And Bob's just been livid about that for years.

Ingo Preminger, from "Remembering *M*A*S*H:* The 30th Anniversary Cast and Crew Reunion": The amusing thing is that Michael Altman made more money out of this picture than his father.

Robert Altman, from "Remembering *M*A*S*H:* The 30th Anniversary Cast and Crew Reunion": Oh, by a long shot. I'm cool about it all, because what I got out of it was better than money.

MICHAEL ALTMAN: I squandered the money away. All of it.

Here's what happened. After I got out of school and got this paper signed saying that I was responsible for myself, they released the money to me and I bought a big camper thing, a big hippie van. You know, like the Magic Bus. It was a converted bread truck. I cut the back of it off and put a loft in it and put a ship's wheel on the front and a couple of two-man saws on the side. Just painted it all up and hopped in the thing and traveled for several years and just caravanned around the country. And every three months we'd get a check for about twenty-five, thirty grand at a pop, which was a lot of money back then. And I just partied it away. It was tragic really, the whole thing was really too bad. There was no telling me what to do and so they just stopped trying and basically let me go. It was a great retirement plan, which I would love to have now, in retrospect. So anyway, I had never paid taxes; they just used to send me checks. They did for years. And then like ten years later I was up in Washington state and I went down to a car lot and I decided that I was going to buy a car. I go, "I'll pay cash." And the guy goes, "Just bring in your income-tax returns and we'll use that to get you a loan." And I go, "I don't have any income-tax returns." I started thinking, "Hmm, I wonder who's been doing that all this time for me." So I call up the IRS and they go, "Well, all right, with the penalties and interest you owe a quarter-million dollars." And so I disappeared for another ten years and didn't bring it up again. And then I tried to get it straightened out and by that time it was like close to half a million dollars.

It took years to straighten it out. I went to Bob for help. He got some of his lawyers and his army of guys on it. And they made this deal. So I did a bankruptcy. Bob bought the song from the trust-deed guy for thirty thousand dollars. He bought the rights to it, or bought the royalties off. So he finally ended up getting the royalties, and he still has them, or his estate does, I guess.

Sally Kellerman as "Hot Lips" Houlihan in the famous,
or infamous, shower scene

I was irresponsible and unbalanced to begin with. The money certainly flavored it and shaded it, but it wasn't the cause. I take responsibility for who I was. I don't blame it on Bob or on my mom or on the business or on anything. That's bullshit. I might have done that a few years ago, had I not tried to get involved in a program where you take responsibility for your own actions and become accountable. But I don't believe any of that anymore.

Have I published any other songs? No, nothing that's gone out. I've put together quite a few. I've got a ton of stuff. I've worked with a few other songwriters and put some stuff together. And quite honestly, by my personal standards, I never liked the suicide song. I wasn't that impressed with it at all.

*   *   *

Dialogue from *M*A*S*H:*

HAWKEYE PIERCE (*Played by Donald Sutherland*): I knew it.
    I knew you had a—had an attraction for Hot Lips Houlihan.
TRAPPER JOHN McINTYRE (*Played by Elliott Gould*): Hear, hear.
DUKE FORREST (*Played by Tom Skerritt*): Go to hell, Captain
    Pierce. You know I damn near puke every time I look at her.
    'Sides, I'll bet she's not a real blonde.

SALLY KELLERMAN: So now I've committed to doing this part, and I'm absolutely horrified and humiliated that I'm going to have to do this shower scene. I knew there was no getting out of it—it was one of the central things that moved the fun and the story along. I was horrified because I was always ashamed, you know, because I was fat as a kid, about thirty pounds more than now. And people would say, "You're not fat, you're just big." And that was even worse, you know? So I went to my shrink and I don't know what I said. I was hating myself so much. I went to my shrink and I dropped my pants and I said, "There." And he said, "So?" And that was it. That was my preparation for doing the naked shower scene.

Robert Altman, from DVD commentary: Sally was very nervous about this. I don't think she'd ever been naked in a film before or publicly, and she said, "I don't know how to do this, I don't know how to do this." And I said, "Listen, you just go in there and take your shower and when the curtain flies up, protect yourself at all times and it's no big deal."

Well, the first shot we made, the tent thing went up—Sally looked at us and she hit the ground in the tent so fast that we couldn't even tell what she was doing. She was on the ground before the flap came up.

SALLY KELLERMAN: When I looked up, there was Gary Burghoff stark naked standing in front of me. The next take, he had Tamara Horrocks, she was the more amply endowed nurse, without her shirt on. So I already had a penis in my mind, from Gary, and now I thought I was looking at a hermaphrodite. So I attribute my Academy Award nomination to the people who made my mouth hang open when I hit the deck.

RENÉ AUBERJONOIS: When they drop the tent and she's naked, my character covers the face of the houseboy. In that sequence, it's like a *Mad* magazine cover, in which everyone does something that illuminates their character. It's worth looking at that shot because it shows the gift that Bob gives actors.

SALLY KELLERMAN: He kept the camera rolling, by the way. Nobody said anything, no cut. And my character goes into the colonel's tent, and I suddenly realized that she was losing everything.

Dialogue from *M*A*S*H:*

MAJOR MARGARET "HOT LIPS" HOULIHAN (*to Colonel Henry Blake, played by Roger Bowen, in bed with Lieutenant Leslie, played by Indus Arthur*): Put them under arrest! See what a court-martial thinks of their drunken hooliganism! First they all call me "Hot Lips," and you let them get away with it! You let them get away with everything! If you don't turn them over to the MPs this minute, I'm— I'm gonna resign my commission!

COLONEL BLAKE: Goddammit, Hot Lips, resign your goddamn commission!

*   *   *

SALLY KELLERMAN: And I said, "My commission . . . my commission." I broke down, and I backed out of the tent.

Robert Altman, from DVD commentary: Sally's such a great actress, and this scene of her anger is, I think, one of the high points of the film.

SALLY KELLERMAN: After I did the shower scene, Bob ran around the tent and said, "I had no idea you were going to do it like that. You can stay in the film now—you've changed, you're vulnerable." She giggles and gives in—that was one of the things Bob taught me. And she gets to be a cheerleader, to play poker with the boys, to sleep with all kinds of cute guys, which she never could before. Well, I mean except for Rob Duvall, who played Frank Burns, who was as uptight as she was.

ROBERT DUVALL: *M*A*S*H* was a lot of fun. The only problem I had with military films was the higher the rank of the character, the more buffoonery set in. People don't understand the military. But since it was a spoof . . .

BUD CORT: I kind of never emotionally had a father, and that's where my hookup with Bob really had resonance. I would look at Bob and say, "That's my father. He picked me out of nothing and put me in a movie." It became my focus to make him crazy with my acting. He got every single thing that I did, and when it was time to do my big scene with Robert Duvall—my one line in the movie—I was psychotic with fear. My big scene was where I cried because Frank Burns—Duvall's character—says that I killed a guy due to my incompetence, and Elliott's character sees the whole thing happening and calls Frank out and punches him as hard as he can.

Apparently, before the scene Bob said to Duvall, "Fuck with Bud a little bit." Duvall just grabbed me and called me every word in the book. I went completely pale and we did the scene in one take. That's what Bob wanted—me frozen with fear. Once that was under my belt, I experienced a freedom and an elation in the work that I had never experienced before. It was bonding, like actually a family.

*   *   *

Robert Altman, from DVD commentary: I remember speaking at a college, oh, over in an auditorium of over five thousand people in Wisconsin or someplace, and somebody got up and said, "Why do you treat women the way that you do? You're a misogynist." And I said,

"Well, I don't treat women that way, I'm showing you the way I observed that women were treated." And that was the way women were treated and still are treated, especially when you get into these Army situations where you've got so many males with egos, with fourteen-year-old development. I think the whole point of this film was to show those attitudes toward women.

MATTHEW MODINE (actor): People got it backward. He appreciated women, he showed their character and strength. It's the men who are so fucked up, not the women in his films. The men pull back the curtain on Hot Lips. It's the asinine ridiculousness, the prank of men acting like Boy Scouts jerking off in a pup tent. He's exposing something about men, not about women.

SALLY KELLERMAN: The question of misogyny, right? People have written about "the humiliation of Hot Lips." I didn't get that at all. The shower *changed* Hot Lips. And me, I couldn't have felt more loved and more appreciated as a woman and as an actress.

*   *   *

Robert Altman, from "Remembering *M*A*S*H:* **The 30th Anniversary Cast and Crew Reunion":** This is the first time that the word "fuck" was used in an R-rated film. That was John Schuck in the football game, and I don't even know where that came from. I mean it certainly wasn't written and I certainly didn't tell him to do it.

Dialogue from *M*A*S*H:*

(The 4077th M*A*S*H unit is playing football against its rival, the 325th Evacuation Hospital.)
CAPTAIN WALTER "PAINLESS POLE" WALDOWSKI *(Played by John Schuck)*: All right, bub, your fucking head is coming right off!

JOHN SCHUCK: Yes, Schuck says "fuck." We were in Griffith Park shooting stuff, second-unit stuff for the football game that Andy Sidaris was in charge of. I had never played football. I was a soccer player. So you find yourself lining up against Buck Buchanan and all these pro football players. So Andy says to me, "Now just go up and say something really nasty about his mother or what you're going to do to him or whatever." And so that's what I did.

He just knocked me for a loop. Came up, he's saying, "I'm sorry, I'm sorry. It's instant reflex, anybody says that to me." So that's how that came about. I thought, "That will never be in the movie."

DANFORD GREENE (film editor): Oh yeah, I couldn't wait to cut that in. I knew it would get a laugh at the dailies.

GEORGE LITTO: I heard that at a screening, and I turned to Bob and said, "It's too bad you can't use that in the movie." And he said, "Why not?" Being as contrary as he was [laughs]. If I wasn't sitting there saying he can't use it, he might have taken it out.

ROBERT ALTMAN: Because of that, my father told his sister not to see M*A*S*H. He told her, "Bobby made a dirty movie."

* * *

DANFORD GREENE: When we ran the film for Ring Lardner, Jr., the lights go on and we walked out. I was walking in front of Bob and Ring, and Ring said, "It's not my script."

ELLIOTT GOULD: Ring Lardner, Jr., came out and walked up to me and said, "How could you do this to me? There's not a word that I wrote on screen."

DANFORD GREENE: I remember before we went to the Academy Awards—M*A*S*H was nominated for Best Picture, Best Director, Best Editing, Best Supporting Actress for Sally Kellerman, and Best Adapted Screenplay. I remember Bob said, "I don't think any of us will win except Ring Lardner, and he didn't even like the movie." And he was right. Ring was the only one who won anything.

Ring Lardner, Jr., letter to the editor headlined, "On Improving a M*A*S*H Script," The New York Times, June 15, 1997: Jesse Kornbluth quotes Robert Altman as saying: "When Ring Lardner read my draft of 'M*A*S*H*,' he said: 'You've ruined my script! There's not a word of mine in it.' Then he won the Academy Award for best screenplay and didn't thank anyone." I have always regarded Bob as an imaginative fellow, but this goes beyond his previous efforts. I not only never said

Editing M*A*S*H *with Danford Greene*

anything remotely like that; I couldn't have, because there never was an Altman draft to read. As for the Academy Award, I was almost certain that later in the evening Bob would be given the directorial award he deserved. Had I known that was not going to happen, I would have thanked him despite my distaste for the standard acceptance speech made up of one thank you after another, which had already become a cliché. However, I have frequently spoken publicly and written about his many improvements and much smaller number of negative contributions.

Ring Lardner, Jr., three years later, shortly before his death in November 2000. From unused footage from Fox Movie Channel Documentary, *Robert Altman: On His Own Terms*: I think Bob should have gotten some kind of cowriting credit since he did add so much, but he didn't ask for it. . . . I think after all these years my greatest regret . . . (is) not giving Bob Altman enough credit for the contribution, the writing contribution.

Ring Lardner, Jr., accepting the only Academy Award given for M*A*S*H

BARBARA ALTMAN HODES: When Bob was up for the Oscar for *M*A*S*H*, I was so excited. When he didn't win, I was so disappointed. I called Bob and I said, "Oh honey, you should have won." He said, "Oh, I'm thrilled to death. Honey, if you're on top, which I would have been, it's awful hard to stay up there. You've got to come down."

*   *   *

GEORGE LITTO: Bob did a brilliant job casting and directing the movie. Another thing Bob did that was brilliant was he solved the problem of an episodic script. Since the story and the characters and the plot didn't propel you, he used sound and music as the motor for the transitions between scenes and characters. He created that whole other voice of the loudspeakers on tent poles. All the way down to the end.

JOHNNY MANDEL: When I first started seeing blood spurting all around the hospital, I said, "God, how in the world are we going to handle that? I certainly don't want to write score to that." I remembered around 1949 I heard something that just about made you soil your pants—Japanese dance bands trying to play jazz. I said, "Shit! That's it!"

I had a Japanese friend take me to Little Tokyo to look in the Japanese records stores, and I went back to Altman and played this stuff. He said, "Great, but how do we use it?" I said, "Why don't you have it coming over the loudspeakers, from Radio Tokyo." His brain starts working, and it became the greatest cutting device he ever had. It allowed him to get from one scene to another. He was open to everything, but only Bob had the imagination to pull it off.

ROBERT ALTMAN: I knew I could use those loudspeakers, and I went around and shot them. For a while, I didn't know what was going to come out of them. But I knew I had to have connective tissue, and that worked.

Dialogue from the last scene of *M*A*S*H*:

P.A. ANNOUNCER (*Voiced by David Arkin*): Attention. Tonight's movie has been *M*A*S*H*. Follow the zany antics of our combat surgeons as they cut and stitch their way along the

front lines, operating as bombs—[*laughs*]—operating as
bombs and bullets burst around them; snatching laughs and
love between amputations and penicillin.

STAFF SERGEANT GORMAN (*Played by Bobby Troup*): Goddamn
army.

P.A. ANNOUNCER: That is all.

[*A gong sounds and the screen goes black*]

* * *

GEORGE LITTO: Dick Zanuck, he's going to hate you for this, but fuck
him. He and David Brown and all the guys at Fox first saw the movie
and they gave Bob, I don't know, ten pages of notes for cuts and
changes they wanted made. I said, "Ingo, you got to get in there and
get a preview or something. You got to do something." He got them to
agree to a preview in San Francisco. We all went up there. And I'm sitting right behind Dick Zanuck.

The picture goes on, and you know one of the other controversial
things is Bob was showing lots of blood, right? I mean it's all outrageous and people are walking out. I'm saying to my wife, "Oh my God,
the pains are coming back. They're going down my chest." And then
there's the scene where Don Sutherland steals the jeep. And then the
audience applauds, and then the audience is screaming. Next thing you
know it's a standing ovation, and Dick Zanuck turns around and he
says, "Hey, George, we got a hit. Tell Bob to forget about my notes."

RICHARD ZANUCK: The marketing people at Twentieth Century Fox
were scared. Some people were really shocked by it because it was so
stark, so bloody. They thought audiences would get up, throw up, and
leave. They had always been very skeptical about the picture. They
first challenged the title—"What is this? Mash potatoes? We can't sell
this." But it was a massive hit at that preview. They got the humor. It
was very reaffirming.

It was great fun for me seeing the picture come to life in his hands.
He added a much more cynical spirit to it than was ever in the script
and a liveliness to it that neither the book nor the script had.

ROBERT ALTMAN: I always said *M*A*S*H* didn't get released. It
escaped.

RENÉ AUBERJONOIS: You know the famous story about the executive from Twentieth Century Fox coming up to Pauline Kael and saying, "What do we do with this film?" And she said, "You release it! What are you, crazy? You release it."

* * *

GEORGE LITTO: Remember we were talking about what Bob said about Kraft cheese? He did it again. After *M*A*S*H* came out, I'm negotiating with Dick Zanuck and Ingo Preminger to get Bob back his five percent. While this is going on, Bob gave an interview and he said something like, "Fox is going broke, and I'm glad."

Linda Stein, story headlined "Altman Is Determined to Make Pix Own Way," in *Film/TV Daily,* **March 3, 1970:** "All studios are going broke . . . and I love it," stated Robert Altman, the director of Twentieth-Fox's *M*A*S*H.* "The studios waste their money. When they go on location it costs them a fortune. When I go on location I know my costs even before I begin to shoot. It's the independent guy that makes the money."

GEORGE LITTO: I don't know how much that cost Bob. It cost me a million dollars, I figured [*laughs*]. Dick Zanuck sends me a copy of the interview. He says, "George, you can forget our negotiation." I thought back to the Kraft cheese and said to myself, "This is where I came in."

RICHARD ZANUCK: I threw him up into the big time but he never looked at it that way. I don't say this in an unkind way. I always liked Bob. I liked the fact that he was so independent. I don't think it was a good trait that he was always pissed off.

He was a lucky guy in that he got the full backing. I fought for that picture—I fought the board of directors. My father, who was chairman of the company, thought it was insane. I fought for it, and he never appreciated it. Never once did I ever hear either personally or in print any appreciation whatsoever or any recognition of it. That's what really launched his career. I don't blame him. I know that kind of personality. I wasn't singled out. He didn't want to be any part of a system. But it fed him. He seemed to piss on all of that. But, all in all, he was a huge talent. I forgive him for some of his surly behavior.

GEORGE LITTO: Now we're showing the picture in New York and the old man comes in, Darryl Zanuck. They run the movie, and he loves the picture. He says, "We're going to put this in the Cannes Film Festival." Now, comedies never won, and we looked at each other. I said to Ingo, "A comedy at the film festival?" Ingo says, "Hey, he's the boss."

DENISE BRETON (publicist): I was head of publicity for Europe for Twentieth Century Fox, and when Bob flew here to France I was told to meet him at the airport. When he arrived I just looked at him. I was so surprised. I said, "I thought you'd be much younger" [*laughs*]. I couldn't believe a man his age had made a film like *M*A*S*H*. He was much happier with me when I told him we had gotten *M*A*S*H* into Cannes.

GEORGE LITTO: I'm on my belated honeymoon at the Hôtel du Cap in Cap d'Antibes. A friend of mine has got a villa a couple of doors down, we're having a nice lunch in the garden. And my friend says, "I just got a phone call for you, George, to give you a message—*M*A*S*H* won the Golden Palm." That's the whole story arc.

*   *   *

JERRY WALSH (friend/lawyer/executor): The film *M*A*S*H* came out and was a big success. I said, "Well, B.C., what's it like having a famous son? Look at this—I read all about him in *The New York Times* and everything." And B.C. said, "Well, the biggest difference I've noticed is I got a check from him for ten thousand dollars that I thought I'd never see again."

REZA BADIYI (director): I had an appointment in New York and I ran into Bob in the lobby of the hotel. He says, "Come on, let's go." We got in a taxi and went to this theater. They're showing *M*A*S*H*, and there's a line going around the block. And he says, "I wish Dick Sarafian could see this!" [*Laughs*]

*   *   *

MARTIN SCORSESE (director): I remember seeing *M*A*S*H* at a *Time* magazine movie screening, in the old Fox building in New York. It had an Egyptian theme and the screening room was beautiful and the screen was enormous and the nature of the film was something completely foreign to me and new to me. I hadn't experienced anything like that before. And I liked it. My take on the world was rather different, so I couldn't quite get into the rhythm of it and the nature of the characters, but I really enjoyed it. I'm not a sports fan or a person who understands sports, but that's the only football game I ever understood.

GARRY TRUDEAU (cartoonist and writer): I saw *M*A*S*H* as an undergraduate at a sneak preview in a suburban theater outside New Haven. I must have seen something in the press about it that drew me to go see it. But there is that moment that anyone who saw the film experienced, when all the principal characters converge on the mess tent—Colonel Blake and Radar and Hawkeye—and they've just shown up and they're trying to get information and everybody starts talking at once. And I had this sense that something had gone terribly wrong in the projector booth. You think about it later on and it was real life, but you don't expect to see real life on the screen. That's not why we have movies. The idea that everybody could finish each other's sentences or talk over one another, or that they would get just the amount of information they needed before they would begin talking, that was revolutionary in film.

The way he gave you the freedom to listen to whatever it was you wanted to listen to, and to track which conversations you wanted to, it was very liberating. And of course, perfect for the times, the cacophony of American culture at that time was being brilliantly reproduced on a screen. And he did it with such artistry. Kind of jazz-like—even if you didn't listen to the individual through lines, the individual melodies, there was a beauty to the jazz of those voices coming in and out.

It made me think about dialogue and what it could be. It had a lot of impact on me. Just the use of black humor and satire, and that has been a continuous thread through my work. The idea that black humor is a kind of last resort, and it's a way to keep the madness at bay and to survive.

GEORGE W. GEORGE (writer and producer): When I worked with him, in the forties and fifties, was I aware he was someone with talent who could make it there in Hollywood? No. Later I found that out—when I went to a screening of *M*A*S*H*. That was the biggest revolutionary experience I ever had. I went into the theater expecting nothing and I came out expecting everything. What that did was prove to me a theory that I had had for a long time. The reason most people can't compete successfully is they are born at the wrong time or the wrong century or the wrong moment for what they're doing. If you get lucky, you are born into a period where you get the most opportunity to do the work you want to do. In the movie business, Bob Altman was born at the exact right time.

After *M*A*S*H*

*

ROBERT ALTMAN: The problem with so many artists today is if a guy succeeds at something in an art form, he feels he is obligated to repeat it. I can't tell you the amount of money I was offered to make another *M*A*S*H* or another picture like it. I wouldn't even mess around with that television series. I mean, I've never seen one of those episodes all the way through—never seen a whole one. I don't like it and I don't like any of those people. And it's jealousy, too, that drives me to have those opinions. It's, "How dare they walk into my studio and look at my easel?" Or, if you're a baker and someone down the street comes up with a bigger sign and is making more money doing what you did first. "What the fuck are they doing? They took my idea! I made cream puffs!"

It's also my attitude that *M*A*S*H*, this movie, was about foreign wars. And then, every fucking week on a Sunday night, to have a drama about that, in which they had these platitudes about liberalism and whatever the current issue is. It's still bringing a foreign war into your home every week for twelve years, and even though the bad guys in the script were from your own military hierarchy, you're really presenting the bad guys as the brown people with the slanted eyes who you're fighting. I don't get the joke, and I don't like the joke.

KATHRYN REED ALTMAN: I never dreamed—though he probably did—that a picture like *M*A*S*H* was going to change our lives completely. Turn him into a star and set up all kinds of problems [*laughs*]. Well, not so much problems but situations that we hadn't dreamed of dealing with. Or I hadn't.

GEORGE LITTO: In this business, before you're somebody they're always taking things away from you. And now you finally get recognized. Now you don't want to give anything up. He won the award at Cannes and he became almost like an international legend overnight. For us, though, it was the start of the end. Suddenly, you know, he got so serious. He wasn't the same, you know?

Bob was contrary. He could be perverse, he could be charming, he could be brilliant, he could be funny. He was all those things. Some days you didn't know what you were going to get. We used to rent yachts, we'd go fishing, go off of Catalina, go swimming in the ocean. I would cook breakfast and everything, he would skin the fish, and we'd cook and we'd eat, we'd drink, and he'd do card tricks, he'd tell stories, he'd do pantomime, he was hysterically funny. He was great to be with. We all had so much fun. Until he started reading his reviews [*laughs*]. Then he became the great filmmaker.

Part of why I invested myself in Bob was because I thought he was this brilliant talent. I never made a lot of money with Bob because he took up so much fucking time. But I did it because we had this—what shall we call it—this adventure. We had this sense of adventure together. It was all a challenge. I liked the challenge because I thought he'd do great things. And I was all for his becoming a great filmmaker, but part of how you endured all this stuff is you had a lot of fun in between. And suddenly it got a little bit too stuffy for me.

COREY FISCHER (actor): There's always the shadow, in Jungian terms. Someone that big, who lives that big and publicly, it's not all sweetness and light. The more someone like him has to maintain a strength and power to see these enormous projects through, there is going to be dark stuff happening. If one is super-enlightened, or really self-aware or incredibly mature, maybe one can deal with that shadow without acting out. But for most of us, it can catch us unawares. And we wind up doing things that, politically, much later we will say, "I was young and irresponsible."

I think film and the industry and the medium, because it involves so many issues of power, the complexity of film, the expense of it, the size of the undertaking, when you are able to pull that off, make a film and make a film like *M*A*S*H* that becomes a cultural artifact, you're vulnerable to inflation, to believing your own legend.

ROBERT REED ALTMAN: The minute *M*A*S*H* was made we moved out of Mandeville Canyon and started renting beach houses down here in Malibu. Then they built their big Malibu house, the one my mother called "the movie-star house." Everything did get very chaotic and different.

KATHRYN REED ALTMAN: Big offers were coming in. He wanted to move to Canada—he was mad at America. He wanted to become a landed immigrant in Canada. He had already gotten the documents and I was trying to sell the house. I was ready for an adventure. We ended up not doing that.

We built what I laughingly call "the movie-star house" in Malibu. By that I meant it had the tower, the gallery, the swimming pool, the gym, the sauna, the hundred feet of beachfront, blah, blah, blah. All in cedar and glass and ferns, up on pilings. It was gorgeous, a great party house, and there were great parties there.

MICHAEL MURPHY: *M*A*S*H* catapulted him into the stratosphere. The guy became the hottest director in the world. And this leads to the next remarkable thing about Bob Altman. A lot of directors—I could name a few, but I won't—would be thinking, "Let me be careful about my next film and who is in it and who can help me remain successful. Let me get Clark Gable in this thing." You know, they want somebody, a big star, that can share the burden. That's what all these guys do. Instead, Bob's next picture is *Brewster McCloud*, with me and Sally Kellerman and Bud Cort. He was just, "Yeah, let's make this."

Brewster McCloud *(1970)*

Vincent Canby, review in *The New York Times*, December 24, 1970: Robert Altman's "Brewster McCloud," the director's first film since "M*A*S*H," attempts to be a kind of all-American, slapstick "Orpheus Ascending," a timeless myth about innocence and corruption told in the sort of outrageous and vulgar terms that Brian De Palma and Robert Downey do much better.

Brewster McCloud (Don "Bud" Cort), a virginal young man who is protected by the gods (but only up to a point), lives hidden inside Houston's Astrodome, that extraordinary enclosed-environment-within-an-enclosed-environment, where he secretly prepares to fly with his own man-made wings. Terrible people, however, keep getting into Brewster's way. . . . Wherever Brewster goes, he is followed by a mother-protector named Louise (Sally Kellerman), who has once had

Bud Cort flying around the Astrodome in Brewster McCloud

her own wings (there are scars on her back to prove it), and her crow, which flies overhead to excrete on the people who would put an end to Brewster's dream, just before they are mysteriously strangled. "Brewster McCloud" has more characters and incidents than a comic strip, but never enough wit to sustain more than a few isolated sequences. . . . Even so, I must admit that I laughed out loud at "Brewster McCloud" . . . largely because Mr. Altman has a gift for occasionally stuffing the screen and the soundtrack with all sorts of crazy and contradictory details, some of which are most attractive and quite dirty.

Lou Adler (producer): I was basically in the music business, but I had done the *Monterey Pop* documentary. Whatever success I had in the music business prompted some agent to send me the script. I sent it to Bob and he liked it. Then we met at MGM and they agreed to go ahead and make the picture. I think anybody would have made a film of his choosing coming off the success of *M*A*S*H.*

He was exciting. He was full of enthusiasm but with a confidence about him. I liked him immediately as a person and he seemed to like me also. I don't think he would have worked with me at that point if he didn't. He was taking a chance with me as a producer. He actually made me a producer. He allowed me to solve the crises—be it dailies that went wrong or something that had to be delivered immediately from L.A. He didn't step in and have somebody handle it—he allowed me to become a producer.

BUD CORT: Once *M*A*S*H* was over I went to New York to audition for a play. I went in and auditioned for David Merrick. I killed. They went with someone else. Bob called and said, "I heard you didn't get the part. That's great because I got an idea for you. Just hang tough." I did some episodic television and Bob said, "Don't do television. You're a movie star. Trust me." I said, "I trust you."

Bob says, "You're going to play a mass murderer and it's going to be a whole reaction to how sick society is right now." Then he would call me two or three times a week and have me for dinner—tell me what was going on. At some point I went to Bob and said, "I want to ask a favor." I took my clothes off. Naked. "I want a trainer." Bob looks at me and says, "Oh yeah, I get it." He got me a trainer, a guy named Buddy Brando, at the Beverly Hills Athletic Club. I instinctively knew that I had to get bird-ripped to play Brewster.

Bob asked if I had any ideas for Suzanne. I sent in some wonderful actresses—Annie Lockhart, others—but I could tell Bob was not a hundred percent sold. Couple weeks later, he said he had found Suzanne.

Shelley Duvall to Lawrence Eisenberg, story headlined "Filmdom's Most Unlikely Star," *Cosmopolitan,* **August 1981:** I was twenty and living with Bernard (an artist whom the actress later married and divorced) in his parents' house in Houston, and we used to give a lot of parties to show off his paintings. Friends would invite other people, and one night two guys showed up saying they knew a patron of the arts and could I bring some paintings to show him.

ROBERT ALTMAN: Tommy Thompson and Bob Eggenweiler, who were my associates on that picture, told me, "You've got to see this girl, she's really something."

Lawrence Eisenberg, story headlined "Filmdom's Most Unlikely Star," *Cosmopolitan,* **August 1981:** The next afternoon Shelley loaded thirty canvases into her car and took them to the appointed spot, where the "patron" turned out to be Robert Altman, in town casting *Brewster McCloud.*

ROBERT ALTMAN: I met her and I thought she was just full of shit. I thought she knew what she was doing, pretending to be that way. And I was really rude to her. But she turned out to be what she turned out to be.

LOU ADLER: She was real interesting, great eyes and an interesting look and particularly interesting in her presentation of the art of her boyfriend. The paintings were very bizarre, but she sort of made them accessible. Bob kept on saying, "Tell us more, tell us more." At the end he said, "I think she should be the female lead of the movie." She wasn't even thinking of herself as an actress.

Shelley Duvall to Lawrence Eisenberg, story headlined "Filmdom's Most Unlikely Star," *Cosmopolitan,* **August 1981:** Actually, I was pretty suspicious. I thought he was making some kind of porno movie or something. Then somebody shouted, "But this is Robert Altman. He directed *M*A*S*H.*" I hadn't seen the picture, hadn't heard of him and couldn't have cared less. Anyway this same person asked for my tele-

Shelley Duvall and Bud Cort in Brewster McCloud

phone number, and just to get out of there I gave it to him, figuring I was safe. After all, my father's a lawyer.

MICHAEL MURPHY: He's intrigued by her and gives her the starring role [*laughs*]. And she has to start shooting in like three days. The closest she's been to a movie is in the theater, sitting in a chair. Of course she was great. She had that real, natural way, and Bob was the kind of guy who could get that out of you. He had her so relaxed and easy. She blew everybody off the screen in that movie. She was such a natural and she was with the right guy.

BUD CORT: We got off the plane and there was this little baby giraffe—eyelashes down to her chin and up to her forehead. And Bob said, "This is Shelley Duvall." She says, "Hi, y'all!"

Shelley Duvall, to Patricia Bosworth, from *Show*, April 1971: Nobody else calls him "Pirate" 'cept me. That's 'cuz I think he's the bravest, toughest, most imaginative man I've ever met. . . . No matter what "Pirate" asked me to do I could do it—easy as pie. Acting isn't difficult. I'd never take lessons. You just do it, you know? Everybody in life acts anyhow. President Nixon, the Pope, even John Lennon.

MICHAEL MURPHY: It was one of those movies where it just got wilder by the minute. I mean I haven't seen the movie in many, many years, but I don't know if anybody has a clue what any of it is about. I don't remember if it was drug induced or what [*laughs*]. This is my own take on it, but I think it was kind of a look at the insanity of all of that period in time, you know? Guys were really breaking loose and doing their "dream films" and doing nutty stuff. Things were getting off the page more and more, and he was in the vanguard of all that.

LOU ADLER: The original script took place in New York in the TWA building. Next thing I knew he was filming in Houston in the Astrodome. That was the beginning of a lot of changes that would come about in that script.

We'd do the day's shooting—a lot of it was improvised—and then at the end of the shooting we'd meet back in Bob's hotel room. At first, that would include the screenwriter, Billy Cannon. He wasn't around very long when he saw how different it was from what he had written. A few of the actors would be there, and Lou Lombardo would be there. Louie Lombardo was assembling the film as they went. Bob's confrontations with Louie were interesting. They were both very strong men. Louie had his own ideas on how things should be. I think it was a love-hate situation between those two guys. They both enjoyed it being a love-hate, and they enjoyed the hating part as much as the love part.

Anyway, Bob would make the best Bloody Mary I've ever tasted. Then he would stand up and make a speech, pretty much the same speech every night. "No one in this room knows what this movie is about except me." Then he would retire to his room and write the next day's pages.

*　　*　　*

Doran William Cannon, *Brewster McCloud* **screenwriter, essay in** *The New York Times,* **February 7, 1971:** Recently, I enjoyed an altercation on the phone with Mr. Altman. He claimed I should take my name off the screen since, in fact, he himself had written most of the film. I told him that if the Writer's Guild . . . would allow a credit such as "Based on an Original Screenplay by," I would be happy to take that credit since it more closely approximates THE TRUTH than "Written by," which implies that the film kept to my script, which is not a true fact.

ALTMAN: Your screenplay was a piece of crap!

CANNON: My screenplay was perfect.

ALTMAN: It was crap.

CANNON: You bought it!

ALTMAN: You sold it!

He accused me of selling a script he had bought! Surely, I am his SOURCE, and that embarrasses him; oh, Hollywood!

ALTMAN: I will continue embarrassing you to the press.

CANNON: I'm hardly embarrassed, but you were embarrassed when I came to Houston. You were embarrassed to think that people might learn I exist. You felt exposed!

ALTMAN: I was embarrassed *for* you.

CANNON: Ha! You remind me of Otto Preminger. He was also embarrassed because I had written "Skidoo" as an original, and he screwed up my vision.

ALTMAN: You put me in the same class as Otto Preminger?

CANNON: Yes!

Silence.

I suggested that we talk the whole thing over when it becomes history, perhaps in a year.

ALTMAN: See you in a year.

*   *   *

ROBERT ALTMAN: I forget what the writer's name was, but he has sole screen credit. Cannon, yeah, Cannon. It was just a dreadful piece, I thought. But it was a kid flying, a gem of an idea I could work off.

*   *   *

MICHAEL MURPHY: One night towards the end of the movie, I could tell he was getting sick of being in Houston. It was a hundred and forty degrees and we're in those hot clothes. It was a hard grind out there. We're in a restaurant and he was giving an interview at one table and I was sitting across the room with some actors. The idea of my character was that he would come into town and Brewster McCloud would get screwed and he would get in his hot car and leave. From the other table, Bob says, "I'm going to kill you tomorrow." I said, "Kill me? Why, what do you mean, kill me?" He says, "Yeah, it'll be great. We'll run your car into that lagoon down there in the park. You're going to kill yourself. It'll be great." I knew that part of it was he just wanted to end this movie and get the hell out of there.

So all this stuff was kind of being made up on the fly. I think probably for the historians, the interesting thing about that movie is, aside from a lot of experimental things that he was kind of fooling with, I think it's interesting knowledge that he really winged it. He would just come up with these ideas and we'd shoot them. Bob would see a fountain and put Sally in it.

SALLY KELLERMAN: Okay, *M*A*S*H* was a big hit, so let's do something obscure. I think he just made up my part because he wanted to work together. I loved it. He gave me wing scars and let me sing "Rock-a-bye Baby" to Bud. I stopped people on the road to tell them about Bob and how I loved Bob and how I'd do anything for Bob. And of course he took full advantage and he put me sitting naked in the fountain. To his credit it was a long lens and there was nobody in the streets, and I was this bird, this fairy godmother. Why I did these things . . .

All I know is we had a great time. I remember Bob had the police chief come over and he'd have these big bowls of grass sitting around. I don't remember if the guy knew or if he didn't.

JOAN TEWKESBURY (screenwriter and director): If you look at René Auberjonois in *Brewster McCloud* and you look at the development of that character, you have to say that is fucking brilliant.

RENÉ AUBERJONOIS: I think I know how Bob thought of me for that. We were at a party at their house in Mandeville Canyon, all stoned and drinking and having a good time. I remember being in the swimming pool. I remember goofing around on the diving board and being a bird.

René Auberjonois as the Lecturer transforming into a bird
in Brewster McCloud

Flapping my arms and showing off. I wasn't trying to prove anything. Bob was this person you wanted to please. I could tell that he was enjoying it. Months later, when he said, "You're going to do a bird lecturer and turn into a bird," I thought, "That party scene got me the part."

It was one of the most incredible experiences. In one day, we shot like thirty-six different scenes of me turning into a bird. I did my own makeup, my own costume—feathers in my hair—and we put birdseed in the chalk tray in front of the blackboard. At the end of that day Bob said to me, "I don't know. I'm shooting this to be safe, and I don't know if any of this will be in the film."

It's a rare thing to get into a situation where you truly feel like a collaborator with the director. He was so brilliant at knowing how it was all going to come together. He was so flexible, and in my life the great directors I've worked with are always directors who know exactly what they want but will change on a dime when they see what the actor brings to it. They are supremely confident that they know what they want, but at the same time open to knowing what might be better. That's what Bob was.

Lou Adler: If I were to plan a vacation and think, "Why don't I do a movie at the same time?"—this would have been it. We had a suite in the Astrodome, we got to watch the ball games, the dailies were a party, and the meetings in Bob's room were a party. The premiere was a major party. It was quite an experience that I've never matched.

We did two endings. The ending that I wanted was the last scene to be silent except for "Somewhere Over the Rainbow" playing. Bob wanted the ending we ended up with. The way he decided on it was we showed it in two theaters next to each other in a multiplex, five minutes apart, so that we could see the reaction of one theater and then judge the reaction of the other. I always thought mine was a better reaction, but he went with his.

Joan Tewkesbury: In *Brewster McCloud*, those beautiful wings were made by the designer Leon Ericksen. Leon always knew that Brewster was going to crash and those wings are going to get broken. And to me, that's the saddest event in any of Bob's movies—when he falls out of the sky.

John Schuck: It's my favorite film. I just find it magical. It's like a little fairy-tale story. But it's so outrageous. It's sort of satirizing movies and society and our inability to truly move forward as human beings.

Michael Murphy: I thought, "It can't miss." Bob was flying and there was so much enthusiasm. Of course, nobody came to see it. It was a huge flop. Floperama. It was a good lesson. It doesn't always turn out the way you hope it's going to turn out.

I look back and I think, "What the hell were we doing?"

Robert Altman to Bruce Williamson, the *Playboy* interview, August 1976: I wouldn't say it's my best film; it's flawed, not nearly as finished as some work I've done since, but it's my favorite, because I took more chances then. It was my boldest work, by far my most ambitious. I went way out on a limb to reach for it.

Peter Newman (producer): The last time I saw Bob my son was seventeen—he really wanted to meet and hear Bob. We went to the Museum of Broadcasting, where Bob was doing a panel with Garrison Keillor about *Prairie Home Companion*. At the end of the evening I brought my son up, and said, "This is my son, Griffin, and I just want you to know his favorite movie of all time is *Brewster McCloud*."

Bob grabbed the bottom of his beard, stroked it a little bit, and smiled. He said, "You have excellent taste—and terrible judgment."

Robert Altman: The greatest films are the ones that leave you not able to explain, but you know that you have experienced something special. I've always had this feeling that the perfect response to a film or a piece of work of mine would be if someone got up and said, "I don't know what it is, but it's right." That's the feeling you want— "That's right"—and it comes from four or five layers down; it comes from the inside rather than from the outside.

CHAPTER 14

McCabe

*

McCabe & Mrs. Miller *(1971)*

Andrew Sarris, review in *The Village Voice,* **July 8, 1971:** *McCabe & Mrs. Miller* confirms the impression of striking originality that goes beyond the Beetle Bailey mechanics of *M*A*S*H* to the more controlled horror and absurdism of *That Cold Day in the Park* and *Brewster McCloud.* . . . *McCabe* succeeds almost in spite of itself, with a rousing finale that is less symbolic summation than poetic evocation of the fierce aloneness in American life. I can't remember when I have been so moved by something that has left me so uneasy to the marrow of my aesthetic. Unlike so many of his contemporaries, Altman tends to lose battles and win wars. Indeed, of how many other films can you say that the whole is better than its parts? [Warren] Beatty's reluctant hero and [Julie] Christie's matter-of-fact five-dollar whore are nudged from bumptious farce through black comedy all the way to solitary tragedy imbedded in the communal indifference with which Altman identifies America. However, Altman neither celebrates nor scolds this communal indifference but instead accepts it as one of the conditions of existence.

* * *

DAVID FOSTER (producer): I had been in Paris meeting with an agent named Ellen Wright, who was the widow of the famous African-American author Richard Wright. She represented a guy, an American novelist named Edmund Naughton, who wrote a novel called *McCabe.*

Listening to bearskin-wrapped Warren Beatty while making
McCabe & Mrs. Miller

She said, "You ought to take this book and read this." She started throwing names around to direct—John Huston, Roman Polanski. It was a great book. I read it on the plane home, over the pole, from Paris to L.A. I got off the plane and called my neighbor and attorney and best friend, Frank Wells. I said, "I've got to get it."

We bought the book. Now what do I do with it? John Huston—he was off doing some picture. And Polanski I really didn't know. Fabulously talented guy. Through connections I got word to him that I optioned this book called *McCabe*. I never heard back. I had a friend named George Litto. Crazy son of a bitch. A madman but I loved him. He said, "I have a client who wants to do a Western but not a traditional Western." *M*A*S*H* was in the can but no one had seen it yet. He said, "His name is Robert Altman." I said, "Who's Robert Altman?" Nobody knew who he was.

I got a call from George saying Bob was going to show *M*A*S*H* to the composer Johnny Mandel. He could sneak me in if I sat quietly. Which I did, and I fell in love with it. Afterwards I met Bob. Litto looked at us and said, "Are you guys committing to each other to do this movie?" I said, "I am." Bob said, "I am." George says, "Okay, you've got to sit still for the next three or four months. If this movie is as good as you think it is, everybody will want Bob Altman." That's what happened. Everybody wanted Bob Altman at that point because *M*A*S*H* put him on the map. And I had him.

M*A*S*H was going to be screened in New York for Darryl Zanuck. Fox wouldn't pay for Bob to go. I'm not a studio. I'm scratching for money. I scraped up enough money for both of us to go to New York, and Darryl Zanuck didn't know what they had. He thought it could be interpreted as anti-American. Honest to God. We get to the hotel—I was paying for all this—and Fox wouldn't pay for shit. The phone rings and it's one of the executives at Fox in New York. "Bobby! Bobby!"—nobody called him Bobby—"we got a great advance in *The New York Times*!" Now suddenly he's Bobby. It was a fucking joke, and on the Sunday that it opened, we went back to L.A.

People who had passed on it earlier suddenly wanted *McCabe* because it was Bob Altman. He was the flavor of the week. There was an agent at William Morris, a guy named Stan Kamen. He was a phenomenon. He had Steve McQueen, Warren Beatty, all these guys. Warren was in London when Stan called him, "Got this script, it's called *McCabe & Mrs. Miller*. It's going to be directed by Bob Altman. This is going to be the new giant director. You've got to see this picture, *M*A*S*H*." Warren flew from London to New York, got off the plane, went to a theater on Third Avenue. Got back on the plane and flew to L.A., met with us, and committed to do it. He committed for himself and for Julie Christie, who he was living with.

*   *   *

JOAN TEWKESBURY: I went to his office and I simply asked for a job. I had directed Michael Murphy in a one-act play that Bob came to see. He barely remembered who I was. He said that he was going to

Canada to shoot *McCabe & Mrs. Miller.* He said, "You can't just come and observe." He said that's like being a groupie. But he said the script girl he was planning to use was now one of the hookers in *McCabe.* Bob wanted this chorus of accents. Nobody spoke English English. The reason he wanted the script girl to be one of the hookers was because she was from Australia and she had the accent. Basically he was developing this town full of people who were all from someplace else. It was all part of his idea about how to make a Western that wasn't a Western.

ROBERT ALTMAN: They were all first-generation Europeans. There wasn't anybody who spoke Texas: "Howdy, pardner." That didn't exist.

JOAN TEWKESBURY: So, if I wanted to, I could be the script girl. By the time I got there, he had forgotten who I was, as only Bob can do.

Bob's idea about the script was that the church was the focus of the town—the town's name was Presbyterian Church. The film was originally going to be called *The Presbyterian Church Wager.* At the end of the movie, he knew he was going to burn the church and what people would discover was that there was nothing in the church. It wasn't a sacred place. There was just this guy, the preacher character, who was half crazy, living inside this shell.

COREY FISCHER: He gave me the role of the preacher, the Reverend Elliot. The preacher was clearly nuts, a fanatic, an obsessive. He was like McCabe's shadow, something from McCabe's unconscious rearing up.

I think Bob was disappointed with me because the biggest moment for that character was when he hauled that cross up to the church, that tremendous shot. That wasn't me. That was a stuntman. I have a terrible fear of heights. No way was I going up there. Bob had a macho side. He tried to shame me into getting up there, but no way. Nobody knew the difference, certainly not the audience, but he knew. I know he was disappointed. I always joked that after that I was replaced by Jeff Goldblum as the tall young Jew. I never really saw Bob again.

KEITH CARRADINE (actor and songwriter): I was told there was a role for a young cowboy. He was supposed to play the banjo and Robert Altman was going to be directing it. Did I play the banjo? As all young actors will say, I said, "Absolutely." Well, I didn't play the banjo. I played the guitar and piano and harmonica, but I'd never picked up a banjo. Immediately I went out and bought this really cheap Kent banjo and a banjo book, and I started learning to play. I was told I was going to have a meeting with Robert Altman and I was told to go to his offices, which were the Lion's Gate offices in Westwood. And they occupied this little office suite off of Westwood Boulevard, south of Wilshire Boulevard.

I went over there and I went to the main reception and they told me, "Oh yes, Mr. Altman is upstairs." So I went up the stairs and I knocked on the door, and at this point I had done one part. I had done my first movie, which was a gunfight with Kirk Douglas and Johnny Cash, but I was still sporting my long hair because I had just come off of a year in *Hair* on Broadway. So my hair was probably about eighteen inches long at that point. I was a hippie. And I walked into Bob's office. It was actually an apartment that he had where he would stay if he decided not to drive home at night. I opened the door and he was standing at the foot of his bed and he was unwrapping this brown-wrapped package, and he was wearing a bathrobe and a T-shirt.

He said, "Hi, you're Keith."

And I said, "Yeah."

He said, "I'm just unwrapping this—I just came back from the Cartagena Film Festival in Colombia."

And I'm thinking, "He's unwrapping a bale of dope." But in fact it wasn't dope. He was unwrapping some pre-Columbian art that he had bought down there and had shipped back. He sort of looked at me as he was looking at his stuff.

He said, "So, we're going to do this movie."

And I said, "Yeah."

He said, "We're going to shoot it up in Vancouver and it's a Western and there's a part for this kid who comes into town. Basically he comes into town because he's heard there's a whorehouse."

And I said, "Yeah, yeah. I heard about it."

He said, "So, do you want to do it?"

I looked at him like, "You're asking me if I want to do the part?" I didn't say that. I said, "Sure."

And he said, "Okay. I don't know about the hair. Maybe we'll keep the hair. I think the hair is good."

Which was a great relief to me, because at that point I was nineteen, twenty years old and my long hair was my identity. It was my badge.

That was the beginning of my working relationship, friendship, love affair with Robert Altman. That was how he worked. He cast essence. He wanted pure behavior and he wanted the essence of people and that was his genius. You didn't have to audition for him to know if you were the right person for the part. He didn't really cast actors so much as he cast people. He loved actors and he stood in awe of actors. He didn't understand how they could do what they did and he found it a baffling mystery and a wondrous thing and he just loved to create an environment where he could take people who did that and give them the freedom to do that in their own inimitable way.

Thank goodness that's the way he worked because that really was the beginning of my validation in Hollywood terms. He validated me because I was chosen by Robert Altman. That gave me a credibility in the community that I could not have gotten any other way, a particular kind of credibility.

When I first got there, they had a big trailer set up, a makeup trailer, and Bob came over to me and he said, "Come on, let's go in here." He put me in the makeup trailer, he sat me down and he said, "Cut his hair off." He saw my look in the mirror, you know? And he said, "Kid, if that's where your ego is, it's in the wrong place." I've never forgotten that.

*   *   *

René Auberjonois: I learned a big lesson there about Bob and why you should never read a script of a film that Bob is about to direct. It's a waste of time and it's counterproductive to you as an actor. In the script, my character, the bar owner, Sheehan, was supposed to come upon Warren Beatty's McCabe and find him wounded and finish him off. I remember Bob taking me aside and saying, "We're not going to do that." That was deep into the film. I was deeply disappointed because I thought that completed the arc of the character. I was heartbroken, but that was stupid. I think it's his best film.

Joan Tewkesbury: Ideas were discussed with Julie or with Warren and they would go off on drives or would come over for dinner. Everybody would come over for dinner. And members of the chorus—who were really members of the repertory company—they would be included. Half of Bob's work was always done over dinners or, in quotes, parties or those kinds of preparatory things, where everybody would get to meet one another or talk to each other. As those relationships would form they would inform the story they would tell. Julie had one of her friends there, and she and Julie were rewriting dialogue for Julie. There would be Saturdays where I would go to the house and Bob would dictate scenes, and that would be the work we were gonna do the next day or the following Monday. Then Warren would bring in his stuff and then there would be times when Bob and Warren would come together and do stuff.

MICHAEL MURPHY: When you weren't in his movies it was upsetting because you knew there were a lot of people out there having a hell of a good time and you weren't. That was the big draw. In the usual manner, I get a call from Bob one day.

"Murphy, you want to be in this film, this movie?"

And I said, "Yeah."

He says, "Okay, I need my car up here. I'll give you six hundred fifty a week."

So I drove his car up to Vancouver from L.A. It was a nice trip, too, up that coast. I went up to work on *McCabe & Mrs. Miller* for a few days and I stayed for months just hanging around. He cast me as this young guy who comes into town with the older man, a partner in the business, to offer McCabe money. We want to buy him out. We represent the industrialists, the movers and shakers. We offer him, I don't know, fifteen hundred dollars or something and he passes. He's bluffing. He wants more money, and so then we send in the killers, to wipe him out. We were just talking one night and I said to Bob, "What do you think about this guy?"

He said, "He's somebody's nephew" [*laughs*]. That was all the direction he gave me. It was perfect. I knew exactly what he was talking about. You know, send the kid on this job, see how he does dealing with this rube out in the middle of nowhere.

JULIE CHRISTIE (actress): He gives you a little clue—like when I had to say a whole lot of stuff about numbers and money. I couldn't remember it because I'm innumerate. He made me look for something I'd lost on the ground. He solves his problems with actors quite practically, very often with physical stuff.

ROBERT ALTMAN: I sent to Warner Brothers for wardrobe. I told them to send up a truckload of clothes and things for a Western for that period. I told the actors, "Okay, everybody, go to the wardrobe truck

Speaking with Julie Christie, as Mrs. Miller

and pick out your clothes. You can have one pair of pants, you can have two coats of different weight—one that you can put over the other. You can have one shirt, a pair of boots, a pair of pants." Of course the smart ones picked out the most distressed stuff, the clothes that had the most character. And then I said, "Now, you've got to live in these clothes in this fucking weather, so you'd better get out there and sew those holes up." So they all went out and repaired their own clothing. And they picked out little artifacts that made their characters more real. I said, "These are yours. And you can't have anything else in the picture, and you can't get rid of these. You have to take care of this stuff." So the cast and the wardrobe were terrific because there was a reality to it.

The set designer, Leon Ericksen, was a genius. He was a big, big influence on me in terms of how to approach that kind of reality. Just to walk on the set and have there be trash in the trash can. He'd have stuff in the drawers, whether or not those drawers were going to be opened. There was a museum quality to it. He was the purest of all the people that I worked with, other than occasionally actors. He taught me how to deal with artifice, with sets. I was doing these films inside this reality that Leon created. In *McCabe*, we shot the film in sequence as the town was built. All of the carpenters, all the workmen, lived there. They actually lived in the place and they were all hippies. They were all Leon's friends.

JOHN SCHUCK: You walked through these two wooden gate doors and you were back in the 1800s. There was no question about it. We got behind schedule in building the town—it grew as the movie went along—because the guys were throwing away their power tools and wanted to do everything by hand.

KEITH CARRADINE: The sets for that movie in West Vancouver were up above a housing development. It was right around the corner from where the newly built houses stopped and the road sort of turned to the left and there was a little gatehouse and there was all this parking out there. You left your car, you walked through this gate, and about twenty or thirty feet after you walked through the gate, you went around the bend and it was 1901. It was absolutely magical.

He had all these carpenters and craftspeople and artisans from Vancouver that came up to work on the set and build the place, and they were invited to stay. All you had to do was put on period clothing and you could hang out here and keep working on the building you're building and that's how he had this incredible atmosphere of a town sort of rising out of the mud. It was a living place. People would spend the night there. They would sleep in their tents or their tepees.

MICHAEL MURPHY: So then the actors come to town and they wanted to live in it, too. René wants to live in a saloon. The crew guys are like, "Goddamn actors." They had to go find another place to live. The actors would live in the place two nights and decide they don't want to do that anymore, they want to go back to the Hilton [*laughs*]. Then you'd go to work. You'd shoot and the next day you'd go to work and the whole town would be framed. Every time you'd come to work the set looked different—fifty new townspeople had moved in. I don't think there are a whole hell of a lot of guys that could shoot a picture that quickly and keep that working as well as Bob did. When you have those big changes on a location, it really freaks people out. The reason he could move the way he did was he always had the picture cut in his head.

*   *   *

VILMOS ZSIGMOND (cinematographer): That was the luck of my life, actually, to do *McCabe & Mrs. Miller.* I was shooting in Santa Fe, and he calls me up and says he had this movie, it's an old Western. He described it in images, very old, like antique photographs and faded-out pictures, not much color.

ROBERT ALTMAN: I had seen something. I think it's in my dreams. Or I'd seen a Western in which the way the buildings were built or the way the people walked looked real. And I don't know when I saw it, or where I saw it, or even *if* I saw it. But I had that look in my mind.

VILMOS ZSIGMOND: I said, "Bob, I have the right thing to do. I just read an article about it and I will make tests about flashing the film." He said, "How is that done?" I described flashing the film and what does that do to the film. It makes it sort of grayish, very grainy, especially if you underexpose it and push the film, and you are going to get this old look that way. He said, "Yeah, that's fine, that's great. We are going to do that."

He made the test before I even got to Vancouver. I described what to do, and then he actually hired the standby, and told him how to flash five percent, ten percent, fifteen percent on the test. That's how we decided fifteen percent of flashing would be just perfect for the movie. But he loved this whole process.

The studio hated it. It was Warner Brothers. Some executives said, "This guy doesn't know how to expose film! Everything is underexposed, it's grainy, we have to reshoot everything!" And Bob said, "No, no, no, understand something. We have a new lab here in Vancouver. They don't know what they are doing. The film is going to get to Hollywood, it's going to be great. You'll love it." So they left us alone. He was conning them. He didn't want interference from anybody. Any studio executive, he could not stand them to come on the set and watch what he was doing because he would not let that happen. So this way we basically escaped letting the studio correct us and go back and reshoot things to make it look like all those movies in those days with Technicolor, saturated colors. We loved so much the way it looked, but the studio hated it. They didn't want anything new.

I don't think we ever really had a real argument. I loved him so much. I listened to him and I learned a lot from him. I learned how to use the zoom, because he really used the zoom way before anybody else was using the zoom—the way he used it in *McCabe*, for example.

Because he loved to dolly and zoom at the same time he could actually create live, dramatic moves. I mean that was the whole idea. He showed me a couple of times, the very first week I was there to learn what he wanted. After the week was over, he let me do it. He realized that I learned what he wanted—to tell me what it should look like as far as composition goes, as far as the camera moves go, and then from that point he hardly ever even looked into the camera.

Afterwards I used the zoom lens all the time because it's convenient, it's fast, you get everything that you want. Yes, it's not as sharp as regular lenses, but who wants sharpness anyhow? I was always on the soft side of things. I liked it not as brutally sharp as many cinematographers do.

* * *

ALAN RUDOLPH (director): Bob wants everybody to come to dailies for the collective energy, the collective thrill. But it's more than that. He wanted a democratic sense where everybody was rooting for everybody else, where you didn't bring your ego to dailies. If you're sitting there and you watch some minor character doing something—'cause Bob's camera would find that person doing something kind of clever—even if you were the big star you'd support it, you'd love it because you knew it was going to be part of the fabric. There was this camaraderie, this spirit, so that nobody felt more important than anybody else. He really wanted it to be a team rooting for each other instead of about me and mine.

VILMOS ZSIGMOND: He always liked to have a lot of people see dailies. Sometimes he had forty people. Everyone from the actors to the crew to the extras. And their children. Dogs, cats, roaming around in the screening room. It was like a happening every night. And we had drinks, you know. Some people were smoking. Bob was into Scotch and everything. Those were really, really glorious days. It was the end of the sixties, basically.

KEITH CARRADINE: He expected you to be there. That was a part of the communal experience of filmmaking as far as he was concerned. You'd show up on the set and you do your work and also you come and you watch everyone else's work. They're going to watch your work and you're going to watch their work and we're all going to watch each other's work and it's all going to be great. Julie didn't go. She didn't like to look at herself. Somehow she got away with that. I know there are people who would not go to dailies because they just—they were afraid it would affect how they approached their work, and Bob would grudgingly accept that, but he didn't really buy it.

JULIE CHRISTIE: I don't like parties, for a start, especially when everybody is more or less congratulating themselves. These are congratulatory parties. I can't bear watching me do things all wrong. I can't bear it. He's someone whose approval everybody sought. I think he made it clear when his approval wasn't wholly there. I think I could have sucked up to him more by being at the rushes. But I just hate them, so there's no point in doing that.

* * *

JULES FEIFFER (writer and cartoonist): Within a few miles of each other, these two marvelous films were being shot at the same time—*McCabe & Mrs. Miller* and *Carnal Knowledge*. As different styles as possible, because Mike Nichols organizes everything and knows everything that's going to happen and plans it all; that's the way he thinks and that's the way he works. Altman works in a pigpen.

Altman loved parties and he loved to party. He invited me to a party one weekend and I invited everybody from the company. Jack Nicholson and Artie Garfunkel were the only two that wanted to come along. We stood outside the party and I still remember Jack looking at Warren Beatty and saying, "He's the right height for a movie star." He said, "I'm too short." And I introduced them.

* * *

RENÉ AUBERJONOIS: I couldn't believe when Bob said he was going to use Leonard Cohen for the score. I thought he would be using fiddle music and flute music. That was the genius of it. Now it's unimaginable that that wouldn't be part of that film.

LEONARD COHEN (singer and songwriter): The first time I heard from him I was recording a record in a studio in Nashville. I was living in Tennessee, a little town outside Franklin called Big East Fork. I had come into Nashville early one day and gone to a movie called *Brewster*

McCloud. It was a grand movie, as you know. There was a phone call. Somehow he tracked me down to the Columbia studios in Nashville.

He said, "This is Bob Altman. I'd like to use your songs in a movie I'm making."

I said, "Okay, that sounds good. Is there any movie you've done I might have seen?"

He said, "*M*A*S*H.*" I told him I hadn't seen it. But I heard it had done well. Then he said, "I also did a small movie that nobody saw— *Brewster McCloud.*"

I told him, "I just saw it this afternoon—I loved it. You can have anything you want."

I saw *McCabe* under very bad circumstances, and he warned me that the circumstances were bad. He invited me to a screening in New York and it was for some executives of a large studio. The atmosphere was

With Leonard Cohen, several years after Cohen's music
became the sound track for McCabe

tense and the projection was bad and the sound was very bad. And I didn't have a positive feeling about it. Then, later, I went to a theater and it was glorious. I phoned him—I felt that I had to rush to a phone to tell him.

*   *   *

RENÉ AUBERJONOIS: When *M*A*S*H* opened, Bob and I were walking down Eighth Avenue and he said, "Did you hear that?" He was talking about the people who were walking uptown as we were walking downtown. The conversations that we would hear pieces of—"and she needs a hysterectomy" . . . "his brother-in-law." He said, "That's the key to it. You don't need to hear everything people are saying to know the world they're living in." That's what he was always looking for, and that's what he did in *McCabe & Mrs. Miller*. That drove critics crazy. And now it's recognized as a breakthrough.

VILMOS ZSIGMOND: The sound track was very, very courageous because he deliberately made the sound so too many people are talking at the same time. I even questioned him myself. I said, "Robert, the sound mix, I can't understand what they're saying." He said, "But have you ever been in a bar where there's so much noise, so many people arguing, do you hear everything that they say three tables away? Well, that's what I try to do. That's exactly what I want to have, the feeling of reality. Not that clear, perfect, beautiful sound recorded on a soundstage."

He recorded on sixteen tracks. He needed the separation of the tracks, because in the mixing stage, he could actually bring one forward and leave the others in the back. So he would select which voice should be dominating and the other ones secondary. That was brilliant, and nobody else used the sixteen tracks in those days, only music recording did.

JOAN TEWKESBURY: Warren was used to clean, Hollywood sound, and Bob was encouraging a mess. And yes, there were drawbacks to that. But there was also Bob fighting—literally fighting—with the mixer to pull stuff out, and he couldn't do it. It was frustrating for him too, but I think probably more frustrating for Warren because he was used to a whole different kind of technology.

JULIE CHRISTIE: The sound? I thought that was how Robert liked it. I know that the sound is on top of other sound, all multilayered. It's not doing what films have done more or less, which is each person talking after another so the audience can hear every word. Robert was into creating more of a tapestry sound. It never mattered what anybody said. It gets the atmosphere. So when you're in a bar you really get it.

KEITH CARRADINE: Bob was developing his style, a sort of cinema verité approach to the way people actually talked to one another. People don't stop and listen, people talk over one another all the time. He mastered that technique and there is a heightened sense of reality you get when you see one of Bob's movies because of that. I think Warren was very, very mistrustful of what he was doing in that regard. He was afraid that no one would be able to hear, no one would be able to understand the movie.

* * *

JOAN TEWKESBURY: During *McCabe*, I remember Aljean Harmetz coming to do an article about Bob for *The New York Times*. We were in the car and Bob was railing on about something involving her. I can't remember exactly, but it wasn't very complimentary about her—and she was in the backseat! When he realized, Bob was like, "Oh shit." And she still was worshipful in that article.

KATHRYN REED ALTMAN: Joan's got that wrong. That wasn't Bob. That was Tommy Thompson. He was the one driving the car.

Aljean Harmetz, story headlined "The 15th Man Who Was Asked to Direct 'M*A*S*H' (and Did) Makes a Peculiar Western," *The New York Times*, **June 20, 1971:** It is 4:30 on a Friday afternoon in late December, and the Canadian darkness has fallen like a stone. Water pours down Robert Altman's Mephistophelean beard, and an incongruously thin string of love beads circles his massive neck. At 2 a.m. the preceding night he lurched to bed, a last glass of Scotch in one hand, a last joint of marijuana in the other. But the indulgences of the night have no claim over the day. He was the first man on the set in the winter darkness of 7 a.m. He will be the last man to leave in the slippery frozen twilight. . . .

In the few hours of daylight, he has completed 34 camera setups.

He is pleased with himself, and he does not try to hide it. Later tonight, swacked on Scotch, grass, red and white wine, he will announce, "I was so good today it was fabulous. I embarrassed myself."

At 46, Robert Altman is Hollywood's newest 26-year-old genius. The extra 20 years are simply the time he had to spend, chained and toothless, in the anterooms of power—waiting for Hollywood to catch up to him. While he was waiting, he made a million dollars as a television director and spent two million; fathered four children on three wives; gave up the last remnants of Catholicism for hedonism; and occasionally lost $2,000 in a single night in Las Vegas without losing half an hour's sleep over the money. Eighteen months ago, Hollywood caught up—with a vengeance.

* * *

DAVID FOSTER (producer): Warren and Bob started to work together about the character. Bob and Warren got along and then something went astray. Warren was very bright and is still a bright guy. We got him at a time when he was a writer, producer, director, star, marketing maven, and he wasn't going to do that in this picture. We had a director, and we had two producers, me and my partner, Mitch Brower. He wasn't going to do any of that. It was hard for him to accept. In his mind he was doing everything—he thinks that he directed himself. It's just a load of bullshit. I just don't know why a guy would say that. Even if it was true. Bob's great facility as a director is he would get the actors to do the things he wanted them to do, but they thought they came up with the idea themselves.

I was trying to be a peacemaker. Bob was so smart—whatever was going on he would never show it to Warren. With me he would say, "That son of a bitch, I'm the director." Bob *was* the director. Make no bones about that. The only actor he ever had a problem with was Warren Beatty.

RENÉ AUBERJONOIS: When Bob and Warren met he was really on the ascendancy. *M*A*S*H* had announced him as a major talent. Warren was at his peak as a major Hollywood star. It was like a meeting of two titans. Bob in his later films worked with a lot of celebrities. In the beginning he invented actors. His work with Warren Beatty was like a grain of sand making this pearl. There was a lot of tension there.

ALAN LADD, JR. (producer): He wouldn't take Warren Beatty's bull-shit. Warren wanted to discuss every scene—Warren wants to negotiate over everything. Bob just wanted to get on with it.

JOHN SCHUCK: My experience with Warren was he was a perfectionist all right, but he's such a subtle actor that there were lots of differences, you know? But I found him very, very easy. What I did sense overall was for some reason I don't think they trusted each other.

JOHNNIE PLANCO (agent): Julie was always best on the first take. It took Warren fifteen, twenty takes to warm up. Julie would get a little less fresh. One night at three a.m. Bob said, "That's it." Julie was wiped out. Warren kept saying, "One more, Bob, one more." Bob went over to Warren and said, "Look, Warren, I have to get up in three hours and

Julie Christie and Warren Beatty at the premiere of
McCabe & Mrs. Miller

I think we got the shot. But if you want, I'll leave the cinematographer here and you can keep shooting." Bob told me later, what Warren didn't know was that there was no film in the camera.

VILMOS ZSIGMOND: I know that Warren for some reason didn't like to work with Robert. Robert was probably too good, too strong, maybe, for him. He always thought about himself, Warren, that he's the director, he's a producer, he knows about everything. Maybe that was the conflict. I don't know.

Warren was happy because he was in love with Julie Christie in those days. But he was not happy about himself I think, because Julie was such a great actor. She did it the first time like this—perfect. And the second time was still good. The third time, she gets bored by the thing. She doesn't like to repeat. And Warren gets bored only after take ten. But he did a great job. I mean a fantastic job. With Robert's help, of course.

I remember once Warren went something like forty-five takes. He started in the morning. It's a long scene and he's in his room and he's talking to himself and he's going on for like seven minutes, without a cut, actually. And we shot it with two cameras, and we shot it and we printed I don't know how many times, but I know that we shot from eight o'clock in the morning until like ten o'clock at night. That one scene. Then after, I don't know, forty-five takes, Warren said, "Let's do one more." And Robert said, "No, Warren, I think we got it on take seven. And if not, definitely on take nine. I'm not going to do any more shots. If you want to do some more, go ahead, but I'm going home." Bob told people that Warren kept shooting? No, Warren actually got the message. He was ashamed, really. He wasn't going to do it without Robert. See, Robert's memories are, well . . .

But Julie was so great. My God, Julie was unbelievably beautiful and I was in love with her, but the terrible guy Warren was with her [laughs]. There's this one shot when Warren is coming into bed, and before he goes in the bed Julie points to the money. Warren gets up and Julie puts the cover up to her eyes, and you see those eyes laughing, smiling. It's such great acting, those eyes, you know? That's why I fell in love with her like that.

JULIE CHRISTIE: Warren liked to be perfect. I liked to get the hell on with it. It's all too painful—let's get out of here.

You had two very different types of ego working in a small area. I'm not going to go any further than that. To my mind it's Bob's best film. It needed the tightness that Warren brought to it and it needed the expansiveness that Robert brought to it.

I think he's a great director, a great, unique, adventurous, experimental, confrontational, provocative director.

JOAN TEWKESBURY: The thing that I watched that happened between them—which I thought was pretty good for both of them—was that Warren presented Bob with a kind of discipline and Bob presented Warren with a looseness and an ability to stretch or grow or have a sense of humor about some things that possibly Warren hadn't been able to have before. It was really kind of lovely to watch that unfold.

Shelley Duvall, to Patricia Bosworth, from *Show,* **April 1971:** How'd I like working with Warren Beatty? No comment. 'Cept he's difficult. "Pirate" and he didn't get along at all. It was terrible. Warren shouting and cussing. Julie was nice. Warm. "Pirate" told me once, "You'll make out OK in this business as long as you don't take yourself seriously. If you do—you're lost."

ROBERT ALTMAN: We shot the whole picture in sequence. . . . I remember calling for a coat—it got chilly out there—and I thought, "Jeez, what's the temperature?" And it was twenty-eight degrees and I just started seeing these snowflakes. I said, "Get the guys out here with the water hoses." And these guys were out in their black slick raincoats spraying that water. The next day we're up there and crystals were frozen on the trees, on the wagons, and it was just beautiful, fantastic, and it was just starting to snow softly. I ran to Warren's trailer and he was sitting there in his makeup chair and I said, "Warren, get ready—this is beautiful."

And he said, "We're not going to shoot today."

I said, "What are you talking about?"

He said, "Well, it's snowing." And he laughs and said, "What happens if it doesn't continue?"

I said, "We don't have anything else to shoot, so let's just do it." And it kept snowing and snowing and snowing.

VILMOS ZSIGMOND: This was the part at the very end when he decided to not flash the film. In the snow. Think about it—the whole movie basically is like a pipe dream, a fantasy, and now we are real, now

Directing on his knees in the snow during McCabe

McCabe is in danger. And that's what happened. It becomes very stark, not hazy anymore, not foggy. It's real.

JOAN TEWKESBURY: It made the movie. What would have been a gunfight, just another gunfight in the town of Presbyterian Church, became this event in the snow. They were like animals tracking each other, and it's fascinating to watch. This was when Bob was truly in his element the most, because he could just go out and make images. Warren's death in *McCabe*, you know, sitting in the snow and freezing to death, never would have happened if the snowstorm hadn't occurred.

*　　*　　*

MICHAEL MURPHY: Warren got mad because he thought the picture was too dark or something, and he yelled at Kathryn one night.

KATHRYN REED ALTMAN: When we had the premiere in Vancouver, Bob for some reason couldn't go back up for that. Mike Murphy accompanied me and it was important that the actors show, because it was a fund-raiser, it was a big deal that we'd been committed to. We were up in the balcony of this big old beautiful theater and it was completely sold out. The sound was not good and it hadn't been refined as I guess it was to some degree later. And Warren had been difficult, as his reputation had preceded him—with many, many takes and lots of controversy and wanted it done his way. The party was tented next door to the theater. The lights went up and we stood up in the balcony and were waiting to get out. I guess Julie had to be with Warren. Anyhow, they were coming down the stairs and I was coming out of the aisle and before he even got down to me he hollered and pointed his finger and waved it in my face when I got out. "You can tell your fucking husband . . ." Some very profane stuff, I can't give it to you exactly. But it was all about the sound. And it was all so hurtful and it was so loud and it was so embarrassing and it was so tasteless, it was so thoughtless. And he just considered himself such a bon vivant.

ROBERT ALTMAN: Warren was terrific in the film. He had an attitude about it that I liked, and I thought he was right for it. . . . I don't know why he and I didn't get along too well.

Robert Altman, to David Thompson, from *Altman on Altman*: I don't think Warren would be happy with *anybody's* methods. That's him. He wasn't happy with *McCabe*: he didn't like the way I mixed it, that you couldn't hear every word, with a lot of lights. It was scary for him, because he hadn't done that before and he wasn't used to it. Yet he was the one who sought me out for the film. He chased the picture; I didn't go after him to do it. He was great in *McCabe*—the film would not be what it is without him. . . . But he just isn't much fun to work with. He's kind of a control freak and he can't let go because he's a director, a producer, and was the last movie star of an era. The best thing he did was to bring Julie Christie in. These affairs of the heart help. Sometimes they're better than the film, you know—"I got to do the picture, but I had to use the girl." But this girl was better than *he* was.

DAVID FOSTER: I would say part of it was that Julie got nominated for an Academy Award and it drove Warren mad.

Dialogue from *McCabe & Mrs. Miller*:

JOHN MCCABE (*Played by Warren Beatty*): If a man is fool enough to get into business with a woman, she ain't going to think much of him.

KEITH CARRADINE: You look at that movie now, it's absolutely brilliant. I'd love to know if Warren can look at it now and go, "You know what? I was wrong." It would take a huge man to say it, but Warren's a big guy in many ways. He has room to admit that he was mistaken about that. I wonder if he will.

WARREN BEATTY (actor/producer/writer/director): Julie Christie and I were going to make *Shampoo* together, but we couldn't get to a script. So I sort of gave myself a deadline and said, "If we don't have a script by that date, Julie and I are going to do another movie." I was offered a movie called *McCabe*. I didn't know who Bob Altman was. I couldn't have chased the film. I talked to Stan Kamen, who said, "He's done a very good movie, *M*A*S*H*. You should go see it." I had come back from London that day and I went to see it in New York and I thought it was terrific. I thought he did a terrific job. I went to the hotel and said, "Say yes, we'll do the movie." With all due respect, Bob Altman didn't have the reputation at that point that he quite deservedly acquired. The picture was kind of me and Julie, on the basis of what we'd done. This thing that I chased the movie is quite an invention.

The movie came out of whatever Bob brought to it. It was extremely relaxed. Sometimes extreme relaxation can bite you in the tail. In the sound mix of the first two reels, it bit.

I attribute the whole making of the movie to the art direction with Leon Ericksen and the whole thing to Bob's approach to work. And what I have called his flexibility. He immediately saw in Julie Christie—who was totally enamored of him—that he had a great thing here. "Let's make her English and go with the Cockney rhyming slang." I always felt that one of Bob's greatest gifts, maybe his greatest gift, was that he knew talent when he saw it, and you can see it throughout his movies.

That's the fun part—having the freedom to be loosey-goosey—and so I felt a little bit required to be structural and conventional in the circumstance, which I didn't mind being. I felt it was very respectful of him to sort of defer to me in that area. And when I say defer to me, I mean welcome my contributions. Together we had a really constructive relationship. I felt he knew how to deal with me in the most constructive way possible, and out of the dialectic in a situation like that comes quite a bit of creativity.

I couldn't agree more about Leon Ericksen. It was a brilliant job on the part of Leon and Bob to have built that town the way it was and have it come to fruition the way it did. I think that Bob was an extremely talented man who was really gifted at seeing what actors brought to him. Same with a cinematographer in the case of Vilmos or the other cinematographers he worked with. I thought Bob's flexibility was wonderful. There were times when that flexibility, I felt, needed to be pinned down a little bit. I thought that the dynamic, the end result, was good. I thought it was very intelligently cast on his part.

I didn't control that movie. I participated actively. When they wanted to flash the film, they flashed the negative. I said, "Why flash the negative? You can never retrieve it. Why don't you do it in the printing?" They said they wanted to flash the negative—okay, do what you want to do. It seems strange to me. You want to get rid of information on the negative that you might someday want?

Why would I say something to Kathryn Altman, who is just the loveliest thing? Why would I do that? I'm a nice, polite boy, particularly with an innocent bystander.

That screening was not in Vancouver. It was in Los Angeles. And that's just not my style. I can't imagine saying that to Kathryn Altman. Why would I do that to Kathryn Altman? That just seems totally rude. It's just not possible, and had I done that Julie Christie would have hit me over the head with a hammer. It's just not possible. What I said was directly to Bob Altman.

It was at the end of the screening. I remember we were in a balcony and I said, "I can't hear"—I might have said "a fucking word"—"in the first or second reel." There were lines, particularly in the beginning, that needed to be clear so people will know what is going on. I didn't want to really hear the background dialogue over the foreground dialogue. I said, "Is there any way you can change it before it goes into theaters?" He said he didn't think so but he would check into it. I was very angry with Bob Altman and it's the only time that I ever did that with him.

It seemed it was an irretrievable situation and I thought it was—he was a relatively new director. I don't know that the picture's financing was dependent on me, but I was an established producer. It was careless. I don't think that he meant to do that. I think it simply slipped through the cracks. There's no question he would have remedied it if there had been time. I thought it was complacent to not show it to me or somebody else earlier than he showed it. And I probably overreacted because I was so fond of the picture and we had all worked very hard on the picture. In the long run when you mix the sound in a picture everything you've done for a lot of months is dependent on a couple of days.

If you have dialogue and people can't hear it, it makes people crazy. If you do that, then you have to let the audience off the hook—put music over it so they know they don't have to work on it. You couldn't understand the dialogue in the first two reels, and that's quite a bit of time, and that's certainly enough time for the audience to give up on the movie. It wasn't that you couldn't hear *every* word. I thought you couldn't hear *any* word. I don't want to denigrate the job that Bob did. I thought he did a wonderful job. But I thought that the mix was extremely unfortunate because people would quit on the movie after a reel or two or three.

I pretty much like everything else about the movie. I thought it was a brilliant choice on Bob's part to have Leonard Cohen's songs. Bob did all that. Bob was a very, very collaborative filmmaker. He was spectacularly collaborative. That's why I really enjoyed working with him. I thought he wanted to get the best—he wanted to get it up on the screen. He wanted the result to be as good as it could be. And I felt that truly Bob was asking me to be as active as I could. And I responded. I worked very hard on that movie. I worked at night on that movie.

I think it's a very, very good movie. John Huston once said to me he thought it was the best Western he had ever seen.

*   *   *

DAVID FOSTER: The picture's coming out. We're in New York at the Regency Hotel. Warren and Julie and Kathryn and Bob and my wife and I, we have a big screening at the Criterion Theater in Times Square—and the sound is a disaster. We reserved a table at the Russian Tea Room. Bob was beside himself. This is going to sound like a joke—he ran out into Fifty-seventh Street and said, "I'm going to get a cab and I'm going to JFK and I'm going home to Kansas City to see my mother."

I said, "C'mon, get back in here. We're having a party, for God-sakes."

I must confess, the sound was fucked up. I kept saying, "What did he say? What did he say?" But that's what Bob wanted.

ALAN RUDOLPH: When we were doing *California Split*, Bob said, "Listen, I've got a lot of phone calls from Warner Brothers. Warren Beatty wants them to remix, he thinks *McCabe* should be rereleased, and they want to remix it. I won't have anything to do with this but I'm going to send you to watch the movie with Warren Beatty and then report back."

So I sat in the Warner Brothers screening room with Warren Beatty, the first time I'd ever met him in my life, and that may be the last time, watching *McCabe & Mrs. Miller* with him. And he kept saying, "I don't understand that. I can't hear that. Can you?"

And I said, "That's what I like about it."

He said, "The footsteps are louder than the dialogue."

I said, "Yeah, but that's kind of good. I don't know if it's important to hear what they're saying." I was Bob's party line, you know, and Beatty was all frustrated with me.

I think Bob would never admit that he wished that the sound quality was better, but what he loved about it was it felt real. It certainly didn't detract from the heart and soul of that movie except it made it annoying for ears that weren't in tune to that.

*   *   *

MICHAEL MURPHY: Look at all his pictures, ninety-nine percent of them are American society, Americana, these subtle moments when everybody moves into McCabe's town and you see like six Indians leaving. It's all the human condition, I guess. But he was very much like that. Julie at the end of *McCabe* goes down and gets on the pipe, you know? I think you see it again and again. He always sort of finds that place to go.

KEITH CARRADINE: Why did Cowboy have to die on the bridge? Well, that was the core of the movie. The movie is really about loss of innocence and the savagery of the natural world, and I think it was a human reflection of the savagery of nature. I mean, wolves go out and kill because they're hungry. People kill for the same reason, it's just a different kind of hunger or fear. That moment where my character is an innocent victim of random and arbitrary violence, that was the denouement of the film, really, that's where the whole film turned.

VILMOS ZSIGMOND: It's an incredible movie. If you watch it today, it's as good today if not better than in the old days. If you really look at it politically, the message is there for all times. Capitalistic society, whoever is the power and buyer of things, is in control. The little people don't have much chance. McCabe tries to believe they do, to be a hero, but you know how it ends.

MARTIN SCORSESE: *McCabe* gave you a different point of view completely of what the American experience was at that time. It was, in other words, very different from the Westerns we had grown up viewing.

Here you have a movie coming into the American mainstream and the hero winds up dead, killed by a bully and a Western gangster, so to speak. And the heroine of the film, the last time you see her she's in an opium den and she's floating away. It's very moving. We'd never really seen the West that way.

DAVID FOSTER: Pauline Kael was so insistent on making people aware of this picture. She went on *The Dick Cavett Show*. He said, "Seen any good movies lately?" She went off for like ten minutes on network television. People were raving about it.

Peter Schjeldahl, essay headlined *"McCabe & Mrs. Miller:* **A Sneaky-Great Movie,"** *The New York Times,* **July 25, 1971:** To say that *McCabe &*

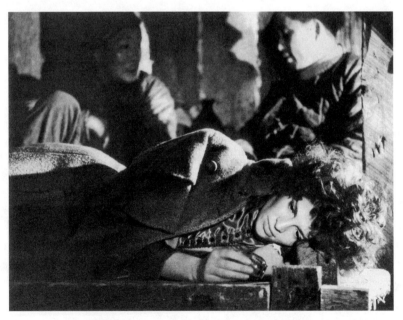

Julie Christie, as Mrs. Miller, in the opium den

Mrs. Miller is no ordinary Western is to put it very mildly. It is no ordinary movie. As a Western, it rather seems to have been made by someone, a sensitive and ambitious artist, who never saw a Western before, who had no idea how such a thing should be done and who thus had to put the genre together from scratch.

This can be confusing until you get the hang of it, which a lot of critics haven't. Only Pauline Kael in *The New Yorker,* of those I've read, has zeroed in on Altman's studied avoidance of convention and has identified it as a key to the film's wonderful, bemusing power. The result of this audacious strategy is a brilliant work of art about the American past, a work to which "a slightly dazed reaction is," as Miss Kael concludes, "the appropriate one." . . .

It is a film which seems to have, in addition to sound and image tracks, a kind of "feeling track," a continuous sequence of fugitive emotional tones that must be laid to the extraordinary sensibility of Altman, whose mind looms in his work like the Creator's in a sunset.

*   *   *

DAVID FOSTER: It didn't do much business. It was so disappointing.

Dialogue from *The Player:*

GRIFFIN MILL (*Played by Tim Robbins*): It lacked certain elements that we need to market a film successfully.
JUNE GUDMUNDSDOTTIR (*Played by Greta Scacchi*): What elements?
GRIFFIN MILL: Suspense, laughter, violence. Hope, heart, nudity, sex. Happy endings. Mainly happy endings.
JUNE GUDMUNDSDOTTIR: What about reality?

ROBERT ALTMAN: It was a very unsuccessful movie. The studio was wrong about the marketing when they put it out. The audience had to catch up. It was ahead of its time, as they say. Later it became what they call a cult film. To me, a cult means not enough people to make a minority.

CHAPTER 15

Fatherhood I

*

JOAN TEWKESBURY: He loved his family. Oh God, he loved them dearly. But to his core he was a filmmaker. One of the things that drew people to Bob was he was a big man physically, so everyone felt protected. He became the umbrella for everyone to stand underneath. Whether you were the cinematographer or the grip or the actor, for the most part everybody was invited to stand under the umbrella. That's a lot of responsibility. The job came first, so often the family was on the fringe of the umbrella.

MICHAEL ALTMAN (eldest son): I never questioned where his loyalties lay. He was his work, that's all there was to it. That's what defined him and that's who he was. That was going on back then and it went on until the day he passed away. That never changed.

As a child, to me he was just this kind of elusive enigma, this god, you know? I was as much in reverence of his work as he was. I didn't have any kind of feeling like, "Oh gee, I wish I had a dad that would take me to baseball games." I didn't want any of that shit. I had no regrets or remorse or feelings of inadequacy on his part or on my part at all. None. I mean it just wasn't there. I was totally accepting of him as who he was, glad to be around him when I could and fine when I wasn't. That probably summarizes it as best as I can recall.

I left when I was sixteen. I didn't reappear again until I was twenty or twenty-one. I had my first son when I was like nineteen, delivered him up in the mountains in the back of the truck in a snowstorm. I was doing the whole hippie thing and the alternative lifestyle and making moonshine and shit like that. I persisted and pursued it and Bob gave

Three generations of Altman men: from left, Matthew, Robert (Bobby),
Stephen, Michael, Bob, and B.C.

me a chance and I blew it and went away and I came back and he gave
me another chance and I blew it. I came back and all right, this time
I'm really going to do it right, and I blew it again. He was acting all
tough and everything like that. But he would eventually give in. It
wasn't just me—we kids were pretty embarrassing to have around.

I run a studio downtown. I have two screening rooms over there
that I maintain and I operate for them and I go into people's houses
and do it. It's a gravy job. It's a union job. I've got full benefits and I've
got a retirement and a pension and the whole thing. It's terrible. I'm a
machine operator. And the thing is, the money is so good that it pre-
vents me from doing other stuff.

STEPHEN ALTMAN (second son): It's very tough not having a father. I
missed having a dad. It was always good for me every time I hung
around him. You know, as kids you don't judge. Things are the way
they are and that's it. I didn't have any animosity, or "Why am I not
with you?" kind of thing. That's just the way it was.

We weren't his priority. His priority was himself and his job. At one point, I think I was around ten, though maybe I was a little older, he had everybody sit down in his Malibu mansion, the movie-star house, and told us all that if it ever came down to it and he had to choose between all of us and his work, he'd dump us in a second. We were like, "Oh, okay." And we went back to playing. But it was something I remember always. I understood where he was standing for the rest of our lives, and kind of treated it accordingly.

I don't know, maybe it was alcohol that made him say it. It's hard when you're young to know when people are drunk and belligerent and surly or hungover. Who knows?

Robert Altman, quoted by Aljean Harmetz in story headlined "The 15th Man Who Was Asked to Direct 'M*A*S*H' (and Did) Makes a Peculiar Western," *The New York Times*, June 20, 1971: "If they should ever say to me, 'You'll never see your sons again or your wife unless you get out of the business of making movies,' I'd say, 'Sorry, Michael, Bobby, Matthew, Kathryn. It will hurt me not to see you again. But good-bye.' "

STEPHEN ALTMAN: I ran away from home at sixteen and went up to be a hippie with Michael, who was a better hippie than me. It was up in Stanwood, Camano Island, up in Washington. There was a little plot of land, kind of a semi-mini commune, and we were all vegetarians and long-haired pot smokers and that kind of thing. I had to get a dentist appointment or something and finally my mom talked me into coming back down and getting that, and she suggested I go visit my dad. He said, "You want to work on my next picture?" And I was like, "Oh yeah, that's a good idea." Tired of living in a tepee and sleeping in a sleeping bag and eating granola.

I was a seventeen-year-old kid. I was into having fun. The crew was always a blast. It was a fun deal and I got a salary. Not very much, but I was working with my stepdad before that. He was a brick mason and basically I was making as much money with him in cash as I was starting with Bob. I think I made eight dollars a week more with Bob, a hundred twenty-eight dollars a week. And he would bill me out for a higher price. He did that all the way through my career with him, right up to *Fool for Love*. I was property master starting on *Quintet*. I'd make five hundred dollars a week and he would, through his company, pay me the five hundred and bill me out at two thousand and keep the rest.

That's how he made his money. Off us kids and whoever else was stupid enough to go along with it.

I'm sure he was hustling everybody. It wasn't a personal thing. It wasn't because I was his son that he was doing that. Whoever would let him get away with it, he would get. It still pisses me off. In fact, it maybe pisses me off more now because it's kind of an advantage taken. Then it was like, "Here's the deal, you want it?" Better than doing brick masonry. Or so I thought.

ROBERT REED ALTMAN (third son): My relationship with my dad? You know, he was working so much I don't really know. For me it was hard. My mom was always right there for me. I'd see my dad, he would come in and then they'd go out to dinner. So there wasn't a lot of time I spent with him.

Throughout most of this time he was so busy always working that I knew he was my father, and I had him as a father, but I think it was probably a bit of a problem for me. I remember one time my mom and dad got into some kind of a fight, and I was scared, in Mandeville Canyon, and I hid behind the bed in my room, afraid that he was going to come and yell at me. I would hear him getting mad about some producer, some deal, because when he drank, not that he was a bad guy or anything, but I remember getting scared about how powerful his anger would come out about things. "That motherfucking son of a bitch . . ." For me, to hear that as a little kid, that was scary.

Graduation came around grade twelve, and my dad called up and said, "Sorry I can't make it—we're about to start shooting *A Perfect Couple*. But happy graduation and I got you a present. I got you in the union." And I'm like, "What does that mean? I can work on your films legally now?"

I've always had to work harder to prove myself. Because when I was younger on a set, people were like, "Oh, we know how you got in, your dad got you in. You're just like all the rest of those producers' kids and blah, blah, blah." I got into a habit of not letting them know who I was, and just doing the work. Then they'd find out and go, "Holy shit, your dad is Robert Altman?" But by then I've already proved that I can do it. So I think I had to work harder than other people, learn faster and be better than other people.

My relationship with him was pretty amazing as far as working together. Even though we were father and son, when we worked together he wasn't my father during those periods, he was the director Robert Altman and I was working with him and for him. I got to spend all this time on a lot of his movies, and I got to learn how to be discreet and how to do things without causing much commotion, and I got to learn what he likes and what he was looking for. I got to a point with him when I was the operator where I became his eyes. I could really tell the way he wanted the camera to move. He wanted it to move the way it would move if the audience was running it depending on what they were seeing and what was happening while it was running. If something blew up and you felt like you needed to back away from it, I could back away from it. And if something intimate went on here and you really wanted to know what it is, I could just move in without hesitating, right into the eyes if I wanted to, and then snap back. That would freak anybody else out. If I were on another movie and I went with how I felt, I would be fired for that.

It's been a good path; it's been very interesting. I did eight years as a second assistant, ten years as a first assistant, and now I'm into like ten or eleven years as a camera operator. But a lot of that time I had a lot of problems with drugs, and now I've been sober for four and a half, almost five years. I really saw a lot of crazy shit and did a lot of crazy shit and really wasted a lot of time. But now I'm doing great.

MATTHEW ALTMAN (fourth son): I don't remember him telling us he'd choose his career over us. But his whole life was not about family, it was about his career, which is something I think he came to regret later on in life. We've got a very dysfunctional family. I think when he became sick in the last five years or so, and maybe even longer, and when I was in trouble with various things, he regretted not spending more time with us and not paying more attention to how we grew up. He didn't force us to do anything. He never made us go to college, so subsequently none of us did. I think he regretted that because now we're all in the same business, which was his business, and that's not easy.

For one thing, for all the money that we've made, none of us seems to be able to support ourselves. And we've all had our divorces and our squabbles between us, like everybody else's family. Bob never guided us or helped us or forced us to learn about money or learn about the stock market or buying houses on our own or any of that stuff. If we ever had a problem, we came to him and he would have a plan and he would fix it. And subsequently it wasn't to our collective best interest later in life. And we all had our substance-abuse problems and things of that sort, which haven't helped. But he was always there if we ever needed him, which was a kind of a crutch. I think he felt guilty, especially in the seventies, that he wasn't there when he was younger. It was all about his career.

We went on an eight-day fishing trip to Alaska. We took fly-fishing lessons in the valley someplace for a day or so or two days. He went and bought all this expensive Orvis fishing gear and waders and cold-weather gear. We flew from here to Anchorage. I was fourteen. We took a little pontoon plane to a lake, landed on the lake. He had organized this whole thing. He and I would sit out at night and talk. I don't remember anything we talked about. I think we smoked a little pot together. And you'd be tired and cold and it was really the best father-and-son thing that I can remember that he and I did together.

On the set of M*A*S*H *with daughter Christine, grandson Dana, and Michael Murphy*

I definitely got involved with smoking pot through them, I think. He had a box in Malibu Cove of pot, and I would go in and take some and smoke. I think I was about thirteen. And then my friends from Mississippi came, we all went to Hawaii and then we came back and I think I had a fort underneath the house and that's when my parents found out that I was smoking pot. They sat me down and said, "We know you're doing that and we don't think that's good for you, but as long as we know you're doing it under our roof, that's okay. But you're not doing it someplace else and being dangerous." Eventually I learned how to roll a really good joint for my dad.

Even if he wasn't there, he was always available. He wasn't there physically but he was always available. He never said no. I loved him very, very much.

CHRISTINE ALTMAN (daughter): I think I was like twelve or something and we took a ride to Las Vegas, and there was some other woman with us. We went and stayed at this hotel. I couldn't go into any of the casinos, so he taught me how to play backgammon. We were doing okay, and he would go out at night. We were only there three or four days, but by the time we left I could beat him at backgammon. While he was teaching me he'd pay me when I won. By the time it came to leaving we had to leave fast because he was broke. He lost all of his money. The only money we had for gas was the money I had won from him. He had to borrow the money from me to get us out of there. We lost the woman somewhere along the line.

KONNI CORRIERE (stepdaughter): It was like we were down on the ground where it's kind of mundane, and day to day, but I always envisioned Bob walking, being with us but six feet off the ground, so he was just up higher. He couldn't speak our language. He didn't know what we were up to. He had his own way of seeing things, his own way of relating, which was kind of limited, let's just be clear. He just hovered over the earth but he never came down to earth until he turned sixty.

SUSAN DAVIS (actress and cousin): He said to me, "I'm not a good father." That got to me. I think it was that he wasn't around all the time. He taught them a craft, and he supported them. I think maybe Bob expected everyone to have his courage and his sense of drive and it bothered him when they didn't. I remember him saying to me, "I can't even tell you which son was on the set," and they were partying that night or whatever, and something was said about the next morning. I

Flying a kite with son Matthew in Malibu in 1972

think Bob's concern was that they hadn't shown up on time. He said, "Listen, I can have as much as I want, because I'll be on that set at six in the morning. You won't." It was about the work ethic. If you asked a psychologist it would probably be something of maleness that he never dealt with within himself, so he couldn't pass it on or help the next male onto it.

CHAPTER 16

Mirrors

*

Images (1972)

Howard Thompson, review in *The New York Times*, October 9, 1972:
This clanging, pretentious, tricked-up exercise, shown last night at the
New York Film Festival, is almost a model of how not to dramatize the
plight of a schizoid. Then how do you? Simply, clearly, with some sort
of progressive story line minus a technical smoke screen. Above all,
don't let the camera have a nervous breakdown ahead of the heroine. . . . As played by Susannah York, our girl is also some sort of
writer, scribbling away furiously in a diary or journal that sounds like
Emily Brontë on pot. After a prologue, crammed with opening doors,
hallucinations and jangling telephones, Miss York and her spouse,
René Auberjonois, slip away to that country retreat, where a dead lover
starts reappearing (walking in and out of the film) and a lecherous
neighbor closes in. . . . As for why Robert Altman, the brilliant director of the comedy, "M*A*S*H," elected to write and direct this mish-
mash, that's his own business. It just doesn't work.

*   *   *

ROBERT ALTMAN: I wrote a poem once and it went, "I'm looking in a
mirror, I'm looking at myself in the mirror, and behind me is another
mirror, and I see myself looking into the mirror, seeing myself." Mirrors always interested me. That's an idea I used in *Images*, where the set
was filled with mirrors.

It all came from a frightening thing I imagined. You're sitting on

Hugh Millais and Susannah York in Images

the bed and you're talking to your wife, who's in the bathroom. And you're talking away and she comes out and it's an entirely different woman you are talking to. What do you do? Do you continue the conversation and think, "I'm wrong," or do you cover and think this is in your mind? Or do you throw her out of the house because she is a stranger? In writing it, I had the woman sitting on the bed and the guy comes out and it's a different guy, and that's the whole genesis of *Images.*

I didn't know I was doing anything about schizophrenia, yet I was pretty accurate in it. It was an instinctive kind of thing.

KATHRYN REED ALTMAN: People said, "Gee, I didn't know that you were interested in psychology," because of *Images.* And he never even thought it was a psychological thriller. He just made things happen that were of interest to him.

ROBERT DUVALL: These guys hate it when you turn them down. I turned him down on *Images.* I read the script and it wasn't right. He said, "Maybe you don't get it. Maybe you need your wife to explain it." Bullshit. I don't need my wife to explain it. I got it, I just didn't like it.

RENÉ AUBERJONOIS: I don't think people knew that it was a comedy. In a way he was doing a spoof on those kinds of movies. I wish more people knew how wonderfully weird that film was.

I remember when we were in Ireland and we were shooting the sequence when the character I was playing was dead at the bottom of the waterfall. It was the middle of December, freezing cold, and I was in a wet suit under my suit. I had to go down into this freezing water with this waterfall coming from way up high and try not to blink because I was supposed to be dead. It was a skeleton crew and I got stoned before I did it, and I never ever got stoned before I did work. I was driving back with Bob to the hotel and he said, "Were you stoned when we shot that?" I said, "You bet. Wouldn't you be?" He didn't say anything but I understood that was not cool. As much as he had a reputation for being able to drink anybody under the table or smoke anybody up the chimney, he did not bring that to work, and you did not bring that to work. That was not cool.

VILMOS ZSIGMOND: He loved the movie. I mean, schizophrenia in those days was never really presented as well as this. It was underappreciated. I don't know why. I mean, you cannot trust the audiences many, many times whether that one is a good film, or it is a bad film. And even in those days, our movies were successful, basically. I don't think that *Images* was unsuccessful. In those days, all movies made money. It cost nothing to make those movies, you know. Not even two million dollars. And then people went to the movie theater once a week at least, everybody. Not anymore.

BARBARA ALTMAN HODES: I walked out of that show and I looked at Bob. I said, "I don't believe you."

He says, "Honey, what are you talking about?"

"You know what I'm talking about. A man comes in and his wife, she's got a little mental problem, probably like me. Then you finally get into her head, right? And you're with her, you don't know what's real or not, but it's not normal." Correct me if I'm wrong. A man comes in and takes off his coat and his hat. He leaves his gloves on? He goes in the bedroom, gets undressed, and he's still got his damn gloves on? Is that normal? That is strange. And of course that makes me think, "Somebody with gloves, they're going to kill me, you know?" Bob knew that just drove me nuts. When anyone comes in, the first thing you take off is your gloves. I mean, come on.

HENRY GIBSON (actor): He would have been a lousy gift-wrapper. He didn't like tying strings. He loved to let strings dangle and let you wrap the package in your imagination. He invited his audiences to think, to participate, to explore. Oh my God, was there ever a film that you were more invited to explore than *Images*? And the actors were exploring till the last day of shooting.

ROBERT ALTMAN: *Images* I thought was perfect. I said, "Oh boy, this is it. Everybody in the world is going to see this." Nobody did.

*　*　*

The Long Goodbye *(1973)*

Gene Siskel, review in *The Chicago Tribune*, March 27, 1973: "The Long Goodbye" borders dangerously on being totally mystifying, much in the manner of "The Big Sleep." One of Marlowe's best friends is hunted on a murder rap. Marlowe's pursuit of the truth involves him with the wife, a robust yet half-crazed writer, and a positively ugly loan shark who delights in cruelty. . . . Elliott Gould, now recovered from his own psychological problems, plays the Marlowe character with surprising finesse and reserve. . . . All of these elements—the acting, the threat of violence, and the photography—make "The Long Goodbye," despite its convoluted and too quickly resolved plot, a most satisfying motion picture.

ELLIOTT KASTNER (producer): It was my project and I wanted Robert Mitchum as Philip Marlowe. My partners at the time were United Artists. David Picker was the head of United Artists, and he didn't want Mitchum. I then said I would like Walter Matthau or Elliott Gould. I met with Walter Matthau at a delicatessen in Santa Monica after he read the screenplay. He didn't want to do it because he was frightened, actually. He fancied himself a leading man but didn't want to step up and be one. From Mitchum to Matthau it went to Gould. I loved the idea because he had a kind of dandruff on his shoulders, if you know what I mean.

　　Then we went to Altman. He wasn't in demand at the time. He had made an unpleasant relationship with himself and the major studios. *McCabe & Mrs. Miller* was a financial failure. The vicissitudes of the industry would come into play. He was a tough sell, but to David Picker's credit he went with him, and it was brilliant.

DAVID PICKER (studio executive): I could have gone with a bigger name at the time than Altman, but the director I wanted to do it at the time—Peter Bogdanovich—wouldn't do it with Elliott Gould and I was committed to Elliott.

ELLIOTT GOULD: I'm unemployed. I don't even know that I'm out of the business, out of this world, and I went to see this fellow who was quite nice to me, who seemed to get it: David Picker. David was running United Artists and he gave me Leigh Brackett's script of *The Long Goodbye*. I thought it was quite old-fashioned, but I was charmed by it, and something I would have loved to have done. Picker told me that Bogdanovich said that I was too new and he wanted to go with someone like Robert Mitchum or Lee Marvin. I love Robert Mitchum and I love Lee Marvin, and I couldn't argue with them. But you've seen them and you haven't seen me.

Then out of the blue, Bogdanovich wasn't doing the picture and Robert Altman was going to do the picture. Bob called me—he was doing *Images* in Ireland—and he said, "What do you think?" Now I'm getting moved, you know, because it's bringing up this stuff. I remember exactly where I was, in this kitchen of this place where I lived in the West Village, at 58 Morton Street.

And I said to Bob, "I've always wanted to play this guy."

Bob said, "You *are* this guy."

So that was the beginning.

ELLIOTT KASTNER: I didn't agree with some of Altman's perverse casting decisions. I didn't agree with the baseball player, Jim Bouton.

JIM BOUTON (professional baseball player/author/actor): I had met Elliott Gould at an antiwar rally in New York. His hobby at the time was playing pickup basketball. He wanted to know if I wanted to join his group for a couple of games. I did and we had a good time. We were friendly and he said, "I'm going to California for a couple of weeks shooting scenes for a movie. When I get back I'll give you a call."

A week later, at three o'clock in the morning, the phone rings—it scares the crap out of you when the phone rings at that time. It's Elliott. "I'm here in California and we're on the phone with Bob Altman. Stacy Keach got sick and can't play this role. I told Bob you'd be perfect—it's a guy who kills his wife and runs to Mexico. So throw a toothbrush in a bag and come out here." It's like the Yankees reaching up in the stands to some guy and saying, "We're putting you at third base today."

I flew out there and they gave me a script. Altman said, "Don't worry about the script. The situation is that you and Marlowe are old friends. You haven't seen him in a while. Talk about whatever guys talk about—but at some point in the conversation you have to tell him you need a ride to the border. I don't care what you guys do, what you say, you just have to ask him for a ride to Mexico."

Just before the first scene I'm in—I'm in costume, in makeup—Elliott comes over to me and says, "Did you get the changes?" It gave me a jolt. "Huh? Changes? What changes?" It was a nice rookie trick. He just laughed and said, "Don't worry about it."

Altman always seemed to be smiling. He was always in good spirits, a funny guy, and looking around for stuff that was going on, stuff he could use. When we were down at Cuernavaca, shooting the final scene, there was a funeral coming by. "Sign those people up!" He commandeered the band—he took whatever was going on. And those two dogs that were fucking, that was unbelievable. You'd have to shoot a hundred and fifty miles of film to get that if you tried. He was like, "Cue the dogs!"

My character was faking his murder, so they needed a shot of me lying in a box of ice, naked. Altman says, "You need to come down here and take your clothes off—it'll be discreet. Just a few of us." I can handle that. Two days later we had a wrap party and there were drinks and there were coasters all around. Guess what was printed on the coasters? Pictures of me, naked in the ice.

ELLIOTT KASTNER: I don't think I was wrong about Jim Bouton. A lovely guy, but I thought he was a stiff as an actor.

JIM BOUTON: Pauline Kael gave me a nice review. I cut it out and put it in my scrapbook.

ELLIOTT KASTNER: I didn't agree with Nina Van Pallandt.

ROBERT ALTMAN: I saw Nina Van Pallandt on the Johnny Carson show. She'd been mixed up with Clifford Irving, who did the fake biography of Howard Hughes. I said, "God, that's Chandler's blonde. That's what he had in mind when he said, 'Let there be blondes.' "

ELLIOTT KASTNER: I was wrong about the girl because she was marvelous. And I didn't agree with Henry Gibson as the quack psychiatrist. But I was wrong about Henry Gibson.

HENRY GIBSON: Well, casting me had to be somehow intuitive on his part or for his own amusement. I walked in to shake his hand. He said,

*Nina Van Pallandt and Elliott Gould during the
filming of* The Long Goodbye

"Would you be in my next picture?" We didn't read, we didn't talk, so it had to be something intuitive. He'd known some of my work but I didn't have a great body of work. There was *Laugh-In*, of course. He didn't know any of my personal history. "Would you be in my next picture?" Well, of course, you're ready to go to hell for him at that point.

ELLIOTT KASTNER: Mark Rydell surprised me. He worked, too.

MARK RYDELL (actor and director): Before *The Long Goodbye*, I found myself in London at a command performance for the queen for the picture *The Cowboys*. I ran into Bob in a gambling place, and he looked at me and said, "Let's have dinner." So Kathryn and Bob and I wound up drinking wine and smoking until we were dopey and went to a restaurant. In the restaurant he did the old movie joke [*snaps his fingers, then points his index finger*], he went like that to me, "Marty Augustine." He told me he wanted me to play the villain in his next movie.

Bob sent me the script. I looked at it and thought, "This part is just not well written." So I called him and I said, "Bob, what would you think if I rewrote this part and made it two hundred percent better? I have a concept for a character." He said, "Go ahead." The character in the book was wishy-washy, really, had no character. I was sharing a house at the beach with Larry Tucker, who is now deceased. Larry Tucker and Paul Mazursky were partners in those days. They did *Bob & Carol & Ted & Alice*, so on and so forth. So Larry Tucker and I decided to make him this Jewish gangster who was insanely brutal, completely capable of any kind of brutality, yet at the same time deeply religious, offended that he wasn't in shul, where he should have been on this night. At the same time, the challenge was to make it funny. Make it not only cruel and horrendous, but charming and funny. So we did that. And we sent the pages to Bob. He called back in five minutes and said, "That's it. Throw out everything else, I'm inserting your pages right in the script." That's the kind of guy he was. All he wanted was the best from his people.

One of the first things he used to say on a set was, "I'm interested in everything you have to bring." So he had that remarkably paternal and constructive quality of nurturing people and giving them permission to be as good as they can be. He rarely directed them in obvious ways. His ways were more subtle. He would encourage you. "What've you got in mind?" he would say. "Show me. That's great, let's use it."

His directorial style was improvisational and permissive. And actors loved him because of it. Because they could bring their skills and their instincts, which he admired and respected, to the moment. If it came from you, he was interested. He didn't want to give you something and have you execute it because he knew that anything he gives you is by nature less good than what you come up with yourself. He instinctively knew that the way to get relaxed and realistic performances was to encourage the creative spirit of each individual actor, and he cast that way. He cast in an effort to find people who are inventive.

Sterling Hayden, who played Roger Wade, used to smoke hash all day long. I mean powerful hash—puffing big, billowing hash clouds. I said to him, "Sterling, how can you smoke so much hash and work?"

He says, "It keeps me from being a drunk." He was a drunk before, now he was a hash addict. He was a wonderful guy who suffered with the guilt of having testified in the House Un-American Activities Committee, and he never got over it. He was ashamed of himself, you know? For having protected his career by testifying. So he was a tragic figure and Bob knew that. Bob used him that way, Bob used that element. He's a tragic figure in that picture. A writer who's a drunk and who's lost, and he embodied that. It was perfect casting.

ROBERT ALTMAN: Elliott Gould and Mark Rydell were at my house in Malibu, and we went to a place to have dinner on the beach. We were constructing that scene when Mark's character, Marty Augustine, hits the girl with the Coke bottle across the face.

MARK RYDELL: We were served by this very beautiful girl, Jo Ann Brody. And Bob kept looking at her face, at her nose—she had such a patrician, elegant face. He said, "She would make a very good girl-friend for you to hit."

I said, "Let's see if she's an actress."

So he engaged her in a conversation. "Are you an actress?" No, she had never done anything before. He said, "How would you like to play Mr. Rydell's girlfriend in this picture?"

ROBERT ALTMAN: She said, "Oh, you guys are kidding." Then when it came time to pay the check, nobody had a penny. We had been at the beach. She said, "You guys come in here and talk about giving me a part in a movie, and you say you've got no money to pay the check! C'mon."

MARK RYDELL: One of his major skills was instilling confidence. He said, "You'd be really fine, and Mark will help you and I'll help you." Bob has an eye for that, finding just the right person for the right part and particularly in a part like that where no major acting demands are made. You just need a certain look and an innocence and a kind of, what? She was like a slave. A sexual slave.

And when we told Jo Ann I was going to have to hit her with the Coke bottle, she was terrified. I said, "We're not going to hit you. It's just going to look like we hit you." But she was absolutely terrified. We set that scene up with a big heavy plate glass that was in front of her, and she never knew when I was going to do it. I kept talking about how sweet she is, how beautiful. "See her face, what a gorgeous face."

Whack! It was such a shocking moment that people literally screamed in the theater.

Dialogue from *The Long Goodbye*:

(Gangster Marty Augustine has just smashed a Coke bottle across the face of his girlfriend, to make a point to Philip Marlowe, played by Elliott Gould.)

MARTY AUGUSTINE (*Played by Mark Rydell*): Her, I love. You, I don't even like.

MARK RYDELL: I walk on the street nowadays and people will quote that line to me. The picture was done, what, twenty-five years ago? Thirty?

Jo Ann was so sweet, you know, sitting in the car when we arrive to harass Elliott Gould, and I said, "Turn on the radio. Sit here. Play the radio." It of course gave us an opportunity to play that song by John Williams, "It's a Long Goodbye." I thought that was another brave idea. To make that song the whole score. A million different ways it was played, including with a Mexican funeral band. Doorbells, Muzak, everywhere. I love that idea. See, Bob was always brave. He was audacious. He had a unique, creative spirit that was willing to go anywhere.

JOHN WILLIAMS: The music was a terrific idea—entirely Bob's. He said, "Wouldn't it be great if there was one song, this omnipresent piece, played in all these different ways?" We would go into a dentist's office or an elevator and there would be this ubiquitous and irritating music playing. It was threaded through, kind of like an unconscious wallpapering technique. I think it's completely unique. I don't think anyone has tried it quite the same way before or since.

PAUL THOMAS ANDERSON (director): Bob loved his music, didn't he? My God, he loved his music. And he used it so well, as good as anybody. So naturally. Never wrong. I don't remember any of his movies where the music was wrong. I mean, there might be a thing or two missing in his films, you know, or something that he missed, that he didn't care about. But the music was always good. The best example is the Leonard Cohen songs in *McCabe*. But think of *The Long Goodbye*. People say, "We're going to use one song as the theme and we're going

Robert Altman with Elliott Gould and Mark Rydell on the set of
The Long Goodbye

to play it in all different versions." Well, it's been done. Who did it? Bob.

I showed him *Punch-Drunk Love* here at my house. There were two chairs, and he was sitting in one and I was sitting in the other. I was just waiting for "He Needs Me"—the song Olive sings in *Popeye*—which I used in my film. I didn't tell him it was in the film, you know? And right when the music starts [*laughs*], he started conducting [*waves his arms*]. By the end of it he's applauding—"Yay!" He and Kathryn came over that night with their granddaughter, Signe. God, we got so drunk afterwards. Such a great time.

JOHN WILLIAMS: I drifted away from working with him, not through any intentional decision or conscious decision. After *Images* and *The Long Goodbye*, I got busy with other directors and other projects. Bob chided me about going Hollywood and getting successful. He would chide me or tease me or censure me about pursuing overly commercial projects, probably my work with Spielberg. He saw that artistically as a kind of betrayal of some kind of bohemian artistic principles he clung to.

One of the big contradictions was that he was always fighting with the studios but he sought acceptance. He sought praise of the establishment in his own way as hard or harder than other people did. He craved the approval of the people out here. His bad-boy-naughtiness character not to the contrary. He didn't want to play the game as he saw it being played. Maybe that has connections to his gambler roots.

*   *   *

ROBERT ALTMAN: David Arkin came and said, "I've got this friend, Arnold Strong. He's a weight lifter. He looks great. Can he be one of the hoods in this thing?" And I said, "Sure, bring him along." It was Schwarzenegger.

MARK RYDELL: The governor was my flunky. So Arnold was sitting in the chair when Jo Ann makes her entrance with braces on her face and the brutally broken jaw. I walked her over to Arnold and I said, "Get up! Get up! Give the lady her chair!" It was a terrific moment because it frightened him. Bob threw his head back and laughed. Everybody wanted to please Bob, you know?

ROBERT ALTMAN: Jo Ann was not an actress. She was about at the same level as that person she played with in that scene—Arnold Schwarzenegger. Neither of them had any acting talent.

GRAEME CLIFFORD (director): Arnold was so interested in movies and never stopped asking questions. Even though you couldn't understand his question, and he probably couldn't understand the answer, he never stopped asking. He was completely captivated with the medium and kept saying, "This is what I'm going to do." If you told me on *The Long Goodbye* that he was going to be one of the biggest movie stars in the world and the governor of California, I would have told you, "Fuck off."

VILMOS ZSIGMOND: You know the scene with Mark Rydell and Schwarzenegger? Amazing story. We are shooting that scene when everybody takes their clothes off. And the studio the next morning, they say, "Robert, we don't like that scene, you have to reshoot it." And Robert is pissed off. He just takes off from the set. And he tells the actors, if anyone is looking for him, he's not there, he's not shooting today. He sent the message, "Let me know when you start liking the dailies, and I will be back." A whole day we didn't shoot. The whole crew was waiting there for something to happen. Nothing happened. And now the studio got really, really scared. Tried to find him, they could not find him all day. They were sending messages. "Okay, Robert, you won, come back." He came back the next day and we didn't reshoot that scene. See, he had balls and he knew how to handle something. He knew what was right, what was wrong, and he didn't want anybody to interfere.

*   *   *

ROBERT REED ALTMAN: On *Long Goodbye* the camera never stopped moving. The minute the dolly stopped the camera started zooming. And the end of the zoom it would dolly and then it would zoom again, and it just kept moving. Why did he do it? Just to give the story a feeling, a mood, to keep the audience on an edge. He hated things being master, two shot, over, over, close-up, close-up—cut, cut, cut, cut, cut, cut. He wanted this to be more of an experience than a typical film.

VILMOS ZSIGMOND: On *Images*, when we wanted to have something strange going on, because the woman is crazy, we decided to do this thing—zooming and moving sideways. And zooming, and dollying sideways. Or zooming forward. What is missing? Up and down! So we had to be able to go up and down, dolly sideways, back and forth, and zoom in and out. Then we made *The Long Goodbye* and Robert said, "Remember that scene we shot in *Images*? Let's shoot this movie all that way."

And I said, "Robert, you are kidding? The people are going to get dizzy, people are not going to like it."

He said, "Don't worry about it."

I got the National Film Critics Award for that, which shows you how much I know about it, you know? I still don't think it was the right thing to do, but they don't think so much of what I say.

ROBERT ALTMAN: The zoom lens got me. I used a lot of zooms in those early pictures and got a lot of criticism for it. It was not uncommon when a film of mine would come out and a critic would say, "Altman, with his tiresome zoom lens . . ." But now I look at these films and television shows, and they're doing everything that way. If you shot in a conventional way, the "proper" way from 1975, it wouldn't be acceptable today.

VILMOS ZSIGMOND: We also flashed the film heavily, even more than we flashed it on *McCabe*. And the reason was basically because we didn't have a big budget there for big lights and all that. So we were really very creative about how, with the little amount of equipment what we had, how we are going to do the movie in a professional way. A couple things we invented on that movie—like flashing fifty percent, which is way over the top. But by doing that we didn't have to hardly use any lights when we go from outside or inside and go outside again. It's quite interesting, you know, to do something with less equipment and still being creative and good. Bob loved that idea—solve the problem in a creative way. He just wanted to keep everything very simple.

*   *   *

JOAN TEWKESBURY: Some people are extremely rigid about what they want to see when it comes to a film noir, what they want Marlowe to look like. In Bob's interpretation it just sort of unraveled. And it pissed people off.

HENRY GIBSON: Charles Champlin, the reviewer for the *L.A. Times*, destroyed the picture in Los Angeles. Oh, he was just so pedantically literal. He wanted a literary, visual translation of the novel as it was written, which you couldn't possibly do. And Leigh Brackett did the best she could in the script. Then Altman added all his touches. And it became something totally reinterpreted.

Charles Champlin, review headlined "A Private Eye's Honor Blackened," the *Los Angeles Times*, March 8, 1973: The problem is that [Altman, Brackett, and Gould's Marlowe] is an untidy, unshaven, semi-literate dimwit slob who could not locate a missing skyscraper and would be refused service at a hot dog stand. He is not Chandler's Marlowe, or mine, and I can't find him interesting, sympathetic or amusing, and I can't be sure who will.

ELLIOTT GOULD: There were people who were enraged that we would break the mold, that we would go against the grain, and for it not to be the traditional Philip Marlowe. But people came around. It became a bit of a historic film as to the evolution of the character. Bob and I had talked about the next picture. We thought we'd perhaps make a Raymond Chandler every other year or every third year, but we didn't.

ELLIOTT KASTNER: During *The Long Goodbye* we had a great relationship. I liked Bob so much I gave him another book. You know Tom McGuane's *92 in the Shade*? We had a major train wreck on that. It got physical. It lasted many years. I'll save that story for my own book, and nobody's got a better book than me. I have a very bad reputation in Hollywood, if you haven't heard that already.

ELAINE KAUFMAN (restaurateur): It was funny. It was back there [*she points to the rear of her eponymous restaurant*]. Long after the movie. Bob got mad at Elliott and threw a drink on him. But Elliott's used to that.

KATHRYN REED ALTMAN: We were on a plane coming back from London, and Elliott came into first class. Bob was reading the paper. He looked up, saw Elliott, and said, "I don't speak to scum." And he never spoke to him again.

DAVID PICKER: Altman? On a personal level I disliked him. He would pretty much do anything to put himself in the best light. I never trusted him. We disagreed on the way he handled certain things and for years we didn't talk. He is a complex man. You can get fifteen different reactions from fifteen different people. Obviously there are people who swore by him, and there are people who swore at him.

I found his conduct in relation to us at United Artists and toward me personally incomprehensible. He took credit for something that we did. We're talking about the entire way the picture was released. I liked that picture a lot and I didn't like the way our marketing people initially distributed it. I pulled it out of release and did a whole new marketing campaign, and Altman took credit for it. He didn't have the grace to give us credit for it, and I told him to go fuck himself.

At one point somewhat later in his career he wished me dead. He said it to a very close friend of mine—wishing me dead. I had a gallbladder operation. I was head of Paramount, and I said no to a project of his. He was a performer. He was his own invention. He probably really didn't mean it, but it wasn't something I took lightly. I don't have any standards for conduct other than you keep your word and you deal honestly and straight, and I felt Bob was only interested in Bob.

Sᴜᴇ Bᴀʀᴛᴏɴ (publicist): When he was shooting *The Long Goodbye* they had rented a house out at the Malibu Colony. The fellow who owned it was this real twit, and Bob couldn't stand him. This guy was petrified that someone was going to break into his house and rob him. So after the film wrapped, Bob kept the clicker for the garage door. Every time he drove by he would click-click and open the door [*laughs*].

*   *   *

Thieves Like Us *(1974)*

Kevin Thomas, review in the *Los Angeles Times*, April 4, 1974: The rural '30s gangster movie, with its equal parts nostalgia and social significance, has become so familiar in the seven years since "Bonnie and Clyde" that it's as if director Robert Altman in doing still another, "Thieves Like Us," had accepted a dare. The result, happily, is one of his most affecting films. . . . The people of "Thieves Like Us," based

Applying movie blood to Keith Carradine's face in Thieves Like Us

on an Edward Anderson novel, are not exactly winners. There's T-Dub (Bert Remsen), an irrepressibly self-deluding optimist, Chicamaw, (John Schuck), a heavy-drinking perpetual hangdog, and Bowie (Keith Carradine), a cleancut youth brighter than the older men but too young not to succumb to T-Dub's dreams. . . . They are as pathetic as they are dangerous, especially to themselves, and doomed without realizing it. They haven't got a chance, we know it; Altman knows it, but won't let us deny them their humanity.

* * *

JOAN TEWKESBURY: I met Bob when he was in his mid-forties, so he had already been in the Second World War, he was on his third marriage, he had more children than you can shake a stick at, he was always worried about having enough money, but he was living like a rich man. A guy who would take fifteen people to dinner and he would always be the guy who grabbed the check.

After we finished *McCabe* I wrote this screenplay. And Bob said, "Do you mind not starting at the top?" And I said, "I don't care." We couldn't get my movie financed and he had a book he needed to be adapted, *Thieves Like Us*. I read it and adapted it in about four days for him.

By this time I had been around Bob long enough. It's almost like when you find a really good dance partner—you know where the next step's going to go. It's not that you anticipate it, but you can relax enough to go with it. In the film I always thought that Bert Remsen's character was Bob, reading his reviews—the newspaper stories Bert would read about the bank robberies. You know, "Why'd they say that? They got that part wrong." It's interesting how the personal becomes part of the overall in those things.

The money fell out for the project about three times. It was really by the grace of George Litto and Bob and the other producer, Jerry Bick, standing in a room and practically mortgaging their houses and saying, "Let's go ahead." It was a really good lesson in terms of not backing down. When you're making movies, and even more so today than ever before, there comes a point where you either put it on the line and do it or simply walk away. I always think back on that moment and the three of them and what a brave thing it was to do.

In the last scene, when the police come in to kill Bowie, Bob wanted

With Shelley Duvall and Joan Tewkesbury in Cannes in 1974
for Thieves Like Us

more gunfire because of course we were living through all the assassinations. Bob wanted them to just kill, to kill the house with bullets. Overkill. Without asking any questions they just went in and shot the house until it fell down, literally. And then when Bowie was carried out, he was like another deer they shot while hunting.

JOHN SCHUCK: *Thieves* was a picture that was so non-mainstream that the studio had no idea how to promote it. They treated it like a bank-robbery movie, which it isn't, of course. And thank God for television and cable and all that. It's developed a sort of a cult following and it got extraordinary reviews. Pauline Kael just wrote a love poem to Bob and to us individually as actors, perhaps the nicest set of notices we've ever received. But it was released and went in a few weeks.

Buck Henry (writer and actor): I met Bob in Cannes. He and Kathryn said, "Come to a screening of *Thieves*." We went to the screening and he went nuts because people were still milling around and talking when the film started. He stood up and yelled, "Goddammit, you fucking people. Will you sit down!" Scared the hell out of them—and they did.

CHAPTER 17

Split, California

*

KATHRYN REED ALTMAN: Oh yeah, he knew how to manipulate women—except for me [*laughs*]. . . . Women were always drawn to him, and vice versa, I suppose.

*   *   *

JOAN TEWKESBURY: It was a tough time between Bob and Kathryn. They were going to get divorced and all this stuff was going on. This was while we were prepping for *Thieves*.

POLLY PLATT (art director and producer): I guess he saw *The Last Picture Show* and *Paper Moon,* and he wanted me to come work for him as an art director. At that time I had the highest respect for him. I adored *McCabe.* He invites me to New York to talk about working on *Thieves Like Us.*

The minute his wife went home he had the door open between our two rooms and wandered between our rooms and started talking about why I should sleep with him.

I did not sleep with him. I had already been married to a director, Peter Bogdanovich. So I didn't want any director in my life at all. I never slept with a director after Peter. They don't interest me. They're all alike—egotistical and used to having every word listened to. They're spoiled. The very nature of the job spoils you for personal relationships.

Then I didn't do the picture. I passed.

RENÉ AUBERJONOIS: It never seemed to me to be a big deal. In this business, on location, what happens in Vegas stays in Vegas. I've been

Robert and Kathryn Reed Altman

on so many locations and there's so-and-so leaving so-and-so's room, and these people are happily married to other people. Bob's just a guy, you know, with all the weaknesses of any guy on location.

ELAINE KAUFMAN: I'm not gonna go into this. Let the guys do that. It's a guy thing. Although I saw more than I wanted to, and they all looked like Kathryn. Shit. You know, those kinds of things go with the job. But Kathryn was always there.

LILY TOMLIN: I'm sure he was a womanizer in many ways. You can't judge anybody on one facet. People are too complicated. Maybe I was just more forgiving of things like that because of Bob and the way he was.

*　　*　　*

Konni Corriere: He told me that he loved how my mother sacrificed her whole life for him. He will always just adore her for giving up her life to make his happen, and to make him comfortable, and to take care of him the way she did.

Lauren Hutton (actress): Kathryn was half the team, for sure. I used to call her Kathryn the Great because she was like a queen. Queen Kathryn. She was incredibly gracious to everyone and knew everything that was going on. She had this weather eye and could see, you know, behind her head as well as from all sides. And could be blind when she had to be.

Mark Rydell: Kathryn Altman is one of the most magnificently loyal supporters of Bob. You know, Bob was a very, very quixotic fellow. She hung in. She was his supporter. She rode through all kinds of crises with him. She was the leveler. She was the loving one. She moderated his behavior, his excessive behavior. She was the perfect, beautiful, loyal, decent, intelligent, witty wife. And he knew that. I'll tell you that. He knew it, he hung on to her, despite many crises in their lives. She was the absolute cornerstone of his career. He could never have done what he did without Kathryn Altman. She deserves as much credit as a filmmaker as he does.

Jennifer Jason Leigh (actress): She's so effortlessly graceful and easygoing, and she can party with Bob till dawn and she's so loving. For so many women it's hard when the guy is the center. It can be hard on a marriage. With them it felt completely natural. I'm sure they had been through it, but they came out the other side in such a gorgeous way. She made it possible for him to be that free and trusting because he always had her.

Stephen Altman: I know he loved her. Some people have a personality about having to be in control or having to be in charge. I think she has the type of personality that didn't have to be those things. "Why aren't you taking me here, why aren't you doing this?" I never heard that. She liked her life and liked what he did and trusted him and let him do his thing and they both loved each other. But love is not enough. You got to give each person their space, and she had her own life, too. They gave each other their space and then enjoyed each other's company. I mean it's not like they didn't get into it—"Oh Bob, what are you doing?" Or, "Goddamn it, Kathryn!" It's not like that didn't happen. But jeez, for fifty years. You could have more arguments with your cat than they did with each other.

ROBERT REED ALTMAN: She's always been like the queen mother in charge. She always made sure everything was running smoothly, that Bob was happy, that he could throw his parties and his gatherings with people. He's the guy whose job is to bring total strangers together, find out the ones that work and get rid of the ones that don't. It was a continuous job for her, all the parties, all the entertaining, all the things to remember. She'd help Bob remember all the stuff on the social front, which was really the base to everything. Even though Bob had his office and the people who worked for him, there was also the whole other side, which she definitely took care of and made sure was running smoothly. Every time we'd move from one house to another to go on location she'd find the right house, she'd get all that stuff together, make sure it was good for entertaining, that it had what we needed. She kept this whole family together. Because like we said earlier, Bob was always just making the movies. She really had to run everything. She's like the grease between all the metal gears that kept everything running smooth and perfect.

*　　*　　*

KATHRYN REED ALTMAN: In October of '72, when we were in postproduction for *Long Goodbye*, a whole group of us were at the Lion's Gate office one night. We were all drinking and they were smoking dope and carrying on. A telephone rang. There were two extensions—one on one side of the room and one on the other. I picked it up and a woman asked for Bob. I didn't know who she was, but I could just tell something was up when I saw him pick up the other extension from across the way.

Before the night was over, it all kind of broke that he was having this encounter with Faye Dunaway—she was the one on the phone. She had been at the house a couple of times. She was a real smart-assed bitch and I really didn't like her.

Well, we had a pied-à-terre attached to the offices because we were between owning homes at that point. He stayed there and I went back to the house we were renting, which was the beach house in *The Long Goodbye*. When it all broke, then everybody started opening up about what happened when I wasn't around. I got a version of what happened in Ireland, what went on in Spain, what happened elsewhere.

We were separated about two weeks. Bobby had just started boarding school. Matthew was so little he didn't know the difference. Konni was already off on her way. I was devastated, and so one dear friend, Johnny Williams's late wife, Barbara, suggested I go see this family therapist. I had never been to a therapist before. I liked him. He was saying things like, "Well, he's on a roll, he'll probably get over this, he'll get it out of his system."

Bob was saying, "You're going to a therapist and you'll probably leave me." He consented to go see him, but something about how he said it bothered me. I didn't understand what he was getting at.

I said, "This isn't going to work."

I don't know where it came from. I will never know where it came from. I was heartbroken. I was hurt and I was mad and I was scared. I thought I was too old to have another life. Somehow or other I got very strong and I invited two or three of my girlfriends to *The Long Goodbye* house on the beach. Before they got there, Bob called me and said he had been to see the doctor. He said, "Listen . . ."

He was not going in the right direction.

Out of the blue I said, "This is October. I don't want to have any contact with you until after the first of the year. I'll take care of the boys. I'll have our business manager take care of the money for me. And that is really that. If you need to tell me something, Bob Eggenweiler can be the liaison. I can't go on like this. I don't care what it is you want to do or don't want to do. Call me after the first of the year."

JOAN TEWKESBURY: I think he sat down and really thought about it. I mean, how are you going to replace Kathryn when you're a working director who has six kids in various places and stages and ways of growing up? Plus the fact she's as smart as you are, she's very attractive, she gives a hell of a party, and she's great at mixing people together. Give me a break.

KATHRYN REED ALTMAN: The girlfriends came down and we boohooed and got loaded, and one of my friends, Helen Colvig, stayed all night with me. About six thirty in the morning, he called and said, "Could I please come home?"

I said yes.

My girlfriend Helen jumped out of that bed [*laughs*]. And he came in. He didn't want to talk much but he figuratively got on his knees asking to come back and begged forgiveness and all that stuff. He said all the right things. It was like a little boy who had done wrong and knew it and wanted to make amends.

JOAN TEWKESBURY: I think what saved him was Bob's good sense. I remember saying to him at one point, "You know, if you're going to do this philandering and all, just get a divorce and do that."

He said, "You know I can't do that."

And I said, "Well, then make up your mind here, because this is sort of silly."

LOIS SMITH (press agent): Anytime someone put a choice like that to Bob there was only one way he was going to go, and that was Kathryn. He was offered many choices over the years, but he realized how important Kathryn was to him, so there couldn't really be any other choice.

KATHRYN REED ALTMAN: Well, Faye Dunaway started calling and saying she was coming to the house. It was a whole drama. Sally Kellerman—she's such a dear friend—came and took Matthew to an amusement park just to get him out of the house before Dunaway showed up. It came very close but it never happened. She never came over.

We got through the night in a very healthy way, and the next morning the therapist called. And he said, "I talked with Bob. I think you're going to have to give up on this. I don't see any way for it to be solved" [*laughs*].

We had Thanksgiving at the Williamses' house, and for Christmas we took the boys back to Kansas City to meet their cousins, and we stayed in a big suite in a hotel there. As far as I know, and I would almost stake my life on it, that was the end of that behavior.

Dunaway? I saw her a couple of times at functions over the years, and I avoided her. Then we were at a *Vanity Fair* party at the Mondrian for the Oscars, with *Gosford Park*. Star-studded to beat all. She was at one end of the table and we were at the other end. She came over and Bob didn't acknowledge her. He was like it never happened, which is a good way of handling it. She came around to my side and kneeled down and went through this big apology to me.

I said, "You can't take full responsibility. It wasn't just you, Faye." Bob was the one who should have been down on his knees.

He was feeling his oats, there's no doubt about it. I loved the way it ended. Now I can say I'm glad he got it out of his system, and I'm glad I didn't take a walk. It was close.

FAYE DUNAWAY (actress): I don't have anything to say about Mr. Altman. I never worked with him. I don't have any time to give you on this subject.

Robert Altman, Q & A with F. Anthony Macklin, *Film Heritage*, Winter 1976–77 (*discussing whether the audience could identify with Shelley Duvall's performance in* Thieves Like Us):

F. ANTHONY MACKLIN: Shelley is not a Faye Dunaway, for instance. They [the audience] can relate to a Faye Dunaway.

ROBERT ALTMAN: Why? Because she's not real. Faye Dunaway's not real. There's no such thing as Faye Dunaway.

LOIS SMITH: Kathryn was a rock. She was the hand on the tiller through all of their life, which as you're aware was quite tempestuous at times. Everyone who knew the two of them prayed he would go first, because his life without her would not be possible.

* * *

California Split *(1974)*

Roger Ebert, review in the *Chicago Sun-Times*, January 1, 1974: They meet in a California poker parlor. One wins, despite a heated discussion with a loser over whether or not a dealt card hit the floor. They drink. They become friends after they are jointly mugged in the parking lot by the sore loser. . . . They're the heroes (or at least the subjects) of "California Split," the magnificently funny, cynical film by Robert Altman. Their names are Bill and Charlie, and they're played by George Segal and Elliott Gould with a combination of unaffected naturalism and sheer raw nervous exhaustion. . . . The movie will be compared with "M*A*S*H," the first big hit by Altman (who is possibly our best and certainly our most diverting American director). It

George Segal (as Bill Denny) and Elliott Gould (as Charlie Waters)
in California Split

deserves that comparison, because it resembles "M*A*S*H" in several big ways: It's funny, it's hard-boiled, it gives us a bond between two frazzled heroes trying to win by the rules in a game where the rules require defeat. But it's a better movie than "M*A*S*H" because here Altman gets it all together. Ever since "M*A*S*H," he's been trying to make a kind of movie that would function like a comedy but allow its laughs to dig us deeper and deeper into the despair underneath.

*   *   *

JOSEPH WALSH (screenwriter): I was a child actor, almost a child star, in New York City. I went from the incredible time as a child star, to at eighteen years old, you now are literally a has-been. It didn't mean anything to me because I was a super-duper gambler. I was a great college prognosticator. It was a loss to my father, not to me. When I came out here—not really working—I was always gambling, keeping ahead of the curve and really getting good at that kind of thing. I realized nobody had done a *real* gambling movie. When I see a *Cincinnati Kid* it's like a Western—"Is the hero going to win or going to lose the gunfight at the end?" There's nothing real about that.

I was friends with Steven Spielberg, and Steven and I were going to do *California Split*. I worked in Steven's home for about eight months. MGM said yes, and suddenly everything changed. Jim Aubrey, head of the studio, was the smiling cobra—and the snake struck. He said, "I want it changed. I don't want what's going on here. I want a straight movie. I want the Mafia to chase the two guys—they owe the Mafia money. The Mafia catches the two guys, they get away. And I want Dean Martin to be the star of it. He wears a lucky chip around his neck, and he gets shot and the chip saves his life." He even had the title for it—"You call the movie *Lucky Chip*."

You've got to be kidding me.

I pulled out of it with a hundred twenty-seven dollars in my pocket. People said, "You are one of the great morons of all time. You should do what they want." But to me I couldn't do it. My agent, Guy McElwaine, made a quick move. He sent it to London, to Bob. Within two days he said, "Bob loves this and he wants to do it." We did it with Columbia.

I'm not that familiar with Bob at this point. I've seen some movies I like, some movies I don't like. I certainly knew he was a big talent. Bob and I hit it off great—we both gambled; he loved the price, he loved the odds. But he says to me, "I am supposed to be your enemy. You know that?"

"My enemy? What do you mean?"

He says, "Writers, they don't like me."

I say, "I don't know you. Why?"

Bob says, "I tend to not want to keep to what they've written."

I said, "We can work with that."

It became one of those situations where Bob would come up with something abstract—"Here's a scene. I think we'll have twelve midgets come in and do this."

I'd say, "What? Twelve midgets? Why in the world would you do a move like that? If you do that, they would laugh you out of the theater. Bob, it took me literally two months to find the right motivation for that scene. You can't throw that out in one second."

He would just look at me and storm out and slam his own door. I knew he had to be back. It was his office. He would simmer down and be back in about two minutes and he would harrumph around and say, "Okay, we'll try it that way."

In retrospect I knew that Bob was a great talent because he had the talent not to impose himself on the process. His trust factor was his greatest strength. Bob was in love with being surprised. He was like a great big kid in a cinema candy store. And more often than not his actors threw a sweet and wonderful party for him.

ELLIOTT GOULD: You know *California Split* is semiautobiographical about me and Joey Walsh, right? After Donald Sutherland and I had done *S.P.Y.S.*, the last picture we did together, we went to see Bob, because Bob always had an idea to do a pirate movie about two guys who could take over any ship. I thought that's way on the back burner or in a closet, but I just wanted Bob to see Donald and I were back together. We went to see him as Bob was starting to prepare *California Split*, and he was in the office with this old friend of mine, Joseph Walsh. Bob said, "There's nothing in this picture for you." And I was so hurt and embarrassed 'cause I thought, "I'm not coming in for this picture."

They were thinking about Robert De Niro. Then it was going to be Steve McQueen and George Segal. McQueen wanted writing that didn't exist and he then withdrew from the project. Bob called me in Munich and asked me if I would consider playing the part we thought Steve McQueen was going to play. I said, "I'll do it, of course, so long as it's okay with Walsh."

GEORGE SEGAL (actor): *California Split*? I couldn't make heads or tails of the script. It didn't mean anything to me. I didn't know from gambling. I didn't quite get it, but Guy McElwaine was so persuasive. And I loved Altman's films. As a matter of fact, when I was on the film Altman said to me, "You don't know this but you walked out of one of the first *M*A*S*H* screenings and you said, 'That's one of the best films I ever saw.'" That got back to him.

Our relationship was warm, mutually respectful, and a little distant. I wasn't in his rhythms. Gambling, I don't know. I guess I was more middle-class than he would have liked. Different sensibilities. He was living a seventies lifestyle and I was a little bit behind in that area. He's Kansas City and living by the seat of your pants and making this totally innovative movie, *M*A*S*H*, changing the rules, and I'm a rule player.

Elliott was also an antirules guy and a freewheeling guy, or that was at least his persona. That was Bob's persona too, and I was always a kid from Great Neck. I brought an innocence, and he didn't have time for that. Risk was not a part of my persona and it was a part of his.

Elliott and Bob barely talked. He talked much more with me. They barely talked because they were already inside each other's heads.

If you would look at him while his actors were acting, he had kind of an ecstatic look on his face. He was thrilled that these actors were fulfilling his dreams. That was a childlike thing he brought, and it was infectious. It was without guile.

*　　*　　*

ALAN RUDOLPH (director): Jack Cashin, the sound man, somehow was associated with this organization called Synanon. They had this big building down in Santa Monica. The people there were all ex-junkies, gambling addicts, or whatever. Bob says, "That's where we'll get our extras." He would never hire Hollywood extras. We sort of broke the mold on that. He wanted real people and he didn't want to pay them extra rates. So he said to me, "You'll go down there and you'll convince the people at Synanon to be extras in the movie. We'll give a ten-thousand-dollar donation or whatever to the organization and they'll supply us with however many people we'll need every day."

So I went down there one night with Tommy Thompson and it really was like one of those homeless missions. Here are all these people, and I didn't know what to say. We had to eat dinner with all these people—and I'll never forget what they served there: white bread and brown gravy. I then said, "Here's your chance to be all the things you know about—but for fun. The only addiction you're gonna get is getting hooked on movies, being in movies, and you'll have the best time." Well, they just lapped it up. So throughout that movie all the extras, they're all Synanon addicts—well, most of them, anyway. Real people with real stories to tell that were just fantastic, and Bob just loved it.

JOSEPH WALSH: He didn't film the ending I wrote. In the beginning of this movie, Tommy Thompson, Bob's longtime friend and assistant director, told me that Bob had this kind of strange idiosyncrasy. When his movies got close to the end he had a tendency to rush them to get them over. That's what happened.

Dinner in Las Vegas in 1974: from left, Bob Eggenweiler, Kathryn, Bob, Leon Ericksen, Tommy Thompson, and Joey Walsh

They're talking to each other at the end and Elliott finally says, "You're going home? Oh yeah, where the fuck do you live?" I didn't write that. I'm sitting there and thinking, "What happened to his character?" George Segal stares at him and gets up and says, "Charlie, I got to go," and walks out. Cut.

Elliott bolts over to me and says, "I'm sorry. I don't know where that came from." George says, "Bob, this is it! You must end this movie right here. I never understood it until now!"

GEORGE SEGAL: That was the point. My character won, but there *was* no special feeling. Now he gets it.

JOSEPH WALSH: And Bob said, "You're right. That's the wrap."

Not many movies pull the movie out from under you. Audiences didn't know how to feel about it when they walked out of the theater. Columbia said we cost them ten million dollars right there. Later on, Steven [Spielberg] said to me, "I could have made millions of dollars with the movie." Steven would have built the climax different than Bob built it. He said, "I would have built it up to the greatest orgasm in town. The foreplay would have been so unbelievable that when the orgasm came the audience would have been on the edge of its seat." It would have been a totally different movie.

Elliott apologizes to me every year for that.

HENRY GIBSON: Joey is still telling that story, seventy years later, about how Bob changed his ending. But see, there's only one answer to that. "That isn't what was filmed, Joey. I love you and I know all the processes you went through—selling it, rewriting it, hanging on to it. People wanted to rip it away from you. But that's not what Bob made, okay?"

CHAPTER 18

Nashville

*

Nashville *(1975)*

Pauline Kael, review in *The New Yorker,* **March 3, 1975 (based on a rough cut of the film, before most other reviewers had seen it):** Is there such a thing as an orgy for movie-lovers—but an orgy without excess? At Robert Altman's new, almost-three-hour film, *Nashville,* you don't get drunk on images. You're not overpowered—you get elated. I've never before seen a movie I loved in quite this way: I sat there smiling at the screen, in complete happiness. It's a pure emotional high, and you don't come down when the picture is over; you take it with you. *Nashville* is a radical, revolutionary leap. . . . The funniest epic vision of America ever to reach the screen. Robert Altman's movie is at once a *Grand Hotel*–style narrative, with twenty-four linked characters; a country-and-western musical; a documentary essay on Nashville and American life; a mediation on the love affair between performers and audiences; and an Altman party. . . . The picture says, This is what America is, and I'm part of it. *Nashville* arrives at a time when America is congratulating itself for having got rid of the guys who were pulling the wool over people's eyes. The movie says it isn't only the politicians who live the big lie—the big lie is something we're all capable of trying for.

*   *   *

ROBERT ALTMAN: While we were making *Thieves Like Us* I said to Joan Tewkesbury, "Go to Nashville." I had never been to Nashville in

Henry Gibson, as Haven Hamilton, onstage at the Grand Ole Opry

my life. My idea when they said Country-Western music was hillbilly music. I said, "Go to Nashville and keep a diary. Just from the day you get off the plane start writing down what happens to you. And somewhere we'll find a movie."

JOAN TEWKESBURY: So I went to Nashville with Bill and Taffy Danoff, who were singing with John Denver. We went to a museum and saw Patsy Cline's hairpins and we went to the Bible printing museum. Bill and Taffy were terrific—but I said, "This isn't the real deal." So when we were shooting in Mississippi, I said to Bob, "I need to go there by myself and figure out what's going on."

Everything you see in the movie is what I saw. I was sort of like Opal. I just went there with a yellow pad of paper and wrote everything down. I rented a car and got on the freeway and there was a big accident and everything stopped. It became the opening of the picture—this great place for everything to converge on the highway, a jumping-off point for all these characters to begin bumping into each other and having near misses. I walked up and down the street and saw that a lot of older couples rented rooms to people who wanted to be singer/songwriters.

The most help I got was from a group of technicians. They were the ones who told me about the club, the Exit/In. I went there on their recommendation, and there was a radio station at the Exit/In that was broadcasting everything out onto the airwaves. There was a girl OD'ing on something on the next table. This black guy shoved a joint up my sleeve and said he had just gotten out of jail for premeditated murder. He was an interesting guy. He had gotten himself out of prison by going to the library. I don't know if he was guilty or not, but he had a great appreciation for music and he told me a lot of bands to go to see. There were several people I had seen throughout the day. The city is built in a circle, so if I saw you in the morning and didn't know who you were, I'd see you at least two times before the end of the day.

I walked outside after a couple of hours in this joint and I looked up and there was a full moon. I said, "Shit, everything runs in circles in this town." I said, "Fuck, this is it. It's all about overlaps and connective tissue."

M*A*S*H was one of Bob's greatest movies in terms of that kind of construct. You can pull all of these people together, there can be a very firm mathematical structure, like music. As long as you pulled them together at the end, you could do anything you wanted in the middle. Which was a perfect structure for him.

I came back and said, "I got it. It was a poem, for God's sake. Your movie's in there." He said, "Well, swell."

I turned in the first draft with eighteen characters, and Tommy Thompson read it first and then Bob Eggenweiler said it was terrific. Bob said, "I don't know about this." I thought, "That's odd." So, we rumbled around and he then talked about how somehow it had to be larger than music and Nashville. M*A*S*H has got a big event, war. So this would not be just another movie, a wannabe musical, about a place where people wanted to be musicians. The further that this went on, the more and more we talked about how ridiculous were the politics of the country. He started talking about a political line—"It can't be about a girl killing herself at the end of the movie."

POLLY PLATT: After the incident at the hotel in New York, he approached me to do *Nashville*. Joan wrote it for him and I thought it was great, and I figured he'd moved on and it would be okay, and it was okay. He never made any passes at me on the preproduction of *Nashville.*

I went to Nashville with Joan and the two of us were searching out locations, and he was with us. It was during the Watergate hearings and we could not get him out of the hotel to look at locations. It was infuriating at the time, but in the light of the pictures he later made, I thought, "Oh, I see why." He was really fascinated with dirty politics.

JOAN TEWKESBURY: Bob and I were walking down Madison Avenue. There had been a horrendous storm, the night that Nixon was elected, you know, and all these umbrellas were turned inside out. And Bob said, "It's a sign. You know, we've elected the wrong guy." Bob was looking for an extreme, an explosive ending, in a way. And it sort of came out of that walk down Madison Avenue. And the discussion was about the fact that no one had assassinated a woman. And that people tended to stay away from entertainers.

ROBERT ALTMAN: We had a designer named Polly Platt. And she was the most renowned person at that time in our group. Polly Platt was better known than I was, or equally well, anyway. At a certain point I called Joan and Polly into my office and said, "Listen, I know what's wrong with this. We've got to assassinate the wrong person." And Polly hit the ceiling. Joan came in with her—they came to quit. And I said, "Well, quit. Because I think this is the strongest thing I got here." Joan kinda changed and she stayed and worked with it. Polly quit.

POLLY PLATT: I fought him on it because the original script didn't have the assassination. He added that, and I felt that it ruined the script. I still think it ruins the picture. I just think that it was a beautiful, delicate story of many lives intertwining. Everybody arriving at Nashville, and then this assassination—which obviously comes from his political fascination. It's like a sledgehammer on this delicate, filigreed story of these people arriving in Nashville. I talked to Joan and she agreed with me, but she was afraid of him. She had a chance to get her script made, so you can see why she stayed.

JOAN TEWKESBURY: I disagreed at first, but I stuck around because I got it.

Bob decided that since everything else had happened to this woman, Barbara Jean, she should die at the end. I said, "So who do you

On the set of Nashville *with screenwriter Joan Tewkesbury in front of Nashville's Parthenon, location of the film's climactic shooting*

want to do it?" Bob said, "I don't care who kills her; she's going to get shot." At the time Kenny was the nicest character, so I simply made Kenny a little crazy.

ROBERT ALTMAN: I started casting it, and people would come in. I'd say, "Okay." Then somebody else would come in—I don't specifically know who—and I'd say, "God, we need a part for them. They want to be in the movie and they're good." So we would make up a part.

JOAN TEWKESBURY: It increased from eighteen characters to twenty-four, and I figured that the audience would be the twenty-fifth character. With every addition a little more sophistication, you know, a little more of the outside world would encroach into Nashville, which was exactly what was happening to Nashville at the time.

ROBERT ALTMAN: It gets back to poetry. What we're all doing is basically haiku. You're trying to make a short poem and get everything in. In the first place, in making a film, I have to figure out—I have to deal with the minds and the information that the audience already has. If the audience can't keep track of all those characters, they give up and your picture's over. So, I've got to get it down to size, to where they can embrace it. I think of all of these things like dinner parties. I go to a dinner party with twelve people and Kathryn and I leave and we're going home, I'll say, "Who was that blonde girl that was sitting next to so-and-so?" I may have met one more person, or two that I didn't know before. But basically I walk away and I don't even know the people I've had dinner with. I think a film is pretty much the same way. There's that problem in *Nashville*. But because of being able to stop and see them sing, you learn who that person is because you've got that camera on them for a long time. And that singing is sort of a confession for them. It tells you a lot about that individual.

KEITH CARRADINE: Bob had one of his weekend parties and we were all gathered up there. It was a sunny day, and I had my guitar and I was playing songs. Joan was already researching *Nashville*. In the midst of her doing that, while we were shooting *Thieves Like Us*, Bob heard my music and Joan heard the music and they basically just incorporated it into the film.

I wasn't even supposed to be Tom originally. I was going to be Bill, who was played by Allan Nicholls. They wanted Gary Busey to play Tom, which was much more on the money in terms of Gary's energy and his personality. It would have made much more sense on first blush. Then Gary passed on the movie because he took a pilot called *The Texas Wheelers* with Jack Elam. When that happened I brought Allan out and Bob moved me into the role of Tom, with which I was never comfortable. I never felt right. I didn't like him. And that's Bob's genius. When we were doing the Exit/In scene, where all these women wonder who he's singing to, I walked out and I said to Bob, "I'm really uncomfortable. I don't feel confident about what I'm doing." And he wouldn't even talk to me about it. He just said, "Oh, you're fine, you're doing fine," and walked away.

The genius of what he had done was he put me into that skin, and

The fictional folk trio Bill, Mary, and Tom. In the foreground, from left, Keith Carradine, Cristina Raines, and Allan Nicholls

what you see in the movie is a guy who doesn't like himself. It's brilliant. It's the truth. So I wish I could say I was such a good actor. It had nothing to do with acting. It was the genius of Bob putting me in a circumstance that made me really uncomfortable to have to fulfill the obligations of that character, and then you see that guy who is really creeped out by himself.

Later on I would meet women who had seen the movie, who had seen me in the movie, and who were expecting Tom Frank. It was so weird. There was something so amoral about that guy that some women like. It was a shocker to me. And when that wasn't who I was, the disappointment in them was immediate and palpable. I'm sorry I'm not on the make.

LILY TOMLIN: Bob put me in the movies when nobody else in the world would. I was on *Laugh-In* and I was Ernestine to most people—the telephone operator. I can only guess that Bob either never saw *Laugh-In* or thought it was a typically unconventional choice, which he probably preferred. Just the idea of me getting to be in a movie was a big deal. And to be in an Altman movie was like over the moon; I couldn't believe it. And when I read the script that Joan Tewkesbury had written, I thought, "Gee. I could play a lot of these different people." But as I watched everybody come into town, and everybody was so perfect for what they'd been cast, I thought, "I must be more Linnea than I have any idea."

GERALDINE CHAPLIN (actress): My version of it is I met Bob at a press showing of *Images*. Then we met again in Cannes and he said, "I'm thinking of a role for you." He said, "Just imitate me. I want you to follow me around and act like me. Do everything I do." Of course it didn't turn out like that. He said, "To play Opal, the one thing you have to be is British." I said, "I don't know if I can do that." He said, "Okay, you're an American pretending to be a Brit."

JOAN TEWKESBURY: We took *Thieves Like Us* to the Cannes Film Festival and we watched Geraldine Chaplin be devoured by the press. What Bob said to Geraldine [for *Nashville*] was terrific: "All you have to do is be them." And she did it.

GERALDINE CHAPLIN: I was pregnant—I thought I'd be fired for that. Bob said, "That is just something Opal would do." He'd said Joan was going to go with me to look for the clothes. In London I had bought all these layers and layers of clothes. As Opal, I was supposed to wear these tank tops. Bob says, "What a great idea! She has all the clothes she owns on her back." He was so incredible in that way. If something went wrong he would make the most of it and something imperfect would stand out.

*　　*　　*

RICHARD SARAFIAN (director/actor/former brother-in-law): I was in Kansas City at his dad's house. The next day was the funeral for his mother, and he was leaving that same day to direct *Nashville*. Backgammon is my road game. I skunked him, as usual. It didn't matter how much I beat him out of—he wasn't going to pay me. He had improved since the early days. He was playing in an unconventional way. But anybody who has had too much alcohol is easy prey. He finally surrendered and staggered into the bedroom and went to bed with his father. Crawled in with his dad, to comfort him. I thought that was a loving, touching thing to do.

ALLAN NICHOLLS (actor/music director/screenwriter/associate producer/assistant director): The night before the first day of shooting, there was the kickoff party. It was a big barbecue and Bob made ribs. During that party I got a call from my brother saying my dad had had a pretty serious heart attack and was in the hospital, and that it was fifty–fifty and it looks like I'd have to go home. So I was like, "Oh God, this is my first film, I'm going to have to tell someone." So I told Tommy Thompson. I said, "You should probably write me out or whatever you do, and I don't want to tell Bob 'cause he's hosting this party, but I'm telling you."

So the next day was the first day of shooting and it was at the airport, with mass confusion. And we all show up for our call time, which was pretty early in the morning. And Bob's out there and it's hot as hell. I see him and he was like choreographing the twirlers and the band and stuff. He catches my eye and pulls me over and he takes me aside and he says, "I know what's happening with your dad, and I'm treating it as if it's happening to me. You're not going to have to go home, you're not going to have to do anything. Just don't worry about anything. You're in this movie." My father ended up getting better, and I didn't need to go home. But needless to say, that was probably the thing that locked our friendship from then on.

*   *   *

MICHAEL MURPHY: He said, "I'm going to start this picture on the fifteenth of July, but I'm having a Fourth of July party and I want everybody down here [*laughs*]. So he's got this log cabin–esque but very, very nice big house, and we're all out there meeting each other on the Fourth of July. So now we have eleven days before the picture starts, and he doesn't rehearse or anything, so we're all hanging around this motel together, one of those double-decker motels. It was the cleverest thing because by the end of those ten, eleven days, you knew everybody. We all had interesting relationships. Some guys would be fighting with their wives, some guys would be doing yoga, some guys would be doing deep breathing. Some guys would be learning their lines. But we all had this funny bonding thing that went on and we all got to liking each other.

GERALDINE CHAPLIN: We all arrived together and we had a party at Bob's. He had little condos for everyone and he had a beautiful big house and he had us all over. He said, "Have you brought your scripts?" We said yes. He said, "Well, throw them away. You don't need them. You need to know who you are and where you are and who you're with." I remember thinking, "I can't do this." I thought I was going to be fired. My first scene was with Lily Tomlin after the car crash. I knew I would get fired and it just came out and he started laughing. He said, "Be serious and don't try to be funny and you'll be hilarious." I never worked this way with a director before. He was an incredible audience. It was like being onstage with a full house every second. All the circus acts you had inside your body you'd do just for him.

*   *   *

RICHARD BASKIN (composer): I was a young struggling songwriter in L.A. and had gone to USC film school and was writing songs and playing music around town. I had heard from my sister that Gwen Welles, who was somebody I knew from an acting class, needed somebody to write her some songs for this movie she was going to be in. She told me about the project and I badgered her to get me a script. I read this screenplay, which was phenomenal, and got very excited about the project. I told her I'd write her the songs under the condition that when she presented them to Robert Altman I would get to come in with her. I wrote her the song "One, I Love You," and we had our appointment to go in and see Bob. When I got my moment with him—I was twenty-three or so at the time—I said, "I think you should hire me to do the music and you should do it live." Which got his attention. He kind of looked at me like, "Who are you, kid?"

I gave him this whole plan to do it live. He said, "Well, who would you use?" I said, "I'd like to come back and lay out a whole plan for you." Truth is, I'm a Jewish kid from the Valley. I don't really know anything about country music. I think he recognized my audaciousness and saw some kind of intelligence there.

I called up my friend Curt Allen, the son of Rex Allen, the cowboy singer. He gave me a list of the best players. I wrote them down and went back to Bob and said, "This is who I'd use."

Bob was rather extraordinary in his way of letting people do what they did. He trusted you to do what you did and therefore you would kill for him.

A couple of days later we were on a plane to Nashville. I was the musical director. To me it was an incredible break and an incredible thrill. To him it was a great deal. He paid me five hundred dollars a week, which I thought was a fortune. I didn't realize at the time how cheaply he got me.

ROBERT ALTMAN: For actors, I had two salaries: seven-fifty and a thousand dollars a week. They were sort of arbitrary. Better-known people got a thousand. I paid Lily a thousand a week. She had not ever been in a picture before, but she was known from *Laugh-In*. Henry Gibson I think I paid a thousand dollars. For the killer I hired Michael Burns, who'd been in *Cold Day in the Park*. He came back from West Virginia, or Virginia, or wherever he was teaching. He had long hair. He went and got his hair cut for the part. When he found out that I had him on the seven-fifty list, he said he wouldn't do it. He wanted a thousand. And I couldn't give it to him, I felt, because I had already published that list to my other cast members. He left. Got his hair cut and went back to West Virginia.

ROBERT DUVALL: Yeah, he asked me to be that guy, Haven Hamilton. Something didn't click with me. Was it money? I don't think so. I can't quite remember. Something didn't click.

LILY TOMLIN: We were in Nashville for two months. And it was in the summertime. It was really hot. And most of us were living in this old singles apartment that hadn't been finished yet. And the yards were all muddy, and the décor was all heavy acrylic carpets, and very heavy, dark furniture. So we all kinda started complaining because we would be there for two months. And Karen Black came in to do a part. And she was only there for about five days. And most of us started protesting, and saying, "Well, why does Karen Black get to come in and just be a week? And we have to be here day after day after day, in this hot weather and in this awful place to live?"

And Bob would say, "You're not supposed to like her."

JOAN TEWKESBURY: Karen Black was not allowed to come until the week she was filmed. She was moved into this really nice hotel—given all the perks all the rest of them weren't getting. Everybody was pissed off at her and it was perfect.

HENRY GIBSON: The whole scene was like a beehive. Certain bees would be over here rehearsing because they weren't scheduled to shoot a scene for four, five days. And Barbara Harris was breaking her ass, working out scenes, improvising things. Always with the advice of Joan and the consultation of Joan. I know that Barbara Baxley and I tried to evolve backstories of our relationship. There were certain facts that were given us by Joan. And then we used our imagination and explored those. And out of that would come possible contributions, which you would run by Joan. At least that was the polite thing one did at that time.

JOAN TEWKESBURY: As we began to shoot there was no time for rehearsal, but the actors and I would get together three days before the shoot. And if they wanted to go over stuff we would go over that, and Bob would rehearse them before he shot. Like the day we shot all the love scenes. It was one day in the crappy motel. Keith just stayed in bed and we brought in a different girl every hour. But contrary to popular belief the whole movie was *not* improvised.

HENRY GIBSON: There's a tremendous misconception. And this exists in film departments at respected universities. "Oh, but it was all improvisation, wasn't it?" Bullshit. Improvisation in some actors' minds or some performers' minds is a "gotcha" thing that you take credit for. And Altman doesn't play gotcha because the only person that can play gotcha in an Altman film is Altman—to his audience. And that's part of his magic and part of his trimming what is absolutely unnecessary, of letting his camera seek out as he wants the audience to seek out something in the background of the frame. Even while the performers, right in your face, are reciting dialogue. And he tempts you—"Wait, hold there, what's that? Jesus, look." I love that.

He told us if we walked on a tightrope he would be the net to catch us. And that sustained us. And implicit in that promise was, "I will not let you appear foolish. You will not be made fun of."

What always bothered me a little bit was, some cast members when they were interviewed would describe it as a lark, a wonderful party— "Oh, it was just fun all the time." It's really denying the fact that this was work. The fun, the party, the drinks, they were not even secondary. These were little things that he invented to make life easier for you, but that wasn't it. Some of the press was responsible for that, too. They would describe it as an orgy of booze and drink and drugs and Altman teetering. They turned him into a Falstaff and he's not Falstaff, he was never Falstaff. He may have had a Falstaffian beard at times, but that's as close as he ever fucking was to Falstaff. I hated when people did that. No, working on an Altman picture requires tremendous concentration, tremendous focus, and I felt a heightened obligation because of the trust that he placed in you.

JOAN TEWKESBURY: What he did for his actors—this is what he did for everybody on the set—was to engage everybody's imagination enough that you're all rowing the boat in the same direction. And yet he was insightful enough to get exactly what he needed. I think that came from his days of flying airplanes in the war. He knew what to target. He knew how to get along in situations where he had to survive. When you stop and think about all of those older movie directors, a lot of them had been in a war.

MICHAEL MURPHY: Bob said, "Now you people know your characters much better than I do. I've got all my money in film stock on this picture, so take them as far as you want to go." But, he says, "Remember, I'm shooting a lot of stories simultaneously, so if you bore me I'm going to just go to somebody else." He's laughing, you know. Those of us who spent time with him knew that he was really talking about paraphrasing and a little bit of improvisation. But I remember Barbara Baxley handing me ten pages of single-spaced dialogue. I'm going, "What the hell is this?" But Bob looked at it and said, "We'll shoot it." So we did and there were some really great moments in it, about the Kennedys and the assassinations. Bob knew that would work.

*   *   *

JOAN TEWKESBURY: I had danced in a nightclub, and Gwen Welles's character, Sueleen, was a compilation of a couple of dancers I had known who thought they were going to set the world on fire. One of them agreed to pose for *Playboy* because she didn't think she would have to take her clothes off. It was nuts.

Gwen had taken socks out of the drawer and stuck them in the dress. That tells everybody she hadn't expected to strip. The whole object of this is to show how far we'll go for fame, or how much of ourselves we'll give up for it.

MICHAEL MURPHY: In the striptease scene, all those guys were like from the Lion's Club. They were like pillars of the business world and

Gwen Welles as Sueleen Gay before her reluctant striptease

everything. You'd think they'd come in there, Southern guys, and say, "I don't know if I want to be seen doing this." Bob knew just how to handle it. He said, "Now, this girl is going to come down out of the ceiling and you guys get off on it." And they're going, "Ahhhh." And they got with it. He was very good at taking people who had never worked and putting them in front of a camera and making it happen, making it real, you know? With very little explanation. He always gave you credit for having a brain. That was what I think he did with these guys. He knew they were smart enough guys. Also, he'd been around that behavior. He'd been around those guys in Kansas City when he was young and he knew how they would respond. And they went ape shit, those guys.

JOAN TEWKESBURY: When we get down to shooting the striptease, the first thing after the dress comes off, the socks come out of the bra. And

I just thought, "Oh my God, you're a genius, girl." And she took off every stitch of clothing and walked offstage. And those men stood—it still makes me very emotional—and they gave her a standing ovation.

It was the emotional core of the film. She is every person in that movie. Every person in that movie believes that if they just do that one thing, it won't matter, everybody will forget and they will get famous, or get the job, or will get to sing the song, or they will be the front-runner in the campaign. Everybody in this movie compromises at some point or another. It was also calculated that every person in this movie has a point where they really redeem themselves. Gwen's character was really calculated from beginning to end to have her arc, and at the end of the day she still has the balls to go stand up onstage at the end of the movie and sing her song.

*   *   *

GERALDINE CHAPLIN: His vision, the way he saw things, was so out of sync with the established way of thinking. He would laugh at things— if you tell a story that you think was tragic, he would see the humor in it. It wasn't cruel. It was the way he would read something and see it completely different. That reminded me of my mother. She had a sense of humor even bigger than my father's, I think. My father proba-bly would have enjoyed his films. Because they're funny. They're funny in the right way. Funny in a critical way—of what the world is and the world we live in. They were both geniuses in their way. They alter your experience of reality. They have their world and they have their humor. That humor is so rare. Would they have gotten along? Probably not. But Bob and my mother got on great. They fell for each other.

ALLAN NICHOLLS: So Julie Christie arrives on the scene. And I think about seventeen of us realized we were in love with her. Well, Michael Murphy was already in love with her from *McCabe & Mrs. Miller*, prob-ably.

JULIE CHRISTIE: I remember not wanting to do it at all. "What has he got me doing now?" I just walked through it not knowing what the hell I was going to be doing. I didn't realize that we were there as scape-goats. If I had, I might have been able to have more fun with it. I was cross, actually, because I really didn't want to do it. My reticence was not listened to at all. Robert by no means got his way by being sweet all the time. He could be manipulative.

HENRY GIBSON: On the last day of shooting, the assassination, the clouds were as ominous as that scene, when you see the progression of black cars with the lights on. You just have to underline that with organ music, you know? A crowd was assembling with promises of hot dogs and crap. And all of these extra camera operators had been flown in from all over. And the equipment, we were top-heavy, and the film is scheduled to close. There was no more money. And there was an orchestra. Oh, they put tarps over the instruments and over the stage in case it was going to come pouring down. It got darker and darker and darker. He looked up and said, "STOP!" He was his own safety net. He was going to hold up the clouds if he could [*laughs*]. And they obeyed! All I could think of was, "And the Red Sea parted."

ALLAN NICHOLLS: After that, some attributed to him godlike characteristics. But I think he knew he wasn't.

KEITH CARRADINE: In *Nashville* he was looking at us, he was looking at our culture, he was looking at America. And how prophetic that movie turned out to be. From Jimmy Carter, who came after, to the assassination of John Lennon, which came after, capturing the zeitgeist that was actually ten years hence. Truly extraordinary. The great artists are the ones who see who we are becoming more so than those who see who we are. And Bob was one of those. It's a better movie now than when we made it. That's saying something. I think it's a towering achievement, that movie. Just everybody that was involved in that, Bob tapped into something. He tapped into the American psyche so absolutely directly, and it ain't pretty.

ALAN RUDOPLH: When he was cutting *Nashville*, especially, you'd see the same film—well, not the same film, but different versions—ten or fifteen times a week. I think that was Bob's greatest thrill. It's the fresh-blood thing. If you've seen it you know what's happening, so he'd throw all of his attention to someone who hadn't seen it. He knew what he had was like a new language to a lot of people, so to watch them redefine the experience of watching a film and knowing that they would, in some way, never be the same again was a great high for him. That's how he got energy.

LILY TOMLIN: When we went to the Oscars for *Nashville*, it was my first Oscars, and so I dressed up as what I thought of as a fifties movie star. I wore a tiara and big faux fur and I was going to have big Harlequin sunglasses. And Lee Grant won for *Shampoo*. I was going to say, "Some of you will say I've gone Hollywood." That kind of thing just pleased Bob. Anything that's a bit outside he got a kick out of.

RICHARD BASKIN (composer): There were two sets of reactions. When we were making the movie it was real pleasant and convivial. People I don't think understood the outsider context of it until they saw the movie. Once they saw the movie, they said, "This isn't really Nashville." And it wasn't Nashville, they were right. The songs were musically correct, but they were character driven. There was a consciousness to them that wasn't entirely of Nashville. I think people were responding emotionally to what was quite an intellectual film.

JOAN TEWKESBURY: There were a lot of tried-and-true Country-Western people that just hated our guts and hated the movie. Thought it was terrible. Thought that we were making fun of people. But basically no, because it became a microcosm of a kind of change that was happening in the United States.

Robert Altman, from DVD commentary: A few years after *Nashville* had come out, when John Lennon got assassinated, I got a call immediately from *The Washington Post* and they said, "Do you feel responsible for this?"

And I said, "What do you mean, 'responsible'?"

And they said, "Well, you're the one that predicted that there would be an assassination of a star."

And I said, "I don't feel responsible." But I said, "Don't *you* feel responsible for not heeding my warning?"

The statement here is that these people are not assassinated because of their ideas or what they do. They're assassinated to draw attention to the assassin.

*   *   *

ROBERT ALTMAN: It didn't make any money. It wasn't a mainline movie. But the critics treated it well. It didn't have any stars in it.

Ronee Blakley as doomed singer Barbara Jean

Maybe that's why that picture's so good. Maybe my reputation comes from just being right about the casting.

M*A*S*H, of course, changed things the most. But I was perceived differently after *Nashville*. It just verified in the critics' minds that I had some sort of value, and that *M*A*S*H* wasn't just an aberration.

CHAPTER 19

Diamond Cutter

*

ALLAN NICHOLLS: Whether you like it or not, Bob was always Bob, and Bob was always the Bob he wanted to be. He was never anybody else. He was never anybody's version of him, either. He was just him.

STEPHEN ALTMAN: There'd be times at Lion's Gate where all of a sudden the smart people realized, "Oh, he's got that look in his eye. All right, stay out of his way because he's going to nail somebody and just lambaste them and rip them to shreds and let's not be that person." But once he stopped drinking he pretty much didn't do that anymore. He didn't suffer fools, but he didn't go looking for a fight.

Some people took it personally but hung around anyway. There's a lot of hanger-on-ers around him and a lot of leeches, and a lot of "What can you do for me?" types. And a lot of times he was right. It's just, do you have to do it like that? Go up to the crafts-service guy and say, "You're just a crafts-service guy, that's all you are." It's like, "What did I do? I'm just making coffee." I think he had a fear of being found out that he was just a normal person and wasn't a genius.

To me, he was like the typical con man. Like how he would get his movies together and get the people involved. He was like Tom Sawyer painting the picket fence. If the movie was made, and everybody made money, he wasn't a con man anymore, he was just a great director and leader and salesman, you know? If it all falls apart and everybody loses their money, then he's a con man. Most of the time he made it work, so that's why everybody kept hanging around. I mean, if he wasn't successful, most people wouldn't be hanging out with him. No, no, no, we wouldn't be here at all. So that's the way it goes.

Seeing the world through a lens

JOAN TEWKESBURY: You know how a diamond cutter knows exactly where to cut the rock so that it doesn't fall apart? He will see a glimmer of something where no one else does. That would be Bob in a crowded room. He could tell you who would fall in love with who, whose marriage was over. He had this uncanny ability to foresee human behavior. That was why it was really difficult when he would have too much to drink and call you a fake. It cut to the core because you had seen him be so spot-on about calling behaviors. So you'd say, "Oh gee, I must be a fake."

It was a favorite word of his. I came to understand it was part of a projection of himself. He was afraid of not being completely real. Bob was a big guy and he had gone through the war and he had done all this stuff. But deep down inside, as there is in many of us, there's this voice saying, "I wonder if they're going to find me out?"

He had dark stuff in there and who knows why. But men of that age didn't talk about their interior life or their stuff, but his interior stuff would come through.

MICHAEL MURPHY: He could cut you. He could do that look and say one sentence. I saw him reduce an obnoxious but famous publicist to tears that fast in the lobby of a theater one night. She said something or did something he didn't like, and he turned on her and he said one sentence and she just came unglued. He was a very powerful guy. But I think he had much more of a reputation than anything else. Anybody with half a brain could get along with this guy. He was not a hostile person. He didn't look for trouble, really. He was certainly ready for it, and as I said before, alcohol was not his best friend in that department. But he had a lot of good times when he was drinking, too. I can't think of too many people that were the subjects of his wrath that didn't deserve it. It was always some stupid Hollywood kind of thing that would start it.

JOHN SCHUCK: There's a real dark side to him. I only saw it personally because it was directed against me at a Christmas party when we were making *McCabe & Mrs. Miller.* It was a wonderful party, and there's eighty people there up in Vancouver, and I'd gone to the bathroom. It was fairly late, so the party had been going on five or six hours. I was coming back through this room and Bob was there getting something out of his desk, and he looked up at me and kind of walked up to me very close and said, "I don't like you very much." And I said, "Well, that's your loss." End of exchange. Never mentioned it again. Never felt any dislike from him again.

He continued to hire me for a couple more films. I don't think it was directed at me at all, but for a minute there I was hurt by it, of course. But then I never saw any indication of it. Don't know what prompted it. I just happened to be in the room at the right time. It could have been the combination of alcohol and whether he was smoking that night, I don't know. But there was that personality change that often happens with people that are heavy drinkers.

ALAN RUDOLPH: The key to Bob is he and his movies, everything about his movies and everything about him, were completely inseparable.

Another key to Bob is that you were always a guest in his world. He never entered yours. He entered yours but only on his terms, whether it was personal, public, professional, intimate I'm sure, or intentional. Bob would never surrender to anyone else's world, ever. I don't think he was capable of that. I think Bob heard his voice and his calling and never varied. He was different, and it'll take your book to try and define it, and it will be elusive and you'll never get to the center of it because you shouldn't be able to.

I don't care what their title was, who they were, I've never been in any room with anybody where Bob wasn't at least tied for the most powerful force in the room. I've been with him with governors and senators. His X-ray vision not only encompassed his ability to react, digest, react, and control a situation, but he also knew where to go inside of any person and what he could tweak. Because he didn't have any decorum rules, he could challenge people on an emotional, personal, political, creative level. And then be in control of them. The restrictions and restraints that a lot of people put on themselves when they're in public prohibits them from being so free. But there were never any rules for Bob on any level.

In the Bob world, the biggest mistake—I think it's the biggest crime maybe committed in humanity—is betrayal. So if you were working on Bob's behalf and did not bring your own priorities there to overwhelm his priorities, and you were working for the common good and you made a mistake, he may be annoyed by it, it may have to be corrected, but there was no anger. No true anger. If you betrayed the trust of the gift of this human interaction and creative process, then, basically, Bob couldn't abide that.

He didn't have to work at being who he was. One of the first things I remember was him quoting Abraham Lincoln, where he says, "You just have to tell the truth and you don't have to remember anything else." And that was how he lived. That's why there was no effort. That's why Bob could create things lying on the couch and not getting up. And there was no tension. There wasn't that stress that killed people. What killed him was bad chemistry, you know, bad pharmaceutical chemistry and a life of just diving off the deep end every time. I mean, it's going to catch up with you if you live to the max.

PETER NEWMAN (producer): The way he ran his life and his business was sheer anarchy. It was a circus with this artistically gifted presence in the center of it. He could be incredibly generous and outrageously cruel. It seemed to me at the heart of it was Bob was very, very, very sensitive. My appraisal was that even though he would make jokes about things, he was very sensitive to the fact that he didn't get to direct a feature film until his forties, and his first was such a hit and he barely got paid for it. He was also incredibly sensitive that he had been mistreated by the studios. He had a real dislike for business.

I think anyone who worked with Bob went through a period of having great love or great anger toward him. It depends on what point in time you talk to someone about Bob.

I was quoted once saying Bob called me "the Jew with the money." Bob was totally irreverent. First of all, I didn't have any money. More important, some people saw an implication that it was anti-Semitic. Nothing could be further from the truth. God knows he wasn't anti-Semitic. He was just outrageous.

PETER GALLAGHER (actor): He would say, "Every morning I wake up and I'm at the bottom of a very deep hole. And I scratch and claw all day long, and by the end of the day if I'm lucky I get my eyes above the edge and I get a glimpse around before I end up at the bottom of the hole again." So as gruff and as sort of outsized as Bob can be, there is a tremendous compassion that informs what he does.

MATTHEW MODINE (actor): On the outside he had this confidence and strength and wry sense of humor, but all of that stuff was like the shell of a crab. Inside it's really soft, sweet meat. To protect that he had to create this strong, I-don't-give-a-shit attitude. For an artist to suc-

Robert Altman, scowling on the set of McCabe & Mrs. Miller

ceed as long as he did, he needed a strong shell. Life, let alone the industry, will crush that and make you cynical and make you think about dollars and cents. A filmmaker whose films don't make money in this business is discarded faster than a used piece of toilet paper. But Bob always found a way to finance his need to tell a story.

BUCK HENRY (writer and actor): In the back of my head I was always aware that he could turn on a dime if someone said something that really irritated him or had an opinion that didn't make him laugh. I think he had very strict rules of behavior—I would imagine having something to do with his childhood.

His rage against the establishment was one or two parts bullshit. Everybody kissed Bob's ass. They realized that he was an important filmmaker—regarded as that around the world. He liked the feeling of being really angry.

*   *   *

LILY TOMLIN: I had optioned a book in 1971, *Maiden*, by Cynthia Buchanan. I was crazy about the book, and Jane Wagner, my partner, wrote a screenplay. And as it happened, Bob was looking for something for Joan Tewkesbury to direct, and we had the same agent, Sam Cohn. Bob read that screenplay of *Maiden* and wanted to produce it and have Joan direct it. So Bob said to me, "You'll come to Nashville this summer and we'll do *Maiden* in the fall."

He had just finished *California Split* and that was a Columbia picture. Columbia optioned the book and the screenplay for *Maiden* and then Jane and Joan had begun working on the shooting script for *Maiden*. I went to Nashville, and the guys from Columbia, the suits, came to town and wanted Bob to cut six minutes out of *California Split*. He punched one of them in the nose, and he fell in the pool. *Maiden* never got made. It's still sitting on the shelf at Columbia.

JOSEPH WALSH: It was something the way he'd go after studio executives.

I'd say, "Why do you go out of your way to knock them in print? Why are you building up the animosity?"

He said, "The suits know nothing. If you had to deal with those kinds of people you'd understand."

I really never knew what the psychology was. Maybe he liked the friction, to keep him on edge with his talent. I felt he did a disservice to himself. I'm saying, "Don't fuck it up, Bob. Don't do it when you don't need to. I'm certainly not asking you to kiss anybody's ass, but do you have to always kick it?"

ROBERT DORNHELM (director): Maybe you have to be playful, dangerously playful, to beat the Hollywood system. He enjoyed making enemies. Offending people was something he had great appetite for. It's quite American, quite individualistic. I grew up in a totalitarian regime, in Austria, and we are all kind of beaten down by authority. He was kind of the opposing way. He was needling, provoking, questioning. He was what a true artist should be.

He shouldn't be put in for sainthood. He had a monstrous side to him and he was also a sweetheart. A man of contradictions. Like any creative person, you have to be monstrous in your beauty and in your ego to accomplish it. Yet at the same time I have seen him be very gentle and sweet.

KEITH CARRADINE: Bob could be very tough, you know. I know there are people who had run-ins with him over the years and he could be very, very harsh and tough. He could cut you off. I never had anything like that with Bob, never. Maybe because I never crossed the line? And I know there was a line you could cross with Bob.

I think probably the people that had problems with him at any point were on some level either fools or just assholes. Not that Bob was a saint and not that he was always right. We all know that. And he also gloried in defying authority. But that's what made his work so brilliant. Even the failures were brilliant.

WREN ARTHUR (producer): On some levels he was the easiest guy on the planet, on others he was absolutely the most difficult, complicated guy on the planet. He was the girl with the curl in the middle of her forehead. He was so great and so much fun and could be the most entertaining, intriguing individual when he was good, and when he was bad he was just the most terrifying, really bad, scary person to be around. On some level, he was the midwestern everyguy. And he could also be Bob Altman the big, fancy director. He was so many different things inside of one person, as we all are. And what made him special is he really saw that. Everybody had the potential or was interesting on some level, or they were absolutely boring and he would sort of torture them or ignore them. But if you showed an interest and you weren't scared of him, he wanted to know what you could bring.

He definitely had a mean streak. I only got it a couple times. I think a lot of other people got it repeatedly, and that was their relationship. I can give you a million psychological reasons for it, but I think it was never black or white. A lot of times it was out of frustration. He was a man, absolutely, but he was also a boy. He had a real boyish streak. And it was sometimes just out of literal frustration, and so it was whatever was in the way. Or whoever was in the way would get it. And sometimes it was all chemicals. A lot of different chemicals in his body, you know, I mean literally, between the booze and the pot, it was just like whatever was happening chemically. I understand moody. But sometimes it could just be the chemicals. And that's almost scarier because that means maybe he really doesn't have control. That would be the frustrating part because you love him and you look up to him and he does play the role of big papa. And for big papa to all of a sudden turn around, it could be very sad. Or hurtful.

He sought out conflict. I think it challenged him, it made him think harder, made him have to. I don't think this is original to Bob, by the way. I think it is universal for artists of any kind. Painters, writers, actors, directors, production designers. Anyone who is thinking in a creative mind. It's like your fingers get electric. Everything shoots and fires and it's like when you wake from a dream because you've fallen or you stub your toe and everything goes "Aargh!" That kind of conflict makes that feeling. It's an endorphin, it's an adrenaline rush. So sometimes the conflict is very productive and sometimes it's incredibly counterproductive, and I think Bob had his share of both across the board.

That said, he was one of the most endlessly positive people in the most negative uniform, you know what I mean? He could just keep going.

PAUL THOMAS ANDERSON: I was asking him advice about something, talking about something that was going on with me in my life. He said, "I will tell you this, whatever you do, you have to do what's right for yourself. You can't think about anything else." It wasn't as vague or general as it sounds, 'cause I'm not telling you what we were talking about. But he was very specific in what he was saying. It wasn't just a broad-stroke comment. I felt like he was relaying to me something that he learned through the course of his life. And perhaps suggesting that you have to be selfish from time to time. Perhaps he had been selfish from time to time. But it would be okay and ultimately it would make me happy.

JOHN WILLIAMS: He was very much a man of his time. Shaped by the Depression, sculpted by the war. He didn't look back to earlier times or ahead to other times, but he was showing us how we are right now. He spoke the current vernacular, literally as well as artistically. If he could have been a writer, and I think he could have, he was almost a Sandburg or a Steinbeck kind of character who really knew the people in the middle of this country in the 1930s and '40s. He really had an understanding of the people of the Midwest, the blacks, the farmers, the workers. The farmland bowels of this country were in his blood in

Robert Altman, smiling on the set of McCabe & Mrs. Miller

some ways. He felt like the quintessential midwesterner to me in all these respects.

JULIANNE MOORE (actress): Often I think you find with auteurs or people who are supposedly artists, there's this idea that they carry around and that the world carries around that they're somehow different, therefore more special, therefore are supposed to have special treatment. There was none of that. None of that was present in Bob's personality or his life. Not a moment of it. Not a moment of egomania. I've never known anybody who was more aware of what was going on in a set, like everywhere, with the camera operator and the actors and the makeup person, and he was always exceedingly aware of the psychological temperature of the set. And of everybody on it. And was careful of how he talked to people, how he interacted.

There was a script that somebody had approached him about for me, and he wanted to talk to me alone. He was like, "What do you think, honey?" I remember he was lying down. He was in the last year of his life and he was lying down on the couch and I had come in for a meeting and sat next to him on the couch and he was like, "Tell me what you really think. Do you want to do this or do you not want to do this?" He was really trying to assess exactly what my feelings were about the project, privately. He wasn't somebody who was going to disregard what I felt, ever. And not because it was me, but because that's how he was with every individual, which is really unusual in a person with that kind of breadth of artistic vision.

WOLF KROEGER (art director): He said he never gave a shit. Of course he did. Of course he cared. He was always marked as being anti-Hollywood. But if anyone was Hollywood it was him. The real Hollywood. He wanted to be a famous film director. He was a rebel. But he would never admit that. He had the same weaknesses we all do. We all want to be appreciated. You know, "This whole system sucks and this whole system is unprofessional, and I'm the one who is really working very hard on it. They don't appreciate me, but I'm going to do a good job." And by being difficult he got a lot of fame out of it, too.

He was a human being, a guy you could talk to, relate to. He showed all his faults, he showed all his tempers, he was a person you could relate to.

JOHNNIE PLANCO (agent): One night in Cannes, Bob and Kathryn were having words. Kathryn said, "Oh Bob, get over yourself." And he stood there sputtering and finally said, "Why don't you take a flying fuck off the ceiling?" I burst out laughing because it was such a stupid thing to say. Then we all started laughing.

SUE BARTON (publicist): I had known Bob and Kathryn for years, and I had seen Bob through all kinds of awful things. I was the publicist on *Nashville*, and we used to have these arrangements: if it was somebody's birthday or anniversary a party would be given following dailies. Everybody would stay and have some drinks.

Early that afternoon Bob's secretary said to me, "It's Bob and Kathryn's fifteenth wedding anniversary. Should we do something?"

We got a cake. We did this and it was very unpleasant. We didn't realize how far gone he was, drinking and smoking at dailies. Kathryn was ever cool—"They're playing our song." I was walking toward the office and he was walking away.

He said, "Who arranged this?"

I said, "Well, I did."

He said, "Well, you're fired."

I said, "You can't just say that and walk away."

So he turned around and walked back to the back room. I said something and then he said, "There's nothing to celebrate about marriage. Your mother just died, right?" And she had, a couple months before. He said, "Why aren't we celebrating that?"

At which point Kathryn picked up this great big fruit basket and threw it at him. He walked out.

She said, "He doesn't mean anything by it. Be there in the morning and it'll all be fine."

I thought he was never going to do that to me. I thought, "Fuck, I don't want to do that." I promptly left and went to Nova Scotia. I didn't see him for a long time after that.

Then one night at Elaine's, Kathryn was giving a kind of surprise birthday party for Bob. As the evening progressed Bob came over to me and said, "You've been a wonderful friend."

"That's because I love you and I love Kathryn."

And from that moment on we were fine.

GARRY TRUDEAU: I've done some soul-searching on this because of the whole issue of exceptionalism. Do you excuse bad behavior in some people and not in others? Do you write it off as the price that you pay for doing the work with somebody who is exceptionally talented? And

I wasn't entirely satisfied with the answers I gave myself because there were times when I thought, "This man is not very good to a lot of people a lot of the time." Although he was always capable of enormous generosity and warmth, is there some sort of complicity in just overlooking it?

For some reason, I had immunity. He only exploded at me once. I can't recall what it was over, which is telling. Because it didn't really matter what it was over. He just needed to explode. Generally he'd be tough on others and not on me. That made it more confusing in a way. A tougher call. You can say, "Well, do you put up with this because it's not directed at me?" [*Laughs*] I can imagine myself walking away had I been treated with the kind of cruelty which he was capable of. Just out of self-protection. But I wasn't.

MALCOLM MCDOWELL (actor): He was such a maverick and a "fuck you" kind of person and such a complete individual who very much marched to his own beat. It was very refreshing. He didn't seem to be scared of anybody. He wasn't intimidated by the suits and all that, which was great.

I found myself in Rome while he was there talking about some proj-

At the start of each new film, Altman would ask his wardrobe department for a new hat, which he would wear throughout the shoot. This straw hat with a flower was the choice for The Long Goodbye

ect. And I was there doing a film, a very strange film about a Roman emperor. And it was a strange set. And I was telling Bob about it at dinner.

And he said, "You're all naked, huh?"

I said, "Yeah, yeah."

And he said, "I may come and visit you."

Well, actually there was a big party, so he did get to meet the producer, this man called Bob Guccione. And I was telling Bob all about him. And he was going, "*Penthouse* magazine."

And I said, "They told me to treat him like one of the Warner brothers."

He said, "I see."

And he goes in. He comes in. And there's this big party—there's Pets and the actors, on one of the sets, or whatever. And Bob goes over to Bob Guccione and says, "Mr. Gucci, I like your shoes."

Beautifully put away. Beautifully.

HARRY BELAFONTE: Early in our relationship, I told a joke and it became the metaphor for everything in our lives. These two musicians decided they were going to the jazz festival in Montreux, but they always flew. One says, "We should take one of these cruises, man, and just get out there and have four days and just lay out and see what that side of life is like." So they were out in the middle of the Atlantic. And the water was calm and glassy. The moon hung high in the sky. The musicians broke out a spliff, a reefer, and they lit up and took a hit, gazing quietly out at the magic of the moon and the water.

The first musician said, "Man, look at all that water."

And the second musician said, "Yeah, and that's only the top."

Bob went crazy. He went out. So anytime we were someplace and somebody said something, Bob would look at me and say, "That's only the top." And when somebody would come and aggravate him, and she ran her mouth or something, as she took a breath, Bob goes, "That's only the top."

LEONARD COHEN (singer and songwriter): He came to a concert that I gave at the Troubadour in Los Angeles, which I think still exists. It was a very popular club at the time. I remember an extremely generous gesture of his. I was onstage and I left the stage with a considerable amount of anxiety about the performance I had just given. I was walking offstage, down the hall to this little dressing room, not feeling very good about things. Bob was standing there—he was a big man and I'm a small chap—he just opened his arms and gave me a big bear hug.

He was a very, very good example because he just kept doing it regardless of how it was received. And did it with a tremendous grace and tremendous originality. To see him doing that was always impressive and always inspiring. He was only about seven or eight years older than I am but he seemed to be very much more accomplished and very much more in the world, so he was someone who was a shining example of the combination of integrity, originality, and indifference to the winds of change.

MATTHEW SEIG (producer): The guy had a bad temper and he could explode. And you know it was a long time before he ever yelled at me, a real long time. But I never took it personally. I don't know, it was just Bob screaming. By that time I was so used to seeing him do it that it just was, you know, not a big deal. I wouldn't have wanted to put up with that on a regular basis.

MICHAEL MURPHY: I would have hung out with this guy night and day. He could have been a plumber. That would have been fine with me. He just was that kind of guy. How could you not want to be there? I really did, I wanted to be there regardless of whether I was in the movies or not in the movies or any of it, you know? I loved hanging around with him and ergo I was involved in a lot of things. I was there for a lot of the down stuff and the hard times and I saw a lot of it. I try to be careful with that stuff because you see people at their most vulnerable. That's why I never have liked those kiss-and-tell books. But this guy was just so remarkable.

You know, my parents influenced me, obviously, but I don't know, I was too young to get it, or maybe it was jammed down my throat. But it was something about the way he just let you tag along. You learned by standing there watching it all. I think about this guy, I swear to God, every day. Every day he goes through my mind somehow.

ALLAN NICHOLLS (actor/music director/screenwriter/associate producer/assistant director): We went on a fishing trip once. Bob, Bob Eggenweiler, myself, Tommy Thompson, and Frank Barhydt. One night, we're floating around—we were going to go fishing the next day—off the coast of Escondido. It was about an eighty-foot boat, a luxury boat. I had never been fishing on a boat before in my life, and we were sitting around having drinks at the end of the day, and all sunburned and having a cocktail and Eggenweiler was cooking some great fucking meal. And Bob goes, "This is true homosexuality" [*laughs*].

RENÉ AUBERJONOIS: He had these offices on Westwood Avenue, Lion's Gate Films. If you were in town and drove by, you could just drop in and Bob would be in his office. He would be there and you could walk in and just hang out and eat popcorn and smoke a joint. I can't imagine doing that in any other producer or director's office on the face of the Earth, but that's the way it was.

One time, Henry Gibson was there having a meeting for the film *Nashville*. I felt very uncomfortable. I felt like Bob was showing me what I was going to be missing. The minute I realized I was in a meeting for a film—I never actually told Henry that, how uncomfortable I felt—I made excuses and left. I remember feeling very hurt. Bob was manipulative. He was devilish. He was tricky. He was slippery. He was McCabe. You could sense that you could get on the wrong side of Bob and that could not be good.

HENRY GIBSON: René found that as a source of rejection? Did he say I did anything? Because I don't remember too many meetings there prior to shooting. Oh, what a heartbreak. It could be that he imagined that I was in the room, which is all right.

JOSH ASTRACHAN (producer): I don't know, this may be a little easy, but I feel like Bob never saw somebody who was satisfied with himself that he wouldn't like to pull the rug out from under. But part of it is just this combative guy who couldn't resist taking a swipe sometimes, even if he ended up being the one who got swiped.

RICHARD BASKIN (composer): I had a dream where I'm at a cocktail party and we're at an apartment on the twentieth floor. Everybody's having a good time and Bob is pretty lit. Scotch in one hand and a joint in the other. We end up out on the balcony arguing. He loses his balance and falls off the balcony. Jesus, I've killed Bob. I see Kathryn in the room and say, "How am I going to tell Kathryn?" The door opens and in walks Bob, like a cartoon character. His hair is rumpled and he has a Band-Aid across his nose. That was always the perfect metaphor for who he was. He was indomitable, a force of nature.

BILL ROBINSON (agent): I met him during *The Long Goodbye*. I was an agent trying to sell him a client. He didn't act like he was one of the great filmmakers of our time. Pretty soon we started playing backgammon, and eventually we probably played a few hundred thousand games of backgammon. How was he? Not great. On a ten scale, a ten being a top tournament player, I was probably an eight and he was probably a six. But he had great guts. He was not afraid to make a bet or give you the cube and double you. That was the fun with him. You'd be sitting here, it's his turn and you'd be in a much better position to him. He'd say, "I'm going to turn the cube to sixteen." When you're playing with an opponent not as good as you, you don't want to have the doubling cube go too high. He wasn't afraid or intimidated by anybody, just exactly like he was in the business. And he never cared if he lost. He always paid right then. You didn't wait a day or a week. He got up, got his money, and paid you. Every single time.

Most of us, when we're spending or gambling money, we understand how much we can afford to lose. And I'd rather not lose that much. I guess I can, but I'd rather not. He never worried about that. Let's say he had five hundred dollars in his pocket and he was bringing it home to give to Kathryn to buy something. If on the way home he got in a backgammon game he would just not worry about losing that. He would get in the car and find a way to get what he wanted with that five hundred dollars. And if he didn't, he had the confidence that he'd get it tomorrow. It was confidence, mainly, but it was more than that. He didn't have the fears and the insecurities that the rest of us have. If you don't worry about that, you're free. Your behavior is free. If you're a businessperson, your idea of failing would be, "Did the movie make money or not?" His sense of failure would be if people he knew and liked didn't like his movie. Unless, of course, he really liked it.

HARRY BELAFONTE: Backgammon? He beat me all the time. I mean, that son of a bitch has beaten me when I had just one off left, and he had all his chips still on. He was amazing. In the face of a clear loss he would turn the cube over, a double. I'd say, "Why are you giving it away, Bob? I got you, man." He said, "Let's play."

ALLAN NICHOLLS: There is a sheet of paper somewhere, and I can't remember if I'm up fifteen points or seven points. But he does owe me. And I can't remember if it was five dollars a point or twenty dollars a point. If he was winning, he'd make it twenty dollars a point. And if I was winning, five dollars a point.

STEPHEN ALTMAN: He was a horrible backgammon player. I used to kick his ass regularly. On my nineteenth birthday he bought me this beautiful backgammon board that I still have. And he took two weeks of per diem pay from me that night, gambling. It was like, "If you're going to play with me you're playing for five dollars a point." It was every penny I had, like five hundred dollars or something. At the time that was everything. He really enjoyed that and then enjoyed beating the hell out of me at that game for a long time. But I persevered and at the end I believe I took a lot more from him than he ever took from me. I certainly played by his rules and stuck it to him whenever I could and it was a lot of fun. We had a good time.

Playing his signature tarot solitaire game

JOSH ASTRACHAN: One of the great things was the Bob solitaire game, with tarot cards. It's such a vivid part of who he was on a day-in, day-out basis. It always seemed to me it was kind of the perfect distraction and meditation, because it allowed him to remember whatever he needed to remember. What'd it look like? Oh, the desk was covered. I mean they were oversized cards. He looked like some kind of wizard, you know, with these things. And I didn't even know what those characters were, let alone what the rules were of how you could assemble one on top of the other. And of course he had those long beautiful hands and he would look so great playing solitaire. So it all seemed inscrutable and kind of magical, as if he were summoning, you know, telling his future. And then he'd know what to do and he'd call out in the middle of it—"Get this thing done."

*   *   *

JULIAN FELLOWES (actor and screenwriter): Bob was a very explosive personality. Bob was hot. He was a kind of charismatic exploding lion, and that is something that has to be handled with care.

GERALDINE CHAPLIN: He was such a focus of your attention that when he didn't call you worried you had done something. He was the best person in the world to be loved by. You'd always love him, but you never knew if he loved you or not. I fell out of favor for some reason, I don't know why. I probably got old and I wasn't useful anymore.

BOB BALABAN (actor/producer/director): Well, he had a ferocious temper. I don't think it was an age thing necessarily, but I think for a lot of men anyway, he's their father. Because he's the thing you fear in your father, you need his approval desperately, because people around Bob really, really want his approval, which he gives so lavishly when he's giving it. So the times when he didn't give it, it's like your father has taken away your worth, you know?

PAUL NEWMAN (actor and philanthropist): He was an original. Being an original means that you're standing out there on thin ice sometimes. But at least he was out there skating while everybody else was waiting for cold weather.

HENRY GIBSON: I'm always surprised that people are surprised that an artist has tantrums, has fits, has prejudices, becomes easily exasperated, is impatient, is overly exuberant, loves to entertain, is theatrical, is a gambler. This is human nature. Artists from the beginning of time have been this way. What, are we really surprised? Are they surprised because perhaps in the twenties and thirties and forties the press was not exposed to this? Yes, that's what I think. But did great artists, great conductors, great writers of the last three centuries not have similar characteristics and traits? Yes. This is all part of the fabric of greatness. He was very, very human. He never presented himself as a saint.

Now, his work demonstrates his generosity, the expansiveness of his spirit, his encouragement of others, his taking chances on others, his recognizing talent, his fanning it. He held people up. Yes, there were some actors who gave brilliant performances only for him. And could not sustain it, because perhaps they did not have the technique to follow through, the training, the exposure. What they didn't have was Bob. No, if you talk about the man, I see both sides and I hug both. It would be unbearable if he was treacly. He's not a greeting card. He's not haiku.

He had this gift—which was also an affliction—of people finding in him the father they never had. Because he was by nature in accommodating cast, crew, the people he worked with, paternal. Did this come from his father? I don't know. Normally we do one of two things. We either imitate our fathers or we couldn't stand them and we go in the complete opposite direction. As we mature as kids, we realize that this man that we idolized makes mistakes. He does have clay feet. He does some outrageous things. He's our father. We love him. And then we get a little older, and we say, "You know, we're all made of many strands." So some people might go into shock. Some people didn't mature. Some people were daddy-hung. It sounds like an Indian word, doesn't it? Or something on an Indian menu.

Your capacity for hurt is sometimes stronger than your capacity for love. You're talking about people being so hurt that they remember it for thirty years. Because they refuse to accept the fact that he was human. He never could be a saint. I know some of those people you're talking about. You know, "I can never forgive him." Hold on for a minute. From that one incident, and yet you worked for him here, you've worked for him there? Someone spilled wine on your new burgundy dress? A disproportionate reaction to a larger-than-life soul, I think.

CHAPTER 20

Active Verbs

*

Buffalo Bill and the Indians, or Sitting Bull's History Lesson *(1976)*

Charles Champlin, review in the *Los Angeles Times*, June 30, 1976: When Robert Altman's movies are good, they are very, very good, and when they are bad, they are infuriating because there is something arrogantly self-destructive about them. . . . The Altman successes and the Altman nonsuccesses are linked by his unchallenged ability to make strong images and arresting scenes. His films are sometimes pretentious and sometimes exasperating but they are not often boring, although the latest, "Buffalo Bill and the Indians, or Sitting Bull's History Lesson," is all three. . . . Buffalo Bill is played as one long Homeric hangover by Paul Newman in a shoulder-length curly wig (which he is caught without, self-scalped so to speak, in one farcical early morning confrontation with Sitting Bull).

*   *   *

KENNETH BRANAGH (actor): *Buffalo Bill* is an example of Altman putting an American icon, Paul Newman, into the role of an American icon. He had the ability to attract actors with surprising roles in controversial pieces that were *about* something—in that case a look at show business, a look at history, a look at how America looks at itself, a look at the West. It was a real potpourri of really fascinating, controversial insight. He was unafraid in that picture of presenting disillusion in a

With Paul Newman, as Buffalo Bill, during location shooting universally described as a joyful experience, followed by a ho-hum audience response and a bitter dispute with producer Dino De Laurentiis

very prominent way, and yet it wasn't gloomy. He looked difficult things in the eye.

MIKE KAPLAN (publicist and producer): It was an Altman movie—what you expect is not what you get. Looking back on it I don't know what they were expecting. I just see the film in my eyes. They were expecting much more of a traditional movie that would have more action, maybe—it had Paul Newman and Burt Lancaster. And Bob was making a statement about celebrity and the treatment of the Indians and the nature of America.

MATTHEW SEIG (producer): He was fascinated by the whole role of putting on a show, the whole tradition of showmanship, whether it's a con or not and how very American that tradition is. He's very much in touch with American culture. Whether or not his films are accepted by it is not really the point. It's his interest in America and its institutions, including show business.

* * *

PAUL NEWMAN: The way he chooses his language and his descriptive phrases is amazingly perceptive and helpful. And if you don't listen very carefully, you might miss it. Bob directs using active verbs. You can play an active verb. You can't play an inactive one.

I don't remember what the specifics of the scene were, but Altman beckoned me over. He thought for a minute—I was playing a scene with another actor—and he said, "Crowd him." It was so clear and so defined and so unmistakable what he wanted from that scene and from that character that he made it easy to play. When he tells you to crowd the guy you're talking to, you know exactly what he's talking about. You put out physical presence to bear on the scene. "Back off" you can play in more ways than one. You can play it intellectually, you can play it physically. If he tells you to amuse the other character—almost any active verb you can think of you can find a way to play.

When you needed it, that was the kind of direction he would give. Most of the time he was happy to let you find your own way and to be comfortable. But if you got into trouble he sure as hell could get you out of it.

He knew how to make people comfortable. Even when he disagreed with them he knew how to make them comfortable. It's a great gift, particularly a great gift for someone who has authority.

JOHN CONSIDINE (actor and screenwriter): Newman has a great sense of humor. I think when Newman arrived Bob had his dressing room filled with popcorn. That started this back-and-forth of practical jokes on each other. Bob had this beautiful pair of beaded gloves that an Indian tribe had made for him. He wore them all the time. Somehow Newman got ahold of these gloves.

At his desk in the production office of Buffalo Bill and the Indians,
or Sitting Bull's History Lesson

PAUL NEWMAN: The popcorn, I thought, was a minor insult. But to get
into his bedroom at the hotel and steal his gloves and then have them
French-fried and served garni in a fast-food box I thought was rather
stylish. I've forgotten what he retaliated with. He always had his very
fancy camper. I think I got ten thousand chickens and put them in his
camper, which needless to say was both difficult to clean and to drive.

I had someone tell him that I had an announcement broadcast on
the local radio station—there was an emergency, and the production
department needed four thousand extras the next morning at six
o'clock. He was crazy. Of course he didn't know how to stop it. There
was a flurry of excitement in the production department. I think I let
him off the hook, told him it was a gag.

We had a bad scene, which we finally, obviously cured, but he said,
"The reason I got so pissed off—underneath every practical joke, there
is an element of malice. You're trying to make someone look silly.
You're trying to humiliate them or make them feel bad." And he said,
"Why would anybody want to do that?" And so that was the end of my
reign as the king of practical jokes. Altman was very relieved when he
found out about that, I might add.

ALAN RUDOLPH (director): Bob once suggested to Paul Newman that they form a company together using the first half of Bob's last name and the second half of Paul's. They'd call it the Altman company.

JOHN CONSIDINE: Dino De Laurentiis was the producer, and he expected a shoot-'em-up kind of thing. He came to the set one day. Bob had rented this big place for the whole cast and crew to watch this big Muhammad Ali fight. At one o'clock in the afternoon Bob says, "That's a wrap. We're all going to watch this fight." He and Dino had this huge argument. "Bob, you can't stop shooting at one o'clock!" The last thing I heard was, "Dino, Dino, it's just a goddamn movie." So we all watched the fight.

During the last third of the shooting, Bob was in extraordinary pain from a bad back. He could barely walk, and you could tell he just wanted it to be over. He probably rushed through the cutting process, too, because I always thought if he ever went back and recut it, it could have been a more successful film. It was a colossal flop. It was so wild to have this amazing, wonderful time and then the reception was so bad.

GERALDINE CHAPLIN: He was always at his best when he had his back against the wall with a knife at his throat. He was too excited to get on to the next project always. He had so much talent and he was such a genius, his mind was going much faster than the project. And a lot of times he would be on to the next project before he finished cutting the one he was on. His best projects were when he was out of favor and had to prove himself. That's when he paid most attention.

LAUREN HUTTON: I went to the premiere straight from the airport. I had this giant elephant bone—huge—it was about four feet long, a bull-male tibia. So I went to the premiere with this thing over my shoulder. And then it was a disaster. Then I see Bob and Dino having this huge fight in the lobby. And then I went and got my suitcase, my little duffel, and my bone, and we went to Bob and Kathryn's apartment for the after party. Everyone was so stricken that when I walked in the door, I immediately took my bone off my shoulder and said, "This is for you." And I gave it to Bob, this giant bone. So Bob spent that whole night with that bone on *his* shoulder.

KATHRYN REED ALTMAN: I love that bone. It's been here in my home for more than twenty years.

Bill Robinson (agent): Dino wanted it to be more commercial. He flew over here and almost threatened Bob, "That movie has got to be shorter!" The longer it was, in his mind, the less people would like it. Bob didn't care. "That's my movie. You can't cut it."

Joan Tewkesbury: Dino is a guy who tells a story, and there's a beginning, a middle, and an end. They may have been sitting down at the same table to have dinner, but they weren't having the same meal.

Unbylined story headlined "De Laurentiis Dismisses Altman from *Ragtime,*" *The New York Times,* **June 22, 1976:** Robert Altman, one of Hollywood's top-flight directors, whose credits include "M*A*S*H," "Nashville" and "Buffalo Bill and the Indians," which is scheduled to open in New York on Thursday, has been dismissed as the director of "Ragtime," the movie to be based on E. L. Doctorow's novel.

The award-winning director said last night that he was dismissed by Dino De Laurentiis, producer of "Ragtime," three weeks ago, because of a difference of opinion, not about "Ragtime," but about how much should be cut out of "Buffalo Bill and the Indians."

"He [Mr. De Laurentiis] was disappointed in 'Buffalo Bill' and requested that I cut the film rather drastically," Mr. Altman said. "I did my best to accommodate him, but in the end it's my movie and I had to put it out the way my conscience dictated." . . . "I'm naturally disappointed. I feel like Adlai Stevenson—It hurts too much to laugh and I'm too old to cry. It's not the artists who are disagreeing, it's money."

Martin Scorsese: The big tragedy, I think— well, "tragedy" may be too strong a word and "disappointment" is too light a word. I'm talking about when he was going to do *Ragtime* and he didn't get it. As interesting a film as it turned out to be, with Milos Forman, there's something uniquely American about it, and it had to do with a kind of gigantic fresco of America at that time. The rebelliousness and the nature of the material, and a gallery of characters. Who could handle that better? Who could juggle it better? Who could weave them in and out like a beautiful tapestry? Who else but Altman could do that kind of thing?

I saw him right after that happened. I said, "What do you do now?"

He said, "Punt" [*laughs*]. And even though the only football game I ever understood was in *M*A*S*H*, I got it.

* * *

Story headlined "*Buffalo Bill* Wins Top Berlin Prize," Reuters, July 8, 1976: The United States film "Buffalo Bill and the Indians, or Sitting Bull's History Lesson" won the Golden Bear award at the Berlin Festival, despite an earlier protest by the director, Robert Altman, that he did not want the picture considered for a prize. In a letter to the festival, Mr. Altman said the film had been edited so drastically that it perpetrated "a fraud" on audiences. The version at the festival was authorized by him.

JEFF GOLDBLUM (actor): After *Nashville*, I saw *Buffalo Bill*. I loved it. The guy who played Sitting Bull hardly talked. Altman said, "I learned something from him—he had the courage to be empty."

* * *

Robert Altman as Producer

Welcome to L.A. (1977, directed by Alan Rudolph); *The Late Show* (1977, directed by Robert Benton); *Remember My Name* (1988, directed by Alan Rudolph); *Rich Kids* (1988, directed by Robert M. Young); *Mrs. Parker and the Vicious Circle* (1994, directed by Alan Rudolph); *Afterglow* (1997, directed by Alan Rudolph); *Trixie* (2000, directed by Alan Rudolph).

ROBERT BENTON (writer and director): He produced for me the way he would want someone to produce for him—to be supportive and never lie. Altman taught me how to be a director. It's that simple. I was a writer working as a director. I illustrated a screenplay. He taught me a way of listening to the actors, a way of respecting the actors, a way of letting the picture become a more fluid process. It was great process for me.

On *Late Show*, he was there every day at the end of the day saying, "Great work, you've done a great job." When there were notes they would be extremely good notes. Essentially he said, "The actors are the only real heroes in movies. It's easy for guys like you and me to stand behind the camera and make up a story. If he or she has a question with our logic, we really should listen to them."

There was a tiny scene and Lily Tomlin was in her apartment and these guys came in to threaten her. It was a tiny moment and she said, "No, no, I'd do this." I suddenly realized, only because Altman had made me see that, she wasn't speaking as Lily, she was speaking as Martha, the character. She knew exactly what she was doing, and my job was to let the actors have a safety net so they could risk anything and they could feel secure. I think that's really what Altman did with all his actors, made them feel safe and that he would protect them. And he did.

He was out preparing *3 Women,* and he said, "Show the picture to Warner Brothers." In the back of Lion's Gate there was a garage he converted into a screening room. All the people from Warner Brothers came. They sat down and it was very pleasant. We started running the picture—it was the worst screening. Three minutes in, I felt like I was on the *Titanic.*

I got a call from David Geffen, who was then head of production at Warner's. He said, "If it were up to me I'd bury this. But there is a young executive named Paula Weinstein, and she wants to work with it." Altman's favorite mode is to put on your helmet and get into the trenches and tell them to go fuck themselves. But he listened to me and he listened to Paula and he said, "We have to change the editor." He brought in Lou Lombardo and he was great. From September until Christmas of '76, we significantly changed the picture. It was really Lou Lombardo and Paula who did it.

Altman kept getting madder at me and madder at me. He thought I was listening to just anybody. He didn't understand how desperate I was. And we got into big fights. He would get so mad he would fire me. I'd be hysterical. I'd call Sam Cohn, who was my agent and also Bob's agent, and he would say, "Don't worry." I'd be back at work the next morning and everything would be fine. He loves a good confrontation, and I was the opposite. It worked in the end. Oh God, I drove him crazy. But I still have enormous affection for him. I owe him more of a debt than any other filmmaker I can think of. If that movie is good it's because of him.

* * *

The Fox Five

3 Women (1977)

A Wedding (1978)

Quintet (1979)

A Perfect Couple (1979)

HealtH (1980)

ALAN LADD, JR. (producer): At Fox, we did *3 Women, Perfect Couple, Quintet,* and *A Wedding* together. I started *HealtH* with him, but then I left the studio. I was the only studio head that would hire him at the time. The hypocrisy of this town—so many people took out ads about him when he died, but they wouldn't hire him. The creative community admired him greatly but studios were afraid of him—because of his outspokenness. On some level they recognized that he was a master. To know Bob was to love Bob—but if you didn't know him you swallowed all the bullshit about him in town.

I knew Bob as an agent when he was a TV director. Bigger than life—even then he was a man who did what he wanted, wouldn't compromise with anyone. But he was always on budget—that was all the studio cared about. When I was head of Fox he gave me a call one day with an idea—and he came in and told me the idea of *3 Women,* which I found intriguing.

* * *

Jack Kroll, review of *3 Women,* headlined "Desert Song," *Newsweek,* April 18, 1977: Like any true artist, Robert Altman couldn't play it safe if he wanted to—which he doesn't. His movies take chances, and none of them has risked more than *3 Women.* In this, his tenth film in seven years and in many ways his most personal work, Altman dares to make something beautiful out of the deepest and most all-encompassing sorrow. Bleak visions of life are a dime a dozen these days, and the only excuse for an artist to have such a vision is to turn that bleakness into something blazing with paradoxical light and heat, something to stir and shock us into the exhilaration of discovery. This is what Altman does in *3 Women.* . . . What makes a wasteland is the absence of love, which Altman embodies in a "rehabilitation" clinic for old people in the Palm Springs desert area of California. . . . Here in this hygienic limbo of youth and age, Altman's dream-girls, Millie Lammoreaux (Shelley Duvall) and Pinky Rose (Sissy Spacek), meet. They are ultimate American waifs, crossing paths in these gypsy jobs that are parodies of caring. . . . The third is Willie (Janice Rule), who owns the apartments and a decayed Disneyland called Dodge City where the local studs come to shoot targets, ride dirt-track motorcycles and drink. Willie is a silent, sibylline figure who paints every surface—even the bottom of the pool—with grotesque humanoid figures in which a fierce, priapic male terrorizes three females, one of whom is pregnant. . . . Altman's dream of three women expresses his sense that human beings have become more vulnerable than ever to pain, loss, betrayal, cruelty and shame. He's right, but his film has an originality and beauty of form that moves you beyond the force of its insight.

Robert Altman: I had done a painting years before. There were about two years that I did paintings. And I did a painting of three women, just three faces, and then I had this dream that I was making

Sissy Spacek, as Pinky, and Shelley Duvall, as Millie, in 3 Women

this picture in the desert, and it was called *3 Women* and it was about personality theft. We were living on the beach in Malibu, and Kathryn had gotten very sick—I had just visited her in the hospital.

KATHRYN REED ALTMAN: It happened fast. Sunday night we were walking on the beach and I felt like I couldn't get anything down. I went upstairs and I was just sick all night. I ended up in the emergency room. They finally just had to go in—surgery. . . . They got in there and found a duodenal ulcer. You know it's all the psychological thing— ulcers and problems and stress. But this one was buried so deep it took forever to finally find it. That was when he was at home with Matthew. And he had this dream.

ROBERT ALTMAN: During that time when Kathryn was in the hospital, our son Matthew was spending time on the beach and he had been sleeping in my bed. So there was sand in my bed, which might be why I was dreaming about the desert. I would dream a little, I would think about this, and I'd wake up and I'd go to the pad by my bed and I'd make notes. And then I'd wake up and I'd have Bob Eggenweiler and Tommy Thompson in my bedroom. And I'd say, "Now go down to the desert and find a location that's like this and this and this." And, of course, none of that happened. Neither of them was there, and I never wrote a dream note in my life, and I had no pad next to my bed, even. So I dreamed about making the picture, and the tenor of what the film was. I called Alan Ladd at Fox and said, "Listen, I read a short story and I want to make a film of it." I didn't want to tell him it was a dream. And I kind of made up the story. And he said, "Great. Go ahead and make it."

ALAN LADD, JR.: He didn't mention that it was a dream until later, in Cannes.

SISSY SPACEK (actress): I got to know Bob while we were shooting *Welcome to L.A.* We'd go to Lion's Gate to watch dailies, and it was really like going to the movies. It was a real festive and relaxed atmosphere at that office. There didn't seem to be a real hierarchy, like if you were low on the totem pole you never felt like you couldn't talk to Bob. He made himself accessible to everybody. Granted, he surrounded himself with people he really liked and respected.

I remember he told us about his dream. I did little drawings, little sketches about his dream. Bob would get the seed of an idea and he would let the people he was working with become a part of that. I remember we were doing one scene and I was really upset about how it had gone. It wasn't real, it wasn't authentic. He just laughed. He said, "Once you have done it, it *becomes* real." Part of his genius was making you feel as though you can do no wrong. He was really an artist. He didn't run after what was happening at any time. He was not a formula man. He did his own thing and he trusted that everybody he was working with would pull his weight.

He told me everything he knew about my character, Pinky, and then it was like he would give actors a track, a blueprint. "Now work within these parameters and put yourself into it." He didn't need to have all the answers. He didn't have that disease where as a director you have to know everything.

There was a lot of improvisational stuff. He would give us a scene in the morning and then it would grow. It was so freeing working with him after having worked with other directors. The way he works is all very naturalistic. Everything is natural and the sets are happy and relaxed and he seemed to always be the happiest and the most relaxed.

I don't think I ever knew what the film was about. I remember Bob would say, "Well, if you confuse people enough in the first twenty minutes they'll give up trying to figure out what it's about and they'll just go with it and enjoy it."

Shelley always said the three women were the id, the ego, and the superego. At that time I had never heard of the id or the superego. She was way ahead of me. I just tried to portray the dream that Bob had. I didn't think of it in those kinds of terms. To me it was about this girl who was a bit of a blank page. So young she didn't know who she was yet and she met someone who she was completely enamored with and wanted to be like her. So as young people often do, she emulated her and was playing that part. I wasn't thinking of the bigger picture of what it's about.

When I was sixteen or seventeen I was on a bus in New York. It was pouring rain, and all the people ran under this awning. There was a girl a year or two older than me who had gotten off the bus. I looked over at her and was so taken by her and the way she dressed and the way she wore her hair. I remember thinking distinctly, "I want to be her. I want to be just like her." Already in my life I had experienced something like that. I did become as much like the way she looked as I could.

Shelley was incredible. I remember her always getting her skirt

With Shelley Duvall and Sissy Spacek during the 1977 Cannes Film
Festival, at which Duvall shared the Best Actress award for 3 Women

closed in the car door. I think the first time it was an accident, but that was the thing about Bob. He loved accidents. He loved the things that happened that you didn't plan. Bob would do things over and over hoping that something would happen that was unexpected.

ROBERT ALTMAN: The first time Shelley caught her dress in the door, Tommy Thompson, who was my assistant director, yelled, "Cut!" I loved it. I wanted her to do it again.

SISSY SPACEK: The little boy was very much alive in Bob. Bob was the mischievous kid who would put a plastic turd on the middle of the cake at the wrap party and then would stay nearby. He would get a few of us over to watch as people came. He was just tickled when no one stopped eating the cake, they just ate around it. He took such great delight in playing those kinds of pranks on people.

ROBERT ALTMAN: The reviews were mixed. Pauline Kael said she liked the first half of *3 Women* but she didn't like that last half. I said, "That's like saying, 'I like your baby. It has a cute head. But I don't like her arms and legs.' " I mean, just say you don't like it. Don't say how it should have been done.

*   *   *

Mary Murphy, story headlined "Crisis of a Cult Figure," *New West*, May 23, 1977: As Altman awakes in his New York City apartment, the phone rings. . . . "Don't you realize you are letting history go down the drain?" Altman is shouting into the phone. He is talking to an executive at Fox about the distribution plan for *3 Women*. "I told you this film had to be released slowly. At this rate it will be gone in three months and no one will make a penny." His mouth moves continuously, his head bobs, his feet pace, perspiration dampens his shirt. He grabs a gold toothpick he wears on a chain around his neck and in rapid strokes picks at his front teeth. "I'm so mad," he tells Shelley [Duvall], hanging up, "I could punch somebody."

Within the next two hours a Fox executive calls to inform Altman that *3 Women* is a box office failure in the South and the Midwest, new reviews are read to Altman in which he is attacked as a "middle-class artist," "a megalomaniac," an imposter who is ripping off Bergman and Fellini, and Shelley Duvall, after a four-minute conversation in the bedroom, has broken her contract and walked out on *A Wedding*.

Altman twists the cap off the Cutty Sark and rolls a joint.

*   *   *

JULIANNE MOORE (actress): I was in the theater department at Boston University, and we used to go to the movies in Harvard Square, where they always had revivals. I'd somehow managed to go through high school in the seventies not seeing *Nashville*. But I didn't—I lived on Army bases. You just saw whatever movies were around, and for some reason I hadn't seen that. So I saw *3 Women* and up to that point I wanted to be a theater actor. I never had seen anything like it before.

And it was the first time in my life that I actually noticed the presence of the director in a movie. I felt it really strongly. And I thought, "I don't know who this guy is, but that's what I want to do. I want to do that kind of work." From then on I'd see his films whenever I could, and he was always my absolute favorite director, for what he said thematically and emotionally and how he felt about people. Who people are, what they're capable of—good or bad.

*   *   *

Betty Jeffries Demby, story headlined "Robert Altman Talks About His Life and Art," *The New York Times,* **June 19, 1977:** Movie buffs may take advantage of this rare opportunity to trace not only Altman's artistic progress, but to chart his development as a philosopher and commentator on social mores as well. And in these times of raised consciousness, special attention will perhaps be paid to the director's treatment of women, from the humiliated Hot Lips Houlihan in "M*A*S*H" to the exotically intertwined heroines of "3 Women."

"Women have been subjugated in our society," he says. "Consequently, they've had to become manipulative. They have more disguises and facets than men. Those are the kinds of things that interest me, where we're dealing with disguises, where we make assumptions and we're almost always wrong." . . .

"I cannot do 'Rocky' or 'One Flew Over the Cuckoo's Nest' and all those films where there's no question about the way the audience is going to feel at the end. I think sad people laugh, happy people cry, and brave people are frightened. Cowards are brave. There's total contradiction. The minute you take the surprise away, there's no art. The minute you plot something and say this is going to be this way because of this, you're wrong."

*   *   *

HENRY GIBSON: As with Fellini, people always wanted to explore the symbolism in his films. And people were constantly after him to interpret this or explain that. I loved what he would say in response. Someone would ask him, "In this particular picture, when we see the color red over here, what does it mean?"

And he very cleverly evolved this response. He said, "Well, what do you think it means?"

The person would say, "Well, I think it means it's the sunset of that character's life."

And he'd say, "You're right. That's what it means."

What he tried to tell people again and again is you get from the feast what you bring to it. There isn't a rightness and a wrongness of interpretation.

ROBERT ALTMAN: Most of the people who have looked at my work and don't know me, even the ones who do know me, they analyze it from a certain point of view, which is right and it's wrong.

Asking me what something's *about* will only lead them into misunderstanding. I mean, then you're talking about some kind of logic that doesn't really exist. Take Vincent [van Gogh]. His whole life was the epitome of the failed artist. And then suddenly, after his death, actually, for some reason somebody says, "Oh, look at this."

I don't think I know the truth. Or if I do, I've been disguising it for a long time. I don't know that I want to give that up, this late in the game. But I don't think it makes any difference. My answer is going to be no less valid, or no more valid, than the woman in England who wrote a book about five of my films, writing about what this or that film was in my life, and applying it to my life.

What difference does it make? How close do you want to get? By you, I mean your audience. What is it that they want to know? And what value is it for you to tell them?

The minute I say what a movie I've made is *about*, I've narrowed everyone else's view of it. If I say what it means to me, its range to some extent is limited to the viewer from that point on.

*   *   *

JOHN CONSIDINE (actor and screenwriter): *A Wedding* had a funny genesis. He was finishing *3 Women* in Palm Springs. I had come down there to do some voice-over work. After this one day he was told he had this big interview. He sat down in this living room and these people interviewed him and one of the questions was, "What are you going to do next, Mr. Altman?" He looked down at this coffee table and it had this whole display of wedding magazines. He said, "I think I'm going to do a film on the American wedding industry."

When they left I said, "Really?"

He said, "I just thought of it, but do you want to write it with me?"

So I stayed in a little room in Lion's Gate and started writing. He said, "First thing, I want there to be a lot of characters."

Nashville had twenty-four main characters, so I doubled it to forty-eight.

He came in one day and said, "We need to start the screenplay." He sat down at the typewriter and wrote, "Exterior—Cathedral, day. Church music playing. Limousines and cars parked. A wedding is in progress." Then he got up and said, "Okay, you take it from here." I wish I had saved that piece of paper.

He didn't write much, but some of the biggest turns in *A Wedding* were Bob's ideas. Like the day he came in and said that there was going to be this terrible car crash, and everybody thinks the bride and groom are dead. I thought, "My god, where is our comedy going?"

I started a little card for each character and started putting them up on the wall. He came in and said, "I'd like our characters to have secrets, every character to have a secret. It doesn't necessarily have to come out in the screenplay. But let's give all of them a secret."

It's great for an actor to know something that nobody else knows. I just started expanding these.

He brought in Allan Nicholls and Pat Resnick to help with the script. I didn't love that. We had a little thing about that. That's just the way it was. I had a lot of anger and I wasn't able to really express it to him.

He said, "Are you mad at me?"

I said, "No, not really."

I was at a stage of my life where at least with someone like Bob, I couldn't tell him what I really felt.

One day Bob came in and said, "We have to have a story tomorrow because we're going over to Fox to get the money."

I stayed there all night and came up with twelve pages. The car is ready and we're going and I handed it to him and he said, "I don't have time to read this."

I said, "Bob!"

We meet with Alan Ladd, Jr., and the other execs at Fox, and Bob says, "So, tell them the story, John."

I started telling them; then Bob would get an idea and he would interrupt me. He would finish this and then say, "Tell them what happens next, John." And we kept going. It was this incredible improv. We get outside and he looked at me with a big smile, and said, "Can you believe those guys gave us the money for that?"

*Carol Burnett, Paul Dooley, Mia Farrow, Dennis Christopher, and Amy
Stryker as the Brenner family in* A Wedding

When we started shooting, Tommy Thompson came in one morning and said, "Fox is really pressuring us. They want to know the
schedule. They have to see it, Bob."

Bob said, "Tommy, look, if they don't see a schedule, they have no
idea how we're doing. So let's tell them we're doing fine."

CAROL BURNETT (actress): I remember Lily telling me how wonderful
he was to work with on *Nashville*—"Carol, if he ever asks you to work
with him, say you'd carry a spear." That told me how much he was
admired.

He had the ability to put a key in everyone's back and open us up to
be brave. He created an atmosphere on the set. I've never really
enjoyed the process that much because I'm kind of a creature of theater

and live television, where you learn it, you rehearse it, you do it, and you go home. Movies take forever. Three hours just to light the scene? For me it's boring at times because you just sit and wait. That wasn't the way with Bob. He created this atmosphere that was like recess. You just went in and you knew what the plot was, and you had some lines you were going to do, and the rest was up for grabs.

On *A Wedding* he got all of us in a room. He explained the plot to us and then he said, "Please, if you have an idea for a scene, come to me with it. I want to hear it. Some of the best scenes in my movies have come from the actors' ideas." You never hear a director say that. That was truly an astonishing thing.

The food was fabulous. He brought a wonderful chef. Everybody got the same salary and nobody got a lot. He made it up to everybody with these fabulous lunches. Everybody got along because everybody was happy.

Pat McCormick and I had this story line that he was married to the character Dina Merrill played, and I'm called Tulip and I'm married to Paul Dooley, who's called Snooks, and we're rich Southern trash. They're to the manor born, but they don't have any cash. Our daughter is marrying into that family, to the son played by Desi Arnaz, Jr. So there was a plot point where Pat's character is smitten by Tulip, and she doesn't know this and they're dancing at the reception. He comes over and asks her to dance. He's supposed to reveal his love for her on the dance floor. There were some lines, but neither Pat nor I felt that it was right. We went to Bob and said, "Can we play with this?" He said, "Sure." We went back and found a room and came up with the idea that during the dance he's in a reverie and never opens his mouth and she makes small talk and the more she talks the more uncomfortable she is. He finally presses her into a corner and professes his love.

Bob said, "Great, let's shoot it."

I've improvised a lot with television but this is the first time I've ever done a film where you can do that.

KATHRYN REED ALTMAN: Paul Dooley, in *A Wedding*, was the only casting I ever did for Bob.

PAUL DOOLEY (actor): Sam Cohn is his agent, and Sam's wife and Bob's wife became friends. Sam's wife ran the American Place Theater and I was doing *Hold Me!* there. So Kathryn sees me and she likes me and she knew Bob was looking for someone, a character man for *A Wedding*. So she said, "You've got to come see this guy, I think he'll be right for that movie." . . . He came downstairs and there were four of us and we were more or less in the same dressing room. Anyway, endearing me to all my fellow cast members, he showed tremendous interest in me. "Would you come and see me tomorrow at my office?" The rest of them are looking at me like, "Who the fuck are you?"

On the third visit he says, "Well, I found your daughter." And he says to me, "Who's your agent?" I said, "I don't have an agent. I'm between agents." He says it doesn't matter anyway, it's going to be the same amount of money. And nobody ever does this. He says, "Vittorio Gassman is getting fifty grand, Carol Burnett is getting fifty grand, everybody else is getting twenty-five grand. Then there's a group of people that get ten grand, and that's you." They never do that in the business. He didn't like bullshit. He didn't like games, he didn't like playing around.

Bob likes to do what some artists call working with found objects. An actor does something that's unexpected, and Bob, in some cases, you may not like it, but if he likes it, you know, he puts it right in the movie. But he loves these happy accidents. And I was one of his found objects. He just found me somewhere and put me in these movies.

CAROL BURNETT: Occasionally he would show us one of his movies if we wanted to stay after the dailies. I had not seen *3 Women*. I was fascinated by it. I went to sleep and I dreamed about *3 Women*. It was a funny dream. I went back the next day and I said, "I dreamed that Janice Rule was in the pool painting these murals. I dreamed she was there and there was a tarp and we couldn't see what she was doing. Then she pulled a string and the tarp was raised and it was all Disney characters—Mickey and Donald and the whole gang." He roared.

He said, "Well, if that's what it did for you, that's what it was supposed to do."

ALLAN NICHOLLS (actor/music director/screenwriter/associate producer/assistant director): If anything, *A Wedding* was about gossip and how gossip spreads and how gossip hurts, and how gossip helps and how gossip kills and how gossip kills the right guy sometimes.

ALAN LADD, JR.: I was concerned about the kids dying at the end of *A Wedding*. He got his way. I guess he wanted the end to make a statement, his way of saying, "These things happen."

BARBARA ALTMAN HODES: That wreck in *A Wedding*, and the bride in braces? Well, you know, Bob just took that from his own life, from what happened before he married LaVonne. And the groom's family's name? Corelli, right? Well, his second wife was Lotus Corelli.

Margaret Ladd, actress, from a diary she kept during *A Wedding*: Today they're shooting the car crash. The car, in which the bride and groom are supposedly driving away, crashes into a gasoline truck and burns up. . . . Yesterday they had to show the car careening dangerously, at a very high speed, away from the house. It had to almost hit the stone pillar in front of the house. It was a very scary shot. Well, guess who was driving the car for the stunt shot? You guessed it: Altman. He scared the shit out of everyone. He really almost hit the post, missed it by about two inches at a very high speed. The cameramen almost stopped shooting they got so scared. . . . He got out, very cool, and said calmly to the cameramen: "Did you get that OK?" But there was a little smile on his face that he couldn't quite hide, just creeping up in one corner.

*   *   *

Aljean Harmetz, story headlined "Altman Pledges Profits to Rights Plan," *The New York Times*, June 12, 1978: The latest in a series of Hollywood parties for the proposed Equal Rights Amendment raised $57,000 yesterday—and a promise of as much as $2 million from Robert Altman, the producer and director of "Nashville."

Mr. Altman impulsively offered all his profits, up to $2 million, of his new movie, "A Wedding," which is scheduled to open in New York in September. Later, he said he had "felt moved" by the speech of Carol Burnett, one of the stars of "A Wedding."

CAROL BURNETT: I think I did my speech in character as Eunice talking to Momma, trying to explain what the ERA was. She said she had been learning what it was, and it was nonthreatening, it was just a cry for equality in the workplace. I thought it might be fun to do it as a character who just learned about it, trying to get through to her dense mother what it was all about.

KATHRYN REED ALTMAN: Yeah, he pledged all his profits from *A Wedding* to the ERA. There *were* no profits from *A Wedding*.

Robert Altman addresses the Equal Rights Amendment countdown party
in Beverly Hills, June 11, 1978. Actress Susan Blakely is at left,
and Gloria Steinem is at right.

* * *

FRANK W. BARHYDT (screenwriter): When he first told me about
Quintet he didn't say it's this apocalyptic thing. It really had to do with
adrenaline and people's middle-class lives. They go to college, they get
out of college, they get married, they have children, they buy a home,
they have these very comfortable and very boring lives. And gambling
was an adrenaline that people need, that risk. He equated that with the
feeling after a storm, a violent storm, people feel invigorated because
they escaped death, they cheated death. So that was the premise. These
people really had nothing other than death looking at them, and in
order to experience life they had to gamble their lives.

WOLF KROEGER (art director): *Quintet* was an absolute bore, really.

PAUL NEWMAN: I think *Quintet* was a valid supposition, but I think the details just got away from us. There weren't enough details piled on top of each other to support that as a dramatic supposition. It's a complicated supposition, you understand. It's the end of the world, and if you're going to go out you might as well go out with some excitement. So the excitement is that you have to track down the guy in front of you and kill him. But you also know that there's a guy in back of you who's trying to kill you. You might have gotten that on the second viewing, but most people only get a first. You have to be looking straight ahead but you have to be looking in back of you, too.

I don't think you have to go out to kill for excitement to keep feeling alive, though Bob may have felt that way about the critics.

Vincent Canby story headlined "Robert Altman's Talent Falters," *The New York Times,* **February 18, 1979:** The other day while watching Robert Altman's new film, the end-of-the-world fantasy called "Quintet," I could feel the blood rushing to my feet and my heart wanting to follow. The movie was both leaving me cold and giving me the sweats.

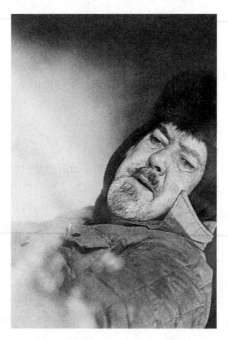

Looking exhausted on the set of Quintet

"Quintet" may be the most aggressively self-indulgent motion picture made in the last 20 years by a major American director.

As "Quintet" droned on in settings of surreal, frozen beauty, and as the characters, the last survivors on earth, play a mysterious kind of backgammon called quintet, or slink around the ruins cutting each other's throats, or talk about life, death, hope ("an obsolete word") and the mystical meaning of the numeral five, I was reminded of all the terrible little-theater plays I'd seen in my youth.

Robert Altman to David Thompson, from *Altman on Altman*: My father died from cancer just before we left for Montreal. My mother had died two years before. I'm sure that influenced the tone of *Quintet*.

* * *

ALLAN NICHOLLS: For *A Perfect Couple*, we came up with the story idea first about two people meeting from very different walks of life. And yet two people firmly involved in family. One of them, the family was a band. For the other, the family was their heritage.

PAUL DOOLEY: I had already made *A Wedding*. Bob's not saying anything to me, like he likes my work, because he had a gruff side, too. So about three months later a friend of mine says, "Buy *Variety*."

"Why?

"Just get the new *Variety*. Page sixty."

So I just went to a newsstand and looked at it and here's an ad with me and Marta Heflin, "Robert Altman announces his next film. A romance. Paul Dooley and Marta Heflin, coming to theaters next year." But he never said a word to me about this.

I called him up. I said, "Who's this Paul Dooley that's going to do that film?"

He says, "I knew I could get you." Then he said, "I wanted Shelley Duvall to do it, but she's got some other stupid job."

He didn't like it that much when his "family," if you will, started going out and working in the other side of the business, because he really invented Shelley. Shelley wasn't available or something, so he was naturally pissed off about that. But he saw Marta Heflin as another girl. He wanted to do a film about people who weren't conventionally pretty people or the right age or just the way Hollywood would do it.

He does most of what he did to say "Fuck you" to Hollywood. He didn't like conventional, formulaic movies, and none of us do, really. Sometimes you put the right hero and heroine together and it's a formula movie, but you know it's George Clooney and someone else and it's still a good movie. But they still spend the last five minutes going back to the girl and embracing her and kissing her. Even if Arnold Schwarzenegger is an alien, he'll do something nice for a girl at the end, especially if she's in a very short skirt. It hasn't changed all that much. Anyway, he didn't use the phrase, but it's almost as if he wanted to show that an ugly duckling has the right to fall in love and be happy.

He was cynical about the idea he was supposed to do things a certain way. It might be antiauthoritarianism or something. "Don't tell me how to make my movies." Well, I got news for you. In fifty years, when people have forgotten many of the current directors who made a lot of money, they might still remember Bob Altman, 'cause there's a body of work you can look at. And there's no one like him, first of all. If a guy makes hit movie after hit movie after hit movie, he's probably doing a formula. Anybody who's an artist wants to do something slightly different next time, whether you're a writer, or artist, or whatever it is. Bob was an individual, an adventurer, and a gambler. And he was willing to gamble other people's money and even his reputation on a hunch, on an idea he had. But I thank God for it because he saw me in certain situations that other people didn't.

ALLAN NICHOLLS: We screened *Perfect Couple* at Lion's Gate for Mick Jagger. It was a fun night. And after that screening Bob and I looked at each other and thought, "We're going to make some money on this one." We didn't. The marketing and distribution failed us. I want to get back at them one day. And the way I want to get back at them, I've been talking to Kathryn and Bob's legal people about doing *A Perfect Couple* as a musical. It is a musical and it should be a Broadway musical. But it takes some time to get that going. Everything else is a musical on Broadway. So why not Bob, who loved Broadway so much, why not his legacy there? It would be cleverly ironic too, if one of his most unsuccessful films becomes a Broadway hit.

*   *   *

FRANK W. BARHYDT: He had just gotten back from shooting *A Wedding*, and I had written this script, for *HealtH*. It was about an election for the president of a health-food convention, and I didn't really know the form. I knew description and dialogue. I didn't know how it really should look. So I just sort of did my own version of it and my parents were out visiting and I asked my father to read this and he found it funny. So I asked Bob if he would read it. He said yeah. Bob has always had a fascination with politics and power. So all political things are interesting to him, and I just happened to tap into that. Four days later he said he was going to make it.

CAROL BURNETT: He was liberal, definitely a liberal. You saw that in *HealtH*. The idea was a convention of health nuts, but *HealtH* was of course really about Eisenhower and Stevenson—Betty Bacall was Eisenhower and Glenda Jackson was Stevenson, down to the part where she crossed her leg and you see the hole in her shoe.

LAUREN BACALL (actress): I didn't really get to know him until he called me one day to have lunch with him and tell me about this movie that he wanted to make, called *HealtH*. Of course he was filled with ideas, and it all sounded very funny to me, which indeed it was. I loved my character, Esther Brill. She was this eighty-something-year-old virgin who says every orgasm takes twenty-eight days off a woman's life! It was a wonderful movie. I loved the movie. Everyone who saw that movie adored it. He used to carry it from festival to festival.

With Lauren Bacall on the set of HealtH

He made movies in his very own original way. If you wanted to try something, go ahead and try it. If you weren't precise about every word, fine. He lived up to his reputation of being this incredibly gifted, original man who was wonderful with actors and who just had a knack for making unusual movies.

WOLF KROEGER: *HealtH*? Absolutely a piece of garbage. There was nothing there. He just made it up. But he must have had something nobody else had, because he always attracted great actors.

DAVID LEVY (producer): With the late-seventies stuff and the Fox deal, there was a certain fly-by-the-seat-of-the-pants quality. He really liked both on-set and off when the unplanned happened; he always celebrated that. And he trusted that. Another person would say that's hubris. A lot of people aren't comfortable in what might be called that unplanned state. He was very much okay with operating in that space. I remember on *HealtH*, Laddie, Alan Ladd, Jr., would be asking, "Could we get a real script on this? Could we get a whole script?" And it was never really forthcoming. It was always a work in progress. That was a thirty-five-day shoot, but after twenty-nine days he basically felt, "I got what I got and I'm okay with it and I don't need to kick this around anymore."

So it was a very free-flowing, controlled chaos. But that was by design, his design, you know? And here again, this was another film that didn't perform. I want to say that the theatrical release for the most part lasted all of a week, maybe two. It played in such a limited way and the studio felt that no matter what they did to get behind it, it wasn't going to reach an audience. So it died a painful but very quick death.

CHAPTER 21

Scotty

*

ROBERT ALTMAN: In all the pictures from *Thieves Like Us* to *Kansas City*, Scotty Bushnell was very, very involved. She was like a producer, a confidante. She did the casting, she did the wardrobe. And, uh, she was a big support. She died not long ago.

* * *

JOHN SCHUCK: We went to Denison University together in Granville, Ohio. Scotty was in costume in the theater department. She was a bit of a renegade. Outspoken, I guess, at times insecure. Different. She had large eyes and huge shadows under them and she was a very heavy smoker. She usually looked unkempt. She wasn't heavy, but she didn't wear tight-fitting stuff. She always looked like she was still in the beatnik age. A lot of black. She was a huge collector of stuff. When you went into her apartment it was filled with interesting things, old washing machines [*laughs*]. She wasn't eccentric in that way, at least I never thought of her as being that way, but maybe she was. She married a man by the name of Bill Bushnell.

BILL BUSHNELL (theater impresario): One night around 1973 I was in Westwood coming out of a movie theater and I ran into Leon Ericksen, one of Bob's designers. He said, "I had a fight with Bob and I'm not going to do *Thieves Like Us*." I called Bob and asked him if he was looking for designers. I said, "I want you to meet a young designer, Jackson De Govia." In the meantime I called Jack and said, "Here's the deal. I can set you up with Bob Altman, but if you get the gig you have

*Producer Scotty Bushnell, with Robert Altman and Elliott Gould,
on the set of* California Split

to hire Scotty as costume designer." Jack said fine. He got the gig and
he hired Scotty to do the clothes on *Thieves Like Us.*

Jackson's relationship with Bob was like oil and water, but Scotty's
was like water and water. She went from there to do the clothes for
Nashville. Next thing you know we were getting a divorce and she was
working with Bob and becoming indispensable to his operation.

Scotty was the only one in that operation who didn't drink or
smoke dope. Bob partied hard, as did his operation. She was always the
one who the next day could say, "Okay, guys, here are all the crazy
ideas you had last night. This one sounds good, this one is crap." And
so on. There was a kind of edginess between Bob Eggenweiler and
Tommy Thompson and Scotty. They were his buddies. All of a sudden
there was this sometimes abrasive female at a critical part of the operation. She was one of the toughest people that you could imagine in
many, many ways. In other ways she was very soft and very vulnerable.
"Feminine" is not a word I would use, but "vulnerable" is.

From wardrobe she evolved into casting director, and she eventually became an associate producer and executive producer. In the process she in effect became his line producer. Scotty became extremely powerful in Bob's operation primarily because she didn't care about the credit. The analogy is Dick Cheney in George Bush's White House. He didn't want to be president, so therefore he isn't a threat. He doesn't care whether he gets any public credit or not. She didn't want Bob's job, she didn't care if she was the producer, and she was prepared to travel anyplace in the world with him. She didn't have any complications of family.

The net result was that both Eggenweiler and Thompson were gone after *Popeye*. That's where Scotty got her infamous reputation as being the black widow spider of Bob's operation. It's probably true.

ALLAN NICHOLLS: She basically gave her life to Bob and became his sole producer. Now, this was over a period of time. She was coproducer when Tommy Thompson was around and Bob Eggenweiler was around. But you could see what was coming. She basically had no other life than Bob. So she became the person he relied on to do numerous things in terms of casting. She was there all the time for Bob, and she was there when others weren't around. She knew Bob's thoughts, Bob's opinions, and so she became the bearer of that news.

JERRY WALSH: Bob frequently referred to her as his artistic partner—far from being an assistant. She didn't have any life other than working for Bob. She was divorced from Bill Bushnell when I met her, and as far as I know she never had any kind of romantic relationship here. She was on top of everything going on in the office. She drove almost everyone crazy, drove many people away from Bob, Tommy Thompson being the first and foremost.

ALLAN NICHOLLS: Tommy was incredible. He was the personality. Big, fun-loving, knew how to run a set. I think probably if Scotty thought of herself as knowing Bob's art, she would probably think of Tommy as not being artistic. But Tommy's creativity was in his personality and his knowing how to engage people, and his charm. So that's where he would totally be a polar opposite of her.

MICHAEL MURPHY: Almost every guy I've known who was a big player like Bob had a woman like Scotty who kind of devoted her life to him, whose whole personality gets taken over by the job and the position and the power of it all. She was very much an integral part of that office, and Bob relied on her a great deal. I got along with her fine. I don't mean this out of school, but she was a lot of the things that Bob wasn't. She was kind of judgmental and you'd see her looking into the lens and she just wasn't the same kind of person around this kind of creativity that Bob was. She was very good at marshaling the army and getting it all together. But she didn't help him in terms of making people feel good on the set or relaxed.

So her style worked at odds with Bob and the way he operated. And, I mean, many times people would say, "Bob, why do you deal with her?" He'd say, "Oh, you know, she's kind of crazy. But I need her for this stuff and that."

ROBERT HARDERS (theater director): She was one of those secretive types who are consolidating their power all the time. When you were jibing with her plans she could be very nice, and when you weren't you might as well be a speck on the floor or worse. Scotty was ballsy. Scotty was true to her convictions. She didn't offer much to people, but I don't think she expected much *from* people.

BILL BUSHNELL: Scotty wasn't nice. Bob's power reflected on her and there was a period of time there in Hollywood and in the film world when she had that reflected power. In some ways, she was one of the more feared individuals in a town full of people who are afraid. And she was never afraid. She was tough. She was Bob's "no" person. She allowed Bob to appear as the good guy. He never said no to anybody. Scotty said no to everybody.

DAVID LEVY (producer): On a pie chart of friends and enemies, the friends slice is very narrow. In my view, she didn't play fair and didn't play by the rules. For instance, if she didn't like the direction a piece of casting was going she might lie to Bob about an actor's availability. Pretty outrageous, you know? Things of that nature. If you're controlling the flow of information in any endeavor you can really stack the deck, can't you? To her credit, was she passionate about the work? Yes. Was she devoted? Yes. Was she in her mind all about Bob? You bet. But I don't think she had the gift of analyzing what was in his or a project's best interest, and there were a lot of unhappy people left in the wake of her involvement.

JOAN TEWKESBURY (screenwriter and director): She did all the stuff Bob didn't want to do. She was the one who tied up all the loose ends.

And he trusted her—which is no mean feat—because he knew that he owned her. She was the "It" person. But it was a dark "It."

Between Bob and me there was a period of time when it was not great. I would try to see him or talk, and he was simply not interested. It was a lot to do with Scott. She had gotten Tommy Thompson out. Bob Eggenweiler left. I mean, these men were his soul, they were his guys, you know, and they were hilariously funny, stupidly funny. A longtime secretary was gone. They were part of the old crowd, with Louie Lombardo. Now they're all dead. All of them.

MATTHEW SEIG (producer): I don't really like getting called at midnight or at two a.m. and yelled at. I would rather keep those things confined to, hell, a twelve- or fourteen-hour day, you know? You know, there's a reason to take it from Bob and there wasn't much of a reason to take it from Scotty.

Those two people, they had no business being together. It was just a disaster. I mean, she was a very smart woman who helped him a great deal, I have no doubt about that. She did many things that he gets credit for. You know, she was behind the scenes and stayed that way. But she was a difficult person and their relationship was bad news, just really poisonous. It was like the worst marriage. It's like a nightmare. I mean people screaming at each other. It doesn't make any sense. Why do people do that to each other?

JERRY WALSH: Initially I got on well with Scotty, but there came a time when she called me to complain about some advice that I had given Bob. She said, "Bob thinks he knows much more than he actually knows, and it is up to me to protect him from mistakes. When you come along and give him bad advice, it just makes my job so much harder. So please, in the future always convey your advice through me so we can avoid problems." Of course, I could not agree to her suggestion, and after that there was a coolness in our relationship.

She was mean and nasty to everybody. Well, that isn't entirely true. She was very nice to actors. Everything and anything they wanted, she would fight to get them and make sure that their lives were comfortable.

PETER GALLAGHER: Scotty was great. I don't think I would have been in *Caine Mutiny*, *The Player*, or *Short Cuts* without Scotty. So I kind of owe her everything. I think that's what kept me being invited back. I mean, I know Bob liked having me around. She was very, very caring, wacky, and smoked too much, which I guess eventually killed her. I thought she was terrific. There's usually somebody, it seems with people like Bob, there's usually somebody in their ear. And if that person is in their ear, it's good if they like you. I don't know for sure, but I suspect that's a big reason why I had such a nice run with Bob while I did.

HENRY GIBSON: She was very good at what she did. And it's the same in art as it is in politics. If you are a staff member of a senator or a president, or a corporate official in business, and a boss responds, you want to do more to please the boss, because the proximity to power gives you power by attribution. And I think that was part of the Scotty story. There's no question she was damned good.

LILY TOMLIN: When we did *Nashville*, the scene in the café when Keith is singing, you did not know where the camera was. . . . When I finally saw how they shot it and they were moving past the other women and pushing in on me, and my eyes were in shadow, I thought, "I've failed this. I've failed this really great moment." I left the screening, which I never did before. I went home and I was in tears.

Scotty called me and said, "Why did you leave the screening? The footage was just great."

I started saying, "No, no, you can't see my eyes." Just crying. It was a terribly important moment in my career at that time, but Scotty tried to talk me out of it and have me see what was good about it.

TIM ROBBINS: She was a facilitator for him. As a good producer will do, she would fight the battles that he didn't have the time for. So I'm sure she was the bad cop a lot of the time. And I don't know that that endeared her to people, but that's kind of the sucky thing about that job. I always liked her and had some laughs with her. I always felt she was part of the machine. She was a part of the artistic process—the adult who would allow the kids to play.

BILL BUSHNELL: Her turf was that office, and I'm sure she didn't make Kathryn feel very welcome. It was the thought that Kathryn held Bob back in a certain way. That his creative choices and the pictures that they were doing were more conservative than Scotty thought he should be doing.

ALLAN NICHOLLS: I saw the disconnect between her and Kathryn. Here were two women in Bob's life, one the best wife, spouse, companion a person could want, and one probably the best producer one could want. They don't like each other, and not many people like the producer.

JERRY WALSH: Bob spoke to me on a number of occasions about the problem of Scotty and Kathryn. Kathryn detested her. How Scotty felt about Kathryn I don't know because I never heard her mention Kathryn's name.

But Bob I remember very well saying to me at one point where there was a particularly big blowup, he said, "I've just told both of them they have to work it out." He said, "I have to have Kathryn to live and I have to have Scotty to do my work, and I'm not going to give up either one. So they have to decide how it's going to work."

MICHAEL MURPHY: I think Scotty was way out of bounds in a lot of ways because she treated Kathryn with a sort of disdain. You'd think she would be trying to make Kathryn real happy. And it's not hard to make Kathryn happy. She's a lovely woman. But there was some kind of possessive thing that went on there. That may be part of even my own dropping away for a while.

ALLAN NICHOLLS: Over the years, her unpleasantness kind of became her. She was wearing all these layered clothes and she started to hunch. She was an incessant smoker. It was like in *Brewster,* you know how René's character transforms? She became the character of the bad producer.

There was one time during *Quintet* where I was getting on an elevator with Scotty, and Kathryn reached out. I think she even said, "Come on, let's just bury the hatchet on this one." I remember Scotty closing the elevator door in her face. So it was clearly not to be. I can remember wanting to be anywhere else at that moment, because I had to ride the next three floors with absolutely nothing to say.

KATHRYN REED ALTMAN: Bill Bushnell came to our house a couple times in Mandeville Canyon in the late sixties, and he brought her and she'd sit over in the corner. She was impossible to bring into the group. We got around the pool, barbecuing and all that, and she'd just take a book and go sit. She had no social grace whatsoever, none. She was like a hayseed. And I worked so hard at that and it just never went anywhere. And so I was starting to resent her right there and then. I mean, it was embarrassing.

She slowly wormed her way into making herself almost—he seemed to feel that she was indispensable. It's a strain, a part of Bob's personality that I was never able to understand. And he was never able to explain it to me or anybody else. And at the beginning when people were questioning him, "God, Bob, what's her story?" and she was turning people off one by one, he would say, "Well, it's good to have her around because she doesn't 'yes' me." I remember that vividly. And he was getting to the point where it was getting to be a little sycophant city around there, that rise to stardom so explosively from *M*A*S*H*. I didn't realize it at the time, but looking back I could see how he didn't need someone to tell him he was right. He functioned better with somebody that would, you know, converse contrarily.

She was a conniver and she was dishonest and she was needy and she was no fun. And she used that power to manipulate all kinds of people—actors, writers. It just got completely out of control and it affected me and my entire family. He lost many friends. Many he's gotten back. He got back Matthew Seig. He got Tommy Thompson, thank God—that was a huge loss. He got back Michael Murphy, David Levy—she dumped Dave. She was just terribly destructive, but also during that time, Bob, he was very successful. You know, he was working one picture after the other. So therein lies the puzzle.

I just went up to her one day after this thing of shunning and shunning and shunning. She was talking to Allan Nicholls—this was in 1979 or something—and she said, "Now, we're going to have the birthday cake for Bob at lunchtime." And I walked in and I said, "Listen, cool it, will you?" Before that, I didn't have the courage to tell her off ever, because I didn't want to rock the boat with Bob. So I said, "Listen, he's my husband. I'll plan the birthdays, you plan the picture." She shriveled up and crawled away or some unattractive thing.

JOHNNIE PLANCO (agent): Bob and Scotty were coming to odds on *Kansas City*. They were hardly speaking to each other.

MATTHEW SEIG: She wouldn't leave and he wouldn't fire her. It was sick. He said for years that he was going to stop working with her and he just couldn't do it. They only separated after she practically died.

BILL BUSHNELL: She was stricken in March 1995, a week from making *Kansas City*. She was on the phone to London to somebody's agent. She suddenly said, "God, my legs are numb," and she fell off the chair. She was lucky there was an ER squad across the street having lunch.

I spoke to the doctors because I was staying in her loft in New York. She flatlined in there for some period of time, and as she was fond of saying, "It ain't white. It's all black."

MICHAEL MURPHY: I went to see her in the hospital. It was an interesting thing. Boy, she really got her priorities lined up because she was nicer than I ever remember her.

BILL BUSHNELL: That was the end. As far as I know Bob never came to the hospital to see her. I think he was so terrified of death that the idea of going and seeing someone who had been with him for twenty-something years at death's door terrified him. Not of being dead but of the process of dying. Because he was having his own problems. Plus I think it was his way of getting rid of Scotty. I think that relationship was over and probably had been over for some time but neither one of them knew how to get out of it.

I don't think she ever talked to Bob again. I think that was a two-way street. She never called him and he never called her.

MATTHEW SEIG: After that happened, for a couple of weeks Bob said that he was never happier on a film, that he was having a great time. Everybody was happier and he was happier and loving it. That changed after a while because we were just really running out of the money and the stresses were growing on Bob. So he was less happy as time went on. But it was a big burden off of his shoulders when that happened, as cruel as that sounds.

I believe that Bob did visit her in the hospital, but I could be wrong about that.

KATHRYN REED ALTMAN: He was ready to let her go. He was ready, [but] he didn't know how, he never fired anybody except cameramen. And I just don't think he had the guts or knew how to do it. I think he was so grateful that he didn't have to do it. He went to see her once in the hospital—I'm sure of that—and that was under great pressure. And he never mentioned her again, after working together twenty-six years.

MATTHEW ALTMAN: That was a strange thing about my dad. There were a lot of people in his life, they were in one minute and then, *boom*, they were gone, never to be talked about again. I never understood that about him.

HENRY GIBSON: She was an arch defender of his vision, of his ability. And she was very clear-eyed except for that one big fault, which was not giving a damn about humanity. And very vulnerable, she was very vulnerable and died alone and sad and uncared for and with very little money. Saddest of endings.

WREN ARTHUR (producer): He was so happy to be free of Scotty, but I think his freedom contained a lot of guilt. A couple of times he did acknowledge that he had put Kathryn and a lot of people who he loved through a lot—Tommy Thompson, a lot of people. He really wasn't respectful to them by keeping Scotty around. Because she wanted them out. I mean, especially Kathryn. Therein lies the hair in the butter, as Bob would say. You don't put your wife through that because of this producer. It's just wrong. There was one specific time, probably the following summer—after work we were all sitting around having wine and he was just talking about Scotty very candidly. About how he wished he'd done things differently and let her go years before and ended the relationship. I'm paraphrasing here, but he said he'd needed her in an old-school way to protect him so he didn't have to be the bad guy.

CHAPTER 22

Popeye

*

Popeye *(1980)*

David Ansen, review headlined "Popeye Without Spinach," *Newsweek,* **December 22, 1980:** Strange bedfellows make strange movies. Take *Popeye* as a case in point. To bring E. C. Segar's venerable comic-strip hero to the screen, proto-Hollywood producer Robert Evans, ironic New York humorist Jules Feiffer and laid-back iconoclastic director Robert Altman joined forces. They employed the services of Robin Williams and Shelley Duvall to play Popeye and Olive Oyl, enlisted Harry Nilsson to write musical numbers and constructed an elaborate rendition of Sweethaven, the cartoon shantytown, on the unlikely Mediterranean island of Malta.

This is high-risk chemistry, and the results are bizarre. The bulging forearms and corncob pipe are in place, but this Popeye hates spinach. The plot hinges on his Oedipal search for his Pappy (Ray Walston), the songs and minimal dances are designed for singers who can't sing and dancers who can't dance, and this gruff icon of pugnacious, all-American goodness has been set adrift on an abstract isle that can perhaps best be described as backlot Ionesco. *Popeye*'s air of alienated whimsy makes for an odd "family movie" indeed.

*   *   *

DAVID LEVY (producer): The Fox pictures were all, I think it's fair to say, budgeted in the high ones, like one-point-eight million, one-point-nine million, to maybe four million. *Popeye* was obviously going to be a very different kind of project, a very different kind of picture. I

Robin Williams, as Popeye, and Shelley Duvall, as Olive Oyl,
with Altman's grandson Wesley Ivan Hurt, as Swee'pea

don't think Bob ever looked at things in these terms, really, but you talked about him being on top of the world a few years earlier. Well, if the five-picture Fox deal left his career in a place where it was on the precipice, this project would be one that would either put him back on top or he'd be falling over into the abyss.

JULES FEIFFER (writer and cartoonist): Maybe it's best to give you the background on *Popeye*. Bob Evans wanted to do *Annie*—I don't know if he told you that—and John Huston had gotten *Annie* at United Artists or Columbia or something. Evans was stuck on the idea of doing a musical of some comic strip and he realized that *Popeye* had been owned by Paramount, where he had just left as head of production and now had a freelance agreement with, and he was working with Bridget Sylbert. [Her husband] Dick Sylbert was a friend of mine—he also was the production designer on *Carnal Knowledge*. And Bob Evans asked Dick who might write the screenplay for *Popeye*, and Dick said I was the only one who could make sense of these characters and put them on screen. So Evans called me and he said, "Would you like to write *Popeye*?"

I said, "It depends on which *Popeye*, because there's E. C. Segar's *Popeye*, the original *Popeye*, which is a work of genius, and there's Max Fleischer's animated *Popeye*, which I'm not crazy about." I might have been stronger. I didn't like it at all.

And he said, and this is virtually a direct quote, "I want to do whatever *Popeye* you want to do." Essentially his attitude remained like that throughout. He was an amazing, important producer for Hollywood or any other place.

Robert Evans (producer): I wanted Dustin [Hoffman] at first very badly, but there were problems between Dustin and Jules Feiffer. What happened? Remember, this was thirty years ago—there are three sides to every story.

Jules Feiffer: I was writing it for Dustin. Dustin and Bob Evans were the best of friends, were very close. I had told Evans after repeated treatments that he kept rejecting that there was not going to be any treatment in the sky that he was going to like. I asked him to give me some money and I'd write fifty pages of script where he would see the relationship between Popeye and Olive Oyl and he would know whether there was a movie there or whether I was the right writer or not. And he agreed immediately, and I wrote those fifty pages. Dustin loved them. Dustin drove me to Evans' house for a meeting, and on the way he kept comparing my script to *The Graduate*, to Samuel Beckett, to Kafka; I mean, he was just going on and on and on. Of course, by the time I submitted the first draft, which was a finished first draft, which Evans and Sylbert loved, Dustin wanted me fired and another writer put on.

Any other producer would have fired me to keep his star. Not Evans. He said, "You know, I'm the producer, Jules is the writer, I'd love you involved but you're not going to . . . this is the script we're going with." Just amazing.

We finally had a script and we threw around names of directors. We got a lot of turndowns. He offered it to Hal Ashby. He also offered it to Louis Malle, and I was afraid Louis, being French, would not get it. I thought we needed someone quintessentially American. At one point Jerry Lewis wanted to do it. And I said, "I'd rather kill myself."

He brought up Altman and I knew two things immediately. I knew that he would put the characters on screen in the most imaginative and vital way possible, and I knew I'd be lucky if I got a word of mine from the script on the screen. But I figured if I got fifty percent I'd be doing very well. And we're out of choices anyhow, and I thought we might just get lucky.

ROBERT EVANS: Bob didn't want to do it at first. He thought it wasn't his kind of picture. He is not a studio filmmaker. He was his own man. A total original. But we got together. The critics were after Bob at that time, I don't know why. He hadn't had a good run right before that, either. And that's why I wanted to get him because I love getting a filmmaker whose last pictures haven't done well. They are usually more collaborative. We got along great, because I only had half a suit on. I was always on his side against the studio.

JULES FEIFFER: Bob Altman and I had met at Elaine's originally. Elaine's at that time was not a glitzy place. It was where a lot of writers

Producer Robert Evans looking over Robert Altman's shoulder,
on the set of Popeye *in Malta*

hung out, and journalists, and increasingly some theater and movie people. My early impressions? Only one impression: jovial and sardonic at the same time. Bearish character—I mean, he seemed bigger than he really was and he gave this impression of size. He was charismatic and highly opinionated and often full of shit, but you couldn't really challenge him because he wouldn't hear it. And you basically accepted him for what he was because it was worth it. He was just good company; he was the real thing in a business where there is so much that is not the real thing. I thought that, while we were friends, it would be insane to ever work with him because he trashed writers. He didn't really believe in words, he believed in images, and his images were often extraordinary.

I didn't go into it with any illusions. And when Evans told me that Altman signed a contract where he can't change a word of dialogue I just laughed [*laughs*].

If you're a writer on a movie, the price you pay for working with Altman is that if there's not constant vigilance to make sure that the script is being followed—Altman with all his gifts, and maybe it's because he's carrying out these gifts, these gifts don't include storytelling. He's not interested in storytelling. His gifts don't include building character. These are just not interests of his. He's kind of a painter on film and he's giving you impressions and visual impressions. He's a little like an action painter. And when it works, it's remarkable, but if you're interested in motivation of character, forget about it.

*   *   *

ROBERT EVANS: I saw Robin Williams on television in *Mork & Mindy* and I said, "He looks like Popeye." They were afraid to put a television actor in a picture this big. Using a television star in those days to play a lead role in a movie was not au courant. That's changed today. But nobody could have played it better than Robin.

ROBIN WILLIAMS (actor and comedian): Evans told me he got Bob. I was excited because he's a great name. All of a sudden I went like, "You're serious."

JULES FEIFFER: I had been thinking of Shelley Duvall even before Altman was involved, because Shelley I knew personally because when she was in New York she'd hang out with Bob and Kathryn. And I loved her in all of the Altman films I'd seen her in and I thought, "My God, she's the perfect Olive Oyl." But they had had a falling-out. . . . I don't remember the reasons for it, but I do know he was down on her and he wanted anybody but Shelley. And, you know, Bob gets petulant about things like this, and his feelings were hurt. I think he felt that kind of a father-daughter relationship and he felt like King Lear. He felt that Cordelia had spurned him and chosen someone else.

Shelley Duvall, to Lawrence Eisenberg, story headlined "Filmdom's Most Unlikely Star," *Cosmopolitan*, **August 1981:** God, as a child I was so embarrassed when the kids would call me Olive Oyl because it meant you were skinny as a rail, you had sparrow legs and an Adam's apple. I mean, who wants to admit she was born to play Olive Oyl?

JULES FEIFFER: When you see the movie again she's the best thing in it. Finally he agreed. He also got Paul Dooley, whom Bob had given some of his best movie roles, as Wimpy. Then Bob Altman found the Pickle Family Circus, which included Bill Irwin at the time.

And for some insane reason, he wanted to shoot it in Malta—I think just simply to get rid of the studio. Malta has no indigenous wood. It's a rock, and we had to import every piece of wood from the West Coast. You know, I've said that if he could have figured out a way of shooting it on the moon, he would have deemed that the perfect location. Just to get away from [Michael] Eisner and [Barry] Diller, who ran the studio at the time.

So all of these young unknowns assembled in Malta—Bill Irwin, Dennis Franz, all terrific talent. It was a family. We set up in this not particularly great but okay hotel, and this guy named Wolf Kroeger created an extraordinary set, the town of Sweethaven. Not the least of which was the score by Harry Nilsson, which was absolutely wonderful. Harry and I worked closely together, and he got Van Dyke Parks to arrange the music and they built a music studio in Malta and they did the recording there. What's great about Altman shooting a movie was it brought to mind all of those MGM musicals I loved as a kid. They were all like Mickey and Judy putting on a show.

ROBERT EVANS: Malta. They told us it never rained between November and May. It rained every day.

When we got to Malta, we were met by all kinds of officials from the Maltese film commission, and they brought Miss Malta along with them. On a scale of one to ten, she was a two. By the time I left Malta, she was an eleven. It was a terribly difficult experience.

STEPHEN ALTMAN: What was the scene like on *Popeye*? It was nuts. I considered it at that time and probably still today as the hardest, roughest time. Nine months on the rock, you know? Gates closed and you're stuck there. It was really bad. Everybody went through changes, everybody had huge changes of life, and people got divorced and married, and very few people were left sane on that island.

KATHRYN REED ALTMAN: Everybody was very loaded. A lot of tantrums and fights and tantrums. A lot of drinking. Bob? He went right with it—he created it. We had one or two kids born, a couple of divorces, a lot of wife-cheating.

ROBIN WILLIAMS: Bob was the ringmaster. I think he was kind of watching it, setting it up, kind of taking delight in watching. I think it was the idea of putting together a three-ring circus as a movie. And I think he loved the metaphor for that, and that the town was full of kind of, you know, strange people, survivors. They're all shipwreck survivors in Sweethaven. I think that was another metaphor he liked. They're isolated and they have their own kind of ways and I come in a stranger, you know?

DAVID LEVY: It's no secret that Bob inhaled. And just because we were in Malta, nearly halfway around the world, life should still go on. And so arrangements were made. This at the time fell on my shoulders to make sure the people over on these shores got something together and put it inside these items that we really did need for the film. We put it inside people-sized dummies. It was a different world then. The Lockerbie flight went through Malta; the explosive device found its way onto the plane in Malta, as I recall. Those were not these times. And we were talking about a situation where we were so ensconced on that island and the authorities were so okay with us that Steve Altman could basically go behind the counter at customs and just sling these things over his shoulder and take them away. A very, very different world.

ROBIN WILLIAMS: When we were on Malta, we were on everything but skates. And then they sent the skates in and it got interesting. The open bar at dailies? I think anything, everything was going on. People smoking a joint or whatever, and then later on when the magic dust appeared in the radios, dailies got more interesting, too. But I think if you're going to watch two hours of a boat rowing, you have to have a little help.

ROBERT EVANS: We couldn't fix Popeye's arms. That was the last thing that worked with the picture. We started the picture without the arms being right. We had a saying: "We're bringing arms to Malta!"

ROBIN WILLIAMS: The initial makeup guy made the arms and they looked kind of like two hazmat gloves filled with putty. They wrinkled all over. It was like I was wearing two long gloves that you use to clean the toilet. Flesh colored but still bad. They had a series of tests and they kept doing things and they just never worked. Finally he let those guys go, I forget who they were. And then they brought in this Italian makeup crew that was amazing. I remember a little old lady punching hair into the arms, kind of like doing it the old-fashioned way, but they made almost da Vinci–type models with arms, with the muscles underneath and then they put the rubber over the top and it worked much better.

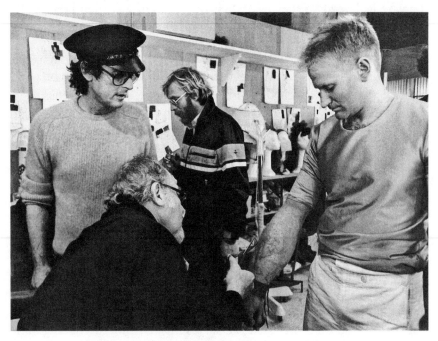

Working on Robin Williams's bulging Popeye forearms

ROBERT EVANS: There were many, many fights on it. But there are many fights on all pictures. The more irreverent you are in a film, the more possibility of turning a bit of magic. We were irreverent, and we thought we turned a bit of magic.

* * *

DAVID LEVY: We were in Malta on Christmas Eve. A group of us were in the prop shop on the set, and suddenly Bob and Kathryn started dancing around the shop like teenagers. The champagne had been flowing. Soon they started twirling each other around, and finally they fell to the floor, with Bob on his back and Kathryn on top of him. They stayed there laughing hysterically, face-to-face, with their arms around each other. We stood there watching.

KATHRYN REED ALTMAN: I don't remember it quite the way David tells it. But yes, there had been a lot of champagne.

* * *

JULES FEIFFER: Bob seemed to be shooting what I wrote, more or less, but since he didn't believe in directing the actors—as he told me—he let them say whatever they wanted to. Particularly with Robin. When Robin meets Olive Oyl, after they meet for the first time but when they first come together . . . this was supposed to be a sweet scene that begins with great hostility and then evolves into the beginnings of a relationship.

ROBIN WILLIAMS: Shelley was brilliant. I think one mumble I had [*in Popeye's voice*]: "Oh God, I've seen better lumps in oatmeal. Together they make one big one."

JULES FEIFFER: Bob let Robin fuck with the dialogue and turn it into a Robin Williams stand-up moment, all of which Bob and everyone else thought terribly funny except me, because it trashed the moment and trashed the scene. And this was the first of our fights.

I went to him after the day's shooting. What happened every night is we had screenings of the dailies. And everybody always loved everybody. And as everybody was loving everybody and laughing hysterically, I was recoiling in horror. Then after, I went to his room and told him what I thought. I told him, "It's no good. It undermines the credibility of the characters. This is where we are set up to believe these characters and go with these characters for the rest of the movie. Instead it's just Robin doing stand-up, and you've got to reshoot it and direct him."

And he said, "I don't direct my actors. I don't believe in directing them."

And so it got rather hostile and angry and I left really bereft and depressed. I remember walking to the set down the hill and just wandering around this empty set, and feeling rather lost.

The next morning at the commissary, there was this big outdoor place where everybody ate, and it was a mob of people, and I sat down next to a member of the crew—I was friendly with everybody—who moved away from me. I started to talk to some others and nobody was talking to me. And I realized in about a minute and a half that I was in Coventry, and I didn't know who put the word out or how the word got out, but [*laughs*]—I had been disappeared.

So I went back to my room and I simmered all day long, and then after we saw the dailies that day I went to Bob's room and I said, "I'm going back to New York. I'm quitting."

And he said, "You can't quit."

And I said, "Well, I can't take this kind of treatment." And he did not know anything about it, and he said he didn't tell anybody about it.

I said, "Well, there were only three of us in the room"—him, me, and his producer, Scotty. And I guess Scotty was the one.

He said, "I can't have you go back"—he was very sweet—"because you're the only man who's not afraid to tell me what's really going on." And he said, "What do I have to do to keep you here?"

I said, "Let's recut the scene." And by that I meant that we all go into a cutting room and put back the dialogue as it was. Because interspersed throughout Robin's gags were some of my lines. Enough of my lines.

Finally we reshaped the scene that's in the movie now as a relationship. Bob saw it and said, "That's good, let's keep it." I was just astonished. And I no longer wanted to leave and also felt terribly moved by this generosity of spirit. The guy was nuts but he was also a brilliant and generous-hearted man.

ROBIN WILLIAMS: We had the Italian stuntmen. That alone was worth the price of admission. There'd be three of them warming up in back and one would just kind of fall in the water. [*Italian accent*] "Okay, he's a-ready. One moment. He's a-ready. *Splash* [*pause*]. He's okay! He's okay!"

We would always make fun of that because it was not like they were Italian war heroes.

And at that point, we had a couple of bad accidents. Doug Dillard, the banjo player, had fallen four floors and survived, amazingly. He even survived the Maltese hospital and the care he got.

*   *   *

JULES FEIFFER: Finally I think I just got worn down. I felt increasingly isolated, and about five weeks before the end of shooting I just went back to New York. And by that time he was ready to have me go back. And by that time it was clear that because of the budget, he was not going to be able to shoot the end of the film. I had written a series of sequences at sea. And the fight Popeye was having with Bluto, there simply wasn't going to be the money to do. I had a scene I loved where Popeye and Bluto on shipboard rip apart pieces of the ship to battle each other, like jousting with each other, and so each one tears off a mast and they're dueling with these masts, and slowly, because they've taken apart the ship, the ship sinks under them. Well, that would have cost zillions. So instead he decided to put it all underwater. The further he got into the movie, the more it moved away from Segar and more toward Max Fleischer. And when I left town, Segar left with me and Fleischer took over, because that was basically more Bob's sense of humor anyway. More slapsticky.

PAUL DOOLEY: The budget went from thirteen million to twenty million. The studio never quite believed it was the weather. They're half a world away, and they figured the director had screwed up several days or was drunk or something or ruined the dailies. He would say it was bad weather, you know? But it really was terrible weather.

ROBIN WILLIAMS: The toughest part was, as we went along the weather didn't play along. . . . And the studio basically pulled the plug at the wrong time, right when we needed the money to finish, and for special effects. They had none. I remember we had a meeting with Robert Evans. I think he was sitting there a bit tweaked, and I said, "How are we going to end this?"

"I don't know. How?"

And then I said, "I could walk on water, like Jesus." I was joking. "That's great, let's do it!"

It was like, "Wait a minute. No, Bob, no, no." I mean, the cartoon Popeye could run on the water, but at that point we didn't have the special effects. In the cartoons his feet would turn into a propeller and he could go flying through the water. But we had three Maltese guys and me on a winch underwater being pulled very quickly.

And they left Shelley in the water with an octopus that couldn't be run. And it was that Ed Wood moment where she's going, "Oh help!" But we kept going and Bob said, "Just shoot it. We got it."

ROBERT EVANS: From the costuming to the casting to the postproduction, I loved the film. I think it was possibly his most ambitious undertaking. Because it was so different but not obscure. It's terribly entertaining. I think Bob was twenty years ahead of his time. I think the picture is terrific. I think he did a wonderful job on it that no one else could have done.

All of the problems you could ever have on a film, we had. From the country not wanting us there, to the weather not wanting us there, to the studio not liking our budget. It was twenty million, and it made money. I defended Bob against the studio, which felt he was too extravagant about things, which he was not. Anybody else would have made the picture, it would have cost twice as much. The picture was a success financially, and I really thought this was going to be the best thing I was ever associated with.

I think they should rerelease it today. I think the picture is a work of genius. And I've watched it recently. If you can see a film and sit there for two hours and laugh and cry during that two hours, and be entertained, I think you have a hit. But I was wrong. It was one of the biggest disappointments of my career. I think it was Bob's best work.

JULES FEIFFER: I only found out five years later, maybe ten years later, that it was one of the top ten moneymakers that year, because Paramount was circulating rumors, calling it Evansgate. It seems to me the combination of Evans, who they hated by this time, and Altman, who they probably hated always, made them want this movie to fail. And whatever I didn't like about the movie, people liked the movie. Kids loved the movie.

I got a call about it a few days after its release, from Chicago, from a woman who introduced herself on the phone as Segar's daughter. She said she had heard me on one or two radio interviews talk about her father, and how I was trying to make this movie a testament to him. She thought this was absolute nonsense and didn't believe it because she had heard people talk this way before and it never, ever amounted to anything. But she'd just come from the screening and she said it was her father up there on the screen, and she wanted to thank me. I thanked her and I hung up the phone and I wept.

Robert Altman: You should watch *Popeye* with a kid. Kids love that movie. They get it.

Robin Williams: It's a beautiful film, man. It's done with the same love he made every other film with. He told me later on, "Don't always go with a critical response. Go with, 'What did you *do* there?' " Yeah, we did do some really great stuff. I think it was just because it was my first movie, it was like the illusion—"I want the studio to make money."

At one point I think he got kind of pissed that I was making fun of it. But I said, "Listen, I'm a comic, I have to kind of do that." I said, "You run it backwards and it has a happy ending."

He said a great thing. He said, "A lot of people in the business are making shoes. I'm in the business of making gloves." I look back on the experience and I go, "Goddamn, man, it was an honor." I think you come away working on an Altman movie going, "Well, that was something." You don't come away blasé, you learn a lot about being gutsy, about putting your ass on the line, trying something. Hey, dude, put it out there.

I think for the first one out of the gate, that's a pretty amazing experience. It's kind of like *Apocalypse Now* without the death. . . . For your first movie to get the shit kicked out of it, it toughened me up. It's kind of, in a weird way, a gift. It was like, "Hey, now you go off and you work. You're no longer a virgin. You've been in your first battle. It wasn't a total victory but we didn't get slaughtered. So keep going."

Stephen Altman: It only made sixty million, and of course it cost twenty million to make. So how that translates into bomb, I have no idea. Still, it wasn't the huge success that everybody thought it was going to be.

David Levy: *Popeye* got a bum rap.

* * *

JULES FEIFFER: Bob must have spent so many years simmering [*laughs*] and building up rage at what he had to put up with to get work from these assholes that when he finally got in a position to do Altman work—and as he discovered how to do Altman work—he was not going to back off for anybody. And he got into endless fights over it and he lost opportunities, I'm sure, and he got fired from things, but he just didn't know how to behave any other way. I mean, maybe he felt that once he starts down that road again it won't stop. I think he was kind of a grown-up Huck Finn.

He was destined to go into the wilderness. If anything, he willed himself into the wilderness. This was his fate, that he had to butt heads, he had to fight the establishment, and he also was a genius and there's only a little of genius that's allowed in American movies. And then we want to go back to doing what we do best, which is *Star Wars 42*.

ACT III

1981–2006

*Robert Altman abandons—and is abandoned by—
Hollywood, sells his studio, sells his Malibu
movie-star house, films plays, films operas, moves to
Paris, becomes a "Player" again, gets a new heart,
loses a kidney, collects his Oscar, embraces his family,
and goes out with his boots on.*

*

CHAPTER 23

The Wilderness

*

ROBERT ALTMAN: It's hard to take the idea that maybe you're not that different from everyone else when you've spent all your life trying to convince other people that you *are* different. And consequently, you're trying to convince *yourself* that you are different. You're trying to live up to the myth, and before that, you're creating a myth. I created this myth and now I have to live up to this myth.

* * *

STEPHEN ALTMAN: After *Popeye*, it got very rough. He was right at the top. *Popeye* spiraled him down to nothing. Nobody wanted to deal with him. I don't know if I would have been able to deal with that.

JERRY WALSH (friend/lawyer/executor): He went through a period where he had a hard time raising money to do anything. He didn't wear his heart on his sleeve, really, but I just knew there were times when he wasn't working on something, he wanted to work on something. He couldn't because there was no money, and people would not answer his phone calls. That's the thing he complained about the most. He always wanted to be in touch. He always answered his phone calls. You called Bob Altman in the middle of a film or when he was juggling fifteen balls at once, and by the end of the day you had a return call—and I wasn't alone in that. He just never ended a day without responding to everybody trying to reach him unless he just didn't want to speak to the person, but it wasn't because he was too busy. He would always make time. And it drove him crazy that Sam Cohn wouldn't answer his

Directing one of his stage productions in the 1980s

phone calls. He forgave Sam for it, but he used to say, "It's just a sickness. I don't understand it."

As he said: "I'm a very extreme personality. I always have been. It's just the way I am." Think about the difficulties he had in the forties and fifties getting started, followed by the tremendous success of *M*A*S*H* and the big contract that let him do four or five big movies. The relief from the frustration and failures of the sixties, released by *M*A*S*H* and those other things, into the seventies where he was the king of the world—buying the studio and going to get into the music business, and the big house in Malibu—the ego was probably just over the top. Then to get into the late seventies and hit the wall, which he did, was probably very hard for him, I think.

SAM COHN (agent): I saw Bob really angry lots of times. It didn't last long, and never on the set. It was primarily at the suits.

One of his precepts was that he was going to create this group of people who would be together—and the demands on him financially were substantial. He thought that was the way movies were supposed to be made—the same guys doing it over and over again. In some instances he had to use his own money to pay them. Bob and his actors always remained good friends—even if the movie was a dog.

He was very important in my life—because of his guts and heart.

MARK RYDELL (actor and director): He wasn't the flavor of the month at that time. But Bob had a remarkable elasticity; his ability to come back was brilliant, it was incomparable. Very few people could survive a series of bad pictures, you know? You make two bad pictures in a row and you're out of the business. It's not so much bad pictures—they may be wonderful. Pictures that don't work commercially and financially. But Bob never let the industry beat him. He created his own initiative. He went out and got the money to make his pictures. He rejected the status quo and wouldn't be deterred. If he wanted to make a picture he would see that it got made. He would fucking get the money somewhere. I admired that immensely.

When jobs were tough to come by, he'd say, "There's no need to worry. I know there'll always be someone to come along and hire me, just to add a little class to their life." You've got to laugh, you've got to love him.

DAVID LEVY (producer): Right when *Popeye* was released we were preparing a film called *Lone Star* based on the stage play by Jim McClure. And that project was put in turnaround, which meant death. Literally the week of the *Popeye* release, or within a week. It didn't live up to the expectations of certain people. Expectations count for a lot, and Bob didn't help his own cause. You know, I remember him around this time, I don't know if you can find this stuff, but he gave an interview or two and referred to Diller and Eisner in uncomplimentary terms. That couldn't have helped matters at all. I think certain powers that be in this town just decided it wasn't worth it to them. It's like, "Fine, I'll take a risk, but I don't need to be called names in the press on top of it." So we had a project put in turnaround right away at that time. And it was very much a time in the wilderness.

After *Popeye* there was that eight-year period where he was grabbing a lot of different kinds of work ranging from operas to television plays to what have you. He would do what he could do, basically. Eighty-one, eighty-two were very painful times. He sold the facility, Lion's Gate. Basically he felt he had to—I still maintain there was a way that maybe it didn't have to happen. I wished that weren't necessary, but he felt it was.

Physically, at Lion's Gate you had three levels going on. In the basement—this seems so funny now—you had wardrobe and a prop shop which was basically chock-full of stuff from movies past that could maybe work again in the future or who knows, be rented or sold or what have you. In the final days of Lion's Gate we literally were taking it out to swap meets in Pasadena. The last months in that building, I turned from his executive assistant to a moving man along with a couple other guys. We put stuff in Scotty's house until the other shoe dropped and he figured out where he was going to be. On the lower level, it was a combination of editorial suites and the dubbing stage. A good one. A place where you could do all the final work on any kind of picture. We certainly did on *Popeye* and others of his, but it was also used by other movies. I know Alan Pakula did *Starting Over* there. So that was the street level, the ground-floor level. And then upstairs was primarily what might be called executive offices, ranging from Bob's and mine, Scotty's, that sort of thing. Bob had his own publicity operation there. He had, in a way, his own distribution entity, although that was starting to go away by early '79, when I got on board. Again, it was supposed to be a studio. A development team, an art department for titles and graphics, accounting department, all this was on the second floor. So the idea being you could walk an idea into the building and it could come out the other side a finished film.

LEONARD COHEN (singer and songwriter): He either told me this or I saw this: While he was sitting with some of his scriptwriters and production people working on one of the next films—this would have been a few years after we met—the creditors were coming and removing furniture. I think that actually happened and he had this wonderful kind of gleeful sense of abandon that things couldn't get much worse.

DAVID LEVY: I think things had gotten to a point where to maintain the status quo was just too hard. At its peak, that place had over fifty employees. The idea was to pay them a salary fifty-two weeks a year. So it wasn't just about, "Oh, you get a check on a project or checks on a project and then you go fallow for six months." So, a lot of overhead. He was a bit of a micromanager. He got too involved in the business aspect of things. He was too—I won't exactly say hands-on—but too interested. Instead of getting experts and letting them do their thing and letting them try and market the thing, it was too much about it being his toy or serving his individual needs. And his career was at a point where that wasn't enough to sustain a facility and a payroll like that. It just wasn't. So it got too hard. It was too grand. When he was going in that building and building that company to another level, he was producing a Robert Benton movie, he had a Bob Young movie, he had an Alan Rudolph picture. It wasn't just about him, but then when those movies don't perform and the thing couldn't grow, it really only had one direction to go because he wasn't interested in just having a building and machines that other people would use. It was never just about, "We'll serve the film community." It was never just about, "Let's turn a profit with this thing." It was about serving him and the artists and the projects that he wanted to do, and they just weren't sustainable from an economic standpoint.

That's sobering, to know that you're turning stuff out and the marketplace is not receiving it, and your reps are not able to make deals on your behalf that are going to enable you to continue bankrolling a business of that magnitude. It was supposed to be a mini-studio where he and the anointed could thrive, do their thing, and create. And he had to turn his back on that notion.

I still remember the day he made the decision. He got on the phone with Kathryn—this would have been, I guess, in '81. He said, "The way I see it, we've got twenty good years left." Well, I'm pleased he was wrong about that—he at least had twenty-five and she's still with us. "And this is what we're going to do. We'll base out of New York and sell the place in Malibu Cove." God, I loved that place. He just had to regroup.

KATHRYN REED ALTMAN: We didn't sell Malibu for money. We were leasing it to Diana Ross while we were in Paris. While she was there, Dyan Cannon married this wealthy guy, and she wanted to know if there was any way she could buy it. They came up with a big offer. We never put it on the market. We just sold it.

DAVID LEVY: I think he was under a lot of pressure and I think he wanted to wipe the slate clean and start fresh. He always had a tremendous belief in himself. Other people might disagree, but he was terribly shrewd about money. I remember he used to say to me, "You never want to be more than this much above water"—holding his hand up to his nose. In other words, he felt the money was there to be used, whether it was in life or in the work or what have you. He wasn't interested very much in this idea of security or nest eggs or anything like that. But I daresay that at the time he sold, the water wasn't up to his nose, it was well over his head.

FRANK SOUTH (playwright): It wasn't an easy time. He and Kathryn and I were in his apartment in New York and he had just gotten off the phone. And he said, "I've got to sell everything." There was a hardback chair right up against the wall, and he just sat down in it. He was going over things in his head and he had hit a point of having to make a decision. He said, "I just can't believe it." He looked at me and said, "I've even got to sell my car." I said, "That was a great car." It was a brand-new brown BMW, and he had loaned it to me when we were in Malibu to drive to visit my great-aunt. He said, "Yeah, it was." Then he said, "I've got to sell the house. I'll get a couple million for that."

Watching the two of them deal with this without any embarrassment was really something. Kathryn didn't say, "Bob, not in front of guests," or "Let's not talk about that now." I can't remember exactly what she said at the time, but it was along the lines of, "It doesn't matter. Just things. Doesn't matter." She was so real. When Bob was at his lowest, she was there. Just a positive force. Just wouldn't ever let him be down on himself or blame himself. He would get kind of lost in the "Oh God, oh God." She was always ready to say, "So what? We'll do something else. We'll be fine." Bob didn't like to be vulnerable very long. He was down and then he said, "Okay, we'll do something else."

KATHRYN REED ALTMAN: There were a lot of those periods and they always scared the hell out of me. But he always bounced back. I don't remember dwelling on that particular one that Frank mentioned, but I'm sure it happened. And then Bob made things happen. But I have no memory of things staying down. I'm sure they did. And I'm sure I said, "Well, where should I cut back or what should I do?" And he never dwelled on it and he never talked about it that much. And it never stayed down. I never had to skimp and say, "We've only got this much money to do this or that." We always seemed to keep on trucking and flying and, you know, doing all the stuff.

FRANK SOUTH: During that time he was really pasting it together and risking a lot. But he walked away from L.A. during this time and I remember him sitting in that chair and realizing that he was going to sell it all. He had managed to beat the odds and thumb his nose at pretension and money-centered nonartist ways of thinking in Hollywood for a good long period of time. But he had to walk away from there.

Aljean Harmetz, story headlined "Robert Altman Sells Studio for $2.3 Million," *The New York Times*, July 11, 1981: Robert Altman's Lion's Gate Films has been sold for $2.3 million to a group headed by Jonathan Taplin, producer of "Mean Streets" and "The Last Waltz." Mr. Altman—the prolific and controversial director whose movies include "M*A*S*H," "Popeye" and "Nashville"—has recently retreated from film making in the wake of a number of commercially unsuccessful movies, including "Quintet," "A Perfect Couple" and "HealtH."

"Suddenly, no one answered my phone calls," Mr. Altman said in a telephone interview from Montreal. "I had no place to turn." The maverick director whose greatest commercial success was "M*A*S*H," 11 years ago, put his company on the block last winter in the wake of financial claims and counterclaims with Paramount Pictures over the budget of "Popeye" and the collapse of his next project, "Lone Star," at United Artists.

"I feel my time has run out," he said today. "Every studio wants 'Raiders of the Lost Ark.' The movies I want to make are movies the studios don't want. What they want to make, I don't."

STEPHEN ALTMAN: He got offered to do *M*A*S*H II* for five million dollars. That was more than anything he'd ever made. He was like, "No fucking way. I'm not doing that. *M*A*S*H* is not my movie anymore. There's a TV series. Everybody took it away from me." He wouldn't do anything like that. He would never get involved in those paydays. He said, "They won't hire me for anything else except stuff they have control of." He needed final cut. He needed it to be his picture. He needed it to be his way, so you know, you only get so much money for working off of your name.

Was he different? No, he was the same all the time. When he was down and out he was still the king and when he was the king he was the king. It was just, he could afford better offices. He lived the same. Everything was always the same for him. That was one of the things about "the genius" and "the failure." I don't think he ever believed any of that. "The award, yes, I want the award. But it doesn't mean anything." He did really believe that. "I don't care what you think about my movie, I'm doing this for me. You know, it would be nice to make some money, but first I'm making the film." I mean, he could always have made the payday. And kept working and segue into a TV series and been fat and rich. But the importance to him was doing what he wanted to do as he wanted to do it, and being in charge.

MICHAEL MURPHY: He's never defeated. Nobody could defeat this guy. He suffered a lot of slings and arrows, but he was never defeated.

Robert Altman, unused footage from Fox Movie Channel Documentary *Robert Altman: On His Own Terms*: In the eighties people would say, "Oh, gee, it's a shame that you're, you know, you haven't done anything for so long." I'd say, "I do two pictures a year." I have constantly got a project.

*   *   *

2 by South—Rattlesnake in a Cooler and Precious Blood *(1982; First presented at Los Angeles Actors' Theatre and St. Clement's Theatre, New York)*

David Sterritt, story headlined "Robert Altman's Sudden—and Auspicious—Stage Venture," *The Christian Science Monitor*, **October 27, 1981:** A few months ago Robert Altman sold his production company— Lion's Gate Films—and hightailed it out of the movie business. This distressed the fans who have cheered such pictures as "M*A*S*H," "Three Women," "Nashville," and "A Wedding," and who regarded Altman as one of the few independent voices in Hollywood.

But it turns out Altman hasn't retired, just altered his course. Hoping to continue his career in the cable-TV and home-video markets, he has meanwhile set his sights on the stage. "2 by South," presented recently at the Los Angeles Actors' Theater, has now arrived Off Broadway, marking Altman's New York stage-directing debut. It is an auspicious occasion.

The evening consists of two one-act dramas by a new playwright named Frank South. Both are cautionary tales, tracing the path of seemingly reasonable men to eruptions of violence. Perhaps more to the point, both provide ideal working material for Altman, who thrives less on plot than on dense characterization and unconventional structure. In this regard, he and author South are kindred spirits.

FRANK SOUTH: I was a writer-slash-waiter-slash-performance artist in New York and we had a space on lower Broadway and we would do our own pieces down there. I was working at Windows on the World as a waiter. One show I did was a one-man show called *Rattlesnake in a Cooler*. Some divine luck stepped in and a woman came in—she saw a review in the *SoHo News*—and she told some friends at an agency. So a bunch of agents came to this little tiny space. They had a client, Leo Burmester, and he was working on *Lone Star* with Bob. The agents showed the script to Leo and said, "This is perfect for you." Leo optioned it, gave me something like five hundred dollars. *Lone Star* fell through and he took it to Bob and they started messing around.

Bob didn't know what he was going to do, but he enjoyed the piece. Leo was rehearsing it at Bob's office. Leo said he put holes in the walls—tore the place up—Bob didn't care. He said, "That's great, that's great." At one point after they were messing with it for a while. Bob said, "I've got to meet this guy, I guess."

I got a call from my agent and he said Bob Altman wanted to talk with me. I said, "Bob Altman, who?" I couldn't believe it was Robert Altman. It was a shock to me because back in my Missouri days where I went to high school and did my knock-around times, I saw all of his stuff, especially *McCabe & Mrs. Miller*, which I had gone to see like five times.

My agent said, "This is a very important meeting." He was really worried. He was an uptown guy and I wasn't at all. He said, "For God's sake, Frank, whatever you do, Frank, don't drink. This is a rare, rare meeting. Keep your head about you."

So I went to Delmonico's, where Bob had an office-slash-apartment, and I knocked on the door—straightening my shirt—and he's in his robe, his hair all over the place. He's on the phone and he's going, "Fuck, fuck. Well, I don't know, I don't know. It was a cabdriver. I don't know how I gave him two hundred bucks!"

He says, "You the writer? Come in, come in." He closes the door. This is around one o'clock in the afternoon.

He says, "I was at Elaine's. Can you believe this guy? This cabdriver? I thought I gave him two tens. And it was two hundreds!" He's mumbling around and he goes over to the bar—"Want a drink? I don't trust anybody who doesn't drink."

We started talking and drinking and he told me he'd been rehears-

ing the play with Leo and he liked it very much and he asked me if I
had any more. It turned out that I had written another play called *Precious Blood*. He says, "So let me read it. Anything else?" I had a short
story. He says, "Let me see that, too."

It was not like any kind of job interview. It was more someone sitting down and wanting to know who you were. And not by asking
directly. After a while we got into this thing where we were quizzing
each other back and forth. There were times he would say, "I don't
want to talk about that." We talked about everything that afternoon
and we kept having drinks. And there was a pasta maker that came out
somewhere mid-afternoon. And he wanted to know where I came
from—family, all that stuff. About writing, about performing.

He asked if I had read Barry Hannah. I said yeah, and he said, "You
remind me of him." I spent twenty-something years in Hollywood
after that, and people rarely read. Scotty one time said he didn't like to
read that much, but I didn't find that to be true. He knew what he was
talking about, about writers. He knew viscerally on a real deep level
what *Rattlesnake* was about. He wanted to know if this was an accident
or there was a genuine human being-slash-writer he could get along
with.

He told me about his kids. We talked about football, just all kinds of
things, just one of those rambling kinds of conversations. I figured this
is going to be a half hour or so. Now it's like four o'clock and I'm
through messing with the pasta machine. Then he pulled out a joint or
two and we talked some more, and I am completely loaded. Then he
started talking about music and what kind of music would go with this.
Then he would ask me—he wanted to know more and more about *Precious Blood*.

He asked me what movies of his I had seen and he wanted to know
what I thought. I said they were wonderful. And he said, "That's bullshit. What did you *think*!" And I would say what I thought and there
were some that I loved and some I really didn't understand. We talked
about Hitchcock and he told me about working on *Combat!*, and now
it's around five or so, and some guys show up and they play some music
and we eat something else. And Bob says, "Let's go back to the scene of
the crime. Let's go to Elaine's."

I'm a waiter, playwright, performance artist, and now it's seven or
eight o'clock at night and we're traipsing off to Elaine's and I'm completely sick. I don't know if it's the nerves or the pot or the drink or the
bad pasta, and I'm throwing up in the bathroom. This is the worst

thing. He's banging on the door—"You alive in there? Come on. We've got to go!"

He starts laughing and I say, "That's about the worst thing I could ever do."

He says, "Ah, I've done worse."

He's telling the other guys, "Do you believe this kid? He comes to meet a big shot and he throws up in the bathroom!"

And then he mumbles to me, "Oh, you've got some on your shirt."

We go to Elaine's, and those guys peel off and then it's just him and me at Elaine's. We're sitting there and we're talking and he starts playing backgammon with some other guys. I'm looking up at the waiter at Elaine's and saying, "I'm a waiter, too," in this drunk voice.

He's putting down the veal in front of me and saying, "Uh-huh." Bob's looking at me and he says, "He doesn't care."

He liked to make observations about people and he was always honest to a fault. And he says, "You're one of those people, right? You want to please people. You want to make them like you." He was basically saying, "You should stop that." It was funny because my whole persona at that time was the leather jacket and the jeans, and when I wasn't a waiter I was a downtown rebel artist.

The night goes on and at this point I'm just watching and he's getting involved in the backgammon game. It's like one in the morning, and I said, "I gotta go."

He says, "Okay, get me the stuff. Send it over, and we'll talk."

I stumbled out of Elaine's, got to the nearest pay phone, and called my friends and woke them up. And I didn't know what to say. "He wants to do this, but I'm not sure what he wants to do."

That's how it started.

*   *   *

So I'm still a service captain up at Windows on the World—the businessmen's club at the World Trade Center. I get a call from him and he says, "We're in rehearsals and I'd really love for you to be out here. We're going to be opening soon." I had what, a hundred and fifty dollars, and I put it in my pocket and they sent me a ticket and I took off for Los Angeles.

I'm broke but I'm not saying anything. I don't know what I'm going to do about a bed, even, that evening. I went out and got myself a couple of cheeseburgers at McDonald's and a Budweiser from a store and sat in the back of the theater and watched rehearsals. Afterward, he said, "So, where are you staying?"

"Um, I haven't really figured . . ."

"Why don't you come home with me?"

We drove out to Malibu Cove Colony—he hadn't sold it yet—and I spent the next two weeks living there, in a room that faced the ocean. He and Kathryn were so loving and so generous to me. It was a stunning experience. You don't see much of that in life. And it was just who they were.

This was not a time when he was doing well in Hollywood. One time we were driving past Paramount on the way to rehearsal and he makes like he's throwing a hand grenade as we're driving by. And he says, "I hope that Katzenberg is dead. Little prick." *[South makes sound effects of a bomb exploding.]*

Throughout all this, there was a guy who didn't have a phony bone in his body. He was so hard honest in my relationship with him, and that's what he demanded of me. That's the only thing he really asked.

*   *   *

Come Back to the Five and Dime, Jimmy Dean, Jimmy Dean *(1982)*

Sheila Benson, review in the *Los Angeles Times*, November 12, 1982: No wonder "Come Back to the Five and Dime, Jimmy Dean, Jimmy Dean" didn't work on the New York stage. It was a film all the time, a rich, funny, touching, insightful film. It needed to blend and move, to fade forward and back, to hold one character in the foreground, then shift our focus to another. . . . Robert Altman has fused his extraordinary cast—Cher, Karen Black, Sandy Dennis, Sudie Bond, Kathy Bates, Marta Helfin and Mark Patton—into one of the finest ensembles I can recall in an American film. But then the high-water marks before this were also Altman films.

*   *   *

PETER NEWMAN (producer): In the early 1980s I didn't know what my career was, but I had managed to get some financial backing—relatively minimal—from Mark Goodson, the game-show guy. Cable tele-

On the set of Come Back to the Five and Dime, Jimmy Dean, Jimmy
Dean, *when Robert Altman's mutual estrangement from Hollywood led
him to create "filmed plays"*

vision was just in its infancy, especially pay television. Goodson said he
would stake me to a little bit of money to create some programming
for cable. I got an office in Times Square and I had no idea what I was
talking about. I had no background in film and so I would go home at
night and watch what the pay channels were showing.

Showtime had a "Showtime on Broadway" series. *Come Back to the
Five and Dime* was in previews on Broadway. It was especially a big deal
because it was going to have Cher in it. I talked my way backstage and
I walked up to Bob, and I said, "You don't know me . . ." I pitched him
on the idea of filming it for Showtime.

He looked at me and said, "You've got to be kidding me. This show
is going to open on Broadway in three weeks." He didn't say, "Get lost,"
but he kind of turned and walked away. I think Bob always believed that
the next thing was going to be a smash.

CHER (actress and singer): My mom was friends with Kathryn a million years ago; they were like crazy girls together when they were young. My mom knew I was doing an audition for Joe Papp and so she called—she thought she was calling me to ask how it went. But somehow she called Kathryn and Bob. Bob was asleep, taking a nap. Bob being Bob, he was all pissed off.

Bob said, "Hello?"

My mother said, "Is Cher there?"

Bob said, "Why the fuck would Cher be here? . . . Georgia, is that you?"

"Yeah. Who's that?"

"It's Bob. You have Kathryn and my number in the wrong place."

My mom told him I was in New York doing an audition for Joe Papp. I come out of the audition and there's one of those memo things—I wish I saved it—"Call Bob Altman."

I called and said, "What are you doing?"

He said, "I'm doing this play. How would you like to read the script?"

"Sure."

The day he was sending it over was the Puerto Rican Day Parade. They couldn't get it over—it arrived late that night. I thought he was just blowing me off.

I read it and I said to myself, "I don't want to do the part he's going to offer me." I knew he wanted me to be Joanne [who'd had a sex-change operation].

He said, "I want you to come over. We're going to have a group of women over to do a reading."

I said, "I am dyslexic. I can act or read but I can't do both." I don't know where I got these balls because no one was offering me anything.

So I go over to Bob's, and I had on a hat and scarf and a leather motorcycle jacket and boots, and I'm on the elevator with Sudie Bond. She doesn't know who I am. She thinks I'm going to mug her in the elevator. She gets out on Bob's floor and I get out and I'm following her up the hall. Now she's *sure* I'm going to mug her. We get to Bob's door and I take off my scarf and she realizes it's me, and I'm probably *not* going to mug her.

Sandy Dennis is there, and I think Karen Black is there, too. So first I read Joanne, and I really wanted to read Sissy. Sandy told me later it was the worst reading she had ever heard. She was fascinated it was so bad. We got to be so close—we were just such good friends.

Everyone left and he kept me behind. He said, "Okay, right, Jo is not for you. I think you might be right about Sissy. I think you *are* right about Sissy."

Then he said, "Tell me about some of my films."

I think I told him that I enjoyed *M*A*S*H*—and that I thought he ruined *Popeye*. I remember that as I did, Scotty Bushnell and a boy that were there just kind of turned around and disappeared. Bob said, "I just can't believe you."

I said okay, and then I left.

I had no idea what was going to happen. Later he called me and said, "All right. You got it."

I went to call my agent because I knew I didn't have the union card to do plays. I was going to ask what kind of card I needed. So I called my agent and said, "I need to know something about the Robert Altman play. I need to get the card, whatever you need to work on Broadway."

He said, "You know, that's really difficult. He's only looking at serious actresses and we can't even get you an audition."

I said, "Go fuck yourself," and I left that agent immediately after.

That Bob gave me the job is insane. *I* wouldn't have given me the job. It didn't make any sense. I didn't know what "downstage" was. I had no idea what anything was. I hadn't even been in a play in school.

* * *

We started rehearsing and I realized the first day he was a genius because he had all these personalities and he could talk to each one in the way they needed to be spoken to.

He made the stage feel like a really fun place. He set a tone for everyone. He wouldn't get cross—though he could get crabby. We all would know that it was just momentary. That's something I learned from him—the feeling on the set or on the stage has to be safe. He created a safe environment. You can't really be great unless you're prepared to be stupid. He would make it safe for you to fall on your ass and then say, "Okay, that didn't work. Let's go on."

Oh, and he saved my life. I'm a complete pussy when it comes to swallowing big pills. We were standing on our feet the whole day, and I had this pack of vitamin pills. I told myself, "I have just got to swallow these pills." There was one gigantic one. Looked like Alka-Seltzer. I swallowed and it wouldn't go down. I literally could not breathe—it went down sideways. I went from person to person for help, and I fell into Bob. He was the last one I went to. He turned me around and did the Heimlich. That popped it sideways so I could breathe. I went to a little emergency place in Hell's Kitchen—they were no help at all. "You can breathe, so go to the ear, nose, and throat hospital." It took forever. I was just getting small little breaths, and it took like half an hour to get there. I started getting out of the car and all of a sudden I swallowed it. But it was him—Robert Altman saved my life.

*   *   *

Then we're rehearsing and rehearsing and it's coming together and then he has people come to watch it. Then he said, "We're going to start doing it without the book. So memorize it."

Every night I was going out and dancing at Studio 54 all night long. Then one night he came to me and he was pissed. I was kind of like his pet. He was always sweet to me. I was crazy about him. I just liked to sit in his lap because he was this big bear and he was so fabulous. And then when Kathryn would come, it was wonderful, like, "Oh, now we can stop and gossip."

But then one day I didn't know my lines. He said, "By the end of this night you better know your fucking lines, and I'm not kidding."

I didn't know anything about anything. So, on Broadway you don't get to do ad-libs. But I started and they were funny and people were laughing. He comes to me another night—apparently Ed Graczyk, who wrote it, was getting mad. Bob came to me and said, "You have to say the fucking script verbatim, understand me?"

I did it verbatim and he says the same thing again.

"I did every line exactly!" I told him.

He says, "Well. Oh. I never read the script all the way through."

"Well, I did it."

We both started laughing.

He said, "I don't know. Do it how you like it."

*   *   *

We went to Broadway. Sandy and I were really close friends by then. Sudie, Kathy Bates, Sandy, and I were pretty close. Karen and I never got along.

It was really fun. It was packed like crazy in previews.

One Wednesday afternoon—blue-hair day—I was really great. Matinées were my favorite—balls to the wall and try something I never tried before. Mike Nichols came. I had gone on an audition for him but he said I couldn't play this part. What he said was mean, so I can't say it. I said, "I'm really talented, so one day you'll be sorry." So now he comes backstage and says, "I was wrong. You're right. And how would you like to do a movie with me?"

"Sure."

"How about me and Meryl Streep?"

"Sure."

"Want to know what it is?"

"Nope."

They sent me the script and said, "She's a lesbian but she's a lovely lesbian."

I said, "Fine."

That's how I got *Silkwood*.

Without Bob I would have never had a film career. Everyone told him not to cast me. Everyone. They said, "This is your first time on Broadway. You're going to put *her* in your play? This is important to your career." He didn't care.

One time in Vegas, before this, Francis [Ford Coppola] came to see me backstage. "Why aren't you doing movies?" I started sobbing. I had tried and tried and tried but nobody would give me a break. I am convinced Bob was the only one who was brave enough to do it.

Then it opened and the reviews came out, and it just was a nightmare. He was so excited and we were so excited and the audiences were unbelievable. I had no idea that in one night everything would change.

Frank Rich, review headlined "Stage: Robert Altman Directs Cher," *The New York Times*, **February 19, 1982:** Neither the gimmicky plot nor its clichéd participants are credible. . . . It's hard to fathom that this is the same director who made such a promising theatrical debut with "Two by South" off Broadway last fall.

PETER NEWMAN: I went the day after it opened and Bob said, "What are you doing here? Didn't you read the reviews? Everyone hates it."

I said, "The offer [of filming the play for Showtime] stands." I said I thought it was pretty good, and you could see the wheels start spinning.

With Cher in the role that launched her film career, as the sassy waitress
Sissy in Come Back to the Five and Dime, Jimmy Dean, Jimmy Dean

He was not in great shape financially or professionally. The thing about Bob was he was such a fighter. Even when the reviews were bad he was trying to keep the play running, even running a deficit. He would never cut and run. He would support the failures. He would never acknowledge they were artistic failures. He would fight just as hard for the movies that didn't have a chance.

CHER: He was so proud and so convinced and so committed that he started putting his own money back into it, so it kept running. The people who came really loved it.

PETER NEWMAN: Within three or four weeks the show had closed and we had moved the set to somewhere in the mid-forties and we were shooting it as a film. Showtime thought they were getting a videotaped version of the show. Little did they know.

Bob was driving the momentum and we were going out drinking every night. He went in and said, "I've got this great idea. We're going to shoot it on Super 16 film." He didn't want this to be for cable television. If he could shoot this on film and if it turned out the way he thought it would, he could get it released theatrically. Showtime agreed to let him shoot it on Super 16, but they made it clear—it's for cable. He said he wanted to release it theatrically and they went crazy.

Bob got Showtime to agree to let him take it to some film festivals. He did everything himself. So we went from Montreal to Venice to Deauville to Toronto, with one unbelievable stop in between. He realized there was a two-day gap between Montreal and Venice. There was a film festival somewhere in Belgium—Knokke-Heist. He just wanted to keep showing his movie. So we showed it in Montreal and the picture played really beautifully. Then we got on a plane for sixteen hours to Knokke-Heist, Belgium, and did a lot of drinking on the plane. I was sort of carrying him off the plane. The organizer of the film festival was seventeen years old and he was wearing a cape. Bob was barely awake and I was holding him up. The kid comes up and says, "Mr. Altman, I must ask you a question." Bob thought it would be something like, "How did you get that shot in *McCabe & Mrs. Miller?*"

Instead, he asks, "Why would you come to my festival?"

Bob was totally comfortable. He said, "You're showing my movie."

* * *

MARTIN SCORSESE: I remember meeting him in New York one night in 1983 and his last picture was *Popeye,* I think, and prior to that was *HealtH* with Fox, and mine was with Fox too, it was *King of Comedy.* And when it opened in 1983, *King of Comedy* was considered a terrible flop. *HealtH* was hardly opened. I happened to mention to him that *King of Comedy* was pretty much dropped from distribution by Fox, and I mentioned the name of the man who did it. And he said, "That's exactly the same person who dropped *HealtH.*" In a way, he was sent to the diaspora for ten years, and so was I.

* * *

Streamers *(1983)*

Vincent Canby, review in *The New York Times,* October 9, 1983: "Streamers," Robert Altman's screen adaptation of David Rabe's tough, bloody, sorrowful stage play, is a maddening movie. It goes partway toward realizing the full effect of a stage play as a film, then botches the job by the overabundant use of film techniques, which dismember what should be an ensemble performance. . . . Mr. Rabe's play, one of the major hits of the 1976–77 New York theater season, is confined to a single set, a bleak room in an Army barracks where five soldiers, under the bleary eyes of two boozy old sergeants, are awaiting assignment to Vietnam.

*   *   *

MATTHEW MODINE: *Streamers* was my baptism. I had a big monologue—my character, Billy, is talking about going to gay bars with his friends and having guys there buy them drinks, then running off. One day, one of the guys Billy was with, one of his friends from high school, says he's going to stay at the bar and go with this guy. I wanted to talk to Bob about what it meant, how to interpret what Billy was saying. So I went to Bob and said, "Could I talk to you about that monologue?"

He said, "Oh shit, are we shooting that today?"

"No, not today. Friday."

"Shit, you scared the hell of out me. Don't do that, man. We'll talk tomorrow."

I went home that night and pored over the monologue. I went to him again and he said, "We'll talk about it tomorrow."

Then the next day and the next day, "We'll talk about it tomorrow."

Thursday night I'm scared shitless. Bob hasn't talked to me about this monologue. I'm trying to prepare, trying to prepare. We come in Friday and I say, "Can I talk to you?"

Bob says, "Let's block this. Where would you be when we shoot this scene?"

"Uh, I'll be in my bunk and at the end I'll lift myself up and get out of the bed."

He says, "Great, great."

He asks Pierre Mignot, the cinematographer, "How do you want to shoot this?"

Pierre tells him, and again it's "Great, great."

"Uh, Mr. Altman, can I talk . . ."

He says, "I got to make a phone call."

He left, came back, and I am fucking shit scared about this situation I'm in. He comes back and right away we start shooting. I think we maybe did three takes, and one was because the camera wasn't focused. When it's over, he sits down on the bunk with me and gave me maybe the most important lesson for a young actor.

He says, "You see, kid, I didn't want to have that conversation with you. That's not my job. I hired you to be an actor. There were things about this role that you could interpret, that you could bring to life. If I was interested in my interpretation I would have played the part." Then he gave me an encouraging pat on the back and left.

Secret Honor: The Last Testament of Richard M. Nixon *(1984)*

Michael Wilmington, from DVD liner notes: *Secret Honor* is not just a record. It's an exploration of the play, of [Philip Baker] Hall's acting virtuosity, and of Altman's most diabolical bête noire. In portraying Nixon as a tragicomic puppet, Altman is ultimately commenting on the American political system—seemingly democratic and egalitarian on the surface, mercenary and elitist below, and completely tangled up in show business and TV strategies and imagery.

But Altman isn't just diving into an imaginary Nixon. He's exploring himself as well. More than a few critics have pointed up similarities between this Nixon—isolated, cut off, ruminating on past glories, playing with video cameras, manipulating his image—and the "exiled" Altman of 1983, at the recognized low point of his career. Perhaps that's the film's darkest, most ruthless irony of all.

ROBERT HARDERS (theater director): I came across a script called *Circe and Bravo*, written by Donald Freed. In the course of putting on a reading for *Circe and Bravo*, I naturally had to meet the writer. We spent some time together and we had begun some kind of working relationship. Sometime after that he called me up and he told me he was very close to finishing another script. He did, and I read it. Not immediately, because it had the name Richard Nixon in the title. I think like everyone I was pretty well saturated with the concept of Richard Nixon at that point in American history. When I did read it, I remember reading it like it was a detective story. The pages whizzing by. I remember being very affected by it. I also remembered an actor that I had worked with on another reading who I thought would probably be really good in the part if he were interested in it—that was Philip Baker Hall. I got the piece to Hall, who had to go through his own thing regarding Richard Nixon in order to be interested in it. We worked on it in Phil's living room and spent so many hours together just really getting to know one another and talking about everything under the sun and occasionally talking about the script.

We had a really great time doing it, and the idea was that we were going to do a reading in Donald Freed's living room and he was going to invite whomever. Phil was, as always, amazing, and I distinctly recall that before the applause had even died down, Bill Bushnell, from the L.A. Actors' Theater, along with Adam Leipzig, they were up and talking to Donald about obtaining the rights. Then it was a matter of putting it on for real as a play. Phil and I had already established a very good working relationship. It was a matter of transition to the half stage at the Los Angeles Theatre Center. This was a dream come true. This was what I always wanted to do.

Bushnell is a bit of a schemer, and he had a plan.

BILL BUSHNELL (theater impresario): The day that Dan Sullivan's *L.A. Times* review came out I called Bob and said, "I have a piece of goods here you ought to take a look at."

ROBERT HARDERS: Bushnell told us that Bob Altman was coming. My reaction was, "You're kidding." He came backstage, said he had seen the piece and really liked it. Bob knew right away what he wanted to do with it.

PHILIP BAKER HALL (actor): He said right on the spot, "I want to take this to New York, off-Broadway, and I want to make a movie about it. I am already visualizing how to film it. I want to see a little man surrounded by the immensity of the office, the desk and the office stuff and the intensity of public opinion that was marshaled against him."

ROBERT HARDERS: When we first went to New York to stage *Secret Honor*, Bob invited me and Phil to his office in the Delmonico building. Kathryn was there, and Bob says, "Let's break out the good stuff." He comes out with this case of wine, two hundred dollars a bottle, and we're drinking this wine. As the evening goes on, he is reaching in— one bottle after another. We're looking at each other out of the corner of our eyes, like, "Wow, do you believe this?" Years later, I reminded Kathryn of this, and she said, "You fell for that?"

Yes, we did! From Bob's end, he knew we were rubes and we were as green as you could get. And he knew we might actually believe that it was two-hundred-dollar bottles of wine and it would be good for him and it would be good for us too, and it wouldn't cost him two hundred a bottle. He was making us feel special. He was making us feel he was special. And that's so much of the key of getting the best work out of people. Oh God, did we laugh when she said that.

BILL BUSHNELL: From the stage, Bob took it to the University of Michigan and shot a film. And that in and of itself is a unique piece of goods.

Letter from Frank E. Beaver, chairman, graduate program in Telecommunication Arts and Film, University of Michigan, June 1, 1982: Dear Mr. Altman: I was glad to be able to reach you today and to learn that you are willing to accept a Marsh Professorship in the Communication Department. . . . The prospect of having you discuss representative films of yours in an "Altman Festival-Seminar" is, quite honestly, thrilling. Already students have begun to flock by to ask how they can be a part of this unusual educational experience.

PHILIP BAKER HALL: He was a visiting professor of film at the University of Michigan, and he knew that if we shot the film there, he could get certain special conditions from the Screen Actors Guild and the crafts guild because he could shoot it as part of his class work, and he could also use the kids. Still, he knew it would cost him a half million dollars.

He was waiting for a check of something like a million dollars from the sale of Lion's Gate. Somebody owed him this money and he needed the money to finance the film. He called me one morning— we were in New York, still performing it there—and we had a date to start filming. He said, "I was going to finance the film out of the check. It's held up. I might not get that check right away. I don't really at the moment have the money to do this movie. Were you counting on that?"

I'm thinking, "Nah, I wasn't counting on being the star of the first one-man movie directed by one of the great directors of the twentieth century." Yeah, right.

He said, "Have you turned down anything?"

"Yeah, I did."

"I guess I could mortgage my house."

A few days later, he said, "I didn't get the check but I'm going to make it work anyway."

When it came down to it he was a man of his word. He knew obviously it would be a big disappointment to me not to do that. From what I heard from others he was in some financial difficulty at the time. I think he was having some second thoughts because I think he expected it to be a big hit in New York, and it wasn't. It didn't do well in New York. The first two weeks it rained every night. Sleet and soaked. People coming to the theater saying, "Why did we come out on a night like this?"

It was a huge departure. If he couldn't get a studio film or raise money to do a film conventionally financed, he had to find a film he could finance himself. A one-man film, filmed on a college campus, using college kids in many important technical jobs, he could do this and still maintain his dignity. He could still be Robert Altman.

ROBERT HARDERS: My point of view was probably very limited, especially in this early period. When I thought of Bob or was in the room with Bob, I was acutely aware of his accomplishments and honestly completely unaware of any career difficulties or unhappiness that he may have been experiencing. Bob gave us that first-meeting persona of his. It works. Let the myth do the talking. Just stand there. We're going to fill it in. Why say anything? We've got a monologue running in our heads, so why should he risk mucking that up? I think he understood that very well. He knew how to use that kind of thing.

PHILIP BAKER HALL: When it was announced in *Variety* that Bob was going to make a film of this play *Secret Honor,* he did receive a letter from the Nixon office. I've seen it, and to paraphrase it: "Dear Mr. Altman, I'm a great fan of your films and I have always been. I particularly like *M*A*S*H.* Sincerely, Richard Nixon." Robert Altman was very proud of that letter—he took it to mean Nixon had seen the *Variety* announcement and he believed something damaging could happen to his reputation. And Nixon, in his way, would write a letter—like, "Don't hurt me, I'm just a nice guy who likes you." That's what we take to be the subtext. It's a good demonstration of the kind of odd cleverness of Nixon's life and career. He's saying one thing and trying to get a different result.

Bob had a complicated perspective on Nixon. In certain ways I think he admired Nixon. I think he admired Nixon's cleverness, his ingenuity, his ability to dance around the truth and to play with the facts. In other ways he thought he was a menace, a dangerous person to the Republic. A person who needed to artistically be whipped into shape.

We filmed it at one of the women's dormitories. They had a room for us off the set. It had two single beds, side by side. They would send us off there when they were relighting. Bob and I spent a lot of time there in the semidarkness, talking about the next scene or talking about life in general. It was very helpful to that part of the *Secret Honor* history. I remember the intimacy of it and the importance of it. One time, one of us was depressed about what had just been shot. There was maybe twenty-four inches between us. One of us reached out to console the other. We held hands. That was pretty unusual.

BILL BUSHNELL: That picture gave Bob's career a tremendous bounce. It didn't pay off right away, but it did pay off down the road. First he went to Europe. And ironically, Philip never worked with him again.

PHILIP BAKER HALL: He put me on the map in big-time features with *Secret Honor*. I was a working actor before that, but after that I became a *special* actor. I just regret that I couldn't have done another film or two with him. He's a great director. I have done like sixty features now, but I have always felt that my résumé is not complete because I didn't get to do another feature with Altman. There you have it.

CHAPTER 24

"I Made This"

The Laundromat *(1984; TV)*

Anne Tremblay, story headlined "Altman Makes a Cable Film Abroad," *The New York Times,* **January 20, 1985:** What is Robert Altman doing in Paris directing a film set in a quintessentially American locale? "I find there's nothing for me to do in America because of the kind of films they make there and the way they make them," Mr. Altman said during a recent interview on the set of "The Laundromat," an hour-long drama he is directing for Home Box Office. . . .

The American director, whose feature films "M*A*S*H" and "Nashville" have attained cult stature, moved here last August and at least for the time being has no intention of working in the United States. . . .

"Artistically, it's just miserable. Everything's based on commerce. A guy can be a rapist or a crook, yet if he has a lot of money he's admired. But that system will fail."

DAVID LEVY (producer): His move to France? Most artists want two things. They want to do their work and they want to have an audience for that work. In saying "audience," you're also talking about a kind of acceptance, aren't you? You're talking about acceptance or appreciation of the work. The things that were being offered here and the things being done here just weren't getting that acceptance and appreciation, and he was very much an icon over there. That audience is different from the audience here and they were very indulgent of and accepting of anything he would do. I think it was largely a case of, "Why not be where I'm wanted? Why not be where I'm appreciated?"

Holding the .357 Magnum used to shoot up the motel and a pickup truck in Fool for Love

He had a bit of the gypsy in his soul. He loved being on location and just going into a place and feeding off it, doing his thing and moving on. I think that was a part of it as well.

KATHRYN REED ALTMAN: What drew Bob to Paris? He could get a deal. I only liked it because I knew it was temporary. I loved the city and all the monuments. Bob didn't even notice; he didn't care. He was just making a movie, you know? He was as comfortable there as he would have been anywhere. And his French was the worst. He would garble it out and they'd get it. It helped being Robert Altman.

GARRY TRUDEAU: His moving to Paris, scaling down the size of the films, doing more modest undertakings, didn't make them less serious as films. I think that there are a great many directors who went through periods where their pride prevented them from making certain kinds of films and they now deeply regret that.

STEPHEN ALTMAN: After *Secret Honor* we went right to Paris and he did *The Laundromat* there. Then he left for *Fool for Love*, to shoot it in New Mexico, but he edited it in Paris and stayed there until after *Beyond Therapy*, when he got sick of it, which eventually everybody does, including the French.

*   *   *

Robert Altman Operas

The Rake's Progress (Stravinsky; 1983, University of Michigan; 1987,
Opéra de Lille, France); *McTeague* (director and coauthor of libretto
with composer William Bolcom; 1992, Lyric Opera of Chicago);
A Wedding, The Opera (director and coauthor of libretto with
Arnold Weinstein, composer William Bolcom; 2004,
Lyric Opera of Chicago).

*   *   *

Fool for Love *(1985)*

Roger Ebert, review in the *Chicago Sun-Times,* **December 18, 1985:** At
the center of Sam Shepard's "Fool for Love" are two people whose
hurts are so deep, whose angers are so real, that they can barely talk
about what they really feel. . . . Robert Altman's movie version of
Shepard's play stars Shepard himself, in a strong performance as Eddie.
But he doesn't dominate the story as much as you might think. The
central performance in the movie is Kim Basinger's as May. Although
she has played sexpots before—indeed has specialized in them—nothing prepared me for the dimensions she was able to find in this
one. . . . Part of her impact probably is because the director is Altman.
Few other major directors are more interested in women. In his films
such as "Thieves Like Us," "Three Women" and "Come Back to the
Five and Dime, Jimmy Dean, Jimmy Dean," he has shown women in
setting very similar to this one: unfulfilled women, conscious of the
waste of their lives, living in backwaters where their primary pastime is
to await the decisions of men.

*   *   *

SAM SHEPARD (writer/actor/director): I didn't know Bob before this.
He was originally interested in my play, and at that time he was doing
a lot of adaptations. At the time I wasn't that turned on about making
Fool for Love into a movie. And if I was, I thought Ed Harris should do
it because he was so great in the play. Bob kept insisting that I do it, and

then he wanted Jessica [Lange] to do it, too. Then Jessica backed out at the last minute and I went ahead and did it.

I still think it was a mistake on my part. I thought Ed was better. He had more of a clean attack on the character than I did. I think I was too attached to the material. I didn't have enough distance from it.

I directed the play. A play isn't designed to be a movie, it's designed to be a play. I don't think the movie works nearly as well as it did onstage. But many people liked it. I think Bob did a commendable job. But in retrospect I don't think it works. I think a lot of people who really enjoyed the film never saw the play.

What didn't work? The physicality of it. Onstage it was huge. It had a frightening physical reality to it, because of the actors, because of the intensity and the presence of the actors. On film it comes across as kind of a quaint little Western tale of two people lost in a motel room. Know what I mean? It doesn't have the power. In the theater it was right in front of your face, it was so intense it was kind of scary.

I don't regret making the movie but I've certainly learned from it [*laughs*]. I personally don't want to try to transform a play into a movie. If somebody else wants to take it and mess with it and do the screenplay and all that, I wouldn't object to it. But I don't have any ambitions to turn these plays into movies. And I've never had any success with it. There's never been any of my plays that was turned into a movie that was worth a shit. A lot of people have tried it and one after another they don't work.

It was weird because he had told me I was going to be involved in the editing process and this and that, and he kind of took the film and went to Paris and cut the whole thing there and that was it. I was disappointed in that. I didn't have anything to say about that. I don't blame him really. Why should an actor be involved in the editing? But he did abscond with it and made his own thing. I can understand he probably got it done quicker, which was probably his objective. It was quite a while before I saw him again.

I did an interview—it's one of those things that smartens you up. I finished the interview. I finished it! As we were walking out of the building, the reporter for *Esquire* said offhandedly, "What do you think of Woody Allen and Bob Altman as directors of actors?" And I said, "Neither one of them knows anything about acting." Which is true! I still stand by that! It's true. They're great filmmakers. Each of them in their own way is a fantastic, unique, extraordinary filmmaker. But they don't know anything about actors. About acting. About how to talk to actors, about how to discuss the premise of the character, the situation of the character, how to find the character. I was spoiled to a large extent by working in the theater, by working with great directors who *do* know actors. People who know actors inside and out. Who have dialogue with them, who spend weeks in rehearsal. You don't have that luxury in film.

These guys want to make a movie. And they're great casting guys. They find the absolute right actors for the job. Those actors know how to do it and they *know* that they know how to do it. But there's no dialogue, there no discussion. It's, "Let's shoot it." They're making a movie! Their focus is the camera, the lights, the set, what's going to be on film. They're not interested in how the actor is approaching the character and what he's trying to investigate or anything like that. Neither one of them would sit down with an actor for six to eight weeks working on a role. There's no way. Altman would pull his hair out [*laughs*]. And I love Bob. It certainly wasn't meant as an insult. It was meant as a perception, mainly having to do with the difference between film and theater. Simple as that.

*   *   *

O.C. and Stiggs *(Released in 1987; filmed in 1983)*

Janet Maslin, review in *The New York Times*, March 18, 1988: "O. C. and Stiggs" rambles a lot and doesn't have a full supply of the Altman alchemy, but it's certainly a lively, colorful satire; its notion of American artificiality runs so deep that the film begins and ends at a man-made surfing beach in the middle of the desert.

*   *   *

PETER NEWMAN (producer): When we made *O.C. and Stiggs*, basically, no studios would work with Bob at that point. I was made aware that Freddie Fields used to be his agent, and Freddie had just been appointed the head of MGM. I called Freddie Fields. He said, "Yes, we'll approve Altman if he can do it for eight million or under, and [if] he promises to shoot the script." Within a month or two we were in Phoenix in the middle of the summer at a hundred and twenty degrees, shooting a film I don't think he really wanted to make. But there were financial considerations.

I felt a lot of anger from Bob. I think he was unhappy making the movie, and I think he was angry that I would even be talking to the studio. He said, "We really shouldn't be talking to those people—not even giving them a shooting schedule." I got the wrath of Bob for trying to figure out what a producer does.

I still can't even describe what that movie is. I don't know if he was trying to do a parody of teen movies that were popular at the time, or what.

When we showed it to MGM, MGM said, "We've got a huge problem here." That's one of the few instances where Bob didn't want to hang around and fight the fight. He didn't finish that movie. The studio finished that movie.

I think this guy had given out his share of abuse, but he certainly had been abused by a lot of big corporations, and he was always certain that it was coming. I wish I had understood that when I saw him going through making this movie.

KATHRYN REED ALTMAN: I remember one summer, he was really depressed at the time, and I'd try to think of things to do with two boys and one granddaughter, Signe. This was right after *O.C. and Stiggs*. We were all stuck in a one-bedroom apartment in the Delmonico. Something had fallen through, and there were no jobs in sight. I got everybody roller skates and then I got remote-control cars for Matthew so that he could run them up and down the hall. I just tried to think of all the different things that we could do. Finally Bob got pissed off with the whole thing. We got a friend of ours, Gillian Freeman in London, to look in the paper and see if she could find an inexpensive place—we had no money—so that we could go to London for a month. She found this place in Earls Court, which is not your greatest neighborhood. And it was a funny little place. And the boys went to Amsterdam on their own. And Signe and Bob and I went to Paris on the hovercraft.

He had been put on the wagon and he wasn't smoking dope then. But anyway, so then he decided that we would take the *Queen Elizabeth* back. With what money? Who knows? I stopped asking. I didn't want to know. And so we did, but he had a horrible time because he wasn't drinking. They had a casino but it was about as big as this table. The kids ended up having a good time, a lot of disco stuff and all that. And I was reading *Hollywood Wives* by Jackie Collins, so that got me through it. It was sort of fun. As soon as we got in the range of telephones he was okay—this was a five-day crossing and you don't get to the phones till like the end of the third day. And then he came to life.

* * *

Keeping Busy

Basements—1987 (TV); *Beyond Therapy*—1987; *Aria*, segment called "Les Boréades"—1987 (film); *The Dumb Waiter*—1987 (TV); *The Room*—1987 (TV); *The Caine Mutiny Court-Martial*—1988 (TV).

Robert Altman, to Sally Ogle Davis, story headlined "Robert Altman Reluctantly Tackles a Classic," the *Globe and Mail*, May 7, 1988: I can't get anything made at all in this community [Hollywood]. I don't even have an agent. I don't bother to go to talk to them. I won't even send a piece of material out to them because I just know it's pointless.

PETER GALLAGHER: *Caine Mutiny Court-Martial* was my first experience working with Bob, but the very first time I saw Bob was at Tufts University, where I was an undergraduate and he came to speak. It was around *Buffalo Bill* time. He was wearing a fringe jacket and I remember he looked like Buffalo Bill. He was all balls-to-the-wall and I thought, "Well, that guy seems like he's awful stuck up. Who does he think he is up there in his big tassels?" That was sort of the scornful, outsider's view of a sophomore or junior in college who was just assuming he wouldn't be able to do what he wanted with his life, and it was all going to be miserable. Of course, what I would have seen had I been a little wiser was somebody who was having a great time and loved what he did and made no bones about it. Little did I know that years later, in terms of my approach to film, he'd be about one of the most important people in my life.

Caine Mutiny was extraordinary for me for a lot of reasons. Bob was looking for this part of Jack Challee and nobody wanted to play it, thank God, which is how I've gotten most of my parts, I think. Nobody wanted to play it because he had all the lines and no laughs. No payoffs. It was all just grunt work. And so I got a call to come in—it was from Scotty Bushnell, who was working with Bob then—and we sat down.

So I sat down, it was at the old office just above the Regency, at the Delmonico, and I went in there and it was winterish, kind of late in the day. He said, "I could really see you doing this part. I'd like you to think about that. Would you like a beer?"

What? Huh? Would you like a beer? "Sure."

He left the room and I said to Scotty, "Did he just offer me a job?" I was so moved that he respected me enough to not just arbitrarily make me jump through hoops just for the sake of it. I thought, "I don't care what kind of part this guy wants me to play, I'll walk on broken glass for this guy." He treated me with respect for the first time in I couldn't remember how long, as opposed to the rounds and rounds and rounds of, "I don't know, try it on one foot."

The greatest thing about working with Bob is you suddenly realize there's a tribe of people out there, and when you're amongst them, you realize you're not crazy. *Caine Mutiny* was really the first time that I experienced the kind of freedom and delight and camaraderie on camera that I had up to that point only experienced onstage. I felt valued, which was a shocking thing.

You can say it was during a lull in his career. But when you're that age and impressed by someone, you don't think of him having a hard time. In your eyes, he's kind of a giant. Did he become less arrogant since I saw him at Tufts? Yeah—well, maybe I just got less stupid.

KEITH CARRADINE: After *Nashville*, Bob never invited me again until he was doing *The Caine Mutiny Court-Martial* for television. He called me to play Queeg and I was absolutely terrified. I was terrified by the ghost of Humphrey Bogart. Frankly, I didn't have the balls to confront that. At the same time, I was married, I had two kids, and I was offered another project, also for television, with Glenn Close. I could either do this movie with Glenn Close for two hundred fifty thousand dollars or I could do this with Bob for sixty thousand. I called him, and I was absolutely straight with him. I said, "Bob, I can't afford it. I got kids to feed, I got to make some money, and I've got this thing and they're going to pay me a lot of money."

And he said, "Oh, I understand, I understand."

He didn't understand. Nobody turns Bob down. And that was the last time he asked. And in retrospect, I should have done *Caine Mutiny*. I regret to this day that I didn't do that. He got Brad Davis, who was terrific. But hey, man, you makes your choices and you lives with them. And that was a choice that I made at that moment in time. If I had it to do over again, I wouldn't make the same choice.

*   *   *

Tanner '88 *(1988; TV miniseries)*

MATTHEW SEIG (producer): So yeah, the eighties were a period with *O.C. and Stiggs*, which was a disaster and a disappointment, and *Fool for Love* and *The Laundromat* and *The Room* and *The Dumb Waiter*, which are crazy. And *The Caine Mutiny Court-Martial*. You know, all just out there. Oh, *Beyond Therapy*, too. Odd. A lot of odd stuff done in odd ways. And whatever way to get them done. And then he was sort of sucked into working in Europe quite a bit. And he came back and forth. He came back to do *Tanner '88*.

John Corry, review in *The New York Times*, February 15, 1988: Call it imaginative; call it satire; call it a mixed result. "Tanner '88: the Dark Horse" is too real to be funny, but it's also not real enough. How can a film make fun of politics when politics makes fun of itself? The Home Box Office presentation does not find the answer, although it may make the year's most interesting try. . . . "Tanner '88" is written by Garry Trudeau and directed by Robert Altman; already that sounds rewarding.

*   *   *

GARRY TRUDEAU: I have a very dear friend from college named Richard Cox, an actor, and he had been in Paris for some reason when he was invited to a party where Robert Altman may have been the host, because Altman was living in Paris at the time. And Bob said something completely random to my friend. He said, "I feel like crap."

Richard said, "Why?"

He said, "I just couldn't sleep last night and I was playing this dream over in my head. I was working on this project with Garry Trudeau."

And Richard said, "Well, he's my closest friend. You know, you're a hero of his."

So yeah, he dreamed me before he met me.

The *Tanner '88* idea came by way of HBO. There was a vice president there named Bridget Potter—remarkable woman—who was in charge of original programming, of which there was very little at that

*With writer and cartoonist Garry Trudeau and actor Michael Murphy,
as the candidate Jack Tanner, on the set of* Tanner '88

time. I think we may have been their first series. She called me up and
said, "We're thinking of a bogus presidential campaign. Would that be
something you'd be interested in writing?"

I had my plate full, as I always do, and I said, "The only way I
would really be interested in doing that is if I could work with Robert
Altman." After the dream thing with Richard, Bob and I had gotten
together and we'd been kicking an idea around for a series called *Amer-
icaville* or something like that. I think it was sort of a precursor to *Short
Cuts* and it was supposed to be this vast cast of people whose lives all
intersected. Not unlike *Nashville* and some of the other ensemble
pieces he worked on. But he thought it could be a TV series, so I knew
he was open to working with me on a TV series. So they called back
and said, "Yeah, he's willing to do it."

Okay, now that's December of '87, so we're about six weeks away
from the New Hampshire primary. We don't have a story. We don't
have characters. We have nothing. And so Bob said, "I'm going to put
this into production with the scraps of ideas that we have." And he
called me up day by day and he'd say, "I've got this great actor, could
she be in it? Named Pam Reed. She's this Broadway actress and I think
she'd be great. I'll introduce you to her and maybe you'll think of a
character for her." And Michael Murphy came in as Tanner.

MICHAEL MURPHY: We were doing *The Caine Mutiny Court-Martial* and I get through a bunch of stuff and we break for lunch one day. I'm sitting there and Bob comes up and sits down. He looked at me with that look and says, "I've decided I'm going to run you for president."

I said, "President of what?"

He said, "President of the country."

I said, "You're kidding."

So, twenty minutes later we're in New Hampshire and I'm standing out there with Bush and Dole shaking hands.

GARRY TRUDEAU: We were really winging it in those first few weeks. When he finally got eight or ten people together, he brought them over to his apartment for costume fittings. We had to decide while they were there who they were going to be so that we put the right costumes on them. Danny Jenkins, who played Stringer, he's this sort of rail-thin, tall guy with a very innocent look. He said, "Well, who am I?"

And I said, "Well, you're Stringer."

"Good. Tell me something about my character."

And I said, "You're tall."

He said, "That's it?"

I said, "That's as far as we've gotten" [*laughs*].

If it hadn't been for Altman's reputation for creating safety nets for actors, for protecting his actors, for keeping them secure and making them safe while they worked, I don't think any of them would have signed on, because they didn't know what they were signing on to. So we started.

Bob moved the operation up to New Hampshire, and then as I generated pages I was sending them up to him. The degree of difficulty was very high. It was very complicated because you're shooting stuff, then seeing what you have, then writing to that. Somehow we pulled that together, we delivered it one hour before airtime. The executives never saw it before it aired [*laughs*].

We never did get ahead enough to send them a script. So they put eleven shows on the air that they had not read or lawyered or anything else. I was faxing pages to Bob on the set, so the actors were often seeing them the day they were shooting them. And you've never seen such stressed-out producers because they didn't know what the set was supposed to look like.

I'd join them on the set for things that I thought might need a writer in place. But of course Bob loves to have the actors find what they need. That was an interesting experience. Imagine my surprise when I found out that certain things that I had written would be shot verbatim and other things would be dropped entirely, and then everything in between. And you could see there was some degree of frustration from the actors because they liked the lines, by and large. Or at least they seemed to. It's not that they minded living by their wits, because most good actors kind of enjoy that. But I could see they were a bit conflicted because there were certain scenes that I'd written that they really did want to play the way it was on the page.

But, you know, mostly they didn't say that. It would be foolish for them to say it. A director is God on the stage. So I just made the adjustment. I have this other life and I may have a little less at stake, perhaps, in my theatrical work because of it. For me it was such a kick working with one of my early heroes that I just made the adjustment to the process.

We had a long scene in *Tanner on Tanner*, which was the follow-up to the series. It was at Elaine's, and I had made a big mistake. I wrote that as an eight- to ten-character scene with a lot of cross action. In my head that was a Bob Altman scene. The problem was that Bob Altman had to direct it in a day because that's all we had. So the complexity of it was just out of reach to us in the amount of time that we had to do it. So Bob, depending on what he was seeing, was just being his genius maestro self and he was grabbing what he saw and also was trying to get through the day.

At the end of the day he kind of looked at me, and I was looking a little depressed, because I had the headset on all day and I was hearing very little of what I had written. And he said, "Do you know why you write that dialogue?"

And I said, "No, Bob, why?"

And he says, "You write that dialogue so the actors know who they are."

I thought about that. That's *not* why I thought I was writing the dialogue. I mean, that would be a by-product certainly, and would orient them, but I don't recall anguishing over every comma with the idea that it's just to kind of let them know who they are. But obviously that's the way he viewed it, and that's the way he viewed all writing. Including his own.

JOAN TEWKESBURY (screenwriter and director): When Alex Tanner tells her film students at the New School to forget all the rest of the stuff and just be brave, I hear Bob's voice talking directly to me.

Robert Altman, from DVD commentary: In my mind, *Tanner '88* was the most creative work I've ever done—in all films and theater.

GARRY TRUDEAU: Bob described it as the most creative work he ever did. He says so again and again. He's also wrong [*laughs*]. I would place *M*A*S*H* and *Nashville* way ahead, and if I thought about it probably some other films, too.

*   *   *

Vincent & Theo *(1990)*

Derek Malcolm, review in *The Guardian* (London), June 21, 1990: The film is one of Robert Altman's sanest and least eccentric. It simply looks at [Vincent van Gogh's] life and work from another angle. It is, as a matter of fact, not so much about van Gogh as his emotional and dependent relationship with Theo, his art dealer brother. . . . But

Robert Altman in a field of sunflowers in France during the filming of
Vincent & Theo

though there is no way you would call it easy entertainment . . . it does explain, with some historical accuracy (for instance, van Gogh did not cut his ear off but did slice a lobe) that behind great art lie human beings considerably more flawed than their creations. What the film also attempts to show us is that masterpieces do not appear out of thin air but as a result of constant and usually enervating struggle, involving both refinement of technique and the capacity of the rest of us to mock them. Just once or twice, Altman seems to be making the point that innovatory work in all fields, even his own, is rarely given the succor it deserves.

*   *   *

JERRY WALSH (friend/lawyer/executor): In the fall of 1988, a young Dutch TV producer named Ludi Boeken approached Bob about directing a multi-hour TV biography of Vincent van Gogh to mark the hundredth anniversary of van Gogh's death in 1889. Almost from the beginning Bob was unhappy with Ludi, while Scotty and I argued that he was a good guy doing the best he could with limited funds. The film was not a financial success, and Bob believed that under the contracts he was entitled to more money than he had received from Ludi.

At the Cannes Film Festival a year or two later, Bob told a London newspaper that Ludi Boeken was a liar and a thief and Bob hoped he would get cancer and die.

Judy Brennan, story headlined "Dutch Producer Boeken Sues Altman for Slander," *Variety,* **June 29, 1992:** Dutch producer Ludi Boeken and his Paris-based Belbo Films have sued Robert Altman for slander after the director allegedly called him a "thief, liar and pimp" in numerous articles published worldwide. Boeken is seeking more than $800 million in general and special damages.

JERRY WALSH: Ludi sued Bob and the newspaper for libel in London, and the newspaper paid a settlement to Ludi. Ludi then made the mistake of having his firm, Belbo Films, bring a second lawsuit, also for libel, in Los Angeles against Bob's company, Sandcastle 5 Productions. By doing this, Belbo Films subjected itself to the jurisdiction of the Los Angeles court to hear Sandcastle 5's counterclaim for contract damages.

I got Bob a first-rate First Amendment lawyer in Los Angeles, who promptly got Belbo's libel claim dismissed, and we then had a trial of our counterclaim, which resulted in a two-million-dollar judgment against Belbo Films. Ludi had by that time sold Belbo Films, which had no assets in the United States, and we ultimately settled with Belbo for a few hundred thousand dollars.

* * *

ROBERT ALTMAN: It's hard to talk about the audience because I don't really think of the audience that much. I really don't. I think they have a responsibility to pay attention and appreciate what I do. It's like all the Campbell soup cans—that's the multitude. They're all the same and they're stamped and turned out. On inspection, one is defined by the one next to it.

I remember when we were up in Calgary and *Nashville* opened. There was a theater near my hotel, and there were people going around the fucking block. I rushed down there but nobody was going to see it. They were going to *The Pink Panther* or something. And to me that was the audience. No individuals. I don't think I would know how to cater to them if I wanted to. If I tried I'm sure I would be wrong. I mean, I've had people stop me on the street and say, "Oh, didn't that scene mean so-and-so?" And I said, "That sounds good to me, but I never thought of that before."

Remember the Abner Dean cartoon? There was a young man and there's a dead tree, and hanging from that tree is a tin can and a spring. And coming around the bend is an endless procession of these naked beings pulling boulders with head straps. The line of them goes on to infinity, it curves around a little hill and goes on and on to another infinity. And next to this tree is this young man trying to enlist the attention of this crowd of people pulling the stones. He's saying, "Look, I made this!" Well, these people didn't look up. Their heads were down pulling their boulders and they were just trudging along. To me that says it all. I've never seen the whole art thing shown more precisely.

Vincent van Gogh never sold a painting. Well, his brother bought one. Had he succeeded as an artist he would have failed. I mean, he would have had to change what he did. Do I identify with him? No. I sold a lot of paintings.

Robert Altman to F. Anthony Macklin, *Film Heritage,* **Winter 1976–77:** There are natural enemies, in which case neither can be blamed.

You can't blame the minnow for being the natural enemy of the bass. The fish are always going to eat him. The artist and the multitude are natural enemies.

Robert Altman, from *The Player* **DVD commentary:** If I had all the movies I'd ever made on a desert island, and a nice theater and projector and everything, I'd never run any of them. But if I had one person who hadn't seen one, I'd stop and spend the two hours and run any film I've made for anybody. If there's a new set of eyes to look at it. And I'll see a different film just because I know it's being perceived by somebody else. . . . And I mean an audience of one person, if I've got one person hooked. But if I was sitting here alone, I'd look at about two minutes and leave. I like to feel their reaction, to know there is somebody that this is bouncing off of, this is reaching a new, another perception.

* * *

Peter Gallagher: I'll never forget, we were both in Paris. We weren't working together. He had just shot or was about to shoot *Vincent & Theo*. I was getting screwed by my producers and he was getting screwed by his producers. It was weird, we were both just getting beat up by these separate European producers. We found out the other was in town and we hung out one night and started writing country song titles. And we had a blast. Mine were lame contributions—"Just 'Cause I Don't Know Doesn't Mean I Won't Find Out." Stuff like that—inspired by these producers who were trying to pull a fast one. His was the best: "I'm Swimming Through the Ashes of All the Bridges I've Burned."

Hal Hinson, story headlined "Robert Altman, His Way; on Art, Money and *Vincent & Theo,*" *The Washington Post,* **November 18, 1990:** As the '90s commence, Altman is the movies' forgotten master. He's on nobody's "A" list of bankable directors. Or "B" list. Or "C" list. . . . It's fair to say that a great painter of oils, unable to afford paints, has been forced to work in charcoal. . . . There is a widely held assumption that somewhere along the line, Altman lost it—that for whatever reason his best years are behind him.

CHAPTER 25

The Player

*

The Player *(1992)*

Terrence Rafferty, review in *The New Yorker*, April 20, 1992: The title
character of Robert Altman's new movie is a young Hollywood studio
executive named Griffin Mill (Tim Robbins), who, for no very good
reason, murders an aspiring screenwriter. The picture is a brilliant dark
comedy about the death of American filmmaking. It's like a documentary about a mirage: the world it shows us is sunlit and shimmering, and
the people have the thin presence of holograms. Altman is doing one of
his specialties here—exploring an odd American subculture—and when
his idiosyncratic realism is applied to the insular, constantly self-
regarding community of Hollywood "players" it has an almost halluci-
natory effect. The movie has the exhilarating nonchalance of the
director's seventies classics, and its tone is volatile, elusive: with breath-
taking assurance, it veers from psychological-thriller suspense to goof-
ball comedy to icy satire. Altman turns the self-reflective world of
Hollywood into a fun house in which every grotesque distortion somehow appears to us as a newly discovered, paradoxical truth. Robbins
gives a layered, richly suggestive performance—the sort of performance
that Altman's style, at its best, produces without obvious effort. At sixty-
seven, Altman still seems like the youngest filmmaker in America.

* * *

DAVID BROWN (producer): I had read a piece in a defunct magazine,
called *Manhattan Inc.*, which was an excerpt from the book *The Player.*
I thought, "How wonderful, this author knows Hollywood." There

Tim Robbins as the homicidal studio executive Griffin Mill in The Player

was a true authenticity. But I didn't see how it could become a film. Most of it is an internal monologue, which makes it impossible as a movie. I set it aside, but a little time passed and I had lunch at the Century Club with the man who published the book *The Player*. The lunch was a social lunch but he mentioned the book. I said I read an excerpt in a magazine and I thought it was quite authentic. I thought about it some more and said, "Why don't I acquire the rights for twenty-five hundred?" The author, Michael Tolkin, was fired by his agent for taking so little.

MICHAEL TOLKIN (author and screenwriter): It took me six or eight weeks to write the script. I was surprised how quickly it turned around. I thought a book that is so internal would be difficult to translate, but what I found was the structure of the plot was sound enough that what Griffin is going through is enough. There was enough suspense and enough pressure on the character so it wasn't internal.

After my agent had fired me, I went to William Morris. And Altman had just recently switched to William Morris after he came back from Europe. Somebody there gave him the script.

JOHNNIE PLANCO (agent): I ran into Bob at the Russian Tea Room after he'd been away for five years. I said, "Are we going to work again?"

He said, "Oh, I just went back to Stan [Kamen]."

I was hurt because he'd said we'd work together when he came back from Europe. But the next morning he called Stan and said he'd made a mistake. Then he called me and said, "Okay, I'm yours. That's the good news. The bad news is that I'm unemployable. They'll hang up on you if you suggest me."

He viewed studios as the enemy. Like somebody scared, he shot first.

I talked to David Brown for *The Player.* I suggested Bob. David said, "I hear he drinks too much and is abusive."

I said, "David, it's not true—meet with him."

DAVID BROWN: We had a number of directors in mind. Sidney Lumet wanted to make the film in France. That sounded good to us, but little by little we exhausted all the possibilities. At some point Bob Altman called me and said, "You own a property I was born to direct, *The Player.*"

I said, "Bob, I agree you were born to direct this, but you have to be a good boy and play ball."

He said, "I will."

JOHNNIE PLANCO: They met at seven a.m. By ten, eleven, I hadn't heard from anyone.

MICHAEL TOLKIN: We had a meeting with Altman and Scotty Bushnell. He had recently had some kind of surgery. He had a boil on the back of his neck and one of his eyes was rheumy. Scotty was slumped in the couch, sitting behind Bob, who was sitting in the chair. And Altman said he wanted to do it. He had some ideas. Any time a director wants to do something, he says the right things. I think he talked about wanting to use stars as extras in the way the book had thrown in a couple of movie stars very casually. He wanted to amplify that.

He left the room and David Brown said, "He's a brilliant filmmaker. He hasn't made a successful movie in a while. There are cycles, and he is due for a success."

Frankly, since we hadn't had luck with anybody else, this was the best chance that we had.

JOHNNIE PLANCO: Just before noon, David called and said, "Who are you going to get for the lead?" He told me, "You know, I've got Bob for the movie."

Robert Altman, from DVD commentary: I'd written *Short Cuts*, based on Raymond Carver short stories, and I'd been trying to get that picture financed. That's what I was really working on. I couldn't get the money to finance that film. *The Player* was offered to me as a picture they were going to make. I was a director for hire. I needed the job—I saw it was an easy shoot. I kinda liked the idea of it, so I did it.

DAVID LEVY: It wasn't a huge budget—it was six million and change: but for the first time in years he had people who had the power on a project say "We want you."

Stephen Cole, story headlined "Going the Distance for *Short Cuts* Director," the *Globe and Mail*, October 16, 1993: Sidney Lumet priced himself out of the impending production of *The Player*, author Michael Tolkin's anti-Hollywood screed. Hungry for work, Robert Altman begged for a chance to direct a film he felt born to make, offering his services at one-quarter of Lumet's $2 million asking price.

JERRY WALSH: One night in New York, Bob said he wanted to go to the movies after dinner. I said, "That's just amazing. I've never gone to the movies with you before. I thought you never went to the movies."

He said, "Oh, yeah, I hardly ever go. It makes me too jealous. But I want to see an actor."

I'm pretty sure he said that Scotty wanted him to see this actor who was in a movie called *Bull Durham* about baseball. I'm pretty sure that Tim Robbins is one actor that he was introduced to by Scotty.

TIM ROBBINS: It was kind of a critical time for me when I met Bob. *Jacob's Ladder* had just come out and had tanked. No one saw it. It was as if the universe conspired to create the worst possible environment for a movie about a Vietnam veteran who was having hallucinations. It was two or three weeks before we went into the Gulf the first time, the Gulf War. So the country was not in the mood for a movie that was in any way critical of the military or in any way questioning the military. I was counting on this movie. So it comes out and I was close to broke. I was broke. And I had a new son. And I had a mortgage and all. So all of a sudden I was running out of money.

He was putting together *Short Cuts*. I got a call from my agent saying, "Do you want to meet Robert Altman?"

I go up there, I park my car, I get out and it was very friendly, it was a very warm environment immediately. The people that worked for him, you could tell there was a decency there. You can tell that kind of stuff. He told me about the movie and it sounded great. And he said, "So are you in?"

I said, "What? Oh. Yeah."

And it was as simple as that. I mean I was kind of shocked. Some directors just put you through so much to get a part. I mean, after a certain point, either you have it or you don't. And some directors need to see audition, audition, don't trust something. So already you're starting this idea that something's not quite right. But with Bob it was immediately, "You're the guy." This is the vibe you got from him— "There's no one like you and you're going to be great in this movie." You immediately respond to that positivity, that belief that he had in you and confidence he had in you.

Well, *Short Cuts* doesn't happen. At least not yet. I'm starting to panic now 'cause I got nothing. There's a really terrible comedy that's presented to me for a ton of money. And it's an offer. I'm not sure when *The Player* became real, but I know I was terrified facing that decision of turning down this thing and worried that I would not get anything else for a while. I went out to L.A. and actually said yes to the job. Went to see a movie that night, I think it was *The Doors*. Went home that night and said, "Get me out, I made a bad choice." I think the possibility existed at that point that *The Player* was going to happen. But it wasn't real yet and *Short Cuts* had already not gotten put together. So it was a choice between the possibility that *The Player* might happen and this million-dollar offer for a comedy that was not so funny.

So I find out later, not from Bob but from other people, that around the time that I was having this dilemma, Bob was having a similar choice. They were telling him, "We'll give you the money for *The Player* if you use this actor, or that actor, a choice of two."

He said, "No, Tim Robbins is my guy."

He could have walked away from me and had his film financed, which nine out of ten directors in Hollywood would do. "Sorry, kid, I can't get it made with your name, you're not worth enough." But Bob had given me his word and he had a belief in me that I was this character. And he turned down the money to do it with these two actors that he didn't feel were right. Or maybe he just felt that he had already told me that it was me.

Robert Altman, from DVD commentary: I think that eighty percent of my creative function or work is finished the moment I get the film cast. And from that time on, I'm passing this idea that came to me from someone else over to someone else or another group of people. So I can't claim any real authorship for it. All I was for it was the fascist that kept everything in line and going while this thing was made. When you really get down to what made the difference, what made this thing better rather than just ordinary, I don't think we'll ever find out, because I think it's a compilation of people.

Tim Robbins: I go out to L.A. and I start going to rehearsals. It's not really rehearsals, it's just me and Bob. And it's just me and Bob in his office smoking pot. I think I first smoked with him the first time I met him, right after that lunch. I'm not sure about that, though, which is the problem with smoking pot.

We start talking about the movie and about this scene; we started going through the script. And from the start he said, "You know, I don't really like this script. I think we can do some really interesting things with it, but I've asked Michael to change some stuff."

And Michael was reluctant. He felt the script was good enough. It was sold to the financiers and I don't think he saw the need to change it. And I guess I was of the mind that I'm working with Robert Altman, dude. That is all I need to know. I'll change anything, you know? If he says we're going to change it, we're going to change it.

It's a live organism making a film, and in Bob's world it couldn't remain static, it couldn't remain the same, it had to keep evolving daily. The basic situations were there, the basic scene structure was there, but I think he thought a lot of it just sounded like written dialogue and it wasn't organic enough and so we had to figure out how to get there.

David Levy: Bob was really loving the picture, but right near the beginning there he felt hamstrung by certain things script-wise, and I remember that he called up Michael Tolkin and said something along the lines of, "You did a great job, it's really terrific, but now I've come to the point where I've got to do what I've got to do." And when he hung up that phone it was like a tremendous burden lifted from him. He was not going to be a slave to the written word. I hope that doesn't seem like any kind of diminution of Michael's contribution at all. I'm just saying Bob really struggled with trying to respect him and what

With Tim Robbins, as Griffin Mill, on the set of The Player

was there and at the same time needing to make a certain departure from what was on the page. That was a pretty glorious experience.

DAVID BROWN (producer): During the production, Robert Altman was an improviser beyond belief. The writer, Michael Tolkin, complained that he went to the dailies and he didn't recognize any of the dialogue. For a while, Michael and I bonded against Altman. We slunk away and said, "Why can't we see the script?" And all that stuff. We were anti-Altman at the same time we recognized his genius.

Finally I said to Bob, "Why don't you show Tolkin the working script?"

He said, "Yes, I can do that, but that's not what I plan to shoot."

He reminded me that Ring Lardner complained all during the picture they made together, *M*A*S*H*, but didn't complain when he won the Academy Award for best screenplay.

PETER GALLAGHER: There's this scene with Cynthia Stevenson and Tim Robbins in a hallway at the studio, and I was sort of hanging out. I wasn't in it. I had just finished and I was up in a couple of scenes and I'm just messing around, hanging out.

"Gallagher!" It's Bob.

"What?"

"I want you to go in there and do something."

"What?"

"I don't know."

"When?"

"Next take."

And I'm like, "Fuck, okay, all right, where am I? Where has the character been, where's he going, where are we in the story? What's happening between them, why would I possibly be there, what would I say to them? My office is over there and the lot is over there, what would I be . . ."

"Ready?"

"Yeah, okay, I got something." And I go by them and it's like, "*Habeas Corpus*, Griffin. *Habeas Corpus*." Because that was a movie he was pitching, but Tim's character was also beating the murder rap, because they didn't have the body. In that minute it's like you pull every molecule of every instinct and training and awareness you have to try to contribute something. And it's not like Bob's sitting back not watching. He's breathing in every single moment.

Tim Robbins: At one point Bob said, "There's going to be people around that are going to be trying to tell us what to do. I just want you to know that if it becomes a pain in the ass and it's not fun, I just want your word that you'll walk off the set with me."

And I said, "You got it."

In other words, I was a coconspirator. And I knew he was up to great mischief and he warned me that there could be ramifications from producer kind of people, or money people. But he said, "As long as we're united, we'll be fine." So that's pretty cool, to have one of your heroes invite you into his mischievous master plan and smoke a joint at the same time.

Peter Gallagher: It must have been a mindblower to write a great book and write a script thinking the script would be developed in that way. Then all of a sudden this eight-hundred-pound gorilla says, "Yeah, I love your script. Hang onto it and tell me what you think of the movie" [*laughs*].

Michael Tolkin: The story of every movie is the same—script changes, writer grumbles. I was one of the producers of the movie. If I hadn't been I would have been banished from the set, I'm sure.

His disdain for plot is something that I think hurt the basic entertainment and commercial potential of some of his films. In the book and the script there is the postcard writer and the police. He lost the perspective of the postcard writer. He trimmed that part of the story in the second and third act, which in the book and the script was keeping suspense while the love story and the business story were playing out. There were three forces—Larry Levy, the cop, and the postcard writer. He cut the postcard writer out of the suspense. I think it would have been five minutes more, if that, of film.

A director cannot improve the structure that holds attention. It's just not possible. Only a script can create or hold attention. But writers get into trouble egotistically when they want to think that if a script wasn't changed everything would be better. It's a balancing act.

Robert Altman, from DVD commentary: Making a film is like painting a mural. You've got this big wall to fill and you've got a subject, and the only difference is, as you go up there and you're painting it, you've got living pigment. So you've let me paint a horse over here in the upper-right-hand corner and you turn around and look back and the horse is moving across the stage and you have to quickly paint a fence. You have to kind of control it, but you're dealing with a living thing that's really forming itself. So you're sitting up there doing damage control all the time. But the style in which one paints these films is . . . their personality, it's what they do, it's their artistry.

* * *

Dialogue from *The Player:*

(Studio executive Larry Levy, played by Peter Gallagher, introduces himself to Burt Reynolds, playing himself.)

LARRY LEVY: Burt. Larry Levy. I hope you don't remember me, and if you do, I hope there are no hard feelings. I was only working for Kastner at the time.

ELLIOTT KASTNER: The line about me in *The Player?* That's Altman getting back at me, but I enjoyed it very much. I found it amusing.

* * *

DAVID BROWN: People came out of the woodwork to work for him. He was extremely popular with actors. We had Bruce Willis, Julia

*Julia Roberts playing a condemned convict and Bruce Willis
as her rescuer, in cameo appearances in* The Player

Roberts—any number of actors who simply wanted to be in a Bob Altman film.

DAVID LEVY: *The Player* was one of those pictures where every day you
felt the magic. I know that word is off-putting and overused, but it was
true. Just that kind of energy on set and then at dailies. I mean, you
were aware of everything coming together just as it should. Once we
started screening it, the buzz in town was just incredible. And even
before that we started getting people to do cameos and play themselves, and then people started calling us saying, "Oh, can I be in it, can
I be in it?" It was nice because they worked it for day-player scale, and
we donated their salaries to the Motion Picture Home, and so it
became a thing to do.

PETER GALLAGHER: I made a point to meet a few studio heads. Not
heads, but close—presidents—because we were just trying to learn
about the system. About Hollywood. One of these guys asks me, "How
did Altman do it? He's got all these people making this movie now for
nothing."

I remember thinking, "Well, he just picks up the phone and calls." I
said, "If you give an actor the slightest chance that they might be able
to do good work, that counts for a lot. If, on top of that, they'll be valued as well [*laughs*], who's going to say no?"

MICHAEL TOLKIN: Harry Belafonte was the first person Bob called. He wanted to be able to say to all the others, "I've got Harry Belafonte." He said, "We're leading a protest march."

HARRY BELAFONTE: I was in the Caribbean and a person in the house where I'm staying says Bob Altman wants to talk to me. So I was surprised. Thought there might be a little prank at the end of the line. But it was him. And he said, "Mr. Belafonte, I'm Robert Altman. I'm calling to get you into a picture I'm doing."

I kind of paused and waited for the other shoe to fall. And I said, "Really? What movie are you doing?"

And then he said, "*The Player.*"

And I said, "Is there a script or something?"

He said, "No. I mean, you could read it if you like. But your part is not in it."

So, okay [*laughs*].

He said, "I only need you for a very, very short time. But I must tell you I cannot have anyone else but you in this scene and doing this."

As he talked, everything became more and more diminished [*laughs*]. No script, I have no lines, and I'm only needed for an hour. So I said, "Well, Mr. Altman, if it weren't for the glory of the honor of talking to you, this would be the silliest conversation I've ever had with a filmmaker."

He said, "Well, I've had my moments."

I said, "Let me hurry up and tell you that I'm very far away. I don't live in L.A., where you're shooting, and I'm not in the United States. That's a lot of work, expense."

So he said, "Well, in this instance, no expense will be too great."

It all comes to about eighty bucks [*laughs*]. So we chatted for a little bit longer. I put aside all the alarms of what I expect to come out of such a thing. I began to pursue the curiosity of it. I said, "Okay, well, I'm down here in the Caribbean. It's going to be a day to get there, a day to rest, and then a day to shoot and a day to get back."

He said, "What's the day to rest for?" [*laughs*].

LILY TOMLIN: During *The Player*, he called me one night and said, "Can you shoot a little thing?"

I asked what the setting was and he said it was an old hotel. Scott Glenn and I were supposed to be in the dailies the suits were watching. I just pulled out an old vintage forties robe from my costume room and went onto the set. I would have done that anytime, and with complete trust. I don't think actors always do that. You have to really have a feeling for who you are going to run yourself over to.

CHER: One day he called me. "I need you in a red dress for a movie."

"All right. Give me a moment and I'll call you back."

It was late. I could have said I don't wear red. But you would do things you didn't like because of him. I was crazy about him.

MICHAEL TOLKIN: Schwarzenegger was the only one who refused, and Bob was really pissed at that. He was really pissed that Arnold had slighted him. He couldn't even get through to him. It was all managers and agents and lawyers.

ALLAN NICHOLLS (actor/music director/screenwriter/associate producer/assistant director): In shooting the most important scene in *The Player*, the execution scene with Bruce Willis, Bob challenged the whole Hollywood system. He shot it in an empty warehouse in Culver City. By shooting it off a studio, he didn't have to pay Teamsters, which would have been an incredible amount of money. He didn't have to pay studio charges. He shoots it on Sunday, on a day off. So everyone—all the stars he got to come—would be available. He encourages them to come already dressed for their parts, and they do. He got everybody to donate their salaries. And he was organized enough to shoot it in one day. The whole day was probably six hours long. We didn't break for lunch; there was no reason to. So nobody went into any kind of overtime.

Nobody but Bob could've pulled that off.

* * *

STEPHEN ALTMAN: You know, his improvisation isn't always pure improvisation each time. It's hard to tell what was the accident and what was planned. For the beginning of *The Player*, he wanted to shoot a ten-minute scene and that was it. He was like, "Stevie, build me a model of the set, the exterior, then build me a model of the crane. And I want all the interiors, of where everybody's going to be."

And he just smoked pot and played with this little thing like a kid playing with a Tonka toy. He worked that out in his mind well before we ever built the set or got out there. So that opening scene was practiced. The actors could say whatever they want, basically, but there was very much already in his mind.

TIM ROBBINS: It wasn't like he couldn't deal with writers. He needed to be in the moment. And the filmmaking process had to be a living organism that is constantly evolving. And so that whole first shot—that long tracking shot that opens the picture—that's completely improvised. I mean, everyone knew where we were going to be, but all the pitch meetings were improvised, all my responses were improvised. All the scenes you see, I don't think were ever written down. We had a day of rehearsal where we just played around.

And then there's the scene where we're sitting around in a conference room talking about the writers and eliminating the writers. That line came to me at the last minute. It was just like, "Well, if we could just eliminate the actors or the writers, we'd have something there." It was all in the moment. And this stuff doesn't happen unless you are free to do it. If you're in a constrained or restricted environment that is telling you, "You must do the script as it is written," none of that stuff would have happened.

BUCK HENRY (writer and actor): For my scene in the famous opening panning shot of *The Player* he called and said, "Come and pitch a project. You'll sit with the studio head—Tim Robbins—and pitch something. You'll be one of three or four."

I said, "Pitch what?"

He said, "Anything you want—it will all be one shot."

I was just improvising. I was pitching *The Graduate, Part II*—as a parody of pitches. In each take I got a little further out. I didn't want Tim to know what I was going to say. I was looking for the hot laugh, looking for the band to laugh, as we used to do in the old days of television.

Dialogue from *The Player*:

BUCK HENRY (*as himself, pitching* The Graduate II): Ben and
Elaine are married, still. They live in a big, spooky house up
in northern California somewhere. And Mrs. Robinson lives
with them . . . her aging mother, who's had a stroke . . . so she
can't talk. . . . It'll be funny. Dark, weird, and funny. And with
a stroke.

BUCK HENRY: Typical of Bob to begin a film with an impossible shot. Everyone was in on it—the crew coming together for the first time. It gave a sense of camaraderie for everybody, that we were all in on this one big gag. There must have been sixty actors in the take—and everyone had to hide behind a tree or in a car or a house or something. It was not like *Rope*—a continuous shot for no good reason except Hitchcock's amusement. This one parodied the long shot, introduced forty or fifty characters, and expressed what the movie was about—the mechanics of filmmaking.

At the premiere of *The Player* at the Ziegfeld, a guy comes up to me and says—apropos of my proposal for *The Graduate* sequel—"I know you were making a joke, but I think we should take it seriously."

Robert Altman, from DVD commentary: It's a very conceited thing, this shot with no cuts in it. . . . It's showing off. And it sets the picture up to be the kind of picture it's going to be and it tells the audience what they're in for. And I knew it would be commented on.

* * *

STEPHEN ALTMAN: Again, when you talk about improvisation, sometimes it's just Bob taking what's presented to him. Think about the Greta Scacchi–Tim Robbins love scene. Where it's focused completely on their faces. Everyone's like, "It's oh so marvelous," and "How did you think of that?"

How? She wouldn't show her tits. She was pregnant at the time and so they were forced into that. He had to figure some way out to get this love scene out and then it's like a work of genius. Actually, it was because we couldn't do it any other way.

TIM ROBBINS: We talked about it and Bob was a real gentleman. And you know, I don't recall him getting pissed off about it. He had envisioned it in a certain way, but he is the kind of filmmaker that as things evolve, they evolve. So he shot that scene in close-up with just the faces. But as he's telling me about it, he's totally excited about it. He says, "It's going to be great. We're going to make this the sexiest sex scene ever and it's going to be just on your faces."

ROBERT ALTMAN: I put Cynthia Stevenson in the hot tub with Tim because she's not the girl Hollywood usually asks to take her shirt off.

Greta Scacchi, as the amoral artist June Gudmundsdottir,
with Tim Robbins, as Griffin Mill, in The Player

When he saw the movie, Paul Newman told me, "I get it. You don't get to see the tits you want to see. You see the ones you don't want to see."

PAUL NEWMAN: Yes, that's accurate. I don't have to clarify it. It speaks for itself.

SUSAN SMITH (spokeswoman for Greta Scacchi): Thank you very much for your interest in interviewing Ms. Scacchi, but unfortunately she is unavailable at the time being. I wish you the best of luck with your book and thank you again.

PAUL NEWMAN: There was a more important point in that movie about nudity, I thought. Tim Robbins' character was talking to this young woman on a cell phone and he was watching her while he was talking to her and moving in closer. It was just the most frightening scene in the world, to realize that you could be observed in your most private place. And of course it raises the specter of all those questions of privacy which are now becoming paramount and the technology that we have today. Just a little hint. Yeah, it certainly wasn't about nudity, it was about how accessible everybody is. It's spooky.

*   *   *

DAVID LEVY: Tim can corroborate this, but I think that Bob and Tim were, shall we say, relaxing. And they cooked up the ending together.

TIM ROBBINS: It must have been one of the last days of preproduction. We went all around the block about the ending. I think it was late in the day, the office was still open, there were still people there, but I seem to remember it was late in the afternoon. And he said, "Come on, we've got to talk about this ending."

And so we smoked a joint. It was like, "Let's figure this out—only one way to do it: Smoke a joint."

So I say to Bob, "I forget, how did *M*A*S*H* end?"

And he goes, "Well, Radar comes on the loudspeaker and says, "This is a movie directed by Robert Altman and blah, blah, blah."

And that's what tipped it for me. I said, "Whoa, whoa, whoa. What if the writer pitches to Griffin the story you just saw of the movie?" And that is a totally stoned thought.

But Bob was like this [*stands up, starts pacing around excitedly, waving his arms*]. He walked out and he comes back and he goes, "I'm never giving you credit for that!" [*Laughs*]

And he comes out and tells everyone, "We've got the ending, we've got the ending!" But it really was his idea because it was *M*A*S*H* reinvented.

I hold those to be some of the best creative moments I've had. He didn't suffer bad ideas. It was like you'd be in the room and someone would say something and he'd say, "No, that's terrible." He was honest with you. Something that's too clever, too thought out, too derivative, he would piss on it in contempt. Not in a mean way but just, "Come on, we're creative people. Creative people create new things, they don't try to do what people have done before and repackage it." That's what's wrong with Hollywood. It keeps telling the same stories over and over again with different actors. And very few people are trying to tell the story in a unique way. And that's the only thing that Bob was able to do. No one told a story like Bob Altman.

DAVID BROWN: Tolkin had to begrudgingly agree that his book was well served by the film. It's a remarkable film and Altman deserves a great deal of credit, but so does Tolkin, whose book it was.

MICHAEL TOLKIN: I can look back and say he changed my life. *The Player* as it is, as a cultural object, exists because of Altman and what he brought to it. Altman was unquestionably a genius and an important artist. He has a few really great movies and a lot of films that are of great interest and are worth watching and watching again, but don't fully work on the terms on which they could have worked because of his disdain for story. Which I think is competition with writers, or anxiety that if he didn't take full credit for the films he was somehow admitting defeat or not being the artist he wanted to be. But the movies are completely collaborative, and that's the great message of human cooperation that comes out of the movies.

*   *   *

TIM ROBBINS: You know, *The Player* was a huge hit in Cannes. He won Best Director and I won Best Actor. And you're sitting there having champagne at your hotel after this fantastic screening. The whole town is abuzz. It's "Altman's Return."

JOHNNIE PLANCO: At Cannes, he was back on top. During that festival everyone wanted to meet him. We sold *Short Cuts*, *Kansas City*, a movie about Mata Hari that didn't happen.

There was a French company who really wanted to meet Bob. He'd sold everything, but they really wanted to meet Bob. He said, "I have nothing to give them."

I told him just to meet them and be polite. They came in, three guys with weird haircuts. Bob said, "Unfortunately, I have nothing to give you, but thanks for coming." As he was ushering them to the door, he said, "You know, you guys look like Mo, Larry, and Curly—you should be in *The Three Stooges*."

He closed the door and said, "That went well, didn't it?"

KATHRYN REED ALTMAN: You talk about how the eighties were hard, and then when *The Player* hit it was a whole other thing. It used to irk him to death when they'd all say, "Yeah, Altman's making a comeback." He'd say, "A comeback? I haven't been anywhere. I've been working."

Robert Altman to Gavin Smith and Richard T. Jameson, story headlined "The Movie You Saw Is the Movie You're Going to Make," *Film Comment*, **May–June 1992:** Every goddamn magazine that you could pick up has it as my "comeback." This is my *third* comeback; whaddya gonna do on my next one?! . . . It's nice, but you know what's gonna happen next? I'm gonna pay for it. But I *know* that. I know that these are the rules of the game and I'm okay with that. I'm not "angry with Hollywood." I'm not a "maverick." I'm not a person who "ran away in exile." I fiddle on the corner where they throw the most coins. Where I can get my work done.

KATHRYN REED ALTMAN: At the Academy Awards in 1993, Bob was nominated as director for *The Player*. Our chances were absolutely nil, and Bob didn't want to go, but he was convinced that it was important that he show up. We had no anxiety. We just knew that we had to do this. So I decided I would bake pot brownies or grass cookies—whatever I was doing at that time in my baking career. We crumbled it up to the size of nuts and had it in a little bag.

The Academy Awards can be the most miserable experience ever because of the anxiety and the fears, and because it takes forever. We left our house at three in the afternoon—Konni was with us—completely made up and dressed up, and it didn't start until seven. Then they break for commercials, and if anyone gets up they slip a stand-in into their seat. It just goes on and on.

So there we were in the very front row. I thought we'd get into our brownie bag later. Bob wanted to get into it right away. Well, every award was for Clint Eastwood, for *Unforgiven*. We'd clap and appreciate, and every time we'd tuck in our legs so he could get by to get his Oscar. The whole time we were munching away on our grass brownies. By the time he got up there to get Best Picture—after he'd gotten all the others, including Best Director—we were all for him [*laughs*]. We were saying, "Hey Clint! Go for it! Way to go! Hot dog!" [*Laughs*]

We went to every party that night—the Governor's Ball and the

Elton John party and Clint Eastwood's party. He had taken over Nicky Blair's on the Sunset Strip, and we talked with him and had a drink. We ended up at Swifty Lazar's party at La Scala—that was the famous party in those days. We got home at three in the morning.

It's a great way to lose.

Short Cuts

*

Bernard Weinraub, story headlined "Robert Altman, Very Much a Player Again," *The New York Times*, July 29, 1993: At 68, an age when most of Hollywood's film makers are retired, ignored or treated like dinosaurs by movie executives and talent agents, Robert Altman has embarked on the most radical and adventurous journey of his career.

"People here have just come to the conclusion that I'm not going to go away," he said the other afternoon. "I seem to have become like one of those old standards, in musical terms. Always around. Lauren Bacall said to me, 'You just don't quit, do you?' Guess not. I guess 30-year-olds out here have decided I'm not just an old man living in the past."

Hardly. . . .

Seated in the garden of a nearly deserted restaurant near the beach in Malibu, Mr. Altman said the success of "The Player," the scathing satire about Hollywood, has enabled him, finally, to work on the projects that have obsessed him for years but proved elusive because film companies found his work too risky and potentially uncommercial.

*   *   *

Television Directing

Black and Blue—1993; *The Real McTeaque*—1993.

*   *   *

Robert Altman and Tess Gallagher, the widow of the writer Raymond Carver, during the filming of Short Cuts

Short Cuts *(1993)*

Kenneth Turan, review in the *Los Angeles Times*, October 8, 1993: The old lion can still roar. Though tradition holds that there are no second acts in American lives, writer-director Robert Altman, never much of a traditionalist, embarks with "Short Cuts" on the fourth or possibly fifth act of a remarkable career. Both building on what has gone before and extending outward to new boundaries, he has made a rich, unnerving film, as comic as it is astringent, that in its own quiet way works up a considerable emotional charge. . . . Altman's co-conspirator this time around is the late Raymond Carver, a groundbreaking short-story writer who called himself a paid-up-in-full member of the working poor and made his considerable reputation with beautifully compressed, unadorned tales of life among the blue-collar classes.

Though this might seem too narrow and specific a base for Altman's ambitions, he and co-screenwriter Frank Barhydt understand that the harder you look at even the most ordinary lives, the more you see. Basing their script on nine of Carver's stories plus a prose poem, they have fashioned a three-hour-plus chamber piece for 22 players, a beautiful and intricate mosaic of character and incident that examines the greatest of all mysteries, that of ordinary reality. . . . Perhaps the most remarkable thing about "Short Cuts" is how effortless it all seems. Made with the unforced and casual command that often comes to artists late in life, it is close to magical in the way it draws us into its web, in how the whole comes to be considerably more than the individual parts. . . . If you want to know what the work of a mature American master is like, this is the place to look.

Rita Kempley, review in *The Washington Post,* **October 22, 1993:** "Short Cuts" is a cynical, sexist and shallow work from cinema's premier misanthrope, Robert Altman, who here shows neither compassion for— nor insight into—the human condition. This long, sour and ultimately pointless film allows Altman, the debunker of Hollywood and Nashville, to put the screws to the common folk of Southern California. . . . Basically, Altman's here to tell us that life stinks and there's not a damn thing to be done about it.

* * *

Robert Altman, from his introduction to a collection of Raymond Carver's stories published in 1993: Raymond Carver made poetry out of the prosaic. One critic wrote that "he revealed the strangeness concealed behind the banal," but what he really did was capture the wonderful idiosyncrasies of human behavior, the idiosyncrasies that exist amid the randomness of life's experiences. And human behavior, filled with all its mystery and inspiration, has always fascinated me. . . . Raymond Carver's view of the world, and probably my own, may be termed dark by some. We're connected by similar attitudes about the arbitrary nature of luck in the scheme of things—the child being hit by the car in "A Small Good Thing"; the marriage upheaval resulting from a body being discovered during a fishing trip in "So Much Water So Close to Home." Somebody wins a lottery. The same day, that person's sister gets killed by a brick falling off a building in Seattle. Those are the same thing. The lottery was won both ways. . . . When I first spoke to the poet Tess Gallagher, Ray's widow, about wanting to make this film, I told her I wasn't going to be pristine in my approach to Carver and that the stories were going to be scrambled. She instinctively recognized and encouraged this, and said Ray was an admirer of

Nashville, that he liked the helplessness of those characters and their ability to manage nevertheless. She also knew that artists in different fields must use their own skills and vision to do their work.

TESS GALLAGHER (poet and widow of Raymond Carver): I'd always admired his work and so had Ray. He began to look more closely at the stories and to try to see what was available. It turned out that a film-maker named Jill Godmilow—she's done some small films—she had optioned a good number of stories. Bob had to choose from what was left. There were a lot of complaints about Bob having chosen the darker stories. The reason he hadn't chosen others was they weren't available. It wasn't Bob saying, "I'm going to choose the toughest, meanest stories Carver wrote."

I had seen *Nashville* with Ray. I found it so affecting the way that the characters were willing to chance everything. They so wanted to fol-low that dream, even if they were not terribly talented, that they would put themselves in untenable situations. They were so fragile, yet they were so invested in the dream of what their life can be, that they didn't see themselves. We saw them, we felt them, we cringed when they tried to sing and couldn't sing. I think that we feel something similar for Ray's characters, how fragile they are, how unprotected, how out there, how they don't know how to do it right, so they cause them-selves more harm and they can't figure out how to get out of their snarl. But we stay with them because we've been there. You don't get through life with everything going the way you think it will or you want it to. Life gets away from you. Like the baker in "A Small, Good Thing." You wake up and find yourself a brutish character who is mak-ing those terrible phone calls. That's not who he set out to be. But you would never have found the tenderness in that scene without Carver. Carver was in there. Carver was working on Altman. People say Alt-man was working on Carver. Well, it worked the other way around, too.

I think Bob and Ray really connected on the basis that in Carver's stories every moment is fragile. . . . You will be on safe ground with somebody and then a word or a notion or something from the past will be brought up and everything is changed. Suddenly the ground has dropped out from under you. We go along as if we know how the peo-ple around us are going to behave and we think we know their motiva-tions, but we don't. We don't always know what is going to be brought to bear, what the possibilities for that person really are. Altman thinks everything comes out of who the character is, and I think so does Ray. The characters are maybe less set in Ray. I think they are even more unpredictable in Ray's work.

ALAN RUDOLPH (director): When Chris Penn's character hit that girl with the rock and she went down, that was one of the most brutal things I'd seen in my life. I remember the first time I saw the screening of it—it was a rough cut.

Bob said, "What's wrong?"

I said, "Man, I wish there was a way you could do that without showing it."

He said, "Oh, you've got to show it."

I saw someone bolder than I could ever be. Because I would have wanted to be overtly liked more than that. Bob just didn't care if you liked it as long as you had to deal with it, because out of having to deal with it on his terms comes respect. And out of respect you can change people.

*   *   *

Peter Travers, review in *Rolling Stone*, October 1993: Stuart Kane (Fred Ward) . . . and his pals Gordon (Buck Henry) and Vern (Huey Lewis) had just walked four hours to their favorite fishing spot when Vern, pissing in the stream, found his urine trickling on the beautiful and dead body of a girl. It's only after Stuart comes home and makes love to his wife Claire (a never-better Anne Archer) that he tells her how he and his friends made the decision to leave the body in the water for another day and keep fishing. She was dead, wasn't she? Claire is shattered; she attends the funeral of the girl but can't salve her conscience.

ANNE ARCHER (actress): I loved playing that part because it had a tragic poignancy. I instinctively knew who she was. She was this woman who felt immediately victimized by what he did because she saw herself as everyone. So this woman lying in the river could have been her, this woman who was treated as a piece of meat. It took all the love out of the relationship because it could never be undone. It showed such a lack of care of the things that would make you want to be in a relationship with a man. It was a very sad, tragic feeling that I felt as that character. It throws her world into disarray.

Yet that's also the fun about Bob. Just as you start to moralize he won't let you do that. That's why he creates such interesting, complex characters. You don't dislike Fred Ward's character. He's not an evil person. He did a thoughtless thing. It's just that the woman he's married to is a very sensitive person and takes it very personally.

TESS GALLAGHER: Altman likes taking the opposite view from Ray. He was really in a dialogue with Ray. When Ray is pointing all the emphasis on the woman in "So Much Water So Close to Home," Bob is saying, "I'm going to focus on the guy." I talked to him about that. Ray really did this from the point of view of the wife. But Bob didn't want us to think that it was all the guy's fault, the husband who continues to fish after finding the body of a dead girl. He wanted to move the two of them closer together so we cannot rest in a pat judgment about what the guy did. When you bring the poles closer together the friction is very moving. It's very unsettling. And you can't tell who is going to come out of it right as easily as you thought you could. Of course, those readers who were very fond of the woman's view weren't happy about having to consider that this fellow, this seemingly good fellow, makes a bad judgment and is really in trouble.

When you have the moment when the guy is pissing onto the body, this was horrible. I instinctively thought, "Oh, God, he's way over the line." But he wouldn't give that up. Not that I asked him to, but I think Kathryn did. He was looking for the image that could show the carelessness, the despicable carelessness of the American male in that situation—where they're all out there, men being men together, and the body of the woman suffers a desecration. He doesn't come on and say this body has suffered a desecration, he leaves that for you to feel. Bob had him do that because he knows what everybody's going to feel. He didn't do that to be a smart-ass.

Robert Altman, to Peter Travers, review headlined "A Robert Altman S*M*A*S*H," *Rolling Stone*, **October 1993:** "I don't think the husband did a bad thing," says Altman. "People say to me, 'Oh, you wouldn't do that.' I say, 'I would do that.'" The movie allows for both points of view, which is Altman's purpose: "It is not my business—nor was it Carver's business—to moralize about these things. I resent in art the definitive explanation for people's behavior—there isn't any."

Anne Archer: I think Bob is right in that sense. He doesn't like it when you make things morally right and wrong. He loved the foibles and the charm of different characters. He didn't create these dark characters that depressed you. He created these flawed characters that amuse you. He could create a flawed character that would somehow mix it up just enough so you would have to get off your moral soapbox and sort of go, "Well, there's a little bit of that in me." You sort of have to forgive them.

Bob was nonjudgmental. Actors are always being judged. They're being watched, they're being looked at, everybody has an opinion, everybody judges the width and breadth of their talents, or lack thereof. Everybody is always judging artists and it's the worst thing you can do to an artist. It's the thing that kills them. There's an active plot to get the artists. Bob doesn't do that. Bob loves actors, and all artists, whether it's the set designer or the lead or the cinematographer.

*   *   *

Dialogue from *Short Cuts:*

(While getting ready for a dinner party, Ralph Wyman, played by Matthew Modine, confronts his wife, Marian, played by Julianne Moore, about an incident at a party three years earlier.)

Ralph: Your lipstick was smeared when you came back.
Marian: How would you know? You were drunk.
   [Marian spills wine on her skirt]
Marian: Goddammit, I wanted to wear this. Shit.
   [She removes her skirt and rinses it under the faucet. She is naked from the waist down]

Julianne Moore: Unfortunately, the way Bob asked me to be in *Short Cuts*, I literally got a cold call. I got a call at home—I was standing in my kitchen—and he was like, "Hello, Julianne. This is Bob Altman. Do you know who I am?"

Which is crazy. I assumed that it was somebody making fun of me. I thought it was a friend of mine making fun of me because they knew what a huge fan I was of his. And I said, "Oh, come on. This isn't Bob."

He goes, "No, no. It's Bob Altman."

Julianne Moore, as Marian Wyman, in Short Cuts

And just, I was shattered. I just didn't—I said first, "How did you get my number?" And I just couldn't believe he was calling me at home.

And he said, "Well, I have this movie and I have this part I want you to do."

And I said, "Yes. Yes."

He said, "No, no, no. You really—you have to read it first." He said, "Because there's something—there's some nudity and it's not negotiable."

And I said, "Yes, yes. I don't care. I'll do whatever you want me to do."

And he said, "Well, sweetheart, really, just think about it. But I'm glad that you're enthusiastic." So he said the nudity, you know, the part, it's bottomless.

And I said, "That's fine. I'll do it."

Bob claims that after this—I don't remember saying this; this is the unfortunate part—I may have said, in my excitement, "Guess what, I'm a real redhead."

I don't remember saying that. But Bob never forgot it. And then the story got bigger. It morphed into—"And then she said, 'I have a bonus for you, I'm a real redhead!'" This is at the very, very beginning of my film career when I'm desperate to be taken seriously.

So basically, I would do a movie and they would call people you worked with and the first person they would call would be Bob. And Bob would say, "Listen to this story. . . . She said, 'I have a bonus for you. . . .'"

And I'd be like, "Oh, my God!" So this story was in *The New York Times*, the *L.A. Times*, *Rolling Stone*, *Premiere* magazine. Basically, anybody who'd talk to Bob, he'd tell that story.

So I didn't know what to do because then people would say to me, "Can we call Bob and ask him for a quote?" And I'd go, "Please don't call Bob, please don't call Bob."

And I thought, "This is ridiculous. I can't, I can't go on like this. I love him. And he means more than anything to me." And I thought, "Just get your courage up, Julie."

And I called Bob. And I felt like such an ass. And I said, "You know, Bob, about that thing that you always say about my being a real red—"

He said, "Oh, yeah, about how you said, 'I have a bonus for you.'"

I said, "Well, Bob, I know it's funny. But I'm kinda sensitive about it, and maybe—maybe you could stop talking to the press about it."

And he said—and in the most gentle, humane, you know, way possible—he said, "Of course, honey, whatever you want."

It was so moving because that's who Bob was. You know, whatever you wanted was great. Whoever you were was great. You never made a mistake with Bob. Bob made you feel that everything you were doing was perfect. He made you feel, once he had cast you, you were what he wanted. He made the decision in the casting and therefore nothing you did on set was going to be wrong because you were bringing your whole thing to it. He didn't want anything different than what you decided to do. So you felt insanely comforted by that because he was so gentle. You know, all this talk about Bob being this kind of irascible, difficult kind of person? Well, he was never that way with an actor or with a creative person that I saw. Never, never, never. He saved all that for the money people.

*   *   *

I remember being really nervous doing that stuff in *Short Cuts*. I said, "Do you want me to do it again? Is there anything else you want me to try?"

He said, "No, you're doing absolutely everything you need to do. You're doing it perfectly." He was so reassuring. But the funny thing was, after I finished, I'd done the big scene, we were in a place called Baldwin Hills, and it was way, way high up in these mountains, so they were counting on all this light coming in. I did all the stuff and it was all emotional and everything and Bob had this tradition that everybody went to dailies. Whoever was working with him that day usually went with him in his car, which was incredibly sweet.

He said to me and Matthew Modine, "Come on, you guys, let's go. Let's get in the car." He said, "I've got some news for you. We have to reshoot that. We lost the light."

I was like, "What?"

He said, "Don't worry, you can do it again."

I mean, I was like . . . I couldn't even wrap my mind around the fact that I had to do it all again the next day in the morning after spending the entire day doing the most emotional part at the end of the day. And Bob was completely calm about it and completely certain that it would happen again. He always gave you an enormous amount of freedom. So much freedom within a boundary. Which is the best situation you can be in. People always assumed with Bob there was all this free-for-all, that there was endless improv and people did whatever they want. I mean, that was only true up to a point. You improvised, but then you'd need to hone it. You were free, but it was Bob's set. He never lost sight of the movie he was making and what your place was within it. It was that sort of thing. You don't want rules that restrict you, you want rules that aid you, that guide you. That's what he was able to do because he knew what movie he was making. Always.

MATTHEW MODINE: The scene is about so much more than Julianne having her pants off. You just know these characters have had this conversation a few times before. You can feel it in the text. Tonight he's going to make his cocktail and sit down in his chair and ask her to tell him what happened. That's what's going to be so unnerving—he's not going to be chasing her around, berating her.

JULIANNE MOORE: So many people asked me about doing that scene.

MATTHEW MODINE: I felt so embarrassed for her when we did press for the movie. The reporters reminded me of President Bush. He always looks like a guy who just heard a really dirty joke and he wishes he could share it with you. So reporters would be sitting there with Julianne and they had this stupid smirk on their faces and they're like, "So, you're a real redhead." And Julianne would handle it, just say, "Well, yeah."

I only wish I had my pants off, so they would have talked about my pubic hair as much as they talked about Julianne being a real redhead.

JULIANNE MOORE: When you read a piece of literature it's a very internal experience. You can talk about the characters' feelings and whatever. But when you're trying to translate that into a dramatic experience, you have to find a way to translate that kind of intimacy and that thought process. So the feeling of being incredibly intimate and knowing somebody, knowing their body, of a marriage, he was able to communicate that in that scene that way, and it was shocking to people. And really, really upsetting because he communicated that in a flash.

So, anyway, it might not have been the last time I had dinner with Bob and Kathryn, but it was after we'd had this conversation about my bush. And we were sitting at the table: my husband, me, another couple, and Bob and Kathryn. And somebody was asking me how Bob and I had met, and how I had ended up in *Short Cuts* and what had happened.

And then *Kathryn* said—I will never believe what she said—"And I have a bonus for ya!"

And Bob said, "Kathryn, we're not supposed to talk about her pussy anymore."

But you know what? I'm really glad he did. I loved him.

* * *

JENNIFER JASON LEIGH: He called me and said, "I have this movie and there's a couple of roles that might work for you." And I was really excited. I read it and I liked Lois, the woman who did sex calls from her house. I called and told him, and he said, "Oh good, that's the only one left."

My research? I went to a bunch of those places. He told me, "The

*Chris Penn and Jennifer Jason Leigh, playing pool cleaner
Jerry Kaiser and phone sex worker Lois Kaiser, in* Short Cuts

script is really a blueprint and I need you to fill it out. I want it to be raunchy and I want it to be real. You figure it out." One place I went was a factory with cubicles. One was a house in the Valley and this was a guy using a falsetto. He was a straight guy with a picture of Michelle Pfeiffer on the wall. And a woman's house. She kept files, which was kind of awkward because I knew some of the people. So now I know what they *like*. I made my script from that.

Dialogue from *Short Cuts:*

Lois Kaiser (*Played by Jennifer Jason Leigh, taking a phone-sex call while changing her daughter's diaper*): Oooh. My panties are getting a little wet.

JENNIFER JASON LEIGH: The great thing about Bob was he would inspire you out of sheer necessity to come up with stuff that you didn't know you were capable of, that you didn't know you had in you. He was so genuinely mischievous and so damn funny.

He had that much faith and trust. Which is nerve-racking. It could be a free fall, which is what I think acting should be. But you need a master to catch you, which is what you had with Bob. You could make these extravagantly spectacular choices, knowing you had this strong, loving man to catch you.

*   *   *

PETER GALLAGHER: The most amazing thing in the world is that we did *The Player* and it was a hit, and then everybody and his brother wanted to be in *Short Cuts*. And Stormy Weathers was a great part and everybody wanted to play it. And Bob said, "No, Gallagher is playing it." Which is maybe one of the most astounding things I've ever heard. That was maybe the only time in my life that somebody with a bigger name wanted a part that I got.

I remember calling Steve Altman a couple nights before the scene where I destroy the house with the chain saw. I was working on the part and Steve is the art director. I said, "Steve, now, what kind of gag do you have in mind for this couch? I don't want one of these frantic, slash-and-hack things. I want to slice that fucker like a pound cake."

And he said, "We're giving you a real couch. I'll just make sure there's nothing that can snag the chain and fly back and kill you, any springs."

Bob said, "I want you to come in here, look there, and then cut the couch up. And we're going to do that in one take."

You just can't ask for anything more than that. Just to get these great, wonderful, cool things to do.

LILY TOMLIN: When we did *Short Cuts*, we weren't all there together. Each couple shot for about a week. Tom Waits and I were the first couple. I was mad for Tom—I loved him as an artist and a person. He had his own kind of underworld eccentricity and private poetry. He would go home every night after shooting and call me and pretend that he was Earl out driving in the limo. The first night he did it I was so surprised. I should have taped it. He was talking nonstop poetry to me as if I was Doreen. He called me about four nights in a row. He was so involved in it. Bob allowed you to be totally in the moment because there was nothing rigid about Bob, about what he was going to do.

BUCK HENRY: He made actors believe that they were doing something for him that they couldn't do anywhere else. I'm not sure that was true—but the belief was true. An Altman set was different because everyone felt they were collaborating—of course they weren't—between the apparent looseness of the day and the possibility of improvising. He backed off from the actors; there was never the feeling of the camera being in your face. Usually it wasn't anywhere near you, so it encouraged you to do things you wouldn't have done if the camera was in your face. And since you were always wearing a mike you weren't worried about not being heard.

TESS GALLAGHER: Bob gave one of the characters he invented my name—Tess. Annie Ross's character. She's falling out of the seams. She's kind of a ruined character, kind of a bellicose, pitiable character, so wrapped up in being this singer and her love for her dead husband. She was full of bathos, like somebody out of Chaucer, almost. Offended? No. I thought they had used my name, but I didn't find myself there. I don't regard Ray in the way in which she does her hus-

Lily Tomlin and Tom Waits, playing waitress Doreen Piggot and chauffeur Earl Piggot, in Short Cuts

band. I'm not maudlin about Ray, and she is rather maudlin. I thought it was a way for Bob to sneak my name in there. I like the toughness about her. It says you have to be tough for life. Altman's right. You do have to have a good amount of stamina. You have to have your compassionate nature in hand but there's a way in which you also have to stand up to life.

ANNIE ROSS (singer and actress): I always had the feeling with Bob that I was on a beautiful schooner and the first in charge was Bob, and I knew he would get us into port with no problems. You knew he knew what he was doing. It's the same way with a pianist—if you have the right pianist, you have a mind thing that goes on. Listening is the most important thing, and that's what Bob did so well. He listened. And it's the same way in singing jazz.

He loved adventure, he loved newness, and he loved that you've got to jump out in the deep water. And he lived by that. You have to be brave and you have to take chances, and that's what he did and that's what he was. And I think it goes with an artist's temperament. Because what you're actually doing is saying, "Come on, crucify me. Here I am."

Robert Coles, essay headlined "Compassion from Carver, Male Swagger from Altman," *The New York Times*, October 17, 1993: The director gives us a movie full of male swagger, with women always at the edge of things; a movie that lacks Carver's gentle humor and prompts laughter at people . . . a movie relentless in its cynical, sardonic assault on anyone and everyone, as if America itself is beyond the pale.

TESS GALLAGHER: I know that Ray would have laughed at the same things that Altman laughed at in this film. But I don't think Altman made fun of the characters. I think he was watching those characters, letting them be as bizarre as they could be. I think their motions are larger and they're stranger in Altman—like the woman who does telephone sex—much more the American grotesque. The things these people are reaching for are not going to satisfy them. The woman who is having one guy after another. The guy who takes a chain saw to the living room. None of their actions are going to move them into a livable space. They're just good at making disasters. And the chaos of Ray's characters didn't make you feel like they didn't have possibilities. The suffering that they had was wonderfully handled so you could respect the suffering.

I think *Short Cuts* is just a classic, and I think it's one of the classic American films because we really do get a portrait of America and we're really looking in the mirror.

Robert Altman to Cathy Horyn, story headlined "Robert Altman Confronts His Critics: *'Short Cuts'* Has Been Called Misogynistic and Callous; the Director Replies, 'So What?'" *The Washington Post,* October 31, 1993: I'm not doing a literal translation of Carver, nor did I ever say I was going to. If anything, the film is a reflection not just of my interpretation, but of those of a hundred other people who worked on it. We were all responding to the material. . . . But you know, so what? We're not saying this film is anything other than what it is. So, maybe all I can say in response to [Robert] Coles is, 'Tsk, tsk, I wish he had got it.' "

PAUL THOMAS ANDERSON (director): The way the characters dressed, the way they looked, the locations in the film, everything about it— God, that is the city, this is the city that I've known, I've been near.

That movie got inside my bones so strongly, and you know, without it I never would have known how to write *Magnolia.* I knew that I had stories that I wanted to tell but certainly didn't know how to do it and wouldn't have known how to do it without that film.

ROBERT DORNHELM (director): He looked at film on one side as a pure, artistic venue. At the same time he was quite happy if the box office was good. Just getting a few good reviews and no audience wasn't enough. It consoled him, but he would prefer to have a hit. With *Short Cuts,* the distributor was begging him: "If you want money, cut a few minutes." Bob just thought the Antichrist was trying to destroy his art. They were well-meaning people who wanted him to get what he deserved, which was a big commercial hit. But when it came down to the art or the money, he was with the art.

*   *   *

DAVID LEVY (producer): As successful as those films were critically, commercially it was another story.

Both *The Player* and *Short Cuts* were released by Fine Line, a new company. I think *The Player* was maybe the second picture they ever released. And we'll never know, but I don't think there were ever more than four hundred prints in circulation. I really think it was the sort of movie that you could have let out in a more substantial way right from Jump Street, and people would have come, such was the quality of the reviews. But in what is now called the specialty world, there was a conventional wisdom that prevailed at that point in time. It was like, you will open in just a few cities, you will start small, you will build. This is one time, and I'm not talking about going crazy wide with the thing, but I think ultimately twice as many people might have seen it in theaters if the approach to the release was different. Similarly, *Short Cuts*. I won't say I feel it had the commercial appeal of *The Player*, but again, here's a picture that gets all that acclaim and what did it do? Maybe ten, twelve, thirteen million box office?

CHAPTER 27

Heart in a Cooler

*

KATHRYN REED ALTMAN: The deterioration was kind of off and on for many years. The doctors said, "Well, you got a little problem there, an enlarged heart—cardiomyopathy—so you shouldn't do this or that, and you shouldn't drink."

So he would not drink for a while and somebody would say something else and then he'd start drinking again. He stopped smoking when he was about thirty-six years old because they detected something. So it was always kind of there. And in '68, I guess it was, he had to give himself Heparin shots, blood thinner, way back then. It would be off and on and come and go, but it never stopped him from doing anything. He never had a heart attack. But the booze is the worst thing for an enlarged heart, and finally the heart just gave up.

Anyway, sometimes he would have to go on these extreme diets because you've got to lose this weight because of your heart. And in '92, before we'd gone to Paris for *Prêt-à-Porter*, he had kind of a semi-stroke here. I wasn't here, Konni was.

KONNI CORRIERE: Mother was in L.A. She couldn't fly. She had just had a medical procedure or whatever. He took me to one party to meet a bunch of bigwigs. Lauren Bacall was there and he just shuffled me around and introduced me. The next morning I heard him yelling. He's like, "I think we have a little problem here."

So I came downstairs and what had happened, we found out later, is that he had a stroke. He couldn't remember my name. He was trying to call me and he couldn't remember my name. I got the phone book and called the doctor and helped him get dressed. I was over him, trying to get him to sit up, so I could do a button or something. And he looks at me and says, "If this is it, it's been great."

Oh, God. It was so sweet and so cute and it was so serious. And it was really terrible.

I got him into a car with a driver and we went to this first doctor for an echocardiogram. They said, "You have to go immediately to the hospital."

I just wanted to keep him engaged and busy. I knew he was scared. I knew I had to seal myself right next to him. I said, "Let's get you an alias." So we ended up with my mother's maiden name as his last name, Reed, and his middle name, Bernard. And he was Bernard Reed for all his medical stuff until he came out at the Oscars.

I knew he couldn't stand to be alone. I knew that all the screaming and yelling and partying and socializing—he hates to be, he was afraid to be, alone. That's what it comes down to, and I knew that, especially at this health moment. So I asked the nurse, "Hey, listen, is there any chance I could sleep here tonight?"

She said, "Sure."

I slept next to him. Later, I went to Paris with him as his assistant. I really was his secret health assistant more than anything else because he couldn't let anybody know he was sick or had a stroke. In Paris, he told me, "Konni, when I woke up in that hospital that morning I didn't know where I was. And I was so scared. I rolled over and I saw you sleeping in that little cot next to me. I want you to know I will never forget that. I will never forget it and I will always be there for you."

He did lose the vision in the right side of his right eye, and after that whenever you walked in the room, you had to be careful because he wouldn't see you if you entered on his right side. You'd startle him. He'd get startled a lot. He couldn't drive after that, either. That was big. But he never complained.

KATHRYN REED ALTMAN: He was weak, he was thin. He was great, though. He was still fun and funny. He started to lose some weight in August of '93 and he looked just great. Then he just did it by design. Then it just started falling off of him and he kept losing. All through *Prêt-à-Porter*, he was very thin. He wore those beautiful suits, Brioni, Cerruti, all these French and Italian designers were making these gorgeous suits for him. He looked like a million bucks. But he got too thin.

* * *

Prêt-à-Porter *(aka* Ready to Wear; *1994)*

Alexander Walker, review headlined "Ready to Wear? Ready to Walk Out," *The Evening Standard* **(London), December 14, 1994:** As a film, it's a huge disappointment—an artistic debacle that spoils its chances by wasting a multitude of stars on itsy-bitsy roles and induces the same sense of confusion that ruled when it was shot in the middle of the Paris spring fashion shows earlier this year. But as an expression of what Altman thinks of the couturiers and models . . . the movie is a gesture of the utmost disdain for everything the rag trade holds dear and profitable. Repeated no fewer than five times . . . is a moment where someone puts his or her foot firmly—and in close-up—into a pile of dog dirt.

* * *

STEPHEN ALTMAN: At the film festivals, when you've got something good there, there's a feeding frenzy. We'd get a signature on a napkin from somebody for the next picture. For making the movie. For all of it. That's what happened at Cannes. We were there with *Short Cuts.* That was a big Cannes hit and they were basically beating down the doors. I think that's how *Prêt-à-Porter* was made. He hated that script. It was like, "Bob. You don't have a movie."

And he'd say, "Yeah, but this guy is ready to roll. Let's just do it. We'll make it up as we go along."

JOHNNIE PLANCO (agent): *Prêt-à-Porter* was very difficult. He hired a journalist who'd never written a screenplay as the screenwriter. No one came up with a shooting script. Lots of people he hadn't worked with—Marcello Mastroianni, Sophia Loren, Julia Roberts. Nothing jelled.

LAUREN BACALL: I was the first person cast in that. We went down to the Tribeca Grill and we had lunch and he said I was going to be this Diana Vreeland character. Of course he convinced me of everything. Like most actors who ever worked with him once. It was a little like actors who worked with John Huston—"Tell me what you want and

*With Marcello Mastroianni, as the mysterious tailor Sergei/Sergio,
and Sophia Loren, as the fashionable widow Isabella de la Fontaine,
in* Prêt-à-Porter

I'll be there." That's the way Bogie was with John, and Bob had that gift with actors, too.

I think the main thing that didn't work was he was ill. I knew he couldn't wait to get out of France because he didn't speak the language and it drove him crazy. There was no room for foreign sound to permeate that Kansas City accent.

I think that in fairness he didn't have enough time or didn't have entrée into what happened in the back rooms of a fashion house. And then what was that with the dog shit? That's a onetime joke. You can't base a movie on a guy stepping on dog shit every five minutes.

Bob had a concept, as he always did, and there was always room for ideas. My part ended up not being what he intended it to be. He got caught up in the little vignettes.

I don't think he was well enough to really cope with it.

Bob and I really got along well except on *Prêt-à-Porter*. We were not so palsy. There wasn't any argument, nothing specific. I felt somewhat at a loss because I thought the character was not what he told me it would be. I wasn't quite sure I was playing the scenes properly. He said, "If you do something wrong I'll let you know."

I was kind of thrown off by it and I don't think he was so thrilled with it, either. When you're physically not right, especially with a man like Bob Altman, anything that would hold him back would be really hard for him.

I walked into his office one day and he was lying on a sofa with a blanket. I said, "How are you?"

He said, "I'll be a hell of a lot better when I get out of here."

SALLY KELLERMAN: On *Prêt-à-Porter* he was so ill. Oh my God. I flew to Paris, went to the production office, walked in, said, "Where is Bob, where is Bob?" I was so excited to be there. I walked down the hall to find him. He had his back to me. And I almost . . . I mean, this is a dramatic way of putting it, but I just thought, "Oh my God, he's dying." He just looked so different. And he managed to make that movie with that crew. I don't know how he did it.

ANOUK AIMÉE: It was thirty years after I met him about *Lake Lugano*. We got on well right away. There were a lot of women in *Prêt-à-Porter*, but I couldn't have had a better friendship and understanding and rapport.

Robert Altman's handwritten acceptance speech when he received the Legion of Honor in 1996. "Gilles" is Gilles Jacob, the director of the Cannes Film Festival, who presented the award.

To work with a man like Bob, that desire was stronger than the desire to portray the part. The part was okay, but the real joy was to be directed by him. If you work with a great director, often something great comes out. If you have a wonderful part with a bad director, you might disappear.

Sick? We never saw it. He was always very strong. I never saw him complain. I sometimes saw him very tired but we never stopped because of him. He was very dignified. It was a very difficult film for him.

HARRY BELAFONTE: When we were in Paris, I had a bedroom that was right down the hall from the main bedroom where he and Kathryn stayed. When his door was open, what you saw was the TV set. He would use the remote from the bed and you could see what program he was watching. One night it was the Winter Olympics, and they showed it in a way where you never saw one full thing. They cut to several events. Bob was into sports. He didn't care what it was. He was really into it.

So he was sitting there. I could see the TV set, and it dawned on me. I got the remote in my room, and I aimed it down the hall, and sure as shit I clicked it and the channel changed. And Bob got up and was clicking back to get back to the station. I'd leave it in place a while and I'd click it again. And click it again. And Bob would click it back.

You have to understand something. Bob was so fucking sharp, there is no con he did not know. He was always so skeptical and cynical in his own great, genuine way, good way. So now, just as the skier took off the ramp, just as he's about to land, I clicked it. And he said, "Aw shit! Kathryn, this fucking set, what the hell's wrong with these French?!"

And I waited. The end of the race, click. And another time when he clicked, I clicked, he clicked it back on, and I clicked it back off again. This went on for half an hour, forty minutes. He was in a rage [*laughs*].

It was Kathryn who walked by just when I was doing it. She saw me, and she said, "Is that you, Belafonte?"

I said, "Me? What?"

She said, "Bob . . ."

Bob looked around and said, "You fucker!" [*Laughs*]

He really got to a state of such agitation. He denounced all the French and the French Revolution. Napoleon was a shit. I mean, you name it.

BUCK HENRY: *Prêt-à-Porter* was really a mess, but there isn't an actor in the world I believe who wouldn't have preferred to be in it.

PETER GALLAGHER: After *Prêt-à-Porter*, we were having dinner at Café Luxembourg. And they were pretty cruel; the reviews were tough. I remember asking him, "Does it get any easier?"
He said, "No. It just gets harder. Just hurts more."
And he's fucking right, you know?

* * *

Robert Altman's Jazz '34: Remembrances of Kansas City Swing *(Documentary for PBS, Great Performances; 1996)*

* * *

Kansas City *(1996)*

Jay Carr, review of *Kansas City, The Boston Globe,* August 16, 1996: Although Robert Altman's "Kansas City" is a labor of love, it's anything but nostalgic. Rich in texture, it alternates druggy reveries and a harsh clarity about some brutal realities of life in the American heartland in 1934 as it unfolds during a single calamitous day. Although Altman was only 9 the year the action of the film takes place, its world of black jazz and white power politics obviously informed his youth. Here he celebrates the former and pitilessly indicts the latter. . . . Its framing device is a kidnapping—tinny-voiced Jennifer Jason Leigh, a Jean Harlow wannabe, kidnaps a Democratic Party bigwig's wife (Miranda Richardson), a sad woman given to swallowing laudanum to forget she's unloved excess baggage. . . . Dermot Mulroney's none-too-bright thug has robbed a visiting gambler, and the local black mob boss—played by Harry Belafonte with an invigorating hardness he seldom has been allowed to display throughout his long career—acts fast to put things right.

* * *

DAVID LEVY: *Kansas City* was a case of him going home. In a funny way, it's sort of like a bit of drama meets a kind of memoir. It's almost like he's operating out of sense memory of his youth there, you know? And so it's not the stuff of biography, but it is like the kind of melodrama that might have played in his head during his formative years.

KATHRYN REED ALTMAN: I can't tell you how many times during *Kansas City* he'd come home and say, "A guy came to the set today who I went to kindergarten with."

FRANK BARHYDT (screenwriter): Kansas City was unique in that first of all, it didn't abide by prohibition. Also, it wasn't affected as much by the Depression. A lot of that is due to the fact they had a political boss here who had connections. Because it wasn't suffering so much from the Depression, this is where musicians came. There were clubs open and you could drink constantly. Bob remembers going into these clubs—a whole lot of clubs just up and down Twelfth Street—and he wanted to show that in this movie.

HARRY BELAFONTE: One night we came home from something and we were sitting there and he broke out a joint. He said essential to this film is this character, a black character, and he's a gangster. And he painted the environment for me and he said, "He's a lethal son of a bitch." He said, "I just don't have the cards in my deck. I can't get to him. And I wondered if you would work with me on it."

Harry Belafonte, as the gangster Seldom Seen, in Kansas City

Coming from a background where my relatives are deeply immersed in the numbers world, small-time racketeers, I enjoyed this because a lot of my childhood was spent around it. And this picture was taking place in 1934, so I could go back into it. We were talking and I said, "Most movies you see, you always find gangsters are dim. They might have some instinct that's sharp, but it's always equated on the side of evil and therefore they're seen in a rather one-dimensional way." I knew guys who were learned men who could quote Socrates and philosophers and play chess, were bright men, and could offer political and social analyses, and they could shoot you in a minute. I said, "If you approach him from the elements in his persona that run against his practice and his culture, you have an interesting character."

So the picture is now called *Kansas City* and the character's name was Seldom Seen. He's called Seldom Seen because he spent most of his life in prison. Other people hardly ever saw him, and yet he ran everything. And in the middle of this movie he becomes pivotal to the plot. And he says, "Belafonte, I want you to play it."

I said, "No. I don't need to go through all that. This character is so against type. My persona in the world at large is all this peace stuff." I told him I would hurt the movie to ask the audience to overcome the popular persona to get into this part that was so pivotal to this movie. And he took a draw on his spliff and he looked at me and he said, "Tell me something, Belafonte, when did you decide you were an actor? You can't play it? And you're an actor? That's interesting."

Well, man, that laid me out. And I said, "Look, Bob, okay. I'll give you my best shot, but stand on notice that I told you I thought it was the wrong way to go." And I got into it. I didn't want to use a lot of makeup. I went in, I got the costume. I had my shirt made a size and a half, two sizes small. And when I pulled the collar together, it started to cut off the circulation to the face. I pulled the tie up a little tighter, and hooked it so it kept in place. The blood began to fill my face. And I always looked like I was on the verge of an explosion. And that's exactly how my uncle looked. He always looked like he was going to detonate. And he was a big, big numbers man up in Harlem.

So I came out for Bob to see, and I said, "Does this get it?"

And he said, "Let's shoot."

I said, "What? I've just gotten in this fucking costume, and I've done no prep. I did this for you to see."

He said, "Belafonte, I'm ready."

It turned out to be—certainly at that time in my life—the best thing I ever did. It was the best relationship I ever had with a director who led me through a development towards the approach of a part that I'd never experienced before. He gave me the chance to do just what I saw. And by and large, most of the critics on that picture were very, very laudatory, and I wound up getting the New York City Drama Critics Award for the best supporting actor.

JENNIFER JASON LEIGH: It's very rare you get to actually work with someone who worked with your parents as artists. He worked with my mom [Barbara Turner] on a bunch of things, and my dad [Vic Morrow] on *Combat!*. After one take on *Kansas City* he says, "Oh, just like your dad."

It felt great because he knew my dad. And I look so much like my dad, and to have someone say it who has the right to say it was interesting and exciting. Someone else might say it and I would be like, "Who are you to talk about my father?"

We had a great time making *Kansas City*. Watching Bob watching jazz was very emotional. It was the music of his youth, which is why he wanted to make the movie. I was so happy to see him move to the music. I really didn't know how sick Bob was. He kind of keeps that from you. I found out later. When we were making the movie, he's just a giant.

JANE ADAMS (actress): He gave my character his grandmother's name, Nettie Bolt. [A reviewer called her "a snooty Junior-Leaguer trying to stuff charity down the throat of a pregnant black girl, whom she views as a trophy."]

Bob told me, "You're going to be playing my grandmother. She was involved in the Junior League, and they smile even when they don't feel like smiling. It's that particular kind of society lady." We just sort of had fun with that.

He was very good at instilling confidence, a confidence I don't always have.

DONA GRANATA (costume designer): *McCabe & Mrs. Miller* was the picture that made me decide to become a costume designer. The visuals were so amazing. Then, right before *Kansas City*, I was ready to throw in the towel with designing. I was very disillusioned. I told myself, "If this is meant to be, some incredible thing will happen and tell me I'm on the right path." Two weeks later, I got a call from Bob to come interview for *Kansas City*. It was a life-changing event.

Bob was such a class act. He had beautiful vision about things, and he inspired you to do your best work. You didn't even know why. You just had to do really great stuff in Bob's presence. He never put the pressure of failure on you. He wasn't tyrannical. Quite the opposite. He wanted you to express yourself and come up with ideas. Every day I just wanted to get in there and keep his vision going.

Bob had this way of using his hands in the most beautiful fashion. When he directed, it was as if he was conducting an orchestra in front of the monitor. You'd just watch his hands go. He was almost coaxing the actors on somehow. On *Kansas City*, the two women were instruments in his mind—one was a saxophone and one was a clarinet. It was all integrated—the sounds, the sights, the color. It was a universe he was creating and you got swept up into that.

Bob had many sides, but he was always Bob. He would be happy with a piece of peach pie and vanilla ice cream, and Kathryn's fabulous macaroni and cheese. Then he'd get dressed up in his white dinner jacket to receive an honor and he'd look like this total movie star. You'd go to France with him and the whole country was ready to kneel at his feet at Cannes. I watched these young people follow him around in the middle of the night like he was the Pied Piper. Yet at the same time, he was just Bob.

MICHAEL MURPHY: One night he was waxing a little philosophical. We were driving along and he says, "Isn't this weird, the way we spend our lives? You get dressed up in these funny clothes and I tell you where to stand" [*laughs*]. Even when he wasn't feeling well, he was always fun on the set.

FRANK W. BARHYDT (screenwriter): He was having trouble breathing. I remember being in his trailer one time and he said, "I don't know what I'm going to do after this. Can't get insurance." He was kind of emotional. Made me feel awful. It was a tough time for him. A very tough time for him. However it is you feel when you're sick. Angry. Like your body is letting you down, I think.

MATTHEW SEIG (producer): During *Kansas City*, he got sick, and a group of us were called to his house in the early morning. I don't think it was light out yet. And we got the call that Bob was sick and the doctor had been there and we should come by. And it was clear that by that time he already knew that he had to take at least a few days off. And you know the whole thing was real shaky. And so Bob says, "Well, we're not going to work. We got to take three days off. And don't file an insurance claim because I'll never be able to work again."

Robert Altman surrounded by jazz musicians on the set of Kansas City

Well, how are you going to not work and not file an insurance claim? We ran out of money. I mean, the budget was like totally shot. We spent the contingencies; there was no money. You can't just take three days off. The completion-bond people get the daily production reports every day. They watch what's going on. If you're not shooting and you haven't filed an insurance claim, you're in deep shit.

He was really sick and he probably wasn't thinking clearly, but that is the first thing that would come to Robert Altman's mind—"We've got to protect my ability to work; that's the most important thing."

He obviously had had heart problems, we knew that. He had to change his diet and he had to stop drinking, which he did by cutting down to white wine for a while. It didn't stop things. But it all fell apart in Kansas City. It was so incredible—between Scotty getting sick and then Bob, it was a really cursed production.

*   *   *

Lynn Elber, story headlined "Movie Snub Spotlights Politics of Oscar Campaigns; Robert Altman's *Kansas City* **Left Out of Race By Distributor,"** *The Associated Press*, **January 31, 1997:** If Robert Altman's *Kansas City* receives any Academy Award nominations, the director won't have Fine Line Features to thank. The distributor of Altman's jazz-soaked movie set in the Missouri city of the 1930s declined to mount an Oscar campaign for the film or its actors, including the critically praised Harry Belafonte. While industry trade papers are thick with ads touting such unlikely Oscar contenders as the Sylvester Stallone flop *Daylight*, academy voters won't have their memories jogged by *Kansas City* hype. Nor will they find Fine Line video cassettes of the movie in mailboxes crowded with tapes from other Oscar hopefuls: Altman footed the $18,000 bill to send the movie to some in the Academy, including the performing branch. "I just think it's such disrespect to Harry Belafonte I can hardly stand it," said Altman. . . . Although Fine Line declined to comment officially, a company executive called its action sensible for a small firm saddled with a money loser like *Kansas City*.

WREN ARTHUR (producer): He was so hurt by *Kansas City*. He felt let down by the people who were releasing it, and he felt let down by the critics. They just really went after it. It was my first experience in any of this and I was shocked because I thought *Kansas City* was a beautiful movie. It was like a really lovely jewel and I thought the performances were great. But everybody went after it with such a passion. And some of them did the same on every film after that, too. Bob got that. His work was always going to be compared to something it wasn't. Why wasn't it *Nashville*? Why wasn't it *Short Cuts*? Why wasn't it *The Player*? He was really hurt. Not that it stopped him.

* * *

KATHRYN REED ALTMAN: He was frighteningly thin. They were trying all kinds of stuff. They barely got him through *Kansas City*. That was a big one. It was the heart. It was giving up.

KONNI CORRIERE: At some point we went to a doctor at Cedars-Sinai and he said, "Have you ever thought of a transplant?" We were elated. Absolutely, positively, one hundred percent yes.

KATHRYN REED ALTMAN: The doctors said one of the main sources of hearts for transplants are motorcycle accidents.

KONNI CORRIERE: On the way home, it was raining. And Bob said, "I hope we see a motorcyclist."

KATHRYN REED ALTMAN: It wasn't very long. We signed up for the program in September 1995. The wait can go on forever—you have no idea how long it can go on. Then December fourth they called and said, "Come right down." Konni, Bob, and I went. He'd taken a sleeping pill, Ambien, but it had no effect on him whatsoever. He drove us to Cedars-Sinai and they put him in a room. We had to wait until the team went up to San Jose to get the heart. I saw the heart come in—in a bucket, one of those coolers.

He was really lucky, never had any rejection. He was home by Christmas, walking around Malibu buying presents. It was phenomenal because I don't know how much longer he could have lasted.

We kept it a secret. There was a big stigma on heart-transplant surgery, more than on bypass or double bypass. He wanted to work more. He wasn't through working. So he didn't want people to know. Until he had four or five pictures under his belt. Then he began slipping it into conversation, and people didn't seem to get it. Once in a while somebody would say, "Transplant?! Did you just say transplant?!" [*Laughs*] He'd tell people it was a young woman's heart, but they never tell you. He made up that story. The original story I gleaned from them was that it was a young man, but we don't really know.

Lois Smith (press agent): I remember getting a call from a member of the press—it might have been Army Archerd—and he'd heard. I said, "That's ridiculous. He was just in and out for a checkup." I don't think he bought it.

Army Archerd, column in *Variety*, December 7, 1995: Good wishes are out to director Robert Altman, who underwent heart transplant surgery Sunday. Altman had known the surgery was necessary since last March, friends say.

David Levy: Bob called Army up and said, "Oh, that's a complete lie. That's bullshit." And he demanded some kind of retraction or correction, which happened. He just didn't want the world to know or think that at that time.

The return of the king, three weeks after his heart transplant

"Celebrity Briefs," *USA Today,* **December 8, 1995:** If you heard Robert Altman had a heart transplant, we happily report it's untrue. Though he has heart problems, he's fine: He'll be fishing next week.

* * *

JERRY WALSH (friend/lawyer/executor): When he first went to work on *The Player* he hadn't done anything that produced any money for some time. I guess *Vincent & Theo* was probably the last thing, and there wasn't a lot of money in that. He got some substantial money in 1989 or 1990 from a project that fell through—about the Italian opera composer Rossini, called *Rossini! Rossini!* Then through '91 or so there had to be two or three years there that were very fallow. Because of the success of *The Player*, Bob got to make *Short Cuts* and then he also got to make *Prêt-à-Porter* and *Kansas City*. All those things brought substantial money. But after that he kept saying, "I can't understand why I don't have more money."

I said, "You'd been building up that debt that we never paid off."

He sold the big Malibu house and he got out of debt, that was in the eighties. And then he started borrowing against the Malibu condominium, and he borrowed against his apartment here in New York, and he had a line of credit with a bank that finally cut that off at some point. And so when we finally did get the money, of course there were substantial taxes to pay on it, and then there was substantial debt to pay off. And he really got pretty comfortable by the middle nineties, but I don't think he ever had more than maybe two million in the bank that he hadn't committed to something. But then, making the next picture was always more important than his bank account.

MATTHEW SEIG: Bob was never a New York independent filmmaker. A lot of people thought of him that way. That's totally ridiculous. He was completely Hollywood. He had big appetites, he liked to spend a lot of money. He liked to gamble. New York filmmakers don't gamble. New York filmmakers don't spend money. Bob would be broke and he'd say, "We're going to Cannes and we're going to rent a yacht."

And he would have no money and yet we would have to come up with some way to rent a twenty-five-thousand-dollar yacht for a weekend, so he could go there and be Robert Altman. That's the way Robert Altman was. You didn't go and sleep on somebody's couch. You went there and put on a party, because you were Robert Altman. And that was part of how he was going to get the next picture, by never admitting that he didn't have any money.

JERRY WALSH: I said to him once, "You know, Bob, I think your ambition is to spend the last nickel you've got on the day before you die."

He said, "Jerry, I'm much more ambitious than that. I want to find somebody to lend me a lot of money and spend *that* before I die" [*laughs*].

*   *   *

KATHRYN REED ALTMAN: After the surgery, he was recuperating, January, February of '96, and that whole year was learning how to live with this and handle possible rejections and medications and a whole regime.

By the end of '96 he had formed a little half-assed company and signed up to produce this TV anthology called *Gun*. He directed the first one between Christmas and New Year's of '96 and we came here to New York for '96 New Year's Eve. It was really exciting, he looked like a million bucks, he was really back with it, in perfect health, and then '97 his first picture started in January, *The Gingerbread Man*.

The Gingerbread Man *(1998)*

Christopher Tookey, review headlined "Branagh's Pursuit of a Hit Is Gone With the Wind," *Daily Mail* **(London), July 24, 1998**: Director Robert Altman and star Kenneth Branagh have had up-and-down careers, and *The Gingerbread Man*, based on a short story by John Grisham, is a low point. It's a would-be thriller about (surprise, surprise) a thrusting young Southern attorney (played by Branagh). . . . He becomes carnally, legally and foolishly involved with a mysterious woman (Embeth Davidtz) who wants him to ensure that her deranged husband and seemingly dangerous father (Robert Duvall) is commited to the loony bin. Does she have an ulterior motive? . . . Why is Branagh's character being set up? Is he going to end, like other Grisham heroes, taking the law into his own hands and turning vigilante? The answers are stupefyingly obvious from the first half-hour. Altman's direction is half-hearted hackwork, terribly lacking in suspense and excitement. It's clear that he is using the picture to finance some movie he really wants to make.

*   *   *

KENNETH BRANAGH: He assumed a certain kind of cynicism about the business and yet he sort of was an embodiment of the phrase "This terrible business has been very good to me." One of the ways in which Bob protected himself from the excesses of his own enthusiasm and vulnerable-making passion was to be robustly practical about it. He might have told himself he was, but he wasn't really capable of being a mercenary gun for hire. What attracted him was the sort of creative partnership of what he naughtily hoped might be the creative collision between him and John Grisham.

It was a script that had been around for a little while that had some notoriety and sort of acclaim because it was by Grisham. And yet I think it was an early screenplay of Grisham's, so some people felt maybe it needed some work. I said, "Come back when you've found someone—a director." They said to my great surprise that Robert Altman was interested in it. It seemed to me to be a very interesting combination. When I spoke to Robert for the first time by telephone, he seemed to believe—in Altman terms—the Grisham structure was terrifically helpful. It was much more structured than Bob might normally allow and he was excited by that.

When I came to work on it, I found that with Bob there were very appealing contradictions. In the work, a man who clearly prepared and worried a great deal about what any particular day or scene would bring. But at the same time, he would leave a massive gap between his preparation and the mood and feeling and atmosphere in the scene. He would leave an enormous amount unplanned, so there was a spirit of creative anarchy. So you were never really sure how much Bob had set up and how much was happening before your very eyes.

He had the paint ready, the palette ready, the colors and the canvas ready, but he wouldn't plan the picture until we were all there.

An example is one short scene in a pet shop with two children. When I arrived on the unit base, they said Bob was down by the river, where a couple of hundred yards of festival was planned, a carnival. Bob says, "I want you to start here, Branagh. I want you to move toward the camera and on the way I want you to make stuff up."

I am in the cliché—I am working with animals and children. And I'm in a foreign accent. And it's not what I've planned for. He said, "That's good for you British actors to experience."

I asked, "Anything set up?"

"Yeah. The phone might ring."

And it did. When he said that, I knew he loved me and I knew it would be fine.

DAVID LEVY: With *Gingerbread Man*, just before it came out, he kind of went to war with Polygram, the financier/distributor of that picture. And it was so unnecessary. . . . After the fourth screening, they took the picture away from him, and they had some hack—I'm sorry, experienced, but a hack—recut the thing. And it was dreadful. And they tested that. And that screening's numbers were worse than the first one we ever did before we started making changes. So, faced with that reality, they gave the picture back to him, but they buried it. I want to say there were never more than seventeen prints in circulation, I think.

KENNETH BRANAGH: I think he was trying to create happenings in the film, to try and capture life in an unexpected way that at the same time worked inside familiar genres. He wanted to work in and subvert those genres. He was not a man who talked much about the first act or third act or the story-arc stuff. He didn't want knowable, tangible coherence. His sensibility was a poetic one that tried to embrace within a passion for cinema the American tradition of moviemaking and to infuse that with the poetic, sometimes anarchic deconstruction of the traditional architecture of genre films.

To have acted with Robert Altman, under his direction, was to have tasted a certain kind of freedom, sometimes a certain kind of fear, knowing that an invisible hand is holding yours through that process.

DAVID LEVY: That was just a horrible, horrible exercise, and he really got upset over it. He got sick over it and he went to the hospital. He was depleted. I don't know what the medical aspects of it were, but he was so depressed and bummed about that whole situation, which was still ongoing when he was in the hospital. He was saying things to me—I don't think I've ever told Kathryn this—that he was so utterly fatalistic. It was really worrisome. He's sitting there. "I've had a good ride, it's her I'm worried about." All this kind of stuff.

That is when Steve Altman and I got on a plane, took ourselves to

Mississippi, scouted the state up and down, seventeen cities and towns, to find the place to shoot *Cookie's Fortune*. We came back to that hospital room, we put a map up, we put the video in, and we had all kinds of pictures, and we put on a dog and pony show for him in the hospital, and he got juiced. He got really excited about making a movie again. I looked at that as a turning point, where he was able to put *Gingerbread* behind him and look forward to the next project. It's a cliché, but the work seemed literally like lifeblood in that instance.

CHAPTER 28

Mr. A and the Women

*

Cookie's Fortune *(1999)*

Janet Maslin, review headlined "From Altman, a Salome Story with Southern Sugar and Spite," *The New York Times,* **April 2, 1999:** The sweet assurance and guerrilla wit of Robert Altman's vintage ensemble films make a serenely captivating return with "Cookie's Fortune." In this seamlessly copacetic treat, Mr. Altman once again dreams up a well-rounded community of symbiotic oddballs, then effortlessly lures the viewer into their world. With a fine cast working on a single, nicely eccentric wavelength, he and the screenwriter Anne Rapp turn picturesque Holly Springs, Miss., into a hotbed of grudges, power struggles, family secrets and historical footnotes, all presented with the same rueful overview.

*   *   *

ANNE RAPP (screenwriter): My ex-husband used to work with Bob Altman on his movies. He was an assistant director. They both loved the ponies and went to the racetrack a lot. Somehow that's how our relationship started. I had been working as a script supervisor for fifteen years, but I never held script for Bob.

A short story that I wrote was published. It was a one-page story—most of the fiction in Gordon Lish's publication was short fiction. I was script supervising on a movie in New York. Bob was cutting *Kansas City* in L.A. His editor at the time was Geri Peroni, and I was able to sublease her apartment in New York because she was in L.A. with Bob. So

Liv Tyler and Charles Dutton in Cookie's Fortune

we were conversing once a week about her mail. That was my very first published short story—so it was a very exciting time for me. I sent her one with her mail one week. I guess Bob picked it up and read it. He called me and said, "I love the story and I love the way you write." We had a conversation about how movies are much more like short stories than novels. I sent him a few more and he loved them.

I said, "Give me some time and let me write some more."

He said, "No, I need to read some more now."

I spent all weekend working on a bunch of stories I had written in

Mississippi. Bob was on a plane to the Berlin or Venice film festival with *Kansas City* and he read them on the plane and he called me from France.

He said, "I loved the stories and I want to put you under contract to write for me."

When Bob first hired me I was in the middle of this short story about an old woman on her way out who misses her husband and is lonely and is starting to struggle up the stairs. She makes the conscious decision that she is ready to join her husband in heaven. She's estranged from her family, but her nieces who discover her body are ashamed—and they cover up the suicide and it backfires.

He said, "How does it backfire?"

I had it one way, but Bob's the one who said, "Here's how you make it cinematic."

I abandoned the short story and wrote the movie.

The making of that movie, from script to finish, was the best time of my life. I've never had as much fulfillment in my heart about something I've done and created.

PATRICIA NEAL: The years pass and Roald is gone. If I have the story correctly, my daughter Lucy sees Bob Altman at Cannes. And he was so happy to see her—he knows her immediately. It was fantastic. They became good friends.

He told Lucy everybody was cast except my part, as Cookie. And she said, "My mommy is perfect for it."

She had a party and she invited him to look at me, and he decided then that Lucy was right. I had a great time doing it. I really did. He was a very good man. He just let you do what's natural. Had I ever played a suicide before? Oh God, I think I've killed myself lots of times.

* * *

Dr. T & the Women *(2000)*

Andrew Sarris, review headlined "When a Man Loves Too Many Women," *The New York Observer,* **November 19, 2000:** Robert Altman's *Dr. T & the Women,* from a screenplay by Anne Rapp, reunites the team responsible for *Cookie's Fortune* (1999), which I did not like very much. Hence my delay in catching up with *Dr. T*, since I do not enjoy bashing a director as admirable as Mr. Altman. To my surprise, *Dr. T* is quite wonderful, and not the least of its delights is the much-abused Richard Gere, in the seriocomic role of a Dallas gynecologist who finds himself engulfed in the world of womanhood until he can no longer think straight. . . . Dr. T does get a break of sorts by going out hunting with the guys, but these interruptions in Dr. T's woman-dominated routines are even more ridiculous and frustrating than the rest of Dr. T's chaotic life. Some critics have complained that *Dr. T & the Women* is misogynistic, but I think it is no more so than Buster Keaton's brilliant *Seven Chances* (1925). Mr. Altman is never condescending to the women, only somewhat fearful of their amazing power and persistence.

ANNE RAPP: I never had any sense that Bob was a misogynist in life or in his work. I know Bob loved women and wanted to be around women. He was more comfortable in the world of women than in the world of men. He would be the first to tell you that. I think what happened was when Bob wrote the scene with Hot Lips in *M*A*S*H*, it was something that no one had done before. It was a shocking thing and no one ever let go of that. I think critics look for a place to call Bob misogynistic. They look for that with Bob because of that one scene. He did the same thing with Julianne Moore with *Short Cuts*—all Bob did was something that nobody had done before. How many scenes have you seen with women naked on top? Another director would have had her spill wine on her top and have a sexy scene with her topless or in a lacy bra. Bob did something different.

At the Toronto Film Festival, before we even started, before anyone even asked a question, Bob said, "I just want to say one thing. If anybody in this room has a question about misogyny, I want to just point out that this film was written by a woman." Everyone in the room laughed. He just set the tone right there.

Announcement headlined "Women in Film to Present 'Mentor Award,' to Robert Altman," November 15, 2001: From Altman's first project to his upcoming release of *Gosford Park*, he has mentored hundreds of women—from producers, to writers, to costume designers. Altman has also directed numerous celebrated actresses in such films as *M*A*S*H*, *Images*, *3 Women*, *A Wedding*, *Nashville*, *Short Cuts*, *The*

Player and *Prêt-à-Porter*. "It is especially fitting for Women in Film to honor Robert Altman with the 2001 Mentor Award since he has been at the forefront of discovering, nurturing and showcasing some of the most important women working in entertainment for more than five decades," said WIF president Hollace Davids.

ROBERT BENTON: Altman was a very complicated person. Altman's history with people is like this. When they did the first picture together, *Cookie's Fortune*, he loved Anne Rapp. She did a great job. The second picture, *Dr. T & the Women*, everything she did he changed. It was as though he couldn't stand that everybody loved the script of *Cookie's Fortune*. He was not going to let that happen again.

He is like the scorpion in the story of the scorpion and the frog. The scorpion says, "I can't get to the other side of the river. Will you carry me across on your back?" The frog says, "What? I can't do that, you'll just sting me." The scorpion says, "Why would I sting you? We'd both drown." The frog says, "Okay." Suddenly, in the middle of the river, the scorpion stings the frog. As he's drowning, as he's going down, he says to the scorpion, "Why?" The scorpion says, "I can't help it. It's my nature."

ANNE RAPP: Bob has a reputation as being difficult on writers. You won't hear that from me. I would show him something, and if I did nine things horribly and there was one little seed, one little character, one line that worked, his eyes would light up and he'd say, "That's it, you hit the nail right there! Now take that and go write that."

I would walk out of his office and feel like I kicked ass. Any other Hollywood meeting I was in, they'd rake you over the coals about those nine things you did wrong. Bob had that ability to make you walk out of his office and feel like running back to your computer. He had an amazing way of dealing with artists in vulnerable positions.

Everyone thinks Bob goes in there and purposely changes it and lets the actors do something different. What he does is tell the actors, "You can do whatever you want in the scene. If you love the script, do it." Luckily enough, on *Cookie* the actors liked the script enough that they could do the script.

I was making less money than I was making as a script supervisor. But look at what I was getting to do: He gave me something that was priceless, to get two movies made in three years. Screenwriters write their whole life and don't get anything made. He started an entire career for me. He gave me the chance. There's a part of me that would have done it for nothing. The reason Bob didn't pay people very well was he often had to scrape to get his movies made. He went the total independent route for the better part of his career. He was making movies on a shoestring, so everybody is going to get shoestring wages. A lot of people bitch and complain a bit because you can get paid in this industry very well. I would hear grumbling and complaining, but it was never an issue for me. He knew that in the movie business, everyone is going to change you and exploit you to the best of their ability. But he never did. He never took advantage of me.

I felt like a good writer for the three years when I was with Bob. I have had nothing but doubts since.

* * *

Obituary in the *Los Angeles Times*, March 8, 2000: Tommy Thompson, veteran producer of television's "The Lucy Show" who also worked extensively on the films of Robert Altman, has died of a heart attack. He was 73. Thompson died Friday during location shooting of the Altman film that he was co-producing, "Dr. T and the Women," starring Richard Gere.

* * *

Robert Altman, from DVD commentary on *Dr. T and the Women:* It's so expensive to make these films that if you don't have success you're suddenly going to be in a position where you can't make 'em. You're not going to be able to raise the money to make the films. That would be a disaster in my life, because that's all I do, it's all I care to do, it's all I desire. It's where I get my kicks. It's where I exercise my mind. To suddenly find out that you can't do that anymore, because people don't like what you do, can be quite dreadful.

DAVID LEVY: His time in the wilderness, if you will, was maybe a bit humbling, and while he remained very, very true to his principles, he wasn't interested in going back to the wilderness, okay? He wanted to keep working and keep making pictures. I can cite you a number of times in the last fifteen years when he walked away from projects he could have had because he didn't like the direction they were going or the way things were smelling. But by the same token, he wanted to keep working, because for him work was play and he wanted to stay in the game. I think he was maybe more observant, maybe more considerate of the other elements in what I'll call the business process of things than he had been earlier. Because the world was his oyster and then that went away, I think he was just a bit more considerate of the money and the suits, because one must be if you're going to continue to get to do this.

ANNE RAPP: Bob made a movie every year. Every time he had one ready to go, all he was doing was talking up the next one. He didn't linger on the past, on successes or failures. I always told Bob he's like a farmer. When it's the season you plant and you water and you harvest. If you have a great crop it doesn't mean you don't plant the next season. And if you get hailed out one year you don't spend the next year licking your wounds over it. You get back out there and plant the next year's crop. A good farmer and a good artist just keep turning out the work. I'm not one of these people who revere the Salingers who disappear for twenty years. And then everybody's like, "Oh my God—the artist is back!" Bob never went into the cave.

David Thompson, story headlined "Robert Altman's Decade of Astonishments," *The New York Times*, June 11, 2000: "Short Cuts" (1993) may be his last major work, and we may not have much reason to expect more from a man his age. But old man Altman is about as easily classifiable as the Luis Buñuel of his own 70's. In other words, watch out, and remember that he has been written off too many times for critics to feel secure.

CHAPTER 29

Home Stretch

*

Amy Barrett, Q&A headlined "Questions for Robert Altman; Arrogance Is Bliss," *The New York Times,* December 16, 2001:

Q: You've made some of America's most celebrated films. But your last couple have had a markedly different reception. Do you have any sense of how your latest, "Gosford Park," might fare?
A: I think every one is going to be the greatest thing since hash.
Q: Since hash or since "M*A*S*H"?
A: Hash, I said.
Q: Right, hash.

* * *

Dialogue from *Gosford Park:*

CONSTANCE TRENTHAM *(Played by Maggie Smith)*: Tell me, how much longer are you going to go on . . . making films?
IVOR NOVELLO *(Played by Jeremy Northam)*: I suppose that rather depends on how much longer the public want to see me in them.

Gosford Park *(2001)*

Stephen Holden, review in *The New York Times,* December 21, 2001:
Robert Altman's film "Gosford Park" . . . is a virtuoso ensemble piece to rival the director's "Nashville" and "Short Cuts" in its masterly

Bob Balaban, as movie producer Morris Weissman, and to his left Jeremy Northam, as actor Ivor Novello, in Gosford Park. *Behind them are Natasha Wightman and Tom Hollander.*

interweaving of multiple characters and subplots. The film, set in November 1932, takes place on a grand country estate where well over a dozen aristocrats and their servants gather for a weekend shooting party during which their host, Sir William McCordle (Michael Gambon), is murdered. . . . Hatreds and rivalries abound both upstairs and below, and sexual shenanigans cross class boundaries. . . . What makes the achievement of "Gosford Park" all the more remarkable is that Mr. Altman is 76. If the movie's cool assessment of the human condition implies the dispassionate overview of a man who has seen it all, the energy that crackles from the screen suggests the clear-sighted joie de vivre of an artist still deeply engaged in the world.

*   *   *

Bob Balaban (actor/producer/director): I met Bob at the Sherry-Netherland Hotel when he was casting *Brewster McCloud*. I was just one of a number of young men who might have been right for the part of the boy who flies in the Houston Astrodome. We got to be friendly over the years, twenty-five or thirty years, because of my cousin Judy, whose father used to be the president of Paramount, Barney Balaban. Judy knew everybody in Hollywood. Over the years we just got friendlier, 'cause he was so friendly and Kathryn was so outgoing and adorable.

I had produced and directed some movies myself and developed some things for television, and I was sitting around one day, going, "What wonderful director do I know who if I came to them with a movie, a movie might actually get made?" And I thought, "Well, there's Robert Altman. I know him, he does brilliant things, he's very outside the box, so he won't mind that I'm not really a producer, exactly."

I thought it would be really, really interesting to put Robert Altman in a very traditional circumstance, which would mean England. And I came in with only the basic germ of the idea, which is funny because my character—this movie producer—says basically the same thing in *Gosford Park*. They say, "What's the movie about?" And basically I just say what I said to Bob the first time we talked about this. You know, a bunch of rich people get together at a country house for the weekend, around 1930. I didn't say this in the movie, but I told Bob it should have as many earmarks of a traditional Agatha Christie plot as we could muster. Somebody gets killed and they think it's one of the party guests, but of course it didn't have to be. And when I said that, Bob was intrigued.

He said, "The only thing is, I don't really like the upper class too much. How about we just have this take place with all the servants?"

And I said, "Well, obviously you should do anything you want, but if you like this idea, I think you're going to enjoy being bound by some of the conventions of this traditional murder mystery, 'cause then you can press against it and destroy the convention if you want. But I think you're going to enjoy the tension that that creates."

One of the things Robert loved to do that I thought just worked especially well in this movie was having two worlds going on at the same time. He loved intercutting back and forth. There was such a great energy and a feeling of life when you have two series of lives going on together.

When we got organized to do *Gosford Park*, there came the point when we needed a writer, and I suggested to Robert that Julian Fellowes would probably be a wonderful choice. So Bob talked to him on the phone. Julian was really aware that this was possibly going to be his big break in show business, which it was. And not everybody is like this, but Julian's ears perked up immediately. "Okay, I'll be there tomorrow, I'll write everything." He was so accommodating. He wrote a two-page treatment, which immediately meant he knew more than we possibly would know. Because you had to know what happened in a British house in the country when you had these parties there. We didn't know. We never would have known. Julian came from that world. He knew.

JULIAN FELLOWES (actor and screenwriter): I was a complete unknown. I had a couple of children's TV scripts made. I thought, "Obviously, this isn't going to happen." It's like something out of a Hollywood musical—a completely unknown actor is invited to write a script and the script gets made and it's a hit.

BOB BALABAN: We thought we had financing lined up. It was enough to get Bob over to London, and we began to spend our own money— Bob and I financed the screenplay, we financed the preproduction, and it was all very frightening. And he was over there in London. Mary Selway, our casting director, a brilliant, wonderful woman, was calling actors, and everybody wanted to meet with Bob. He would have tea in his hotel and actors would come by and he'd just charm them to death. And they would commit to being in the movie without dates or a contract or anything else.

And it fell apart. And in between it falling apart and coming back together, we tried everything. One of Bob's old investors said that if Bob would rewrite the last thirty pages and make it be much more satisfying of a murder mystery, he would give us like eighteen million dollars. Well, that's a lot of money. We could have had salaries. You know, not that it was an uncomfortable shoot, but it would have been nice to have made money. And Bob was like, "No, this is the movie. I'm not rewriting the movie for you."

So then the investor said, "Well, okay, I'll give you twelve million."

At that point Bob said, "We'll get it somewhere else. I'm not going to make the movie with somebody who tells me how to rewrite my movie."

And you know, he was right, actually. So we did end up with about eleven or something like that. But in between it was terrifying. I'd be calling Bob all the time. We'd have our lists—you call this one, I'll call this one. Nobody wanted to invest in it. They didn't like the script, basically.

JULIAN FELLOWES: For the people putting up the money, it was all terribly frightening. Here was this film about this very arcane world that nobody knew the rules about. For one thing, the servants took their employers' names downstairs—it was quirky. The executives couldn't understand it. They said, "Bob, this film already has more characters than the Second World War and now they all have the same name!"

BOB BALABAN: The first thing that struck us, both of us, about the screenplay was the fact that all of the servants are referred to by the name of the person who's their master. They didn't have identities, even. And you didn't even have to comment on it, you know what I mean, it was just like, "Oh, Jesus Christ, these people aren't even important enough to have a *name*. They're just named for the guy upstairs." That said more about Robert's take on the world than anything else you could have had in the movie.

What you couldn't tell when you read the script was the way that Bob would develop these nasty petty little people who lived upstairs, the rich people. Bob was a painter and all of these characters were blips and dabs that all came together, but you couldn't see it until you stood back and looked at the canvas, really. So people who read it didn't like it. There were too many characters, and it wasn't a murder mystery at all. At one point during preproduction Bob laughingly, but seriously, said, "Let's not solve the murder at all."

So Julian and I were like, "Um, maybe it would be a good idea to solve the murder."

And in fact I think it frightened people, the investors, to see Robert Altman directing a movie that you're used to seeing from Merchant Ivory because it had to be respectful and Bob is not respectful.

JULIAN FELLOWES: Every time they wanted to replace me—"Maybe someone could come in to do a little fixing, a little polish"—Bob just wouldn't let it happen. You have to be very unafraid. There is something about the film industry that is very castrating. There's so much money involved, and they're talking to you, and your whole brain becomes this negotiation party. Bob was stronger than all that. I have absolutely no hesitation to saying that—not just keeping me on as sole writer, but also holding on to the details of this obscure way of life, of this class that had been forgotten, in this country that is tiny—that is one hundred percent due to him.

BOB BALABAN: Everything that frightened people about the movie was the thing that Bob loved about the movie. Bob liked large noisy groups of people. And that's how he liked to live. And he liked them in his movies. I know people have said this, but in a way Bob's movies were all one long movie. And it was in some ways like his life. They didn't come to a lot of conclusions at the end. Sometimes it was very hard to tell the good guys from the bad guys—there's not a lot of black and white clashing around. It's all pretty complicated. And he loved large groups of people.

It was fine in the beginning. As we got closer to production and as there was less financing and he was in London and I was here in New York and we were desperately looking for money, the peaks and the valleys were enormous. He could be very quixotic and he could be very temperamental, but it wasn't without cause. And it was certainly understandable. But in a way, you could say he had two different natures. The nature that kept everything in his head and worried and worried and worried, and he was thinking about making the movie and also holding in his mind the possibility that this thing that he had now fallen in love with might not happen. And there he was in England and practically mortgaging his house, as we were all thinking of doing, and so the strain financially was horrendous.

But you must think of movies as childbirth for Bob, which they were, and they were all his children. There were no stepchildren among them. It didn't matter what anybody else thought about the movie, they were all equally beautiful and blonde and blue-eyed, all of them. There was that terrifying period when his child might not get born, and he was in love already and it was the thing he lived for. So he was very irascible when it was shaky.

When we were doing *Gosford Park* I was aware that there were a number of other movies he was also trying to work on. I didn't want them to fall apart but I wasn't unhappy when I realized that the laws of attrition were saying *Gosford Park* is going to be the one that we're going to have to make. And in fact, he had to make the movie. Nobody in their right mind would go sit in London and meet Maggie Smith and Clive Owen and Helen Mirren and a thousand other people. It didn't make sense. Why would you go and do that before your financing was set? How could you do that? And yet, he knew that everything was going to help it move forward. So, as scary as it was, as the tightrope walk was getting more and more dangerous, it was imperative that he be acting as if the movie were going to get made because that would help it get made.

DAVID LEVY: We got to London, three of us, Bob and Steve Altman and I, and I believe it was Halloween night of 2000. We went out with this Sri Lankan guy who was allegedly going to finance the picture. We got back from dinner, the three of us, and it was, "Well, this is going to work out, isn't it?" And I said no. I said, "I don't care how many times the guy's banker called him during dinner, this isn't going to happen with this guy." Sure enough. So we spent a couple of months in a very

Directing Emily Watson, as maid/lover Elsie, in Gosford Park

tough place while all the casting was going on and key crew was being recruited.

STEPHEN ALTMAN: David Levy, myself, and Bob went and lived in a little apartment in London, and he just started reeling in the fish. He had a script and no money and the investors were all fakes or not to be trusted. And it's, "Hello, Maggie Smith? Do you want to be in this movie?" "Is anybody else in it?" "Well, I'm seeing Michael Gambon tonight." As soon as those two say yes, everyone is like, "Oh sure, Bob, anything. If you get a movie we'd love to work with you." Pretty soon he's got thirty-five superstars, all working on his picture. We would put the actors' pictures up on the walls when the investors came over. I made a model of the set, which I actually used for the movie. But it was all dog and pony con show. We were doing *The Sting.* But for a good reason. We wanted to make some money [*laughs*]. We wanted the picture to go, no matter what it was.

BOB BALABAN: The minute we started really getting close to shooting, it was as if somebody had given him a hundred tranquilizers. He was just enormously happy in a way that spread everywhere he went on the set. You could hear it in his headset. Everybody on the set was happy. Everybody who worked on the set was thrilled to see him—the makeup people, the hair people, anybody working on the set actively. He was just gloriously happy. But he was really a mess before we started.

*   *   *

JULIAN FELLOWES: Bob realized it was kind of a minefield, this whole class thing. He knew that if you were doing some world, if you got all the details right, even people who didn't know this world would accept its accuracy. It would smell right. He wanted it to be specific—not BBC servant acting, wandering around with a tray. Part of that was he asked me if I would be on the set for the whole shoot. With Bob this was unusual. He and I said my job was to stop him from making a mistake by accident. Of course, a director says that, but then they want everything they want to do not to be a mistake.

He wanted Mary to be in the dining room. There's no reason for a lady's maid to be in a dining room. We'd have these spats. What amazes me now was in the whole time we worked together he never once pulled rank. He never said or even implied, "I am a world-famous director with a million films behind me, and who are you?" We were just these two fat men fighting. That is a paradigm of the man. He was never afraid to fight for what he wanted, but by the same token he never felt he had to use unfair weapons. And I really love him for that.

The role of the writer in film is an odd one. You are the one part of the creative team that everyone wants to forget exists. The audience wants to think their favorite actor said and did all these wonderful things, and the director wants to think it all came from his mind. And the writer is the one member of the creative team that can be fired up to the last day. We're like plastic surgeons. Hollywood couldn't exist without them but nobody wants to know our names.

Bob Balaban: Bob knew enough about what he didn't know to make sure that Julian was on the set every second. Of course, by the end of it he wanted to kill Julian, which was no surprise to me. Julian would say to Bob, "See that maid in the distance? She's coming down the stairs. She wouldn't be carrying coffee. There would be no toast on her plate. This is eleven o'clock, she would have hard-boiled eggs. . . ."

Julian Fellowes: The standard thing in Hollywood is to direct the camera with a movement on the scene. The dog goes down the walk and the camera follows the dog, and it leads to the body. With Bob, the dog goes one way and the camera goes the other. He creates this illusion in the mind of the spectator that they are directing the camera. It becomes an autonomous being that is moving around the room. Because you are the viewer, you take responsibility for the image. You are given the impression that you are exploring this film.

David Levy: Bob would give a listener the impression that he would show up on a set with a bunch of actors and they'd stir a pot and a movie would come out. Julian comes from the place where he'll tell you that exactly one line of Gosford was unscripted, Maggie Smith's line "Difficult color, green," talking about Claudie Blakley's frock. All I'll say is those are both revisionist histories.

As someone who rode to the set every morning with Bob in the car, I fought hard for Julian's script. But Bob would scribble in the morning and try and change things and Julian worked very, very hard to beat the deadline that morning of trying to take whatever changes there were and incorporate them officially and formally and get those to be the words the actors did say on the day. So I understand what he means when he says every line was scripted save one. But it doesn't give the most accurate impression. But it's more accurate than Bob's assessment of we made it up as we went along.

BOB BALABAN: Certainly *Gosford Park* was not an improvised movie, but you got the feeling when you saw it that it was an improvised movie. There were enough sections that were improvised so that the actors really got in the skins of the people they were playing, even if they weren't playing terribly well-developed characters.

DAVID LEVY: I can tell you one thing that was spontaneous. We were at lunch one day. Helen Mirren had come in for hair, makeup, and wardrobe tests. Eileen Atkins had already been working in the picture. Eileen was in costume because she was shooting that day. And Helen was there in some form of costume and hair and makeup, not fully developed at that point. I was sitting at one table, Bob was a table away from me, and the women were off to one side at yet another table. And I saw his eyes kind of get big and he called me over. He starts pointing at them. "They're sisters. They're sisters."

He thought a large part of that picture's success and appeal in terms of audience was because of that cathartic moment at the end that the sisters had. And you know, it's something that I don't think we'd have seen from the Bob of twenty years prior. Well, he might have thought it, but he wouldn't have said it. I think it really comes as close to wrapping a package and tying it up with a bow as he would ever, ever do.

JULIAN FELLOWES: Those two actresses ad-libbed that. But for the most part of the film that was not so. This was very difficult for Bob in a way. I think he wanted to be an auteur director and it was hard for him to accept the importance of script. That was just difficult for him.

*   *   *

Rick Lyman, story headlined "'A Beautiful Mind' Wins Four Golden Globes," *The New York Times,* **January 21, 2002:** One of the evening's bigger surprises, and the source of the longest ovation, was Robert Altman's winning the best director award for "Gosford Park," a murder mystery set on an English country estate. "Gosford Park" was widely seen as a solid return to form for one of the legendary American directors of the 1970's.

Bob Balaban: The Academy Award thing mattered, if only financially. If it did win Best Picture, that was going to be another twenty-five million. It had already done enormously well. So it was very pressured. It lasted a long time and it went on and there was a lot of dirty fighting during it, which happens in Academy Award things. Trying to dig up things you said and what you did. In Bob's case it was easy to dig up things he had said.

Julian Fellowes: I think it was unfair that I won the Oscar and Bob didn't. I love Ron Howard and thought *Beautiful Mind* was a very good movie. But quite honestly I don't think it was quite as iconic a movie as *Gosford.* I think it was a very difficult time. I don't know about smear campaigns. I think that Bob misjudged the public mood about 9/11. For me, I was an Englishman. It seemed to me a terrible atrocity that had been visited on the United States and I felt very, very sorry for the people involved in it and sorry that it happened.

Bob was a very passionate political man. He had all sorts of feelings about American foreign policy. They were informed, literate opinions. He wasn't a rattling drum. He didn't understand that America wasn't yet ready to hear his reasoned opinions.

We were in Paris together and doing one of those junket things. We were together on the platform, and—"*Monsieur Altman, que pensez-vous de 9/11?*" And he came up with an impolitic answer. At the end of it, he turned to me and said, "Oh God, I think I can taste foot again."

I said to him, "It's just too soon. It's like walking into a maternity ward and saying, 'What's the matter with its ears?' "

Robert Altman quoted by the Associated Press in stories published October 18, 2001: The movies set the pattern, and these people have copied the movies. Nobody would have thought to commit such an atrocity unless they'd seen it in a movie. . . . How dare we continue to show this kind of mass destruction in movies? I just believe we created this atmosphere and taught them how to do it.

Jack Valenti, quoted in *The Daily News* (New York), October 19, 2001: That's a giant leap from movies to Osama Bin Laden.

Bob Balaban: There was a lot of buildup and a lot of lead-in and there was this smear campaign going on. I'm not sure if Robert was aware of the smear campaign. He didn't talk about it ever that I heard. But he probably knew.

It would have just been politic for him to shut up during the Academy campaign, but then, you wouldn't be Robert Altman if you were politic. If anything, when he came up against authority, instead of pacifying, it made Bob want to strike out. It was like flashing a red cape at a bull.

JULIAN FELLOWES: That was the man. If someone said, "Bob, could you tone it down a bit?" Well, he wasn't a big toner downer.

My own belief is that if 9/11 had not happened, the following March he would have won the Oscar.

BOB BALABAN: He was quite adorable the night of the awards. It was great how all the filmmakers and all the creative people weren't in a competition. They were just happy to be with people they respected. It was really nice. But you focus so much on winning, winning, winning. And that's so not what Bob would ever be about, you know? I'm not saying he would throw the race, but Bob would want there to be one giant thing where everybody won something. It didn't appeal to his socialist nature too much, declaring winners. But he was fine during the award.

Soon after, Bob called us all and said, "We're having a losers' party. Come to my house." And he was giddy. I think it was that we all had a reason to be together and to affirm our friendship. Because in a way, us all not winning together—well, Julian won, so in a way that made him persona non grata. But in a way it was a bond, having all gone through this amazing experience with this movie that people adored so much and then not winning anything. I think it almost made it more special. In a way. Because it didn't even have the seal of approval from those silly people who don't mean anything.

*   *   *

The Company (2003)

Roger Ebert, review in the *Chicago Sun-Times*, December 24, 2003: Why did it take me so long to see what was right there in front of my face—that "The Company" is the closest that Robert Altman has come

Neve Campbell and Malcolm McDowell in The Company.

to making an autobiographical film? I've known him since 1970, have been on the sets of many of his films, had more than a drink with him in the old days and know that this movie reflects exactly the way he works—how he assembles cast, story and location and plunges in up to his elbows, stirring the pot. With Altman, a screenplay is not only a game plan but a diversionary tactic, to distract the actors (and characters) while Altman sees what they've got. "The Company" involves a year in the life of the Joffrey Ballet of Chicago, during which some careers are born, others die, romance glows uncertainly, a new project begins as a mess and improbably starts to work, and there is never enough money.... "The Company" is his film about the creative process itself, and we see that ballet, like the movies, is a collaborative art form in which muddle and magic conspire, and everything depends on that most fragile of instruments, the human body.

*   *   *

Neve Campbell (actress and producer): I'd been a dancer most of my childhood and teenage life and moved into acting because I had a lot of injuries. I always had an idea in mind that there had never been a dance film that portrayed the world of dance in a realistic light. I didn't want to do the typical narrative film about one dancer who wants to make it and does.

I thought Barbara Turner, as a screenwriter, was very good at creating worlds—she does a lot of research. Over a period of about four years Barbara would go to Chicago to interview the dancers and basically ended up with hundreds of pages of conversations. We were throwing around names of directors—Barbara had worked with Bob in the past—and as soon as Bob's name came up we knew that he would be perfect.

BARBARA TURNER (screenwriter/actress/producer): I sent him the script mainly because I knew he would be the only person who would understand it. Because it was really about the dancers; it's really about them and it wasn't linear and it was all over the place. It was a year in their lives, basically.

One of the things he said to me was, "Now, Barbara, I want you to know that this is your script and it's wonderful, but it has to be my movie."

No bells went off yet. "I understand that, Bob, blah, blah, blah," I said.

So we get there and we start working. The script was long, and he said it has to be cut. Which I cut. He said, "What I want you to do is to take your ten favorite scenes, and make a list of them, because what's important to you is important to me."

And I did it. And he didn't shoot one of them. So I realized, "That's what he meant by it's got to be his movie."

It was painful but it was funny at the same time.

NEVE CAMPBELL: We knew even going in—not a lot of people are going to be interested in this. He would make it anyway. He was interested in it. That was enough for him, and maybe other people would become interested by seeing it.

Originally, Bob expressed some concern about the fact that he didn't know anything about dance, and he needed to be shown why the film should be made. We started flying to New York and he just asked me a lot about dance—why this film could be important and what it was like to be a dancer. I think the more I talked about the dance world and what sacrifices dancers make, the more he identified with it. Bob was very similar to dancers in that he's an amazing artist, he didn't do many things for commercial value, and he never made as much money as he could have if he had sold out in any way. So I think he related.

BARBARA TURNER: To the dancers, he was already a god when he walked on the set. He treated them with such respect, just the way he treats actors. He's amazing and respectful. They could just feel love pouring all over them.

ROBERT ALTMAN: I'd walk into the studio and there would be these beautiful girls with their legs spread apart, up in the air, and they'd think nothing of it. They'd call out, "Hi, Mr. A!" It made me feel young and old at the same time.

NEVE CAMPBELL: It's true—for dancers it's your tool, you almost forget how normal people behave with their bodies. I don't think Bob minded at all [*laughs*].

MALCOLM McDOWELL: He called me and said, "This young kid, Neve Campbell, she's brought me a script about dance. Can you dance?"

"No."

"Well, you don't have to."

He just loved these dancers. Fell in love with them and what they do—their dedication and their athleticism and artistry. And it was just wonderful to see him working with them.

And I remember my first day on the thing. We were rehearsing—the dancers were rehearsing in an outside theater. And I had to come on and, I don't know, do something.

And Bob sees me. "Mal!" I went over. And he says, "You got the scene?"

And I said, "Yeah, absolutely, I got it."

And he said, "Forget it."

I knew this was coming. I knew it was coming. He said, "Call the company together and inspire them."

Well, I figured that's a week's work. An hour later we had it in the can. I don't know what I said. I have no idea.

NEVE CAMPBELL: I love that it's a Robert Altman film. I like the fact that it doesn't tell you how to feel. It lets you make up your own mind about things. It's exactly what I envisioned and exactly what I wanted in the film. I said that to Bob. "I don't know how you've done it, but you've done exactly what I wanted to happen."

He said, "Well, I just listened."

I don't think there are many people who could have done that, who would have listened to another artist and known how to do it.

I would say Bob is the coolest person I met in my whole life. He wasn't an old-school cowboy. Besides, I don't know any eighty-year-old who could smoke as much pot as he could and still function.

CHAPTER 30

Fatherhood II

*

JERRY WALSH: The influence of Kathryn on him in terms of their children really began to have an effect. He extended himself for his children in his later years in a way that he hadn't before.

PETER GALLAGHER: Bobby was an operator on *The O.C.*, so I'd see Bobby all the time and I'd do impressions of Bob saying, "Cut! Cut!" Bobby in a way reminds you so much of Bob. I was on the phone with Bob a week or two weeks before he died, and he said, "How's Bobby doing?" I said, "You'd be so proud of Bobby. He's doing an awesome job. He's such an important part of this whole team." There was a softness and a naked kind of love in the way he said it. I don't know that he would have allowed himself such vulnerability earlier in his life.

STEPHEN ALTMAN: He mellowed in the last, I don't know, ten, fifteen years of his life, perceptibly. Everybody was like, "Oh my God, what a change!" But he had to stop drinking. I think the alcohol didn't really settle with him correctly.

After he mellowed, it got very good. We were collaborators, and once I got my act together, we started being friends and enjoying each other's company. I learned how to play backgammon, and that was his favorite thing. I would roll his joints for him and so I wasn't the long-haired slob that he was embarrassed to be seen with. But even with all that, the collaboration and the trust and the "What do you think, Stevie?," he always did things his way, no matter what. I still think he always kind of thought of me as a kid running around in diapers at the same time.

I remember him pushing my oldest son in the stroller, and it was

With son and favorite camera operator Robert (Bobby) Reed Altman

just like, "Oh, this is fun." You know, walking with the wife in the Tui-leries and strolling along and him being the granddad. Of course I said something rude like, "Oh, is that the first time you ever did that?" And he's like, "Yes, it is." But we were all good-natured about it.

MICHAEL ALTMAN: He certainly mellowed a lot. He used to be a tyrant, but he became a rather amiable character towards the end. He became very enamored of his family in the last ten years of his life, and that was because they wouldn't go away. He just kind of grew attached to everybody. And you know it kind of got bigger. But the five of us kids—the boys and Konni—early on, kind of like created our own fam-ily unit for lack of any other one. It was the only semblance of family that we had. And I'm not saying that with any kind of remorse or any-thing like that, it's just the way it was. It was fine. Me and Steve grew up with our mom and my stepdad and the summer vacations and holidays were out with my dad—you know, swimming pools and movie stars. And then the rest of the time it was refried beans and pot roast, which was great. We didn't know the difference. Basically, you know, there's the same amount of laughter and tears in both households, right?

The last few years we would have these get-togethers and I would catch him sitting in the corner just looking at everybody with this grin

*Kathryn and Robert Altman on the red carpet at the Berlin Film Festival
in 2006 (above) and at a gala to honor Jack Lemmon, in 1993*

on his face. And he would say something like, "Look what I made." It
was like one of his better movies. And that's kind of how he looked at it.
He became very enamored of the whole drama that he lived in. Like at
the end of his life he became aware that he was in his own movie.

KATHRYN REED ALTMAN: In the last ten years I think he realized how
he'd been as a father. I wish he could have been a little more involved,

but every time he had a chance he would play with them. They had their warm periods with him and memorable family games and funny songs. We had a couple of camping-out things. We did as much as you could do, living with a genius who was making a picture every second.

ROBERT ALTMAN: Looking back, I have great guilt about my lack of attention to my own children. I don't think I did well by my own children, who I think I had a responsibility to. I don't think I lived up to that responsibility. I think I was too busy looking after me. Kathryn and I talk about it now.

To keep the marriage together I'd take the family with me where I went on location. And consequently these kids were in different schools, and we sent them away to school, and they went to schools in Canada, and none of them went to college. Because the minute they were old enough to hold an apple box they were working. Consequently none of them are really supporting themselves, and it's sad. And the sadness is that this is my fault. Yet I don't know how I could have changed it. I was—what I was doing—was much more important than that. To me.

I can't go back up the river and think, "Jesus, I should have done something at that bend—that last bend." Because I didn't do anything at that last bend. As much as those thoughts hit me, they've become part of what I put into the work that I do. Because it's the accumulation of guilt. I don't think it's serious guilt, because I live with it. If you take me to any of those crossroads and say, "Okay, let's go back—now here you can do this," I don't think I'd do anything different. It would be false.

* * *

Dialogue from *Popeye:*

POOPDECK PAPPY (*Played by Ray Walston*): Children. They're just smaller versions of us, you know, but I'm not so crazy about me in the first place, so why would I want one of them? . . . Children. They cry at you when they're young, they yell at you when they're older, they borrows from you when they's middle-aged and they leave you alone to die. Without even paying you back.

CHAPTER 31

Boots On

*

A Prairie Home Companion (2006)

A. O. Scott, review headlined "Altman's Casual Chaos Meets Keillor's Rhubarb-Tinged Nostalgia," *The New York Times,* June 9, 2006: A late, minor addition to the Robert Altman collection—but a treasure all the same—"A Prairie Home Companion" is more likely to inspire fondness than awe. This is entirely appropriate, since the movie snuggles deep into the mood and sensibility of its source, Garrison Keillor's long-running public radio variety show. Beloved by tote-baggers across the land, Mr. Keillor's weekly cavalcade of wry Midwestern humor and musical Americana has never set out to make anyone's hair stand on end. Mr. Altman, a more cantankerous spirit (he comes from Kansas City, Mo., a wilder corner of the Midwest than Mr. Keillor's Minnesota), brings his unrivaled sense of chaos and his mischievous eye for human eccentricity. Together they have confected a breezy backstage comedy that is also a sly elegy: a poignant contemplation of last things that goes down as smoothly and sweetly as a lemon drop. . . . It's not a perfect movie, and it does not aspire to be a great one. It's just wonderful.

* * *

KATHRYN REED ALTMAN: Paul Thomas Anderson was there as a backup director because they wouldn't insure the movie without one.

PAUL THOMAS ANDERSON: Any hesitation? None. None at all, because I knew he wasn't going to die.

*With Lindsay Lohan, playing the downhearted Lola, and Meryl Streep,
playing her mother, the singing sister Yolanda Johnson,
in* A Prairie Home Companion

Bob's influence on me isn't something within his films. It's not the films themselves. It's him and the way in which he has *made* films. Whether the films worked or not was inconsequential to the treatment of the undertaking, the fun and the seriousness and the endeavor. It's not overlapping dialogue; it's not zooms. These are just technical things, you know? I know people feel that way, but I always felt that even more, the biggest thing is just the attitude. The attitude about them.

I just remember laughing with him. I mean laughing with tears rolling down our faces. John C. Reilly had this fart machine that he uses in the movie. No one really seems to know what it is—it's a fart. We wanted it to be like three farts, but I think it's two now. We were laughing so fucking hard. Reilly was laughing and everyone else was a bit like, "Guys, come on. Really? Are we doing this?"

And Bob's like, "Yes, it's great, it's perfect."

KEVIN KLINE (actor): Bob loved the infinite possibilities. The abiding potential of some wonderful accident or nonsensical, unconscious bit of behavior to emerge. Extraordinary.

The script was the script, but anything can happen, anything can evolve, anything can mutate into something else if he sees the possibility because an actor was generating some other thing. It's not largesse, it's trust. It's a willingness not to control, to let things happen that you didn't plan. Whenever I would ask Bob, "What do you think if I wear my hat during this scene? Do you think the jacket should be on or off?," he'd say, "Completely up to you."

It's not something I was terribly concerned about—just needed somebody to weigh in. Just to help me decide because I was teetering on the fence. Or I'd have a line, and I'd wonder, "What if I said . . ." He'd go, "Say whatever you want." Not in a tone that he's disinterested in what I'm saying. No, it's like, "Say whatever *you* want." Wow. Fantastic.

Early on, he was lying on the sofa in his office and he wasn't feeling well. We were talking about the character I play, Guy Noir. Reading the script, I get the sense that he was a detective but now he's been sort of relegated to doorman duty at a theater. And as the actor you don't want to sound too stupid—"So, he seems to be American, mid-forties, early fifties." No, you want to show great insight. So I'm sharing whatever few insights I might have had. And Bob says, "Well, you know, he's a nut."

I was like, "Oh."

It cut to the simple, obvious, core truth—which had eluded me—of the character. He's a nut. Oh.

He said to the whole cast, "There's going to be four cameras, and when the scene is over, it's not necessarily over. We're just going to move away and you will keep doing whatever you're doing because you're still part of the shot. So just keep living." Great, so you don't even know—"This is my close-up, this is my medium shot, this is on her." It's just happening. And the fact that we're in a theater too, backstage, onstage, whatever. Everything was in this kind of wonderfully liberating limbo of reality, unreality. Improvisation. Structure.

Bob loved saying, "You know, I just sat there. I didn't have to direct at all. They don't need me." It was in a self-deprecating way, feigning frustration. Because he had Meryl and Lily and Lindsay and it just happened. That was his way of complementing a well-written scene with highly skilled, inspired actors. But really, I think it's his idea. In other words, he doesn't *have* to do anything. He just knew where to put the cameras to capture what's evolving and to allow what's evolving to keep evolving.

Robert Altman with director Paul Thomas Anderson,
his friend and backup director, on A Prairie Home Companion

PAUL THOMAS ANDERSON: Bob is at his best working with the best actors. If you're mediocre, I don't think he's going to help you get past how much talent you might have. I don't think any director could do that, you know? No one talks about Bob Altman films and how well designed they were, you know? They talk about the performances and they remember the people in them.

ROBERT ALTMAN: Meryl Streep is *the* best. I don't have any idea what she's saying, whether it was in the script or not. I can't say, "Oh, that was good that you changed it there." I just accept what she delivers. And Lily, I can see Lily's mechanics working a little differently than Meryl does what she does. And yet, they're both doing the same thing—creating.

MERYL STREEP: He said that? Oh my. I don't know. I always wanted to work with him. Why? He was the cool guy. There were the auteurs, the grandiose kind of directors and the Europeans and the megalomaniacs. And then there was Bob. Bob just seemed to be the one who everybody wanted to work with, because it was more fun.

Somehow, until *Prairie*, things never worked out for us to work together. We worked on *Prairie* for nine days. *[She goes into a stage whisper]* Here's the secret—he probably said that about me because our time was so quick. I didn't wear him down like everybody else *[laughs]*.

We really hit it off. I loved the way he worked and I think part of it is that I like to work and so does he. He loves the chaos of it. The more capacious a talent, the more relaxed they seemingly are about letting everybody do their thing and invent. So people feel like, "Man, I can do anything I want on this set." When actors feel like they're perfectly safe to make big horrible mistakes, the thing really takes off.

He wants you to make your judgment as an actor but then be wrong about it. He wants you to make the big messy mistake because he might use it. He doesn't want people to be careful. He wants the full-throated performance. "Get out there and sing me the song, babe." He's not afraid as a director, so he doesn't want his actors to be afraid or measured. He had no use for it. He was impatient for just the true things, thank you. Actors love that permission. Give them that and they'll give you everything.

It's sort of like a kaleidoscope—he gets all the colors in there, but as he's shape-shifting it, he's not afraid to let the lights fall where they may. I think that's really it. Other, smaller talents are more jealous of it, and more worried about keeping control. "Are the actors getting together by the coffee machine and talking about a scene without me?" The great ones, like Bob, don't care about that, and in fact they hope you will.

Seemingly, he let the pets take control of the pet store. But he was totally in control. He just loved being the sun and having all these planets surrounding him.

The first day on *Prairie* we had the dressing room set up, with three actors in it. You quickly figure out there'll be a master and a midshot and coverage on three people. It's a long day. Then he says it's a ten-page scene. I thought, "Well, he can't do more than three pages a day."

Bob said, "We're going to shoot all ten pages today."

"No, you're not."

"Yes, we are."

I said, "Well, by the way, you have twenty-seven mirrors in this room, and you're going to have your camera in every shot. You're going to be looking at yourself."

He smiled and said, "No, I'm not."

Lily and I were in flop sweats. We hadn't learned all ten pages. The first day usually people say, "We're going to ease into this. We want you to be comfortable with the crew. Today we'll just have you getting in and out of the car." Who knew we were going to shoot ten pages the first day?! Who *does* that? Bob did.

* * *

ROBERT ALTMAN: I think Garrison Keillor and myself are very much in sync in this picture. When we get together, we do talks together, we don't get along. I don't think we like each other very much. And so consequently we're always vying for position for ourselves. But I think it turned out to be a pretty good piece of work.

MERYL STREEP: Bob and Garrison are both very cranky and they liked being cranky, so in a relationship that can be a challenge. But if there was tension, they kept it to themselves. In front of the kids they didn't fight.

* * *

PAUL THOMAS ANDERSON: The last day we shot the last scene, the one with Kevin with the garbage falling and him playing piano. That was the last thing that we shot. And Bob definitely had a melancholy feeling about him, in his face.

Because of the way the shot was, we were shooting the whole stage, so Bob was tucked over in Guy Noir's office. Sometimes you get in those horrible spaces where you just have to be for the shot. And he had a Starbucks coffee in his hand and his coat was zipped up because it was kind of cold in there and he had his glasses on. He was staring at the monitor and he just looked really sad that it was ending. I think we only did the shot twice. I remember sitting there thinking, "Fuck, do it again, do it . . . do more, do more." I wanted to do more—not 'cause it wasn't good, but I wanted to keep shooting.

MERYL STREEP: On the surface, *Prairie* is like Garrison's show. It seems to be this harmless piece of entertainment. But it has quite a serious intent and sort of a rage underneath it. Both of them brought that rage into it. They recognized it in each other. Bob at that point was rage, rage against the dying of the light.

ROBERT ALTMAN (*October 2006, one month before his death*): I didn't get it until we got to the end. I mean, if at any time in the shooting of this, someone had said, "What is this about?" I could not have said, "This is about death." Now, in retrospect, I can say this is about death because everyone is avoiding saying that. But that's what it's about.

*   *   *

Resurrection Blues *(Written by Arthur Miller, staged at the Old Vic Theatre, London, spring 2006)*

MATTHEW MODINE (actor): For Bob's last experience working as a director, the treatment that he received was cruel and inhuman.

SCOTT GRIFFIN (producer): I had been a friend of Arthur Miller since my early twenties, and while Arthur was writing this play I read an early draft, which I thought was terrific—a bold, different kind of play for Arthur. It's his parting shot at the American lust for money. It's about a South American dictator who decides to crucify a young revolutionary who the peasants believe is the next Jesus Christ, and to sell the rights to televise the crucifixion to Madison Avenue. The only problem is, he really *is* the next Jesus Christ, and problems ensue.

Arthur's wife died in 2002—tragically of cancer—and immediately after, Arthur was encouraged to rush the play into production, which was not necessarily the best move. The script was unformed, complicated, and needed work. The production was not well received.

Years later, Arthur told me they were doing *Resurrection Blues* in San Diego. I was going to California, and he asked me to go down there to check it out. The script had come a long way, but the production was directed with kind of a somber tone not in keeping with the piece. It's a satire, a sharply drawn satire. Arthur asked, "What do you think?"

I said, "It's a wonderful play, but who do you have to fuck to get a laugh in this show?"

Arthur asked me to produce it. I had never produced anything at that time. He was firing major Broadway producers to give me a chance. I began work immediately with Jerry Zaks, who is a very highly acclaimed Broadway director of comedies. We had a reading with Nathan Lane and Julia Louis-Dreyfus and Bill Murray and it was a great success. Shortly after that, Arthur became very sick with cancer, though he continued to tighten and tweak and refine the script. We had begun talking to the Old Vic about producing the play there, and Arthur was very pleased with that.

Bob and Kathryn were like family members of mine. We'd have dinner and I'd be telling them about progress on the play. One day I got a call from Sam Cohn, Bob's agent, saying that Bob wanted to meet with me. Bob told me his feelings were hurt that I had not asked him to direct the play. I was completely dumbfounded. I only hadn't asked him because I figured he was going to go off and direct twenty-five movies.

Jerry Zaks had other commitments going on at the same time. I spoke to Jerry and informed him of Bob's interest, and Jerry graciously handed the reins over to Bob.

In that meeting I remember Bob saying, "Do you want me to do this? The issue is not whether I want to do this, the issue is whether you want me."

I said, "Bob, of course. Why wouldn't I want you? You're one of the greatest directors in the world."

He said, "You may think I'm a bigger name. All I am is a bigger target."

Shortly thereafter I flew to London and met with Kevin Spacey, who's the artistic director at the Old Vic, and his partner, David Liddiment. We made the deal to do the play there.

This is an incredibly difficult play. One of the most difficult plays that Arthur Miller wrote. Arthur always said his job as a writer was to hold a mirror up to society. And he said, "Don't be surprised if they don't like what they see."

Things just didn't come together. Bob worked very hard to make sure that they did. When you're working with someone like Robert Altman, you must put one hundred percent of your confidence and faith in that person's vision. Kevin Spacey did not share that opinion. So frequently, in my opinion, he undermined Bob's attempts to make the refinements we needed by imposing refinements of his own, and it confused everyone.

NEVE CAMPBELL (actress): There were a lot of things going on. There were some challenges with the cast.

SCOTT GRIFFIN: One of the leads was Jane Adams. One time Jane was sitting with Bob and she said, "You have the most beautiful blue eyes. They say when you look into a person's eyes you're looking into their soul."

And Bob said, "Oh yeah? Well, don't look too deep, Jane. You might not like what you see."

MATTHEW MODINE: Jane Adams is a good actor but she is so broken as a human being it makes it difficult to give her direction. She's in a world that nobody else has a key to enter. . . . Eventually Bob told me, "Matthew, just kick her in the balls."

JANE ADAMS (actress): Bob is brilliant, and he likes to use whatever is happening in real life. I can't speak for Bob, but I think Bob thought that Matthew's rage was very useful. I think that Bob would be—and was—pleased that Matthew felt that way about me. Of course Bob would say, "Kick her in the balls." That's what Matthew's character was doing. Arthur Miller was telling a story of a woman who is broken by what she is asked to do, and by the insensitivity of the people asking her to do it. Matthew's character, the producer, was insisting that a petite female director, my character, shoot a real human being as he was being nailed to a cross.

NEVE CAMPBELL: Anytime you take on any project, you never know how it's going to turn out or how the chemistry is going to work. Bob—love him to death—had not done an incredible amount of theater. This play required real kid gloves. Arthur Miller had not finished writing the play, so it wasn't where it needed to be. It needed someone to really sit down with the play and really sort out what it was trying to say.

SCOTT GRIFFIN: The root of the problem was Spacey. He's the Norman Bates of show business. One minute he asks you to come in from the rain, have a sandwich, and talk about his bird collection, and the next minute you're standing there buck naked and he's dressed as an old lady, coming at you with a carving knife. At least that's how he treated Bob.

Throughout the entire rehearsal process, Kevin Spacey was completely uninvolved. When he did see the show at the second preview, he almost was in a complete rage. He came to Bob's dressing room and screamed at the top of his lungs for fifteen minutes. At the end, Bob stood up and said, "This meeting is over." From that point forward, Kevin did his best to take the show away from Bob and direct the actors himself both on and off the stage. Which had the net result of confusing everybody in the entire fucking production.

It was just a big mess. And throughout it all, Spacey was arrogant and cruel to Bob and Kathryn. Publicly, he was something else entirely. At the opening night party, you would have thought he was going to build a shrine to Robert Altman.

STACI WOLFE (spokeswoman for Kevin Spacey): Unfortunately, Kevin Spacey won't be available to take part [in your book], but thank you very much for thinking of him.

SCOTT GRIFFIN: On the night of the press opening, before the curtain went up, Bob and I were sitting on a couch stage right. We talked about what the process had been like, and joked that all the critics in London were in the theater at that moment.

I asked him, "What do you think the reviews are going to be like?"

He said, "I think we're going to get killed."

"Does that matter to you?"

"Nope."

After the reviews came out—he was right, they were terrible—a friend at dinner asked what he thought about the critics. Bob said, "Critics are people who sit on the mountaintop and look down on the battlefield. When the fighting is finished, they take it upon themselves to come down from the mountain and shoot the survivors."

Clemmie Moodie, story headlined "Spacey and His Stars Go to War Over the Big Flop," *Daily Mail* (London), April 14, 2006: Mauled mercilessly by the critics and shunned by audiences, Arthur Miller's *Resurrection Blues* is closing early amid reports of backstage turmoil. . . . During last Wednesday's matinee performance one of the leading actresses, Jane Adams, quit the production after allegedly falling out with Matthew Modine and pushing him so hard that he fell off stage.

JANE ADAMS: I can only say I'm five foot four and a half. At that time I weighed a hundred and five pounds. Do the math.

Scott Griffin: Despite everything, I think it was a triumph for him. The guy is going through chemo, he's suffering through gout, he's dealing with this maniac Kevin Spacey, and he's getting terrible reviews. At the same time, he goes to every performance, eight shows a week, and at the last show he takes a big bow and receives an enormous standing ovation. If Bob wanted to go out with his boots on, those boots were way on. And his head was held high through the whole thing.

CHAPTER 32

Not a Tragedy

*

Robert Altman, to David Thompson, from *Altman on Altman*: Every film I've ever done I really like. That's not very modest and not the way you're supposed to be, but you invest so much in them. I liken them to your children. You might say, "Well, don't you wish he was taller?" He isn't. "Don't you wish she had blonde hair and blue eyes?" But she doesn't. And you do tend to love your least successful children the most. So I love all my films.

* * *

HARRY BELAFONTE: The Oscar having eluded him for so long, he developed this façade. He'd watch it to see what went on, but act like it was this crock of shit. He turned being a nonwinner into a virtue—his work was above all that.

I said, "Look, Bob, if you don't like the shit that much, why do you keep dressing up when you're nominated and go?"

He said, "Well, Belafonte, there's a whore in all of us. It would mean a lot to anything I do from the box-office point of view. But other than that, I don't give a shit."

It wasn't until the honorary Oscar and the way in which he spoke that I understood the real depth of feeling that he had and what the Oscar meant to him.

ROBERT ALTMAN (*Accepting his Oscar for Lifetime Achievement to a thunderous standing ovation, March 5, 2006):* Thank you. [*To Meryl Streep and Lily Tomlin*] You gals are great.

Robert Altman with Meryl Streep and Lily Tomlin at the 78th Academy Awards, where he received his Oscar

[*To audience*] Thank you. Thank you. Thanks very much. I've got a lot to say and they've got a clock on me. I want to thank everybody for this. The Academy. I was really honored and moved to accept this award. When the news first came to me about it, I was caught kind of off guard. I always thought that this type of award meant that it was over. Then it dawned on me that I'm busy in rehearsals on a play that I'm doing in London. It opened last night, Arthur Miller's last play, *Resurrection Blues*. I was doing an interview for my new film that I just finished, *A Prairie Home Companion*, which will come out in the summer, and I realized that it's not over.

Of course, I was happy and thrilled to accept this award, and I look at it as a nod to all of my films. Because to me, I've just made one long film. And I know some of you have liked some of the sections and others of you . . . Anyway. All right. And I want to thank all of the people that have worked on all of my pictures so hard. The brilliant actors, the amazing crews. And I can't name them all, so I'm going to name a doctor that is taking care of me, Jodie Kaplan. So she represents everybody who've supported me and made it possible.

I've always said that making a film is like making a sand castle at the beach. You invite your friends and you get them down there and you say—you build this beautiful structure, several of you, and then you sit back and you watch the tide come in, have a drink, watch the tide come in, and the ocean just takes it away. And that sand castle remains in your mind. Now, I've built about forty of them and I never tire of it. No other filmmaker has gotten a better shake than I have. I'm very fortunate in my career. I've never had to direct a film that I didn't choose or develop. I love filmmaking. It has given me an entrée to the world and to the human condition. And for that, I'm forever grateful.

Finally, I would like to thank my family, which—you're all right up there, all of 'em, almost—for their love and support through the years. And most importantly, I want to thank and applaud my wife, Kathryn Reed Altman, without whom I wouldn't be here today. I love you, Trixie! Thank you.

Oh, one more thing. I'm here, I think, under kind of false pretenses, and I think I have to become straight with you. Ten years ago, eleven years ago, I had a heart transplant. A total heart transplant. I got the heart of, I think, a young woman who was about in her late thirties, and so by that calculation you may be giving me this award too early, because I think I've got about forty years left on it, and I intend to use it!

Thank you very much. Thank you.

ROBERT REED ALTMAN: It was the most emotional moment I had. For him to say, "I want my family there in that box, instead of friends and other people," that meant a lot to me. It wasn't like him. A lot of other things that happened, we were pretty much left out when it came to his work. But this was this Lifetime Achievement thing, and he really honored the whole family by making us part of it and by pointing us out. We were all on television with him, and what he said to my mom, all that stuff, and seeing him getting that Oscar, was a huge emotional, joyous situation. It was incredible.

*   *   *

Robert Altman, Proust Questionnaire, *Vanity Fair*, April 2006:
Q: If you were to die and come back as a person or thing, what do you think it would be?
A: I'm immortal.

*   *   *

KEVIN KLINE: We were on a train to Boston, for an event around the opening of *Prairie Home Companion*. I was getting ready to play King Lear, so I asked Bob, "What's it like growing old?" He says, "It sucks. Everything hurts." Just the terseness, the economy of direction. Pure Bob.

ROBERT ALTMAN (*October 2006, one month before his death*): What have I got? At very best probably five years left. I'm aware of the limitations of things.

I'm not interested in being ninety-five, and that's not very far away. I'm certainly not interested in being ninety-seven, because I know I'm not going to be making films then. I am mortal. But for a while there in the seventies and eighties I was immortal. I did not see the light at the end of the tunnel. Now I see the light at the end of the tunnel.

*   *   *

DAVID LEVY (producer): You can fill some multiplexes with all the pictures we didn't get to do over the years. Too many to name. They fell through for money, personalities, timing, you name the reason. There was the sequel to *Nashville*, and the sequel to *Short Cuts*. There was that project that Alan Rudolph adapted from the book *A Shortage of Engineers*. I feel like that maybe would have been Bob's first antiwar film since *M*A*S*H*.

There was the project that became *An Unfinished Life*, that movie with Redford and J-Lo. He was going to do that with Paul Newman and Naomi Watts. I think he wanted to see where his head would take him in what might be called a fairly conventional family drama. Another movie we didn't get to do is *Paint*, set in the contemporary art world of New York. That was a heartbreaker not to get to do. That would have been fun.

WREN ARTHUR: *Wild Card* was a baseball movie that he was going to do with John Goodman, I think, at one point. Paul Newman, maybe Woody Harrelson. Stephen Altman was in Chicago getting ready, and so was the line producer. Dona Granata was going to do costumes. And then it collapsed.

DAVID LEVY: It's particularly sad we didn't get to do *The Widow Claire*, from the play by Horton Foote. You can look at *Prairie* and it seems like the work of a guy who's thinking it could be his last movie, but I think that he was maybe looking at Horton's picture as that. It would have been the work of two wise old men saying to the world, "Just be careful. Don't send your boys off to war." It's a night before a soldier goes off to war and there's a tone of melancholy and an inevitability that we all need to question. I think that it's too bad. It would have been a lovely way to say good-bye.

At the end we were working on *Hands on a Hard Body*, based on this competition where people try to win a truck by keeping a hand on it longer than anybody else. A documentary had been made about the real event, but this would have been Bob's take on it. That would have been something, just having a bunch of disparate characters thrown together in an environment in a prescribed period of time and just seeing how it all shook out. It was going to be part revisionist faux documentary but also a commentary on the twenty-four-hour news cycle. Ultimately I think he would have ended up going into the impact of everyone getting their fifteen minutes of fame.

PAM DIXON MICKELSON (casting director): I spoke to him about casting *Hands on a Hard Body* two days before he passed away. The reason why he lived as long as he did was he always had something great to look forward to, and he always talked about it, which was great. We had Meryl Streep.

MERYL STREEP: I loved the experience of *Prairie* and found it was just a little too short. I wanted to do *Hands* for the fun, and to be around him. For the laughs.

PAM DIXON MICKELSON: We had Chris Rock, Dwayne "the Rock" Johnson, Steve Buscemi, Tommy Lee Jones, Jack White from the White Stripes, Jack Black, Salma Hayek, Billy Bob Thornton, John C. Reilly, Hilary Swank. Others, too. And we weren't finished.

JULIANNE MOORE: I was talking to him about *Hands on a Hard Body* just before he died.

PAM DIXON MICKELSON: It would probably have been the best ensemble cast in the history of film. People were doing it because it was Bob.

ALAN LADD JR.: I'd say, "What is *Hard Body* about?"

He'd say, "It's a film about a car."
I'd say, "Yes, but what it's *about*?"
He'd say, "I don't know. I haven't made it yet."

Wren Arthur: The story that fits inside of *Hands on a Hard Body*—and what Bob kept going back to—was to watch these people fall apart and what they do when they fall apart. One person turns on another person, one person is an angel. It's the theme of all his movies, every single one of them. He deals with us at our very basic nature. The good, the bad, and the ugly.

Josh Astrachan (producer): The way Bob described making *Hands on a Hard Body* was sly, original, and sprung from the specific possibilities and problems of making that particular film and that particular story. The movie was going to be a three-ring circus—at least three rings. Contests around the car would be the center ring. But there was also the ring around the truck dealership, its owner, the owner's lieutenant—a woman who ran the contest with an iron hand, to be played by Meryl Streep. There was a ring of journalists to cover the event, the center of which was the embittered alcoholic toiling for a Texas television news crew, played by Billy Bob Thornton. There were boyfriends and girlfriends and wives and angry husbands and a contestant who is mistakenly arrested for murder and hauled off the truck by cops. And there'd be bands playing, hot dogs, cotton candy—Bob's favorite foods. All these people, over three or four days, would grow almost as tired as the contestants themselves. A perfect Altman film.

Robert Altman (*November 2006, two weeks before his death*): I think I know how to do *Hands on a Hard Body*. I think I know how to do it like a documentary. What I want to do is set up the event and turn on the switch and let the event happen and film it with several cameras. And then that's it. Not to try to perfect it. The things that we miss—something that's a story line or a point—I have to figure out how to insert that. And if I don't miss anything then I haven't done this well. . . . So I have to tell this story. And I really don't like using the word "story." The word "story" is something I don't like at all.

In other words, I can't control everything. That's what I'm looking for. 'Cause that relieves me of the responsibility of being the author. The author that I'm looking for is the event itself.

I'm getting to the point where I'm seeing it as sort of my last thing.

I don't foresee anything beyond that. So now I'm getting to the position where I want it to be really special. And then I think maybe I won't get to make it at all, which is quite a possibility, too. I'm not running out and taking poison over this. I'm not even depressed by it. I'm aware of the conditions. And I'm—I want to deal with it. I feel I have to deal with it. . . . You have to keep going down the river [*laughs softly*].

* * *

KATHRYN REED ALTMAN: Thanksgiving of 2003, he got sick. We had a big family thing in California and he got sick to his stomach and had to leave the table. Cancer. They took one of the kidneys.

And he worked right through it. Chemo or no chemo. Dr. David Nanus—I have to give him credit—and the Oncology Department at New York-Presbyterian Hospital helped him. They paced him. They provided the quality of life. They were easy on the chemo. They'd lay off for five months and then he'd gain the weight again. He'd look like a million bucks, take another project, and then go back on chemo. It was a three-year ride like that. He had an assistant, Lowell Dubrinsky, who was so great through it all.

Then, in November of 2006, we were back here in New York and he was in preproduction for *Hands on a Hard Body*. He just kept working and getting that going and we were making the trip to California because he wanted to shoot it there—he was going to scout locations. So we'd be at home shooting, which was going to be good. Before we left New York, we had two events that he really wanted to go to. He sweat them out. He was not feeling good. He was weak and half sick and we went to a thing Friday night and Saturday night. Sunday we were supposed to leave and he wasn't up to it, and we delayed it.

We got to California on Tuesday, and Wednesday we went right to the oncologist, who saw that he was completely dehydrated. They tried to hydrate him and sent him home, telling us if he wasn't any better to come back.

He wasn't better, so we went back. We were in the hospital and he was starting to fill up again, his body was filling with fluid. He had that a lot, and we'd have to drain and drain and drain. The doctor called me out and said, "Do you have all the papers? Do you have a living will?"

I said, "Yeah, I've already told them all that when I checked in."

Thinking back, I realize he knew how serious this was.

So they finally drained Bob's stomach, and when he came out of that room he said to Konni and me, "I feel just fine; you girls go on home. I'm just terrific. I'll see you tomorrow." He was kidding around—he stuck his tongue out at me and we had jokes and things.

So the next morning he called me before I could even wake up. He said, "God, I feel like a million bucks, I'm having breakfast. I'm having pancakes."

I said, "Oh, that's great. Boy, that's all it took. That's terrific."

He said, "I got the paper and the game is coming on. Take your time."

So I took maybe an extra hour to take care of some things. I was driving down the highway and I called to say I'm on my way.

He said, "I'm not feeling very good."

Such a blow to me, because he'd felt so great an hour and a half before. And when I got in there he just got sicker and sicker. That was Saturday. And I got a special nurse. Michael came and insisted on staying all night. And Bobby kept coming in with the baby, and Stevie came. Sunday morning he went to morphine. He knew me; I could get through to him. I'd say, "Bob?" and he'd respond a bit, and then Michael would say, "He heard you."

And then when he died, he was just hanging on me. Just lifting himself on my arm. I could hear him go.

Last words? Not really, because of the morphine. He said one thing before he got too heavy into the morphine. I was standing at the window. Must have been Saturday afternoon. It was before he sunk so fast. I was standing looking out the window and he was trying to get comfortable—he was so uncomfortable. And he said, "I'm never getting out of here, I know I'm not."

And I said, "Oh, that's bullshit. You've said that before."

He hadn't said it before. That just killed me. Because he never gave up. He was always so positive and optimistic about everything.

And then after, I closed his eyes and stayed with him awhile. Then I walked out. All the family was standing around the door of the hospital room. That's when I said, "Th-th-th-that's all, folks." I don't know why I said that.

That's when our grandson Christian said, "It's a wrap."

Then Konni, over on the side of the group, used Bob's favorite exit line: "See you in the next reel."

The timing was just . . . it gives me chills to think about it. It was so

Altman. It was such an Altman gathering there. It was like he'd set this scene, you know?

*   *   *

Rick Lyman, story headlined "Robert Altman, Iconoclastic Director, Dies at 81," *The New York Times,* **November 21, 2006:** Robert Altman, one of the most adventurous and influential American directors of the late 20th century, a filmmaker whose iconoclastic career spanned more than five decades but whose stamp was felt most forcefully in one, the 1970s, died Monday in Los Angeles. He was 81.

*   *   *

MARTIN SCORSESE: His legacy? His spirit. His spirit was to make pictures, to say what the hell he wanted to say on film. It may have angered people, it may have unsettled people, but he did it. He made independent pictures in Hollywood, with Hollywood money, ultimately. And he had an individual point of view and a personal statement with every picture. Every one.

On the set of A Prairie Home Companion

Hollywood's become kind of at peace with the independent film as long as it knows its place, you know? And that means a certain level of money, a certain type of production value. With Altman, it didn't know its place. That's the beauty of it.

He's an inspiration. I don't think there's any career like that in the history of Hollywood.

* * *

Tim Robbins, New York memorial for Robert Altman, Majestic Theater, February 20, 2007: There's a hilarious new movie in preproduction up in heaven. Bob has gotten the financing together for his new film, called "The Memorial." And we are making the film as we speak. He's watching the people onstage, yes. But there are other cameras looking around the theater today, at the subplots, the subterfuge, the silliness, the whispered comments, the backstage preening. Kathryn, you have a beautiful close-up and a camera dedicated to you. But everyone else, beware. He's going to find us out, and God will laugh.

* * *

MATTHEW ALTMAN: It was my mom's idea to scatter the ashes from the beach to the ocean, and to divide up his personal things between us. Some *Popeye* memorabilia and clothes and that kind of stuff. She thought it was time. So all the boys and Konni and my mom got together in Malibu in August 2007.

We went out with Dad's ashes, the four of us boys—Michael, Steve, Bobby, and me. It was definitely an Altmanesque moment—four grown men in their underwear and shirts on the beach with ashes of their dad. We divided up the ashes and walked into the water. We went up to our knees and the waves were breaking and it was a beautiful night. We just let his ashes go, and my mom and Konni were on the deck. Steve had brought some white lilies, and my mom threw those in the water. And we all said good-bye.

* * *

PAUL THOMAS ANDERSON: Oh, I didn't figure on this making me sad. I thought, "Oh great, I get to talk about Bob." But it's making me feel like I'm sure everybody feels—they really wish they could call him up. Yeah, fuck! Horrible, sad. He was so indestructible for so long.

Susan Davis (actress and cousin): It seems like everyone I talk to has dreamed about Bob since he passed. He was that kind of huge presence. I went to Italy in January or February, and the first night I'm there I had this dream. It was as real as sitting here with you. I walked up the stairway, and there was Bob in the room.

I said, "What in the hell are you doing here?"

He said, "What are *you* doing here?"

I said, "Bob . . . you're—"

And he said, "No, I'm not. I'm getting ready to do a film, and I can't get the money. Will you get it out of their heads that I'm dead? I'm just trying to get the money to make this film."

* * *

Dialogue from *A Prairie Home Companion:*

(LUNCH LADY, played by Marylouise Burke, has just found her lover dead in his dressing room. The angel of death, called DANGEROUS WOMAN, played by Virginia Madsen, embraces her.)

Dangerous Woman: The death of an old man is not a tragedy.

Lunch Lady (*weeping*): I—don't—want him to—go.

Dangerous Woman: Forgive him his shortcomings, and thank him for all his love and care. Tell him he will be remembered, and turn away and live your life.

Lunch Lady (*Crying—to her lover's body):* Good-bye, baby. *[To Dangerous Woman]* You got anything to drink? Like a rum and Coke?

* * *

Robert Altman: Things never end. There are no ends. There are stopping places. So, you really choose a stopping place.

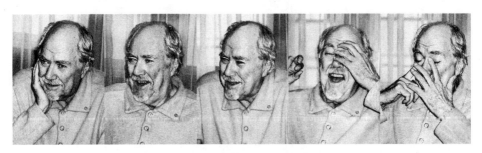

"Giggle and give in."

A NOTE ON METHODS

UNLESS OTHERWISE NOTED, all of Robert Altman's comments are from the recorded talks we had about everything from his upbringing to his next planned film, sadly never completed. Our last conversations took place less than three weeks before his death, making them his final sustained interviews.

For the sake of clarity, I omitted false starts and rhetorical dead ends while doing my best to preserve idiosyncrasies of his speech. I followed the same approach with the nearly two hundred other people I interviewed, some on multiple occasions. The guiding principle was to publish what people said, as close as possible to how they said it, in the context they meant it. Although not all the interview subjects are quoted, all their comments shaped the narrative and enriched my understanding of the man.

When necessary, I reinterviewed sources to untangle word knots in especially awkward quotes. A majority of the initial interviews were done in person, while follow-ups were mostly done by phone. Most interviews were recorded, then transcribed by me, by one of my graduate assistants, or by ace transcriptionist Steve Wylie of Pat Casteel Transcripts in New York.

Entire books have been written on individual Altman films, which means that by design this biography could never cover every one of his filmmaking experiences, collaborators, relationships—or nemeses, for that matter. I apologize to any individual who feels overlooked, and to any reader who feels an anecdote was left untold. The goal was to satisfy the epigram that opens this book.

I worked closely and cooperatively with Kathryn Reed Altman, who was uninterested in hagiography and set no limits on subjects that could be broached or the way they were told.

One challenge of an oral biography is that the form is limited by the availability of sources. Some of Bob's longtime collaborators predeceased him, among them Tommy Thompson, Bob Eggenweiler, Scotty Bushnell, Lou Lombardo, and Geri Peroni, all of whom would have enriched this book. Several others made themselves unavailable, for reasons of their own.

Bob's death also prevented me from seeking his reaction to the comments of others, some of which he might have disputed, dismissed, disdained, or all three. On the other hand, he might well have followed his own oft-repeated advice: "Giggle and give in."

CAST OF CHARACTERS

The following are brief, Altman-centric biographies of people whose interviews are included in this book. Not included are journalists, reviewers, authors, and others whose writings and comments are excerpted throughout.

JANE ADAMS is an actress who played Junior League do-gooder Nettie Bolt in *Kansas City* and director Emily Shapiro in Robert Altman's stage production of Arthur Miller's *Resurrection Blues.*

LOU ADLER is a legendary music producer who coproduced the 1967 Monterey International Pop Music Festival. The documentary of the event led him into the film business and to his role as producer of *Brewster McCloud.*

ANOUK AIMÉE is an award-winning French film actress who became an international star from her role in *A Man and a Woman,* directed by Claude Lelouch. She played the character Simone Lowenthal in *Prêt-à-Porter.*

CHRISTINE ALTMAN is Robert Altman's eldest child. Her mother is the late LaVonne Elmer, Robert Altman's first wife, to whom he was married from 1946 to 1949.

JOHN ALTMAN is a first cousin of Robert Altman. His father, Frank Altman, was the brother of Robert Altman's father, Bernard "B.C." Altman. He is a filmmaker in Kansas City.

KATHRYN REED ALTMAN is the third wife and widow of Robert Altman. They met in 1959 when he was directing an episode of the television series *Whirlybirds,* and were married soon after. She is the mother of two of his sons, Robert Reed Altman and Matthew Altman, and his stepdaughter, Konni Corriere.

MATTHEW ALTMAN is the fourth son of Robert Altman. He was adopted as an infant. He worked on several of his father's movies as a crew member or in the art department as a set dresser, and appeared uncredited in *Thieves Like Us,* as "boy getting free soda."

MICHAEL ALTMAN is the eldest son of Robert Altman. His mother is Lotus Corelli Altman Monroe. At fourteen, he wrote the lyrics to the theme song from *M*A*S*H*, "Suicide Is Painless." He is a film projectionist in Los Angeles.

ROBERT ALTMAN was born in Kansas City on February 20, 1925, and died in Los Angeles on November 20, 2006. His motto was "Giggle and give in."

ROBERT REED ALTMAN is the third son of Robert Altman. He began working with his father on *Nashville*, worked on a half dozen of his father's movies as a camera operator, and was director of photography on *Tanner on Tanner*. He has also been a camera operator on television series including *Lost*, *The O.C.*, *The Wonder Years*, and *Chuck*.

STEPHEN ALTMAN is the second son of Robert Altman. His mother is Lotus Corelli Altman Monroe. He was the production designer on more than a dozen of his father's movies and television projects, including *The Player*, *Short Cuts*, and *Gosford Park*, and worked on a dozen others in the art or editorial departments.

PAUL THOMAS ANDERSON credits the films of Robert Altman with helping him to learn to be a director. Anderson served as the standby director for insurance purposes on Altman's last film, *A Prairie Home Companion*.

ANNE ARCHER appeared in *Short Cuts* as Claire Kane, a woman horrified to learn that her husband left a young woman's body in a river while he fished with his buddies.

WREN ARTHUR worked as an assistant to Robert Altman in the late 1990s and rose to the position of producer on *Tanner on Tanner* and *A Prairie Home Companion*. She acted in *Dr. T & the Women* as a member of the doctor's staff.

JOSH ASTRACHAN was associate producer of *Dr. T & the Women*, coproducer of *Gosford Park*, and a producer of *The Company* and *A Prairie Home Companion*.

RENÉ AUBERJONOIS appeared as sweet-natured Father "Dago Red" Mulcahy in *M*A*S*H*, the man-turning-into-a-bird character called the Lecturer in *Brewster McCloud*, the bar owner/busybody Sheehan in *McCabe & Mrs. Miller*, the unfaithful husband Hugh in *Images*, and as himself in *The Player*.

LAUREN BACALL played presidential candidate Esther Brill in *HealtH* and fashion doyenne Slim Chrysler in *Prêt-à-Porter*. The name Slim was a nod to her role as Marie "Slim" Browning opposite Humphrey Bogart in the 1944 Howard Hawks film *To Have and Have Not*.

REZA BADIYI was Robert Altman's intern and protégé at the Calvin Company and rose to a career as a television director on dozens of shows, including *Mission: Impossible*, *Hawaii Five-O*, *Cagney & Lacey*, *Falcon Crest*, and *Baywatch*.

RICHARD BAKALYAN is a veteran character actor who played gang leader Eddy in *The Delinquents*.

BOB BALABAN is an actor, writer, producer, and director. He produced *Gosford Park* and played the role of the American film producer Morris Weissman.

FRANK W. BARHYDT met Robert Altman as a boy when Altman was working for Barhydt's father at the Calvin Company. Barhydt cowrote the screenplays for *Quintet*, *HealtH*, *Short Cuts*, and *Kansas City*, and had acting roles in *Tanner '88* and *The Player*.

SUE BARTON was the publicist on *Nashville* and appears as herself in the scene where Elliott Gould drops by.

RICHARD BASKIN was music supervisor on *Nashville* and played the role of the studio musician Frog. He was nominated for a Grammy Award for Best Original Score. He was also a composer for *Buffalo Bill and the Indians, or Sitting Bull's History Lesson*.

WARREN BEATTY had already been nominated for two Academy Awards, for Best Actor in a Leading Role and Best Picture, as producer, for *Bonnie and Clyde*, when he played doomed entrepreneur John McCabe in *McCabe & Mrs. Miller*.

HARRY BELAFONTE played himself in *The Player*, *Prêt-à-Porter*, and *Tanner on Tanner*, and the gangster Seldom Seen in *Kansas City*, for which he won a New York Film Critics Circle Award. He and Robert Altman worked for years on an unfinished project on blackface, tentatively called *Cork*. When asked by *Vanity Fair* magazine to name the living person he most admired, Altman said, "Harry Belafonte."

ROBERT BENTON is a writer and director whose 1977 film *The Late Show*, starring Lily Tomlin and Art Carney, was produced by Robert Altman at Lion's Gate Films.

ROBERT BLEES produced the infamous *Bus Stop* episode directed by Robert Altman and starring Fabian, and also produced episodes of *Combat!* directed by Altman.

JIM BOUTON was a pitcher for the New York Yankees who made an indelible mark on baseball with his book *Ball Four*. He played Terry Lennox in *The Long Goodbye*.

KENNETH BRANAGH starred as hotshot lawyer Rick Magruder in *The Gingerbread Man*.

DENISE BRETON met Robert Altman when she was the European publicist for *M*A*S*H*. She remained his European publicist, as well as being a friend and supporter, for the rest of his life.

DAVID BROWN was an executive at Twentieth Century Fox during the making of *M*A*S*H*, after which he formed a production company with Richard Zanuck. After that partnership disbanded, he was a producer on *The Player*.

CAROL BURNETT played mother-of-the-bride Katherine "Tulip" Brenner in *A Wedding*, presidential adviser Gloria Burbank in *HealtH*, and schoolteacher Alberta Johnson in the television production *The Laundromat*.

BILL BUSHNELL was the first managing director of the American Conservatory Theatre in San Francisco, where Robert Altman found several actors for *M*A*S*H*. Bushnell introduced Robert Altman to the play *Secret Honor*, and also to his wife, Scotty Bushnell, who subsequently became Bushnell's ex-wife and Altman's longtime producer.

JAMES CAAN starred as the lunar astronaut Lee Stegler in *Countdown*.

NEVE CAMPBELL produced and starred in *The Company*, playing the poised-for-greatness ballet dancer Loretta "Ry" Ryan.

KEITH CARRADINE played the naïve, doomed Cowboy in *McCabe & Mrs. Miller*; starred as the naïve, doomed bank robber Bowie in *Thieves Like Us*; and played a conflicted lothario, pop star Tom Frank, in *Nashville*. His song "I'm Easy" won an Academy Award for Best Original Song.

GERALDINE CHAPLIN played the impostor BBC correspondent Opal in *Nashville*; sharpshooter Annie Oakley in *Buffalo Bill and the Indians, or Sitting Bull's History Lesson*; and wedding-planner-with-a-secret Rita Billingsley in *A Wedding*.

CHER played sharp-tongued waitress Sissy in *Come Back to the Five and Dime, Jimmy Dean, Jimmy Dean*. She played herself in *The Player* and *Prêt-à-Porter*.

JULIE CHRISTIE starred as the canny whorehouse madam Constance Miller in *McCabe & Mrs. Miller*, for which she was nominated for an Academy Award for Best Actress. She appeared as herself in a cameo in *Nashville*.

GRAEME CLIFFORD was assistant director on *That Cold Day in the Park*, casting director on *McCabe & Mrs. Miller*, an assistant on *M*A*S*H*, and editor of *Images*. He later became a director in his own right, with credits including *Frances*.

LEONARD COHEN wrote "The Stranger Song," "Sisters of Mercy," and "Winter Lady," which together created the haunting score for *McCabe & Mrs. Miller*.

Sam Cohn was Robert Altman's agent off and on for large portions of his career.

John Considine played Annie Oakley's husband, Frank Butler, in *Buffalo Bill and the Indians, or Sitting Bull's History Lesson*. He cowrote the screenplay and played security chief Jeff Kuykendall in *A Wedding*, and appeared in episodes of *Combat!*, *Tanner '88*, and *Gun* directed by Robert Altman.

Konni Corriere is the daughter of Kathryn Reed Altman and the step-daughter of Robert Altman. She was his assistant on *Prêt-à-Porter*.

Bud Cort played timid Private Lorenzo Boone in *M*A*S*H*, then starred as the boy-who-would-fly title character in *Brewster McCloud*.

Norman Corwin has been called "America's Poet Laureate of Radio." His program *On a Note of Triumph*, broadcast upon the surrender of Nazi Germany, is considered his masterpiece.

Susan Davis was Robert Altman's cousin by marriage (his aunt married her uncle) and an actress who appeared in his Calvin Company films and early television work.

Dale Dennison was the pilot on the B-24 Liberator bomber on which Robert Altman was copilot during World War II.

Paul Dooley played pompous father of the bride Liam "Snooks" Brenner in *A Wedding*, unlikely suitor Alex Theodopoulos in *A Perfect Couple*, burger fiend Wimpy in *Popeye*, "little guy" candidate Gil Gainey in *HealtH*—for which he also cowrote the screenplay—and torture target Randall Schwab in *O.C. and Stiggs*.

Robert Dornhelm is an Austrian director who was nominated for an Oscar for his documentary *The Children of Theatre Street*, and a longtime friend of Robert and Kathryn Altman's.

David Dortort was the creator and producer of one of television's most successful series, *Bonanza*.

Faye Dunaway knew Robert Altman but never worked with him.

Robert Duvall played astronaut Chiz in *Countdown*, the supercilious Major Frank Burns in *M*A*S*H*, and the psychotic Dixon Doss in *The Gingerbread Man*.

Shelley Duvall was "discovered" by Robert Altman during the casting of *Brewster McCloud*, in which she played Brewster's down-to-earth girlfriend, Suzanne Davis. She then played reluctant prostitute Ida Coyle in *McCabe & Mrs. Miller*; innocent gun moll Keechie in *Thieves Like Us*; boy-crazy Marthe (aka L.A. Joan) in *Nashville;* Grover Cleveland's wife in *Buffalo Bill and the Indians, or Sitting Bull's History Lesson;* self-deluding Millie Lammoreaux in *3 Women* (for which she shared Best Actress honors at the Cannes Film Festival); and Olive Oyl in *Popeye.*

ROBERT EVANS produced *Popeye* after making a name for himself as the quintessentially "new Hollywood" head of production at Paramount Pictures.

DONALD FACTOR is an heir to the Max Factor cosmetics fortune and was the producer of *That Cold Day in the Park.*

JULES FEIFFER is a Pulitzer Prize–winning cartoonist, as well as an author, playwright, and screenwriter. He wrote the screenplay for *Popeye.*

JULIAN FELLOWES is an actor and writer who wrote the screenplay for *Gosford Park,* which won an Academy Award for Best Original Screenplay, among other honors.

COREY FISCHER played Captain Bandini in *M*A*S*H,* Officer Hines in *Brewster McCloud,* and the mad Reverend Elliot in *McCabe & Mrs. Miller.*

FABIAN FORTE was a teen pop idol in the 1950s who starred in an infamous episode of *Bus Stop* called "A Lion Walks Among Us," directed by Robert Altman.

DAVID FOSTER produced *McCabe & Mrs. Miller,* which launched his Hollywood career. Later films included *The Getaway, The Drowning Pool, The Mean Season,* and *The Mask of Zorro.*

GILLIAN FREEMAN is an author who wrote the screenplay for *That Cold Day in the Park.* An idea given her by Robert Altman became her novel *Easter Egg Hunt.*

HARVEY and **SUELLEN FRIED** were friends of Robert Altman's from Kansas City. SuEllen Fried acted in Altman's productions at the Jewish Community Center of Kansas City and also had a role in *The Delinquents.*

PETER GALLAGHER played prosecutor Lieutenant Commander John Challee in *The Caine Mutiny Court-Martial,* sleazy studio executive Larry Levy in *The Player,* and chain-saw wielding ex-husband Stormy Weathers in *Short Cuts.*

TESS GALLAGHER is a poet and the widow of Raymond Carver, whose short stories were the basis for *Short Cuts.*

GEORGE W. GEORGE was a film and theater producer and writer who helped to launch the career of Robert Altman. His later work included his production of *My Dinner with Andre.*

HENRY GIBSON played mean Dr. Verringer in *The Long Goodbye*, self-important country music king Haven Hamilton in *Nashville*, favored son-in-law Fred Bott in *A Perfect Couple*, and dirty trickster Bobby Hammer in *HealtH*.

JEFF GOLDBLUM played magazine editor Lloyd Harris in *California Split*; the mysterious, magical Tricycle Man in *Nashville*; the neurotic bisexual Bruce in *Beyond Therapy*; and himself in *The Player*.

DR. MARTIN GOLDFARB is a Los Angeles cardiologist who befriended Robert Altman at a poker game when they were young men and allowed him to live in his home for two years.

ART GOODELL was a cameraman who worked with Robert Altman making industrial films at the Calvin Company in Kansas City in the 1950s.

ELLIOTT GOULD played the irreverent surgeon Captain Trapper John McIntyre in *M*A*S*H*, the out-of-time Philip Marlowe in *The Long Goodbye*, incorrigible gambler Charlie Waters in *California Split*, and himself in *Nashville* and *The Player*.

DONA GRANATA designed the costumes for *Kansas City*, *The Gingerbread Man*, *Cookie's Fortune*, *Dr. T & the Women*, and the opera adaptation of *A Wedding*.

DANFORD GREENE edited *Nightmare in Chicago*, *That Cold Day in the Park*, and *M*A*S*H*, for which he was nominated for an Academy Award for Best Film Editing.

SCOTT GRIFFIN produced *Resurrection Blues* when it was directed by Robert Altman at the Old Vic in London.

PHILIP BAKER HALL played a paranoid, confessional Richard Nixon in *Secret Honor*.

ROBERT HARDERS directed Philip Baker Hall in the original one-man play of *Secret Honor* and served as associate director on the film.

BUCK HENRY played a comic version of himself pitching *The Graduate, Part II* in *The Player* and the committed fisherman Gordon Johnson in *Short Cuts*.

BARBARA ALTMAN HODES is the younger of Robert Altman's two sisters.

JOHN HOROSCHAK, JR. was a gunner on the B-24 Liberator bomber on which Robert Altman was copilot during World War II.

LAUREN HUTTON played filmmaker Florence Farmer in *A Wedding*.

MIKE KAPLAN was the publicist for *3 Women* and other Lion's Gate Films releases. He played the Treasurer/Jules Keen in *Buffalo Bill and the Indians, or*

Sitting Bull's History Lesson, and studio executive Marty Grossman in *The Player*. He was associate producer of *Short Cuts* and produced a film based on its making, called *Luck, Trust & Ketchup: Robert Altman in Carver Country*.

ELLIOTT KASTNER is a combative independent producer who produced *The Long Goodbye*. Among his other films are *Where Eagles Dare* and *The Missouri Breaks*.

ELAINE KAUFMAN is the eponymous owner of Robert Altman's favorite restaurant in New York.

GARRISON KEILLOR played announcer/raconteur GK and wrote the screenplay for *A Prairie Home Companion*, a fictional account of the last night of his long-running radio show.

SALLY KELLERMAN played Major Margaret "Hot Lips" Houlihan in *M*A*S*H*, for which she was nominated for an Academy Award for Best Supporting Actress. She played bird woman/guardian angel Louise in *Brewster McCloud*, fashion editor Sissy Wanamaker in *Prêt-à-Porter*, and herself in *The Player*. She also appeared in an episode of the television series *Gun* directed by Robert Altman.

KEVIN KLINE played clueless security man Guy Noir in *A Prairie Home Companion*.

WOLF KROEGER was art director on *Quintet* and set designer on *Popeye* and *Streamers*. He was an associate producer on *HealtH*.

ALAN LADD, JR., is an independent producer who was president of Twentieth Century Fox for most of the period when Robert Altman made five films in a row for the studio: *3 Women*, *A Wedding*, *Quintet*, *A Perfect Couple*, and *HealtH*.

MARGARET LADD played pot-smoking bridesmaid Ruby Sparr in *A Wedding* and kept a diary of her experiences on the set.

TOM LAUGHLIN played college-bound Scotty White in *The Delinquents* more than a decade before being cast in his defining role, as the title character in *Billy Jack*.

JENNIFER JASON LEIGH played nonchalant phone-sex worker Lois Kaiser in *Short Cuts* and desperate kidnapper Blondie O'Hara in *Kansas City*. She is the daughter of Barbara Turner, who collaborated with Robert Altman as an actress and a screenwriter, and the late Vic Morrow, who worked with him on *Combat!*

DAVID LEVY worked with Robert Altman off and on for more than two decades after Altman hired Levy away from his job as an assistant to super-agent Sam Cohn, who represented Altman at the time. He was a crew member on *HealtH* and *Popeye*; associate producer on *The Player*, *Short Cuts*, and *The Gingerbread Man*; coproducer on *Cookie's Fortune* and *Dr. T & the Women*; and a producer of *Gosford Park*, *The Company*, and *A Prairie Home Companion*.

GEORGE LITTO is sometimes called the unsung hero of *M*A*S*H* for having orchestrated the hiring of Robert Altman as its director. He was Altman's agent for periods of the 1960s and '70s, and when the money fell out became executive producer of *Thieves Like Us*.

JOHNNY MANDEL composed the music for "Suicide Is Painless," the theme song for *M*A*S*H*.

LORING MANDEL wrote the screenplay for *Countdown*.

NORMA MARING is alumni director emeritus at Wentworth Military Academy in Lexington, Missouri.

MALACHY McCOURT is a writer and raconteur who says he was the original choice to play Father Mulcahy in *M*A*S*H*.

MALCOLM McDOWELL played himself in *The Player* and mercurial company director Alberto Antonelli in *The Company*.

PAM DIXON MICKELSON was the casting director on *Cookie's Fortune*, *Dr. T & the Women*, *The Company*, and *A Prairie Home Companion*, and helped with casting on *Gosford Park*.

MATTHEW MODINE played the young soldier Billy in *Streamers*, cuckolded husband Dr. Ralph Wyman in *Short Cuts*, and huckster Skip Cheeseboro in Robert Altman's production of *Resurrection Blues* by Arthur Miller, staged at the Old Vic in London in 2006.

LOTUS CORELLI ALTMAN MONROE was Robert Altman's second wife. They were married from 1952 to 1959. She is the mother of his sons Michael and Stephen.

JULIANNE MOORE played the unhappily married artist Marian Wyman in *Short Cuts* and the simple-like-a-fox Cora Duvall in *Cookie's Fortune*.

MICHAEL MURPHY started working with Robert Altman as an unnamed soldier in *Combat!* He played skeptical civilian Rick in *Countdown*, the woman-procuring character called the Rounder in *That Cold Day in the Park*, whorehouse doctor Captain Ezekiel "Me Lay" Marston IV in *M*A*S*H*, suicidal supercop Frank Shaft in *Brewster McCloud*, corporate toady Eugene Sears in *McCabe & Mrs. Miller*, political operative John Triplette in *Nashville*,

Captain Blakely in *The Caine Mutiny Court-Martial*, presidential candidate Jack Tanner in *Tanner '88* and *Tanner on Tanner*, and power broker Henry Stilton in *Kansas City*.

PATRICIA NEAL played Jewel Mae "Cookie" Orcutt in *Cookie's Fortune*. She was the ex-wife of the late Roald Dahl.

PAUL NEWMAN played proto-celebrity William F. "Buffalo Bill" Cody in *Buffalo Bill and the Indians, or Sitting Bull's History Lesson*, and the optimistic Essex in *Quintet*.

PETER NEWMAN was a production executive on *Come Back to the Five and Dime, Jimmy Dean, Jimmy Dean*, and was a producer of *O.C. and Stiggs*.

ALLAN NICHOLLS played cuckolded third wheel Bill in *Nashville*; the journalist Prentiss Ingraham in *Buffalo Bill and the Indians, or Sitting Bull's History Lesson*; security man Jake Jacobs in both *A Wedding*, for which he cowrote the screenplay, and *HealtH*; Dana 115 in *A Perfect Couple*, for which he also wrote the music and cowrote the screenplay; and Rough House in *Popeye*. He was music supervisor on *HealtH*, *O.C. and Stiggs*, and *Prêt-à-Porter*. He was an assistant director on *Streamers*, *Secret Honor*, *The Laundromat*, *The Caine Mutiny Court-Martial*, *The Player*, *Short Cuts*, and *Tanner on Tanner*, and associate producer on *Quintet*.

DAVID PICKER ran United Artists when Robert Altman made *The Long Goodbye*.

JOHNNIE PLANCO was Robert Altman's longtime agent at William Morris.

POLLY PLATT was working as a production designer when she quit *Nashville* over her disagreement about the climactic assassination.

ANNE RAPP wrote the screenplays for *Cookie's Fortune* and *Dr. T & the Women*.

TIM ROBBINS played homicidal movie executive Griffin Mill in *The Player*; priapic motorcycle cop Gene Shepard in *Short Cuts*, and hotel room–bound journalist Joe Flynn in *Prêt-à-Porter*.

BILL ROBINSON worked for a time as Robert Altman's agent and longer as his backgammon partner.

ANNIE ROSS is a renowned jazz singer who played the widowed jazz singer Tess Trainer in *Short Cuts*.

ALAN RUDOLPH was Robert Altman's friend, protégé, and collaborator for more than three decades. He was an assistant director on *The Long Goodbye*, *California Split*, and *Nashville*. He cowrote *Buffalo Bill and the Indians, or Sitting*

Bull's History Lesson. He appeared as himself in the opening scene of *The Player.* Five films he directed were produced by Robert Altman: *Welcome to L.A., Remember My Name, Mrs. Parker and the Vicious Circle, Afterglow,* and *Trixie.*

MARK RYDELL is a director and actor who played the psychotic, observant Jewish gangster Marty Augustine in *The Long Goodbye.*

JOAN ALTMAN SARAFIAN is the elder of Robert Altman's two sisters.

RICHARD SARAFIAN is a director, writer, and actor who worked with Robert Altman making industrial films at the Calvin Company. His films include *Vanishing Point* and *The Man Who Loved Cat Dancing.* He was Altman's brother-in-law during his marriage to Joan Altman Sarafian.

JOHN SCHUCK played the sexually troubled dentist Captain Walter Kosciusko "Painless Pole" Waldowski in *M*A*S*H,* eager Officer Marty Johnson in *Brewster McCloud,* townsman Smalley in *McCabe & Mrs. Miller,* and brooding bank robber Elmo "Chicamaw" Mobley in *Thieves Like Us.*

MARTIN SCORSESE was one of the few directors whose work Robert Altman publicly admired. He played himself in *Tanner on Tanner* and was instrumental in preserving a number of Altman films, including *McCabe & Mrs. Miller.*

GEORGE SEGAL played the conflicted gambler Bill Denny in *California Split.*

MATTHEW SEIG was an associate producer of *Tanner '88,* coproducer of *Kansas City* and *Jazz '34,* and a producer of *Tanner on Tanner.* He continues to manage Robert Altman's copyright and business affairs.

JIM SHEPARD teaches writing at Williams College. His books include *Lights Out in the Reptile House, Project X,* and *Like You'd Understand, Anyway.*

SAM SHEPARD is a Pulitzer Prize–winning playwright who wrote *Fool for Love* for the stage, adapted it for screen (though he says Robert Altman actually wrote most of the screenplay), and starred in the movie version as the tortured, incestuous cowboy Eddie.

TOM SKERRITT appeared in small roles in *Combat!,* then played easygoing, if racist and sexist, Captain Augustus "Duke" Forrest in *M*A*S*H,* and accessory-after-the-fact Dee Mobley in *Thieves Like Us.*

LOIS SMITH is a renowned press agent who spent more than thirty-five years working with Robert Altman, even serving him beyond the grave by helping to organize memorials in New York and Los Angeles.

ROGER SNOWDALL was a soundman who worked with Robert Altman making industrial films at the Calvin Company in Kansas City in the 1950s.

FRANK SOUTH wrote the *2 by South* plays, *Precious Blood* and *Rattlesnake in a Cooler.*

SISSY SPACEK played blank slate/identity thief Pinky Rose in *3 Women.*

JERRE STEENHOF was one of Robert Altman's high school girlfriends.

STEWART STERN wrote the screenplay for *The James Dean Story*, a role for which he was ideally suited, having been a close friend of Dean's and having written the screenplay for *Rebel Without a Cause.*

MERYL STREEP played singing sister (and mother to the character played by Lindsay Lohan) Yolanda Johnson in *A Prairie Home Companion*. News that she had agreed to a leading role in Robert Altman's next planned film, to be called *Hands on a Hard Body*, made him nearly giddy in the weeks before his death.

WILLIAM STUCKEY was the nose-turret gunner on the B-24 Liberator bomber copiloted by Robert Altman in World War II.

JOAN TEWKESBURY wrote the screenplays for *Thieves Like Us* and *Nashville*, for which she was nominated for an Academy Award for Best Original Screenplay. She was a script supervisor on *McCabe & Mrs. Miller*, in which she also played a townswoman. She played "the lady in the train station" in *Thieves Like Us.*

MICHAEL TOLKIN's screenplay for *The Player*, based on his novel of the same name, was nominated for an Academy Award for Best Adapted Screenplay.

LILY TOMLIN played unsatisfied housewife Linnea Reese in *Nashville*, her first film role, for which she was nominated for an Academy Award for Best Supporting Actress. She played herself in the movie within a movie in *The Player*, waitress/accidental killer Doreen Piggot in *Short Cuts*, and singing sister Rhonda Johnson in *A Prairie Home Companion.*

GARRY TRUDEAU, the creator of the "Doonesbury" comic strip, was the writer and a producer of the *Tanner '88* television series and the writer of *Tanner on Tanner.*

BARBARA TURNER played Hildegarde in *Nightmare in Chicago* and wrote the screenplay for *The Company*. She is the mother of Jennifer Jason Leigh.

RAYMOND WAGNER is a producer who was a business partner of Robert Altman in the 1960s. He produced the film *Petulia*, adapted for the screen by Barbara Turner at Altman's suggestion, when their partnership dissolved.

JERRY WALSH was related to Robert Altman by marriage (his uncle John married Altman's aunt Pauline) and later became his friend, his lawyer, and the executor of his estate.

JOSEPH WALSH wrote the screenplay for *California Split*, based partly on his own exploits as a young man with his friend Elliott Gould, whose character is based on Walsh.

JOHN WILLIAMS composed the theme music for *Nightmare in Chicago*, *The Kathryn Reed Story*, *Images*, and *The Long Goodbye*.

ROBIN WILLIAMS starred as Popeye in his first feature film.

RICHARD ZANUCK was president of Twentieth Century Fox during the making of *M*A*S*H*.

VILMOS ZSIGMOND was the cinematographer on *McCabe & Mrs. Miller*, *Images*, and *The Long Goodbye*, for which he won a National Society of Film Critics Award for Best Cinematography.

FILMOGRAPHY

As Director

1957 *The Delinquents* (producer, screenwriter)

1957 *The James Dean Story* (codirector, producer)*

1964 *Nightmare in Chicago* (producer)

1968 *Countdown*

1969 *That Cold Day in the Park*

1970 *M*A*S*H*

1970 *Brewster McCloud**

1971 *McCabe & Mrs. Miller* (coscreenwriter)*

1972 *Images* (screenwriter)*

1973 *The Long Goodbye**

1974 *Thieves Like Us* (coscreenwriter)*

1974 *California Split* (producer)*

1975 *Nashville* (producer)*

1976 *Buffalo Bill and the Indians,* or *Sitting Bull's History Lesson* (producer, coscreenwriter)*

1977 *3 Women* (producer, screenwriter)*

1978 *A Wedding* (producer, coscreenwriter)*

1979 *Quintet* (producer, coscreenwriter)*

1979 *A Perfect Couple* (producer, coscreenwriter)*

1980 *HealtH* (producer, coscreenwriter)

1980 *Popeye**

1982 *Come Back to the Five and Dime, Jimmy Dean, Jimmy Dean*

1983 *Streamers* (producer)

1984 *Secret Honor* (producer)*

1985 *O.C. and Stiggs* (coproducer)*

1985 *Fool for Love**

1987 *Beyond Therapy* (coscreenwriter)*

1988 *Aria* (director and screenwriter of "Les Boréades" segment)*

1990 *Vincent & Theo**

1992 *The Player**

1993 *Short Cuts* (coscreenwriter)*

1994　*Prêt-à-Porter (Ready to Wear)* (producer, coscreenwriter)*

1996　*Kansas City* (producer, coscreenwriter)*

1996–97　*Robert Altman's Jazz '34: Remembrances of Kansas City Swing* (producer)

1998　*The Gingerbread Man**

1999　*Cookie's Fortune* (producer)*

2000　*Dr. T & the Women* (producer)*

2001　*Gosford Park* (producer)*

2003　*The Company* (producer)*

2006　*A Prairie Home Companion* (producer)*

As Producer

1977　*Welcome to L.A.* (director, Alan Rudolph)

1977　*The Late Show* (director, Robert Benton)*

1978　*Remember My Name* (director, Alan Rudolph)

1979　*Rich Kids* (director, Robert M. Young)

1994　*Mrs. Parker and the Vicious Circle* (director, Alan Rudolph)*

1997　*Afterglow* (director, Alan Rudolph)*

2000　*Trixie* (director, Alan Rudolph)*

* Denotes available on DVD

Television

1957–65　Writer, director, producer: various television series, including *Alfred Hitchcock Presents, The Millionaire, Bonanza, Combat!, Kraft Suspense Theatre*

1982　*2 by South: Rattlesnake in a Cooler* and *Precious Blood* (producer, director, with Leo Burmester and Alfre Woodard), Hearst-ABC

1985　*The Laundromat* (by Marsha Norman, with Carol Burnett and Amy Madigan), HBO

1987　*The Dumb Waiter* (by Harold Pinter, with John Travolta and Tom Conti), ABC Television

The Room (by Harold Pinter, with Linda Hunt, Julian Sands, Annie Lennox, and Donald Pleasance), ABC Television

1988　*The Caine Mutiny Court-Martial* (with Brad Davis, Eric Bogosian, Jeff Daniels, Peter Gallagher, and Michael Murphy), CBS Television

1988　*Tanner '88* (written by Garry Trudeau, starring Michael Murphy), miniseries, HBO

1991　*Black and Blue, Great Performances*, PBS

1993　*The Real McTeague* (concept and creative supervision), *Great Performances*, PBS

1997　*Robert Altman's Jazz '34: Remembrances of Kansas City Swing, Great Performances*, PBS

1997   *Gun* (producer) Anthology Series, ABC Television, episode director: "All the President's Women"

1998–'99   *Killer App* (executive producer; written by Garry Trudeau), Fox Television

2004   *Tanner on Tanner* (written by Garry Trudeau, miniseries starring Cynthia Nixon and Michael Murphy), the Sundance Channel

THEATER AND OPERA

1981   *2 by South* (by Frank South, Los Angeles Actors' Theater; St. Clement's Theater, NYC)

1982   *Come Back to the Five and Dime, Jimmy Dean, Jimmy Dean* (by Ed Graczyk, with Cher, Sandy Dennis, Karen Black)

1983   *The Rake's Progress* (Stravinsky, University of Michigan)

1987   *The Rake's Progress* (Stravinsky, Opéra de Lille, France)

1992   *McTeague* (director and coauthor of libretto with composer William Bolcom, Lyric Opera of Chicago)

2004   *A Wedding* (director and coauthor of libretto with Arnold Weinstein, composer William Bolcom, Lyric Opera of Chicago)

2006   *Resurrection Blues* (director, written by Arthur Miller, Old Vic Theatre, London, England)

AWARDS AND HONORS

FILMS and TV

2004 *Tanner on Tanner*
DGA (Directors Guild of America) nomination for Outstanding Television Miniseries

2001 *Gosford Park*
Golden Globe: Best Director (Musical or Comedy)

New York Film Critics Circle Award: Best Director; Best Supporting Actress, Helen Mirren

National Society of Film Critics: Best Director; Best Supporting Actress, Helen Mirren

BAFTA (British Academy of Film and Television Arts) Award: Best British Film

AFI (American Film Institute) Award: Best Director

Screen Actors Guild Awards: Best Cast in a Theatrical Motion Picture; Best Supporting Actress, Helen Mirren

Seven Academy Award nominations, including Best Director, Best Film

Academy Award: Best Screenplay

1997 *Robert Altman's Jazz '34: Remembrances of Kansas City Swing*
Twenty-first São Paulo International Film Festival: Prémio do Público, Best Documentary

1996 *Kansas City*
New York Film Critics Circle Award: Best Supporting Actor, Harry Belafonte

Los Angeles Film Critics Association Award: Best Score

1994 *Prêt-à-Porter (Ready to Wear)*
The National Board of Review: Acting Award for Ensemble Cast

1994 *Black and Blue*
Emmy nomination for Best Director

1993 *Short Cuts*
Venice Film Festival: Grand Prix, Best Film; Grand Prix, Best Acting Award to the Ensemble

Golden Globe: Ensemble Cast

IFP Independent Spirit Award: Best Film

Swedish Film Critics Award: Best Film

Bodil Award, Denmark: Best American Film

Boston Society of Film Critics Award: Best Screenplay

Academy Award nomination for Best Director

New York Film Festival, shown opening night

1992 *The Player*

New York Film Critics Circle Award: Best Film, Best Director

Cannes Film Festival: Best Director; Best Actor, Tim Robbins

Golden Globe: Best Film (Musical or Comedy); Best Actor, Tim Robbins

DGA Award: Outstanding Directorial Achievement

BAFTA: Best Director

Chicago Film Critics Award: Best Director

Boston Society of Film Critics Award: Best Director

Italian National Syndicate of Film Journalists Award: Best Director of a Foreign Film

Bodil Award, Denmark: Best American Film

Academy Award nomination for Best Director

1988 *Tanner '88*

Emmy Award (Academy of Television Arts & Sciences): Best Director

BAFTA: Best Foreign Television Series

FIPA (International Festival of Audiovisual Programs), France: Best Foreign Series

1988 *The Caine Mutiny Court-Martial*

Monte Carlo Television Festival: Best Director

1985 *The Laundromat*

ACE Award

1983 *Streamers*

Venice Film Festival: Grand Prix, Acting, Ensemble

1982 *Come Back to the Five and Dime, Jimmy Dean, Jimmy Dean*

Chicago International Film Festival: Grand Prix

1978 *A Wedding*

New York Film Festival, shown opening night

1977 *3 Women*

Cannes Film Festival: Best Actress, Shelley Duvall

New York Film Festival: Best Supporting Actress, Sissy Spacek

1976 *Buffalo Bill and the Indians, or Sitting Bull's History Lesson*

Berlin International Film Festival: Golden Bear, Best Film

1975 *Nashville*

National Society of Film Critics Award: Best Film, Best Director

New York Film Critics Circle Award: Best Film, Best Director

National Board of Review: Best Film, Best Director

David di Donatello Award, Italy

AFI (Australian Film Institute) Film Awards, Australia, Best Foreign Film

Academy Award nominations for Best Film, Best Director

Academy Award: Best Song, "I'm Easy"

1972 *Images*

Cannes Film Festival: Best Actress, Susannah York

1970 *M*A*S*H*

Cannes Film Festival: Palme d'Or (Best Film)

National Society of Film Critics Award: Best Film

Academy Award nominations for Best Film, Best Director

CAREER HONORS

2006 Hamptons International Film Festival: Golden Starfish Award for Career Achievement in Directing

2005 Honorary Academy Award in recognition of a career that has repeatedly reinvented the art form and inspired filmmakers and audiences alike

2001 Women in Film: Mentor Award

2000 Independent Feature Project: Gotham Awards; Bravo Lifetime Achievement Award

1999 American Society of Cinematographers: Board of Governors Award

1998 Classically Independent Film Festival, San Francisco, California: Independent Director Honoree

1996 Venice Film Festival: Golden Lion

1996 University of Michigan: honorary doctorate of fine arts

1996 American Film Institute: honorary doctorate of fine arts

1995 American Cinema Editors (ACE): award for unique and distinguished contributions to the art and craft of the motion picture

1994 Directors Guild of America: D. W. Griffith Award for distinguished achievement in motion picture direction

1994 Film Society of Lincoln Center, Gala Tribute honoree

1994 Cinema Arts Centre Award for unique achievement in advancing the art of independent film

1992 IFP: John Cassavetes Award, for significantly extending the possibilities of film art

1992 USA Film Festival: Great Director Award

1991 Cinema Audio Society: Lifetime Achievement Award

ACKNOWLEDGMENTS

IF THIS BOOK had above-the-title credits, they would go to Bob and Kathryn Altman. Bob was an extraordinary artist and a remarkable man, and I'm honored to have known him. Kathryn amazed me with her memory, her candor, and her humor. I cherish her friendship.

All the characters in this book were generous with time and memories, and I thank them all. The words are theirs, but any errors are mine.

Marty Asher at Knopf is the editor every writer dreams of, and a mensch to boot. Zachary Wagman of Knopf is a true pal, a ready ear who provided invaluable insight and support. Kudos to Jon Karp, who godfathered this book by persuading Bob to recount his life's work. My friend and agent, the peerless Richard Abate, got me through the door.

I'm indebted to Brodie Ransom of Wholly Cow Productions. In return for boxes of great material, all Brodie asked was that I do good work. Thanks to Tom Ruffner of the Fox Movie Channel for approving Brodie's largesse.

Jerry Walsh, Bob's friend, executor, and cousin by marriage, was a steady hand and a thoughtful reader. Amanda Urban of ICM found this book its home. The contributions and support of Sandcastle producers Wren Arthur and Josh Astrachan are deeply appreciated. Tim McDowell was Bob's jack-of-all-trades, and despite his ill-placed baseball loyalties he played a similar role for this book. Charles Michener provided important early help.

Heather Schultz, Erin Prediger, and Jordan Zappala, my graduate assistants, improved this book with their suggestions and enthusiasm. My colleagues and students at Boston University provide me with a happy professional home. At Knopf, I'm grateful to Peter Mendelsund, Claire Bradley Ong, Virginia Tan, Meghan Wilson, Kathy Zuckerman, Anke Steinecke, and Amelia Zalcman.

For digging into their photo albums, I thank Reza Badiyi, Bill Bushnell, Robert Evans, Art Goodell, Melinda Sue Gordon, Barbara Altman Hodes, John Horoschak, Jr., Jean Pagliuso, William Stuckey, and Danielle Weil.

The lessons of the late Wilbur Doctor guide my work, and I miss him. Thankfully, Christopher Callahan still points true north.

Special thanks to Colleen Granahan, Dan Field, Isabelle Granahan-Field, and Eliza Granahan-Field, and Ruth, Bill, and Emily Weinstein, for their encouragement, gentle mocking, and ready laughter. All right, they can come to the party. Dick Lehr is the best partner in crime I could ask for. Jeff Feigelson goes back to the start, and he'll be there to the end. Naftali Bendavid is that rare thing: a true friend. Brian McGrory is more than an incomparable newsman and sounding board, he's family. Allan Zuckoff will always be the standard against which I measure myself.

My parents, Gerry and Sid Zuckoff, gave me everything that matters.

My daughters, Isabel and Eve, are the joys of my life. They share my sense of direction, which means I'll never get lost alone.

Bob Altman's nickname for Kathryn was Trixie, and as Michael Murphy told me, "Everyone needs a Trixie." Suzanne Kreiter makes everything possible. She's my Rose *and* my Trixie.

ILLUSTRATIONS

INDEX

Page numbers in *italics* refer to illustrations.
Page numbers in **boldface** refer to those individuals interviewed.

Grateful acknowledgment is made to the following for permission to reprint previously published material:

The Academy of Motion Picture Arts and Sciences: Excerpt from the Oscar for Lifetime Achievement presentation speech by Meryl Streep and Lily Tomlin at the 78th Academy Awards, March 5, 2006. Reprinted by permission of The Academy of Motion Picture Arts and Sciences.

The Associated Press: Excerpt from "Movie Snub Spotlights Politics of Oscar Campaigns; Robert Altman's *Kansas City* Left Out of Race by Distributor" by Lynn Elber (The Associated Press, January 31, 1997). Reprinted by permission of The Associated Press.

The Boston Globe: Excerpt from review of *Kansas City* by Jay Carr, copyright © 2008 by Globe Newspaper Company (*The Boston Globe*, August 16, 1996). Reprinted by permission of *The Boston Globe*.

The Christian Science Monitor: Excerpt from "Robert Altman's Sudden—and Auspicious—Stage Venture" by David Sterritt, copyright © 1981 by *The Christian Science Monitor* (*The Christian Science Monitor*, October 27, 1981). Reprinted by permission of *The Christian Science Monitor*.

Roger Ebert: Excerpt from review of *California Split* by Roger Ebert (*Chicago Sun-Times*, January 1, 1974) and excerpt from review of *The Company* by Roger Ebert (*Chicago Sun-Times*, December 24, 2003). Reprinted by permission of Roger Ebert.

Fox Movie Channel: Excerpts from the script from *Altman: On His Own Terms* (Fox Movie Channel, 2000). Reprinted by permission of Fox Movie Channel.

Los Angeles Times: Excerpt from "Losers on the Loose in *Thieves*" by Kevin Thomas, copyright © 1974 by *Los Angeles Times* (*Los Angeles Times*, April 4, 1974); and excerpt from "Robert Altman Finds His Way to Carverville" by Kenneth Turan, copyright © 1993 by *Los Angeles Times* (*Los Angeles Times*, October 8, 1993). Reprinted by permission of *Los Angeles Times*.

The New York Observer: Excerpt from "When a Man Loves Too Many Women" by Andrew Sarris (*The New York Observer*, November 19, 2000). Reprinted by permission of *The New York Observer*.

The New York Times: Excerpt from "*Brewster McCloud*—Movie Review" by Vincent Canby, copyright © 1970 by *The New York Times* (*The New York Times*, December 24, 1970); excerpt from "*The James Dean Story*—Movie Review" by Bosley Crowther, copyright © 1957 by *The New York Times* (*The New York Times*, October 19, 1957); excerpt from "De Laurentiis Dismisses Altman from *Ragtime*," copyright © 1972 by *The New York Times* (*The New York Times*, October 9, 1972); excerpt from "TV: An Hour of Ugliness" by Jack Gould, copyright © 1961 by *The New York Times* (*The New York Times*, December 4, 1961); excerpt from "Robert Altman Sells Studio for $2.3 Million" by Aljean Harmetz, copyright © 1981 by *The New York Times* (*The New York Times*, July 11, 1981); excerpt from "A.B.C. Head Backs 'Bus Stop' Episode" by Marjorie Hunter, copyright © 1962 by *The New York Times* (*The New York Times*, July 25, 1962); excerpt from "*McCabe and Mrs. Miller*: A Sneaky-Great Movie" by Peter Schjedahl, copyright © 1971 by *The New York Times* (*The New York Times*, July 25,